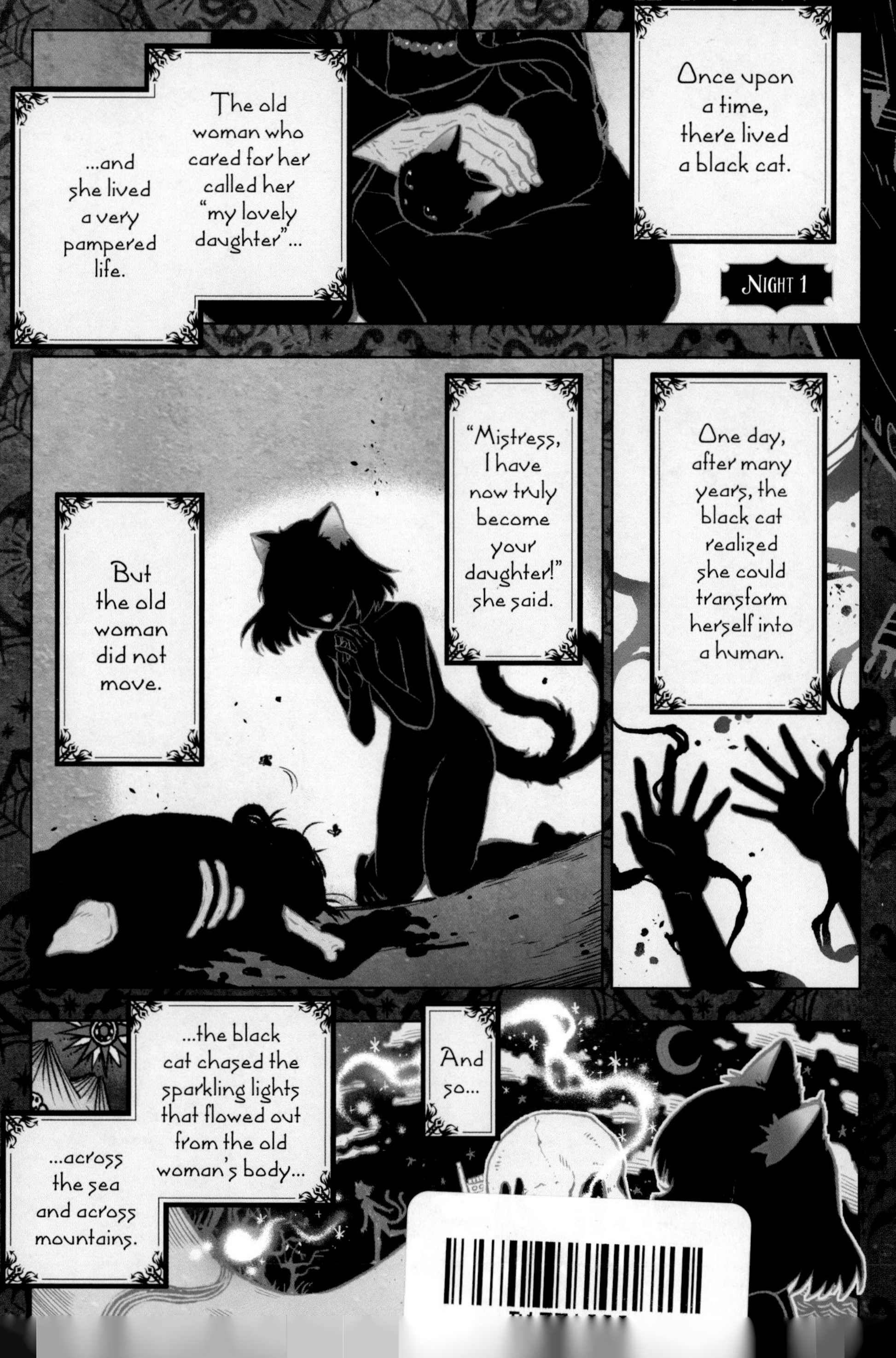
Once upon a time, there lived a black cat.
NIGHT 1
The old woman who cared for her called her "my lovely daughter"...
...and she lived a very pampered life.
One day, after many years, the black cat realized she could transform herself into a human.
"Mistress, I have now truly become your daughter!" she said.
But the old woman did not move.
And so...
...the black cat chased the sparkling lights that flowed out from the old woman's body...
...across the sea and across mountains.

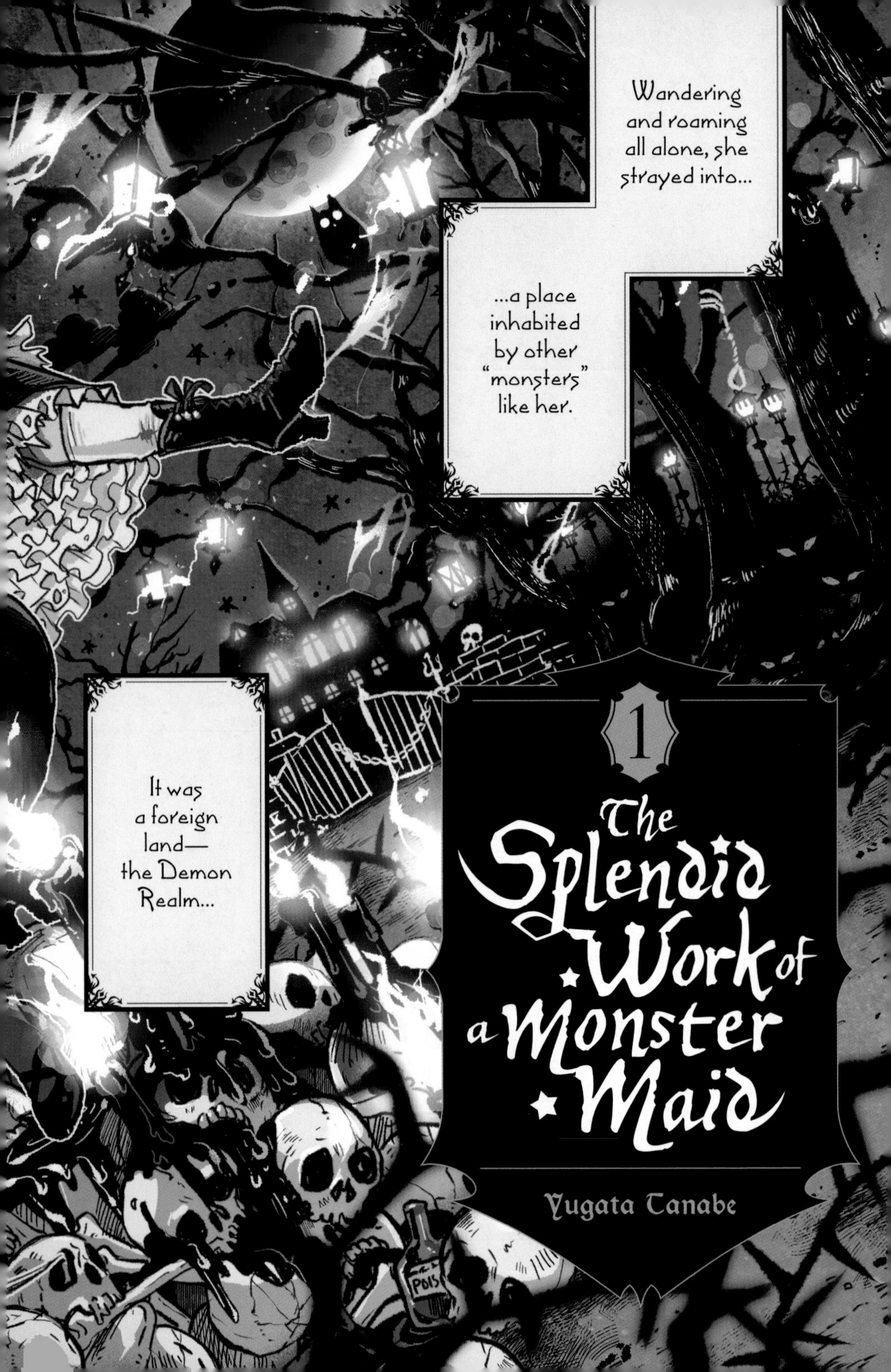
Wandering and roaming all alone, she strayed into...
...a place inhabited by other "monsters" like her.
It was a foreign land—the Demon Realm...
1
The Splendid Work of a Monster Maid
Yugata Tanabe

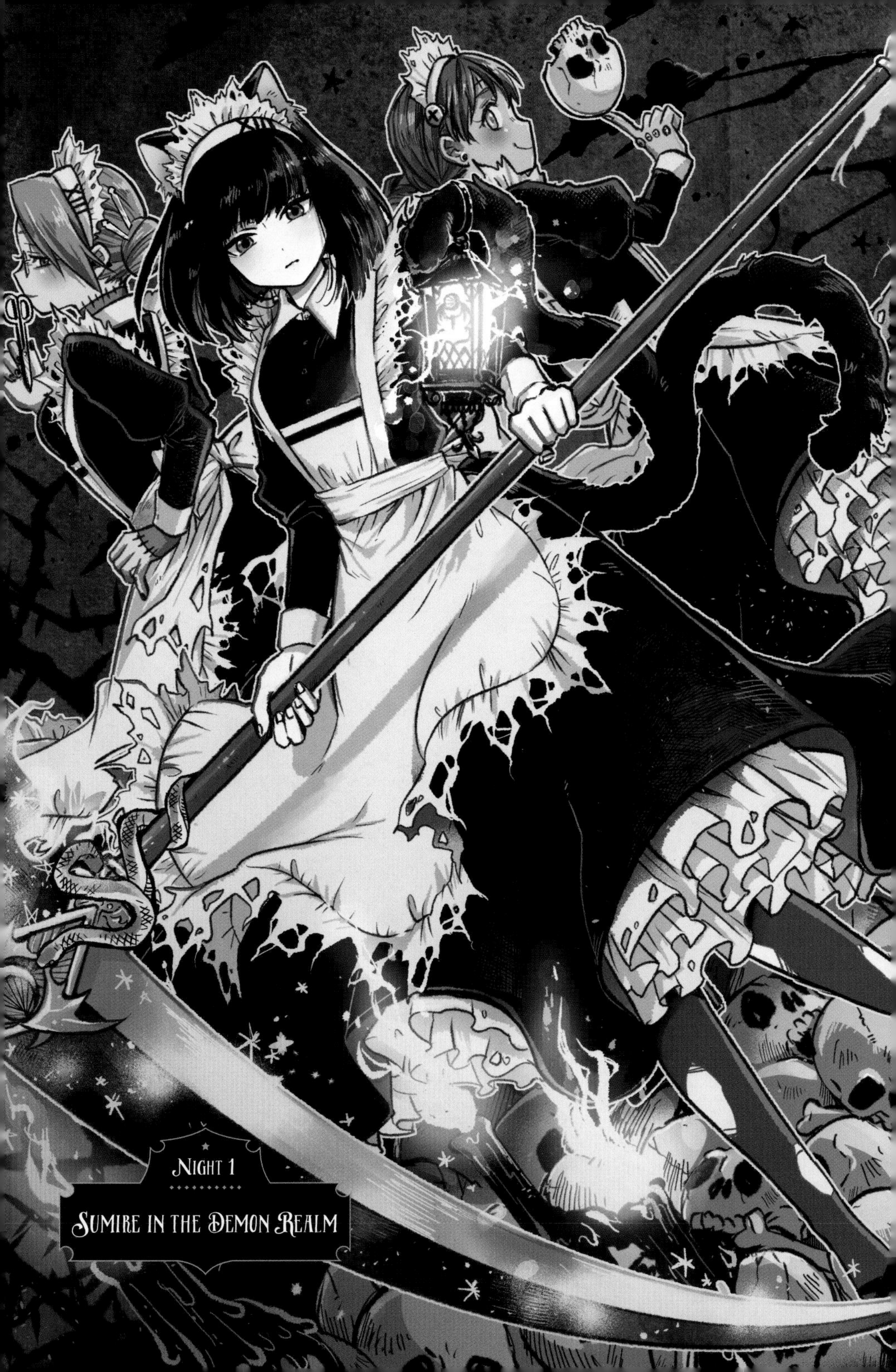
Night 1
Sumire in the Demon Realm

CONTENTS

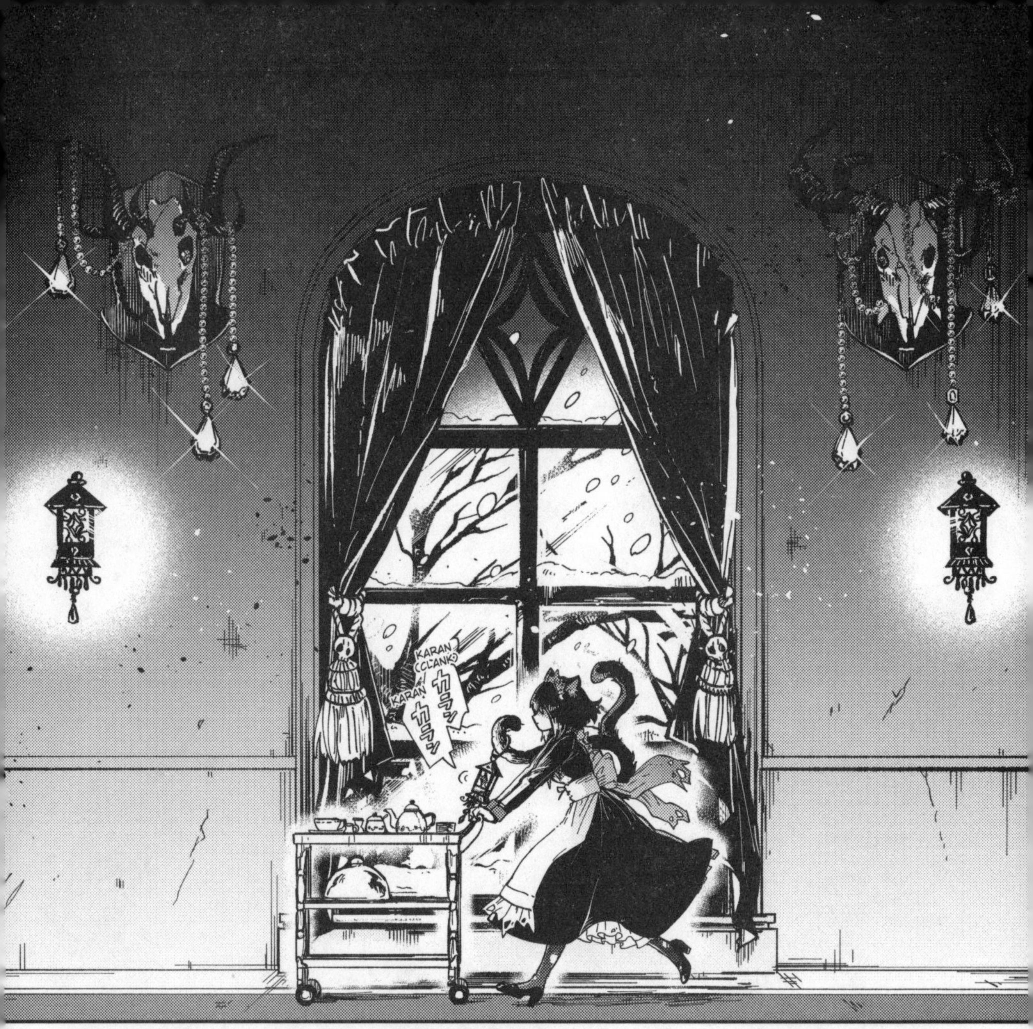
KARAN (CLANK) KARAN
カラン
カラン
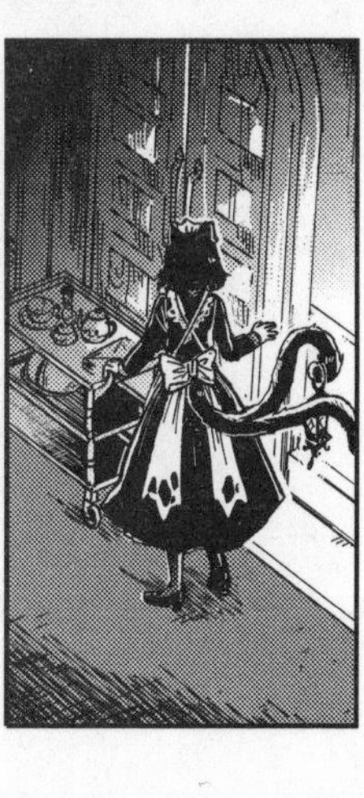
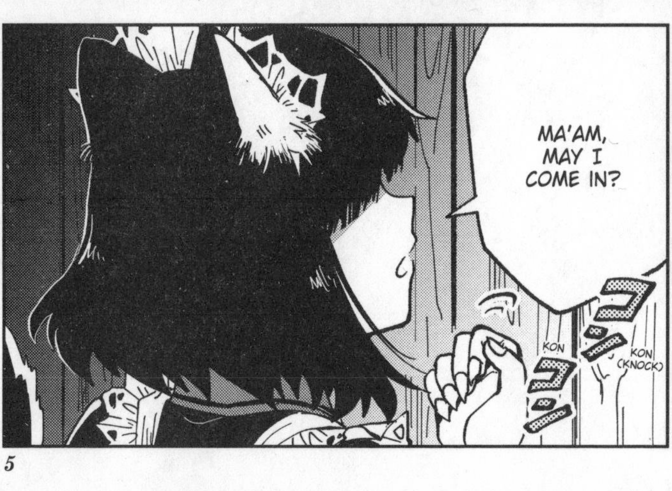
MA'AM, MAY I COME IN?
KON (KNOCK) KON
コン
コン

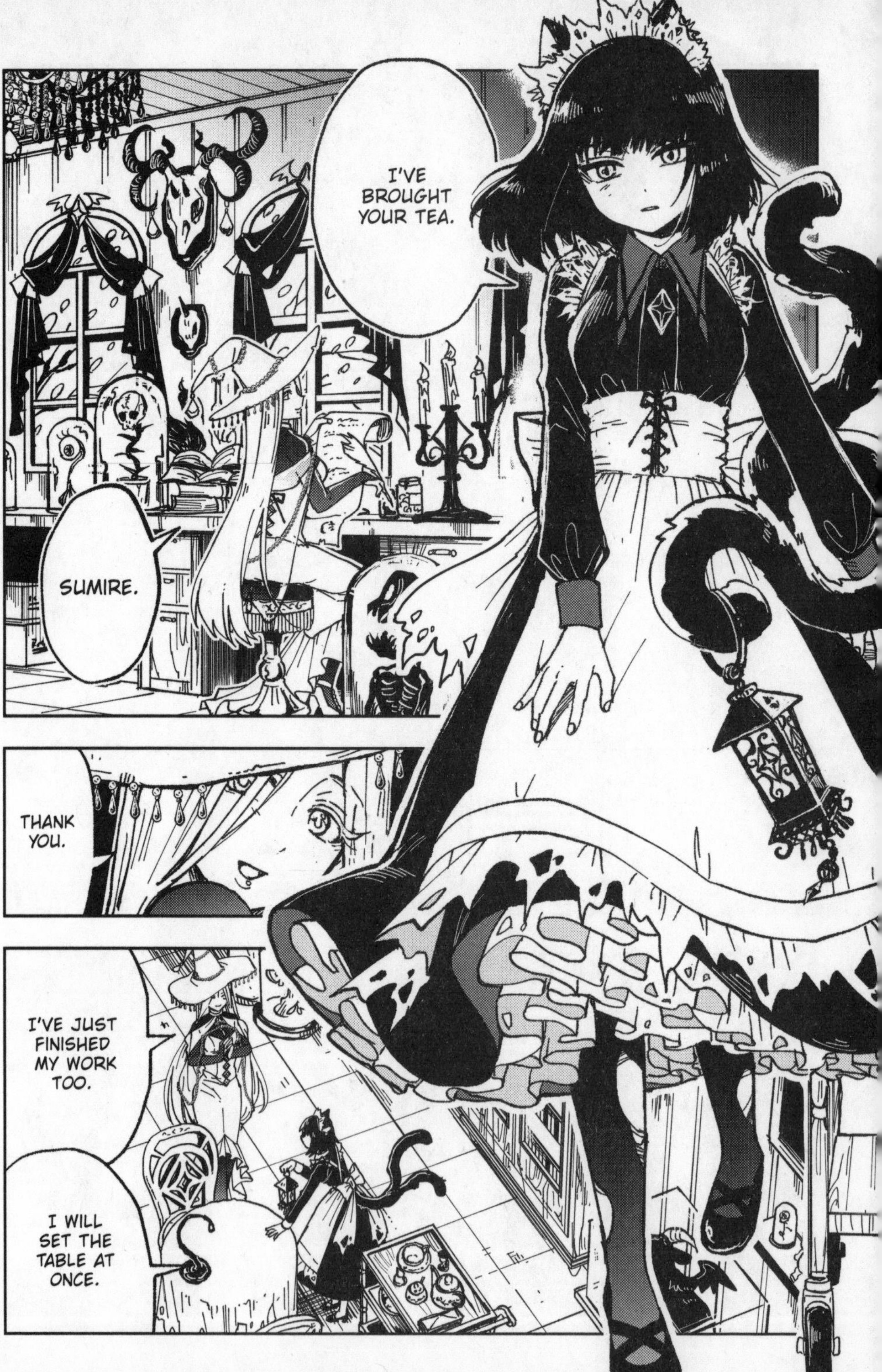
I'VE BROUGHT YOUR TEA.
SUMIRE.
THANK YOU.
I'VE JUST FINISHED MY WORK TOO.
I WILL SET THE TABLE AT ONCE.

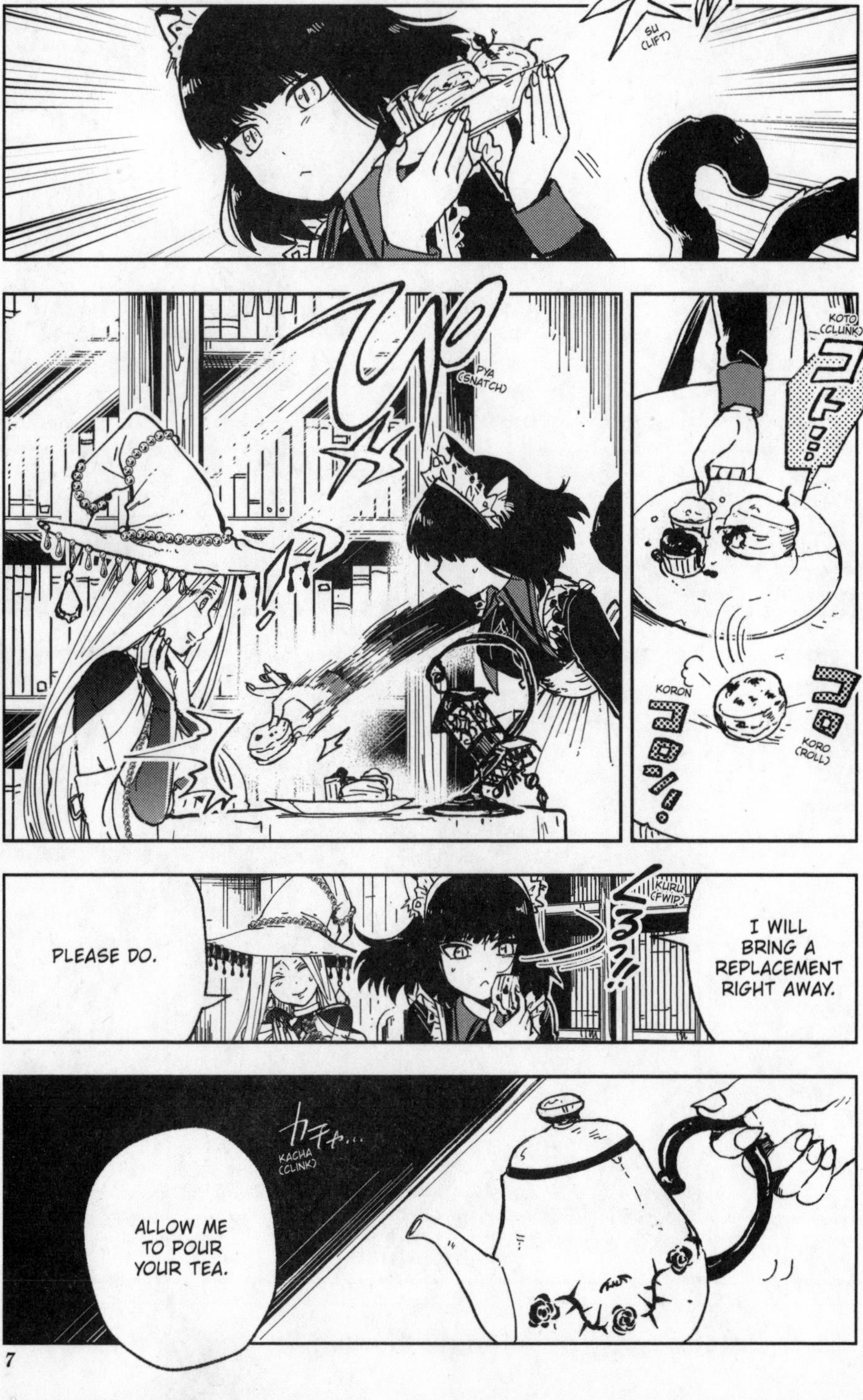
SU (LIFT)
KOTO (CLUNK)
KORON
KORO (ROLL)
PYA (SNATCH)
KURU (FWIP)
I WILL BRING A REPLACEMENT RIGHT AWAY.
PLEASE DO.
KACHA (CLINK)
ALLOW ME TO POUR YOUR TEA.

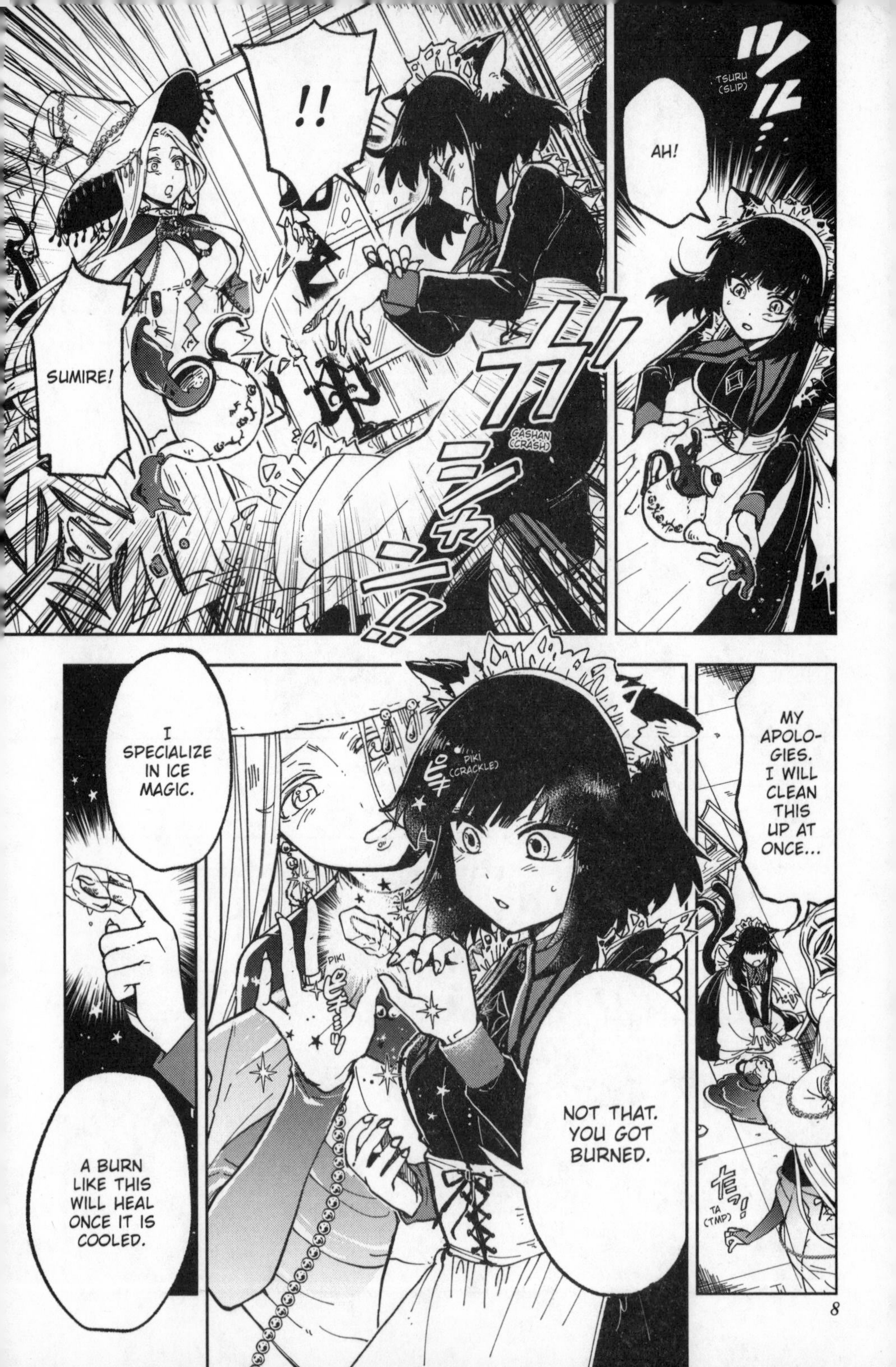
TSURU (SLIP)
AH!
!!
GASHAN (CRASH)
SUMIRE!
MY APOLOGIES. I WILL CLEAN THIS UP AT ONCE...
TA (TMP)
PIKI (CRACKLE)
NOT THAT. YOU GOT BURNED.
I SPECIALIZE IN ICE MAGIC.
PIKI
A BURN LIKE THIS WILL HEAL ONCE IT IS COOLED.

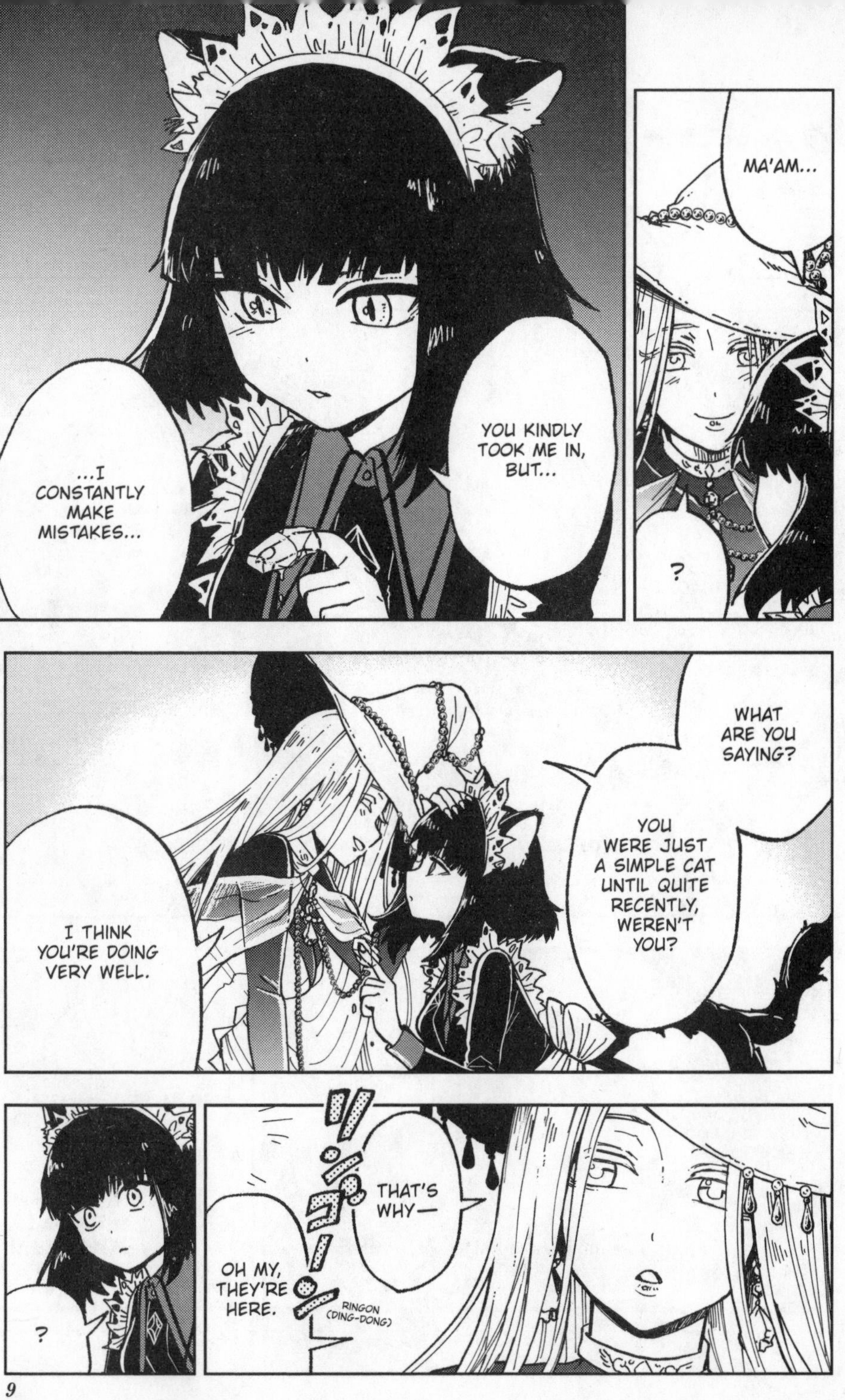
MA'AM...
?
YOU KINDLY TOOK ME IN, BUT...
...I CONSTANTLY MAKE MISTAKES...
WHAT ARE YOU SAYING?
YOU WERE JUST A SIMPLE CAT UNTIL QUITE RECENTLY, WEREN'T YOU?
I THINK YOU'RE DOING VERY WELL.
THAT'S WHY—
RINGON (DING-DONG)
OH MY, THEY'RE HERE.
?

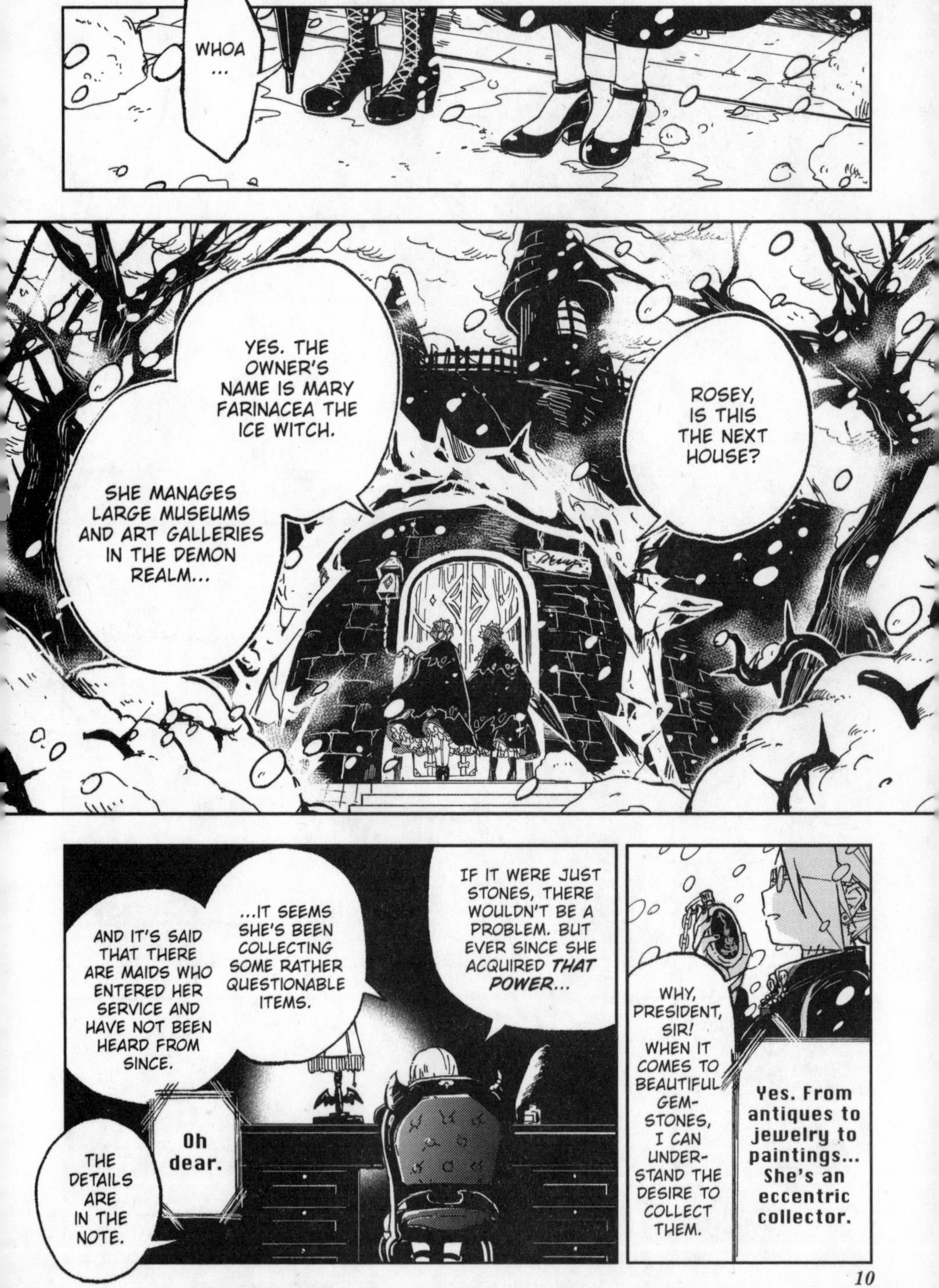
WHOA ...
ROSEY, IS THIS THE NEXT HOUSE?
YES. THE OWNER'S NAME IS MARY FARINACEA THE ICE WITCH.
SHE MANAGES LARGE MUSEUMS AND ART GALLERIES IN THE DEMON REALM...
Yes. From antiques to jewelry to paintings... She's an eccentric collector.
WHY, PRESIDENT, SIR! WHEN IT COMES TO BEAUTIFUL GEM-STONES, I CAN UNDER-STAND THE DESIRE TO COLLECT THEM.
IF IT WERE JUST STONES, THERE WOULDN'T BE A PROBLEM. BUT EVER SINCE SHE ACQUIRED *THAT POWER*...
...IT SEEMS SHE'S BEEN COLLECTING SOME RATHER QUESTIONABLE ITEMS.
AND IT'S SAID THAT THERE ARE MAIDS WHO ENTERED HER SERVICE AND HAVE NOT BEEN HEARD FROM SINCE.
Oh dear.
THE DETAILS ARE IN THE NOTE.

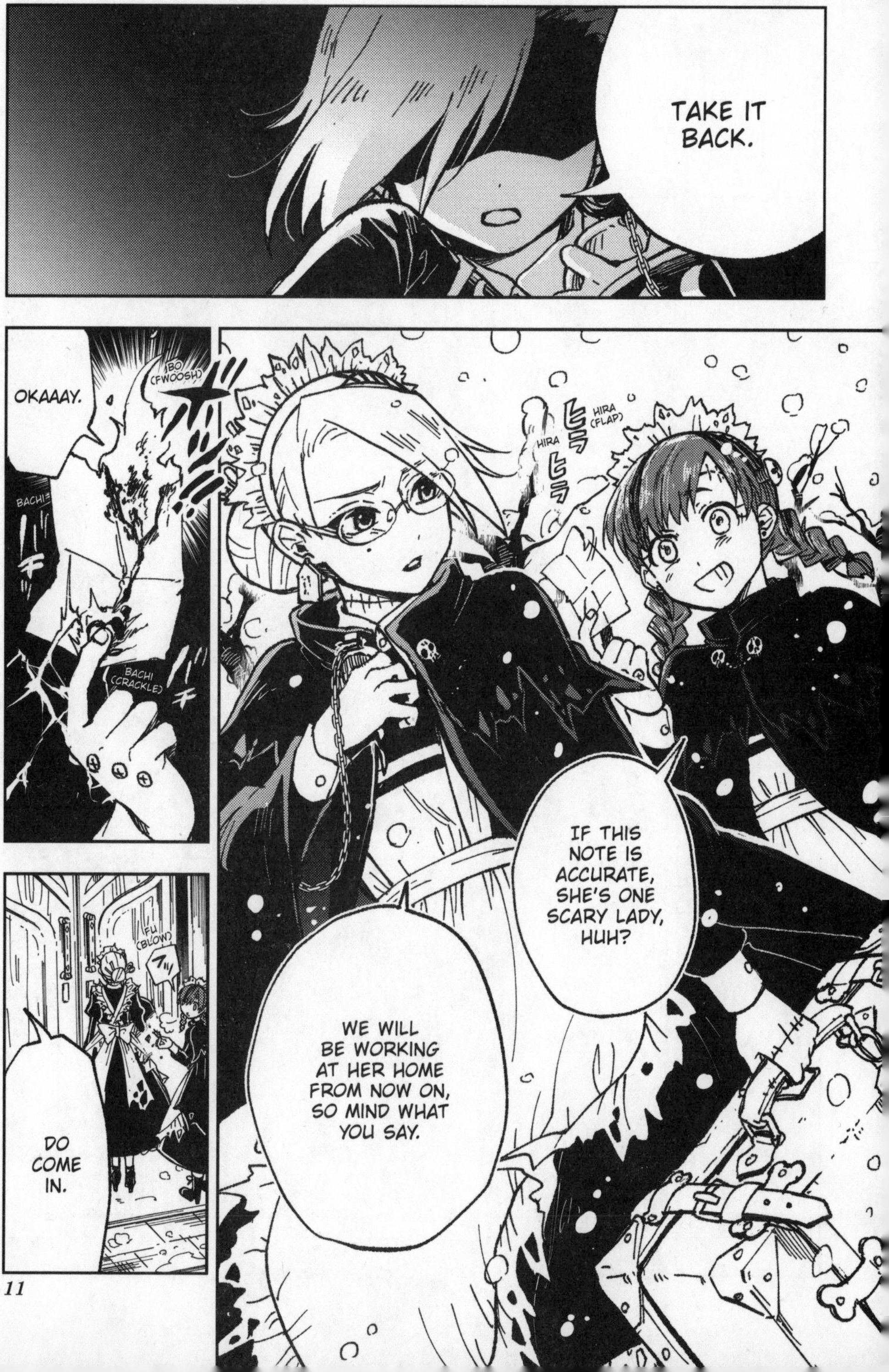
TAKE IT BACK.
HIRA HIRA (FLAP)
IF THIS NOTE IS ACCURATE, SHE'S ONE SCARY LADY, HUH?
WE WILL BE WORKING AT HER HOME FROM NOW ON, SO MIND WHAT YOU SAY.
BO (FWOOSH)
OKAAAY.
BACHI
BACHI (CRACKLE)
FU (BLOW)
DO COME IN.

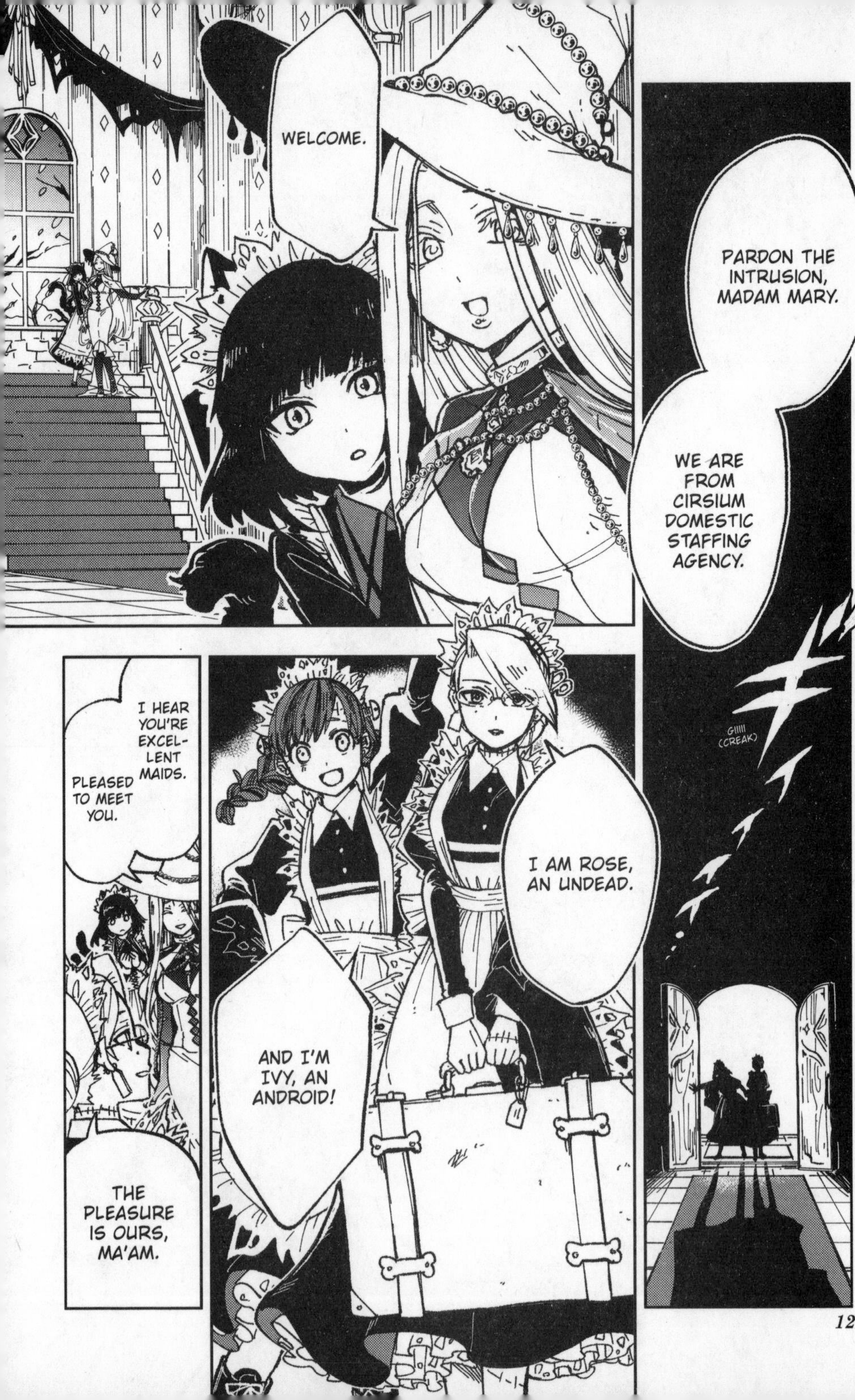
PARDON THE INTRUSION, MADAM MARY.
WE ARE FROM CIRSIUM DOMESTIC STAFFING AGENCY.
GIIII (CREAK)
WELCOME.
I AM ROSE, AN UNDEAD.
AND I'M IVY, AN ANDROID!
I HEAR YOU'RE EXCEL-LENT MAIDS.
PLEASED TO MEET YOU.
THE PLEASURE IS OURS, MA'AM.

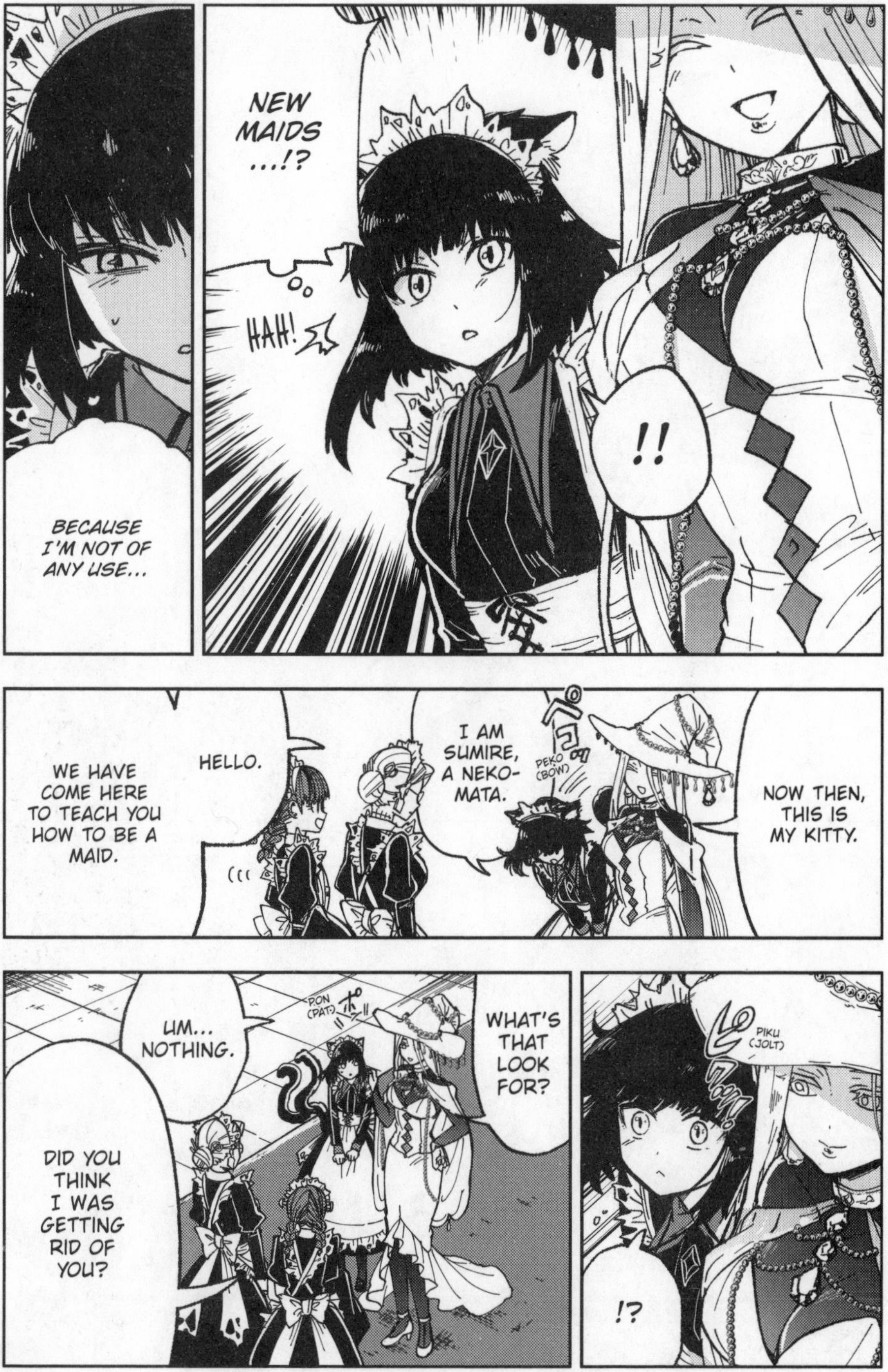
NEW MAIDS ...!?
HAH!
!!
BECAUSE I'M NOT OF ANY USE...
NOW THEN, THIS IS MY KITTY.
PEKO (BOW)
I AM SUMIRE, A NEKO-MATA.
HELLO.
WE HAVE COME HERE TO TEACH YOU HOW TO BE A MAID.
PIKU (JOLT)
!?
WHAT'S THAT LOOK FOR?
PON (PAT)
UM... NOTHING.
DID YOU THINK I WAS GETTING RID OF YOU?

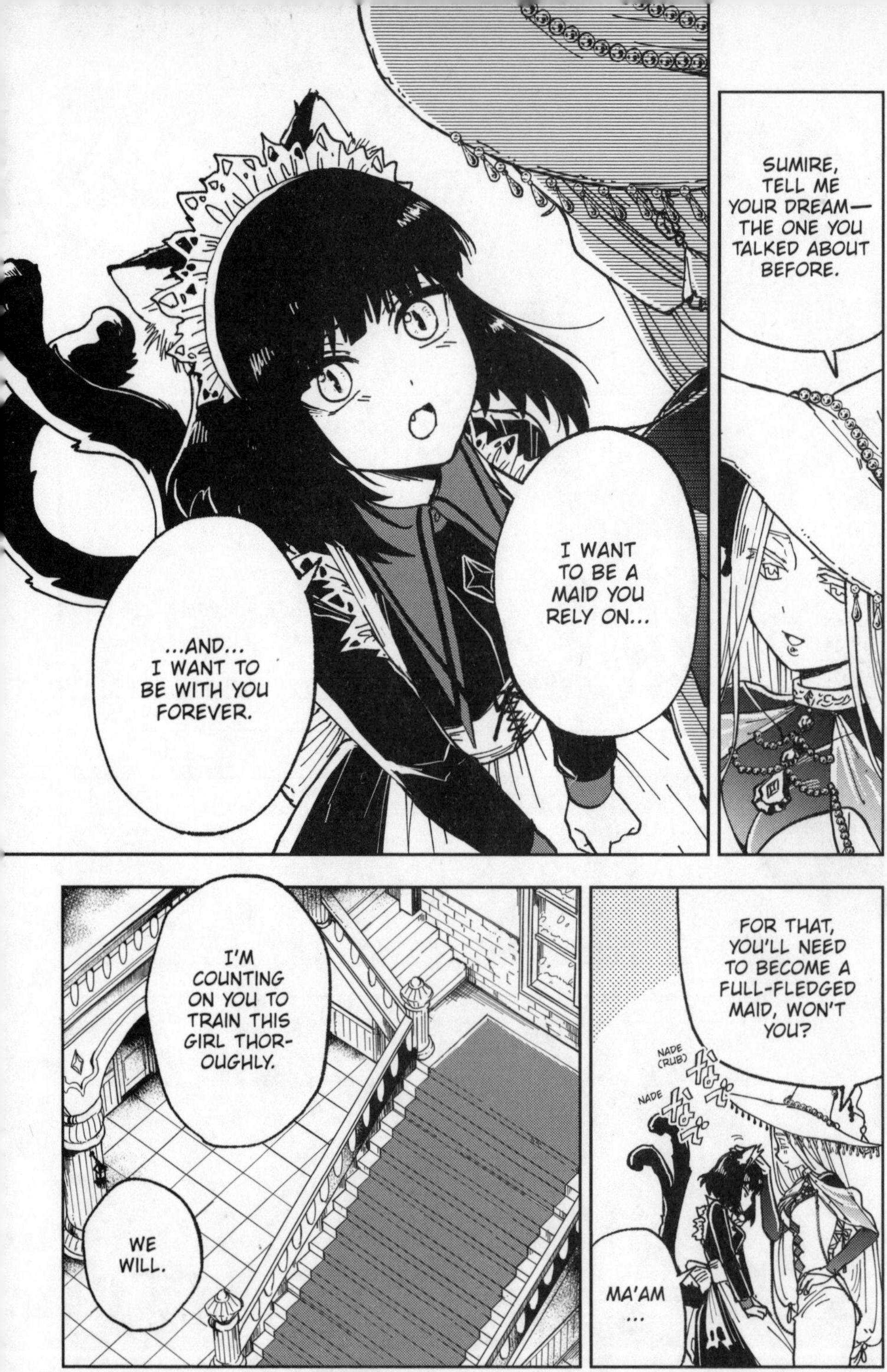
SUMIRE, TELL ME YOUR DREAM—THE ONE YOU TALKED ABOUT BEFORE.
I WANT TO BE A MAID YOU RELY ON...
...AND... I WANT TO BE WITH YOU FOREVER.
FOR THAT, YOU'LL NEED TO BECOME A FULL-FLEDGED MAID, WON'T YOU?
なで NADE (RUB)
なで NADE
MA'AM ...
I'M COUNTING ON YOU TO TRAIN THIS GIRL THOR-OUGHLY.
WE WILL.

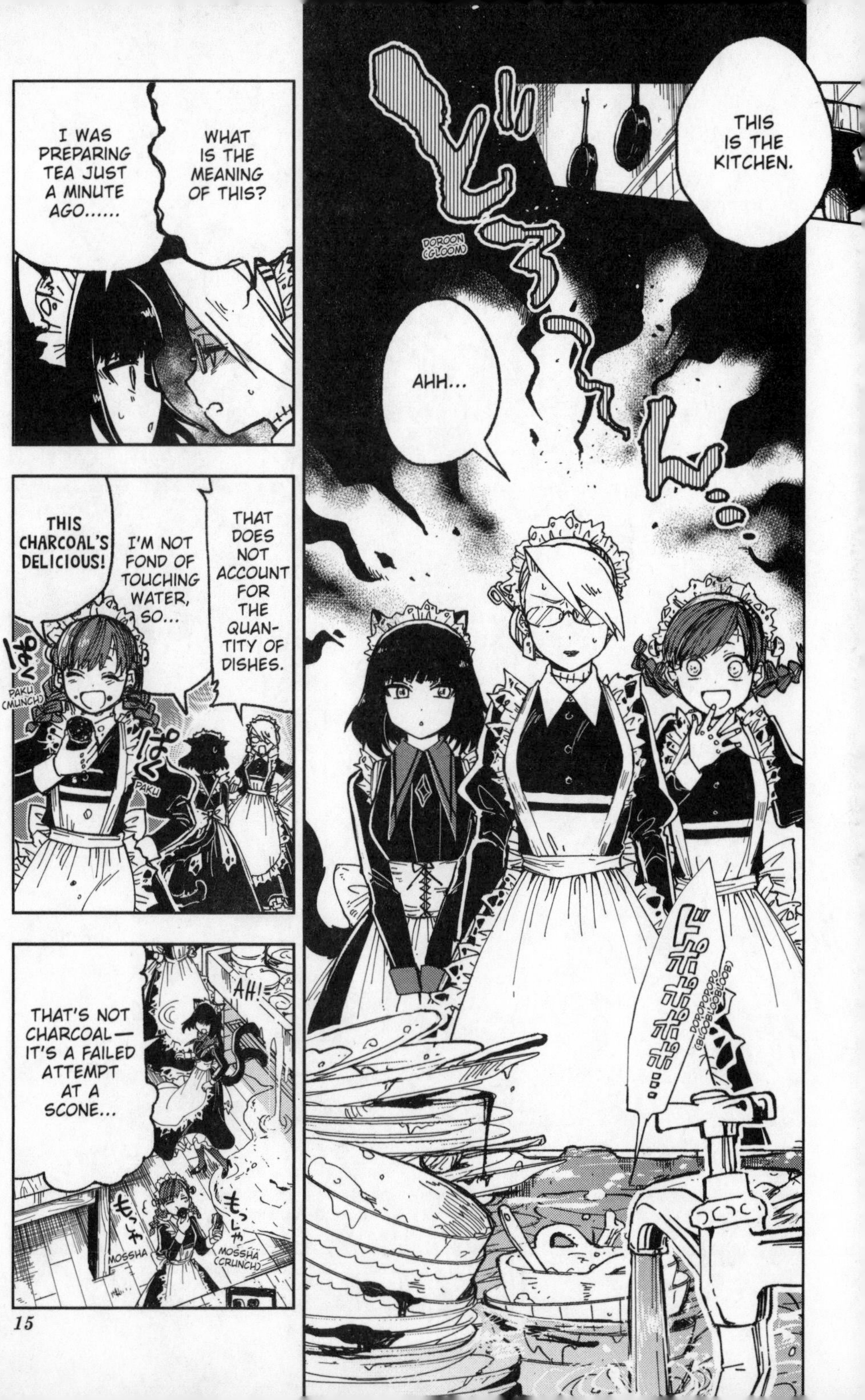
THIS IS THE KITCHEN.
DOROON (GLOOM)
AHH...
DOPOPOPOPO (BLOOBLOOBLOOB)
WHAT IS THE MEANING OF THIS?
I WAS PREPARING TEA JUST A MINUTE AGO......
THAT DOES NOT ACCOUNT FOR THE QUANTITY OF DISHES.
I'M NOT FOND OF TOUCHING WATER, SO...
THIS CHARCOAL'S DELICIOUS!
PAKU (MUNCH)
PAKU
AH!
THAT'S NOT CHARCOAL— IT'S A FAILED ATTEMPT AT A SCONE...
MOSSHA (CRUNCH)
MOSSHA

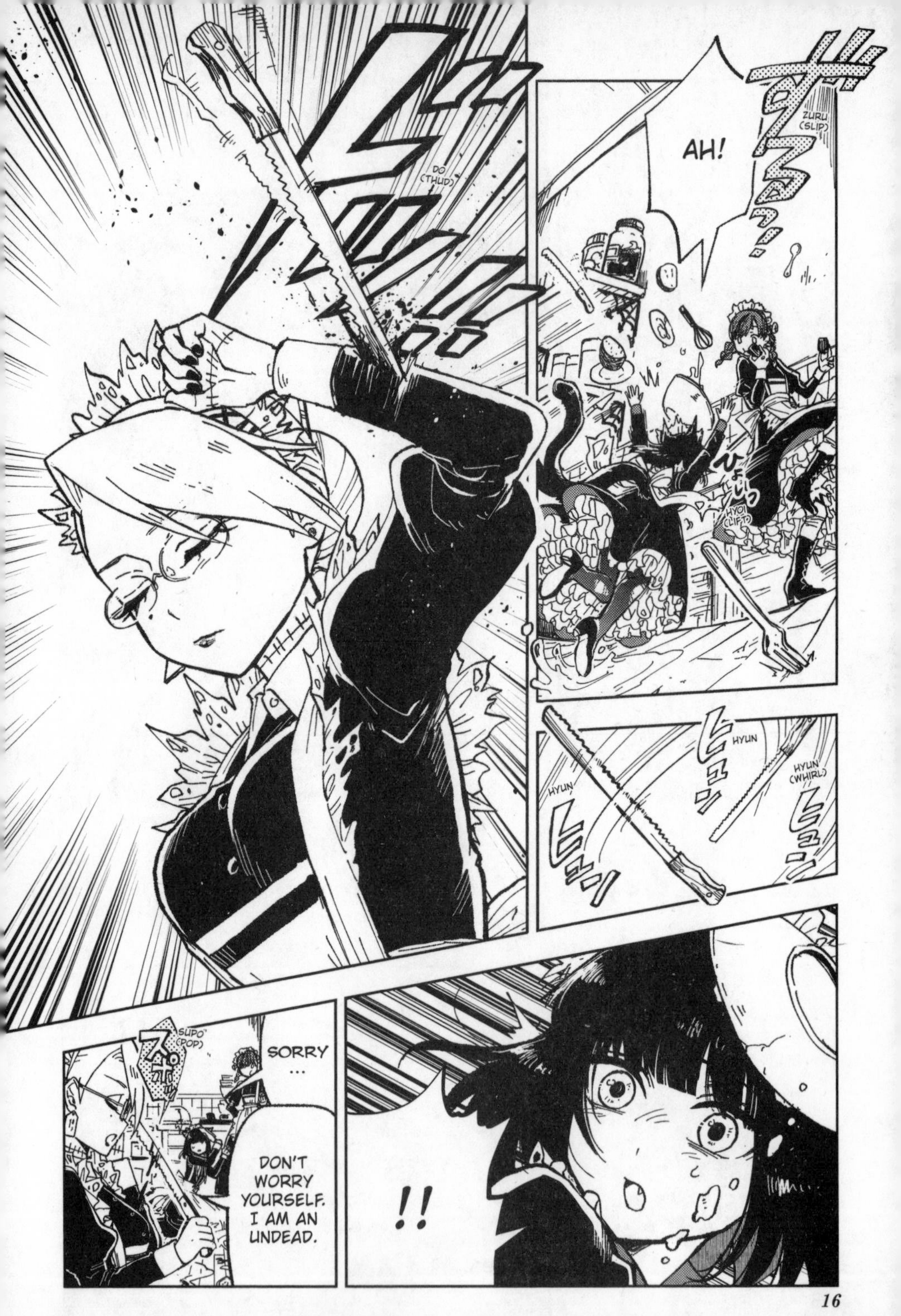
ZURU (SLIP)
AH!
HYOI (LIFT)
HYUN
HYUN (WHIRL)
HYUN
DO (THUD)
!!
SUPO (POP)
SORRY ...
DON'T WORRY YOURSELF. I AM AN UNDEAD.

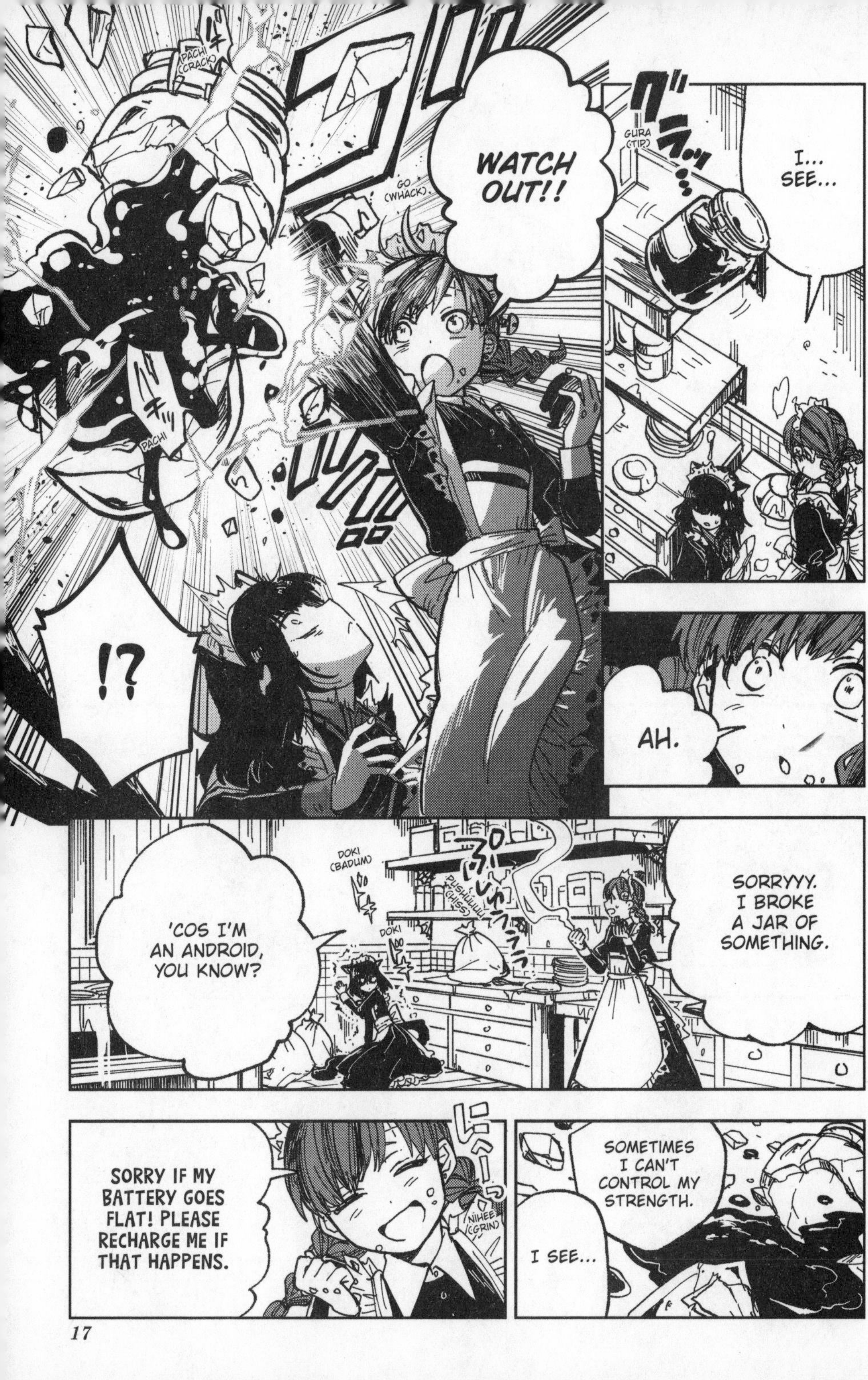
GURA (TIP)
I... SEE...
AH.
WATCH OUT!!
GO (WHACK)
PACHI (CRACK)
PACHI
!?
SORRYYY. I BROKE A JAR OF SOMETHING.
DOKI (BADUM)
DOKI
'COS I'M AN ANDROID, YOU KNOW?
SOMETIMES I CAN'T CONTROL MY STRENGTH.
I SEE...
NIHEE (GRIN)
SORRY IF MY BATTERY GOES FLAT! PLEASE RECHARGE ME IF THAT HAPPENS.

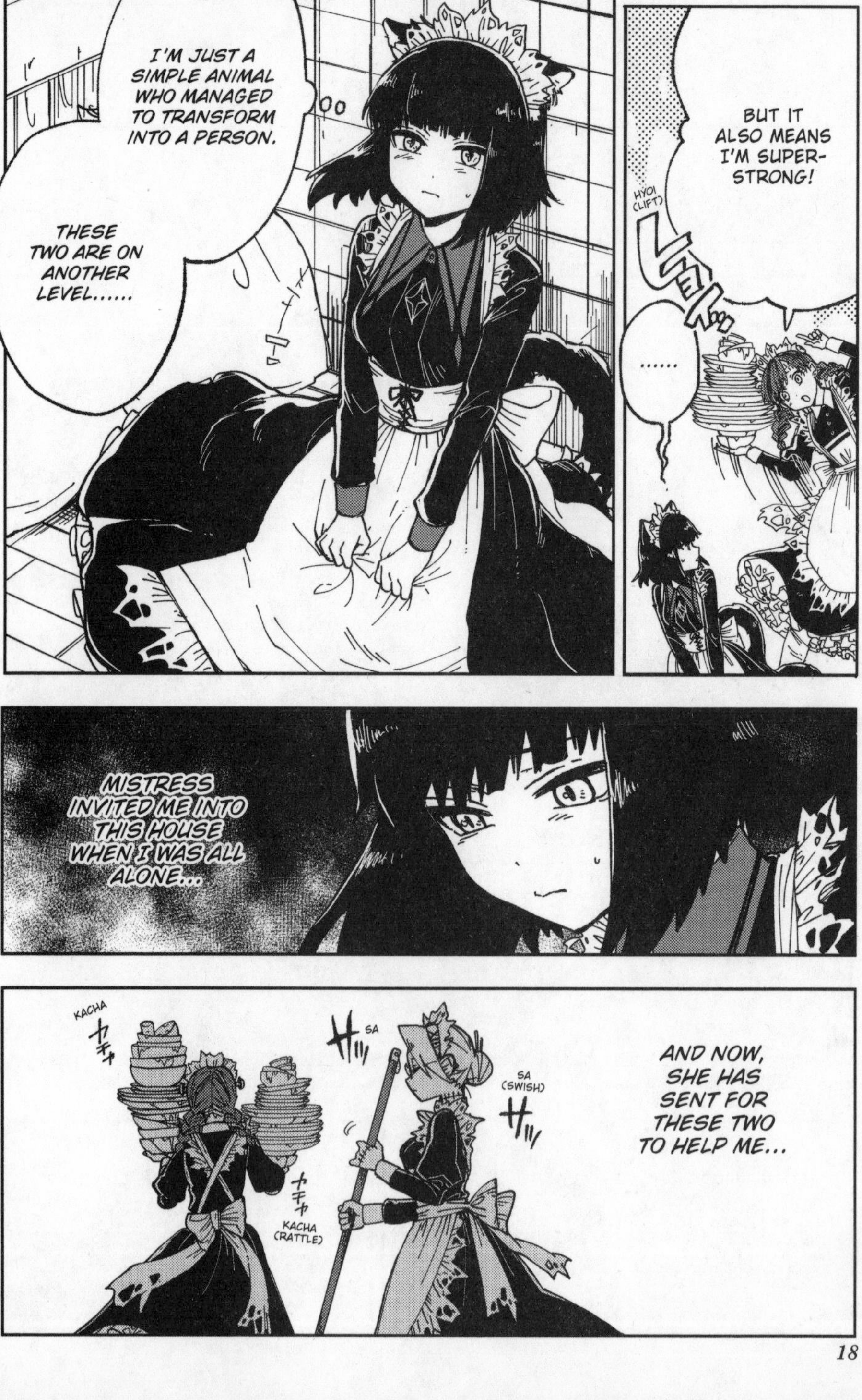

BUT IT ALSO MEANS I'M SUPER-STRONG!
HYOI (LIFT)
......
I'M JUST A SIMPLE ANIMAL WHO MANAGED TO TRANSFORM INTO A PERSON.
THESE TWO ARE ON ANOTHER LEVEL......
MISTRESS INVITED ME INTO THIS HOUSE WHEN I WAS ALL ALONE...
AND NOW, SHE HAS SENT FOR THESE TWO TO HELP ME...
SA (SWISH)
SA
KACHA
KACHA (RATTLE)

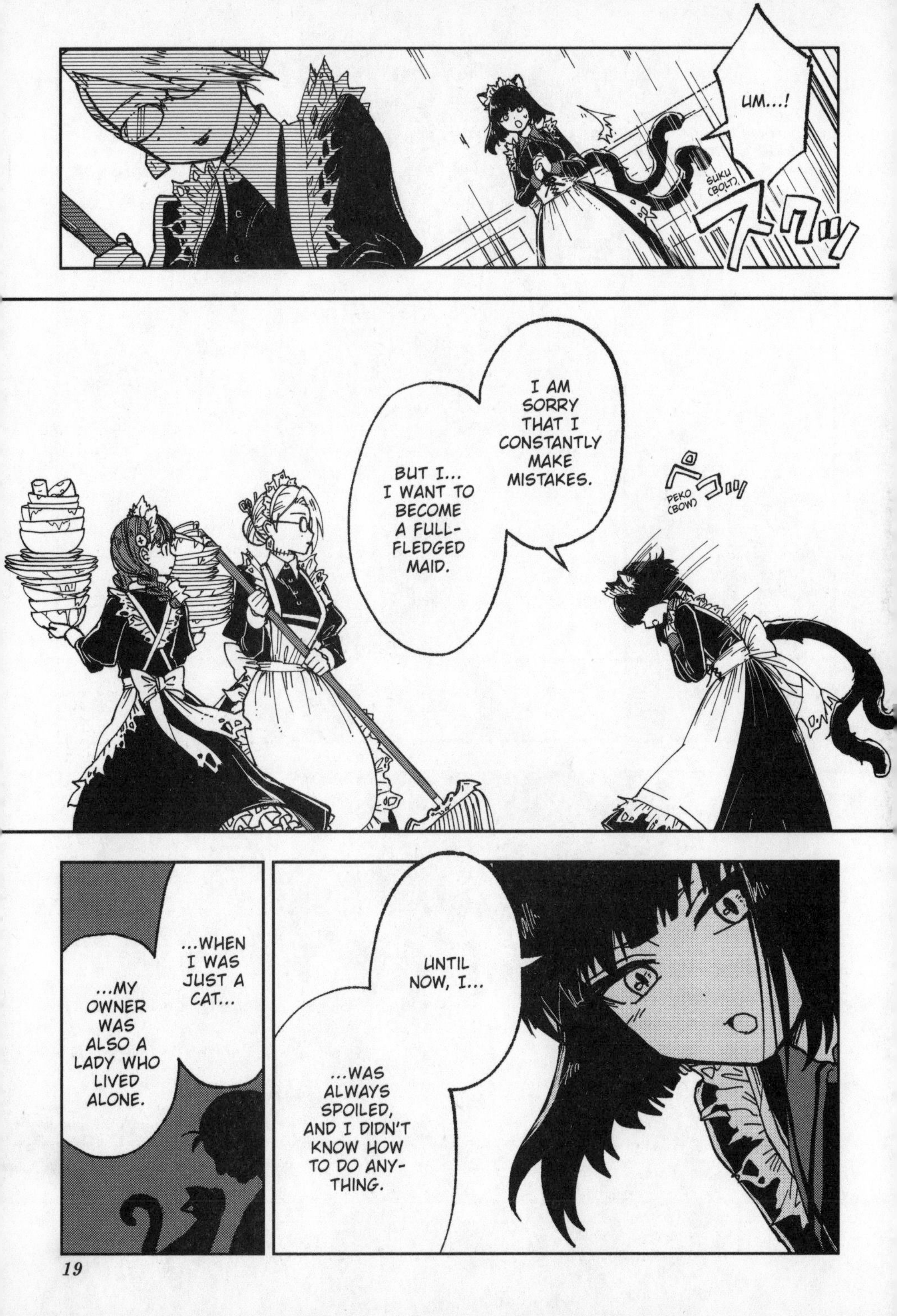
UM...!
SUKU (BOLT)
PEKO (BOW)
I AM SORRY THAT I CONSTANTLY MAKE MISTAKES.
BUT I... I WANT TO BECOME A FULL-FLEDGED MAID.
UNTIL NOW, I...
...WAS ALWAYS SPOILED, AND I DIDN'T KNOW HOW TO DO ANY-THING.
...WHEN I WAS JUST A CAT...
...MY OWNER WAS ALSO A LADY WHO LIVED ALONE.

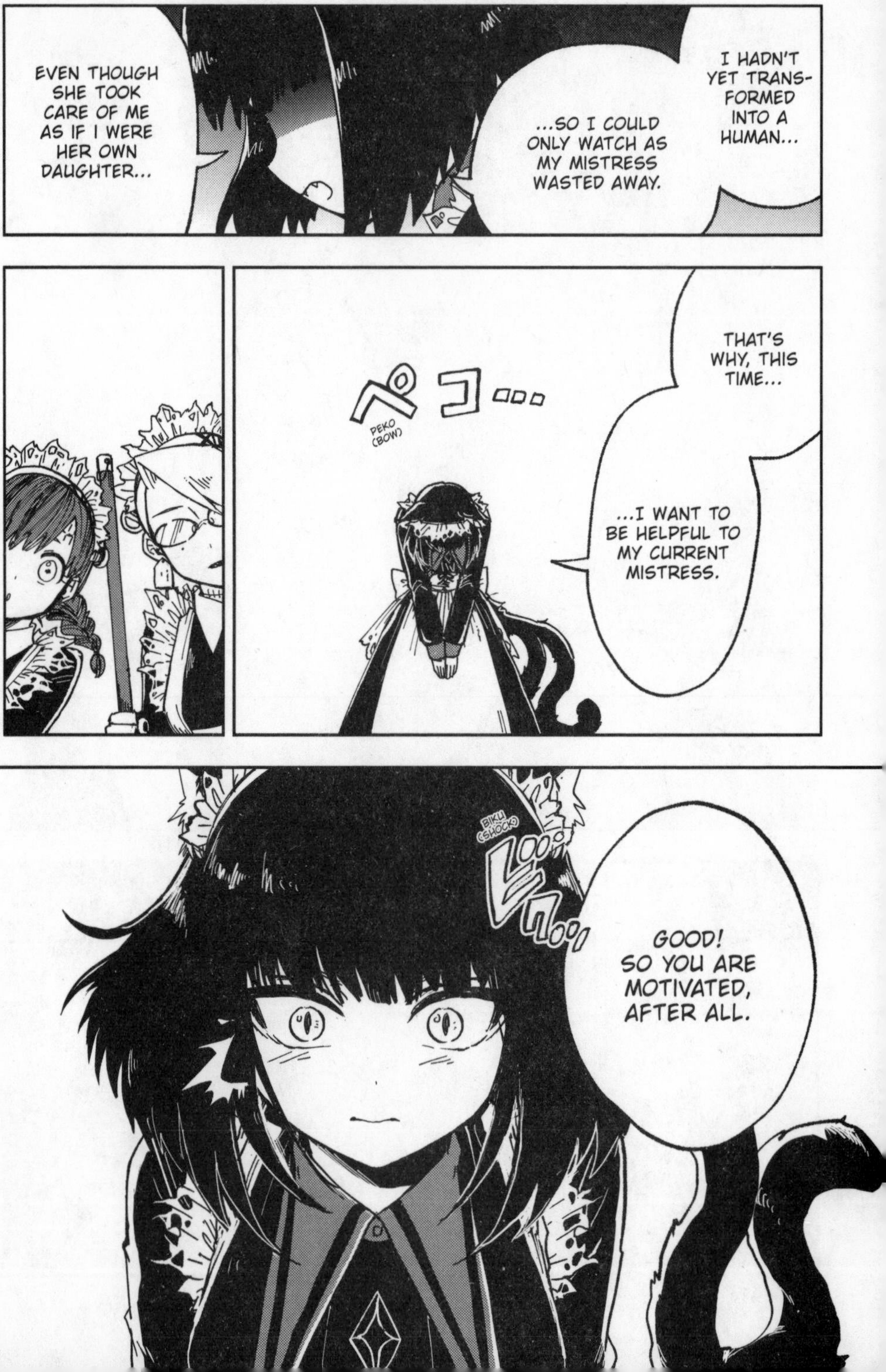
I HADN'T YET TRANS-FORMED INTO A HUMAN...
...SO I COULD ONLY WATCH AS MY MISTRESS WASTED AWAY.
EVEN THOUGH SHE TOOK CARE OF ME AS IF I WERE HER OWN DAUGHTER...
THAT'S WHY, THIS TIME...
ペコ...
PEKO (BOW)
...I WANT TO BE HELPFUL TO MY CURRENT MISTRESS.
BIKU (SHOCK)
GOOD! SO YOU ARE MOTIVATED, AFTER ALL.

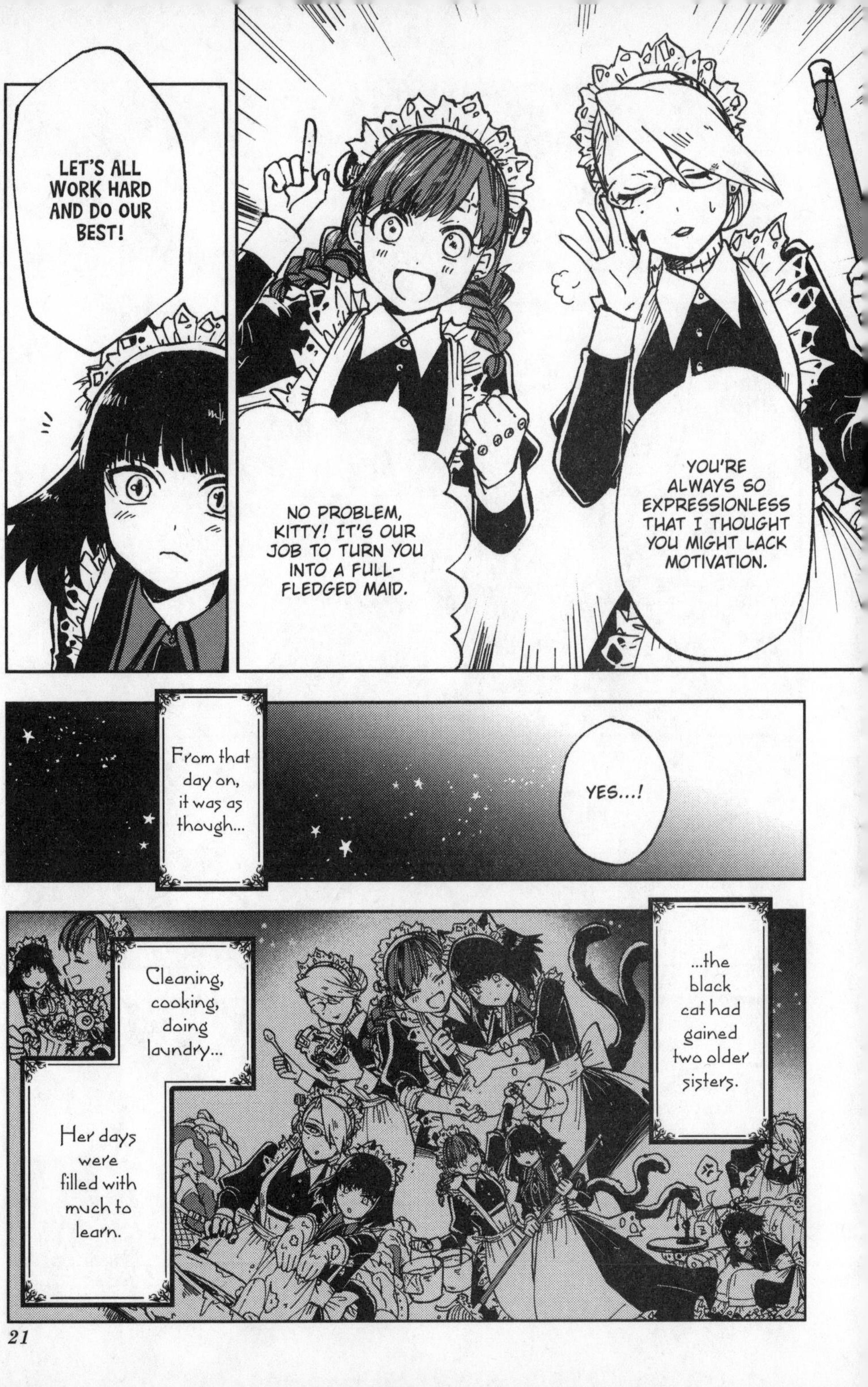
YOU'RE ALWAYS SO EXPRESSIONLESS THAT I THOUGHT YOU MIGHT LACK MOTIVATION.
NO PROBLEM, KITTY! IT'S OUR JOB TO TURN YOU INTO A FULL-FLEDGED MAID.
LET'S ALL WORK HARD AND DO OUR BEST!
YES...!
From that day on, it was as though...
...the black cat had gained two older sisters.
Cleaning, cooking, doing laundry...
Her days were filled with much to learn.

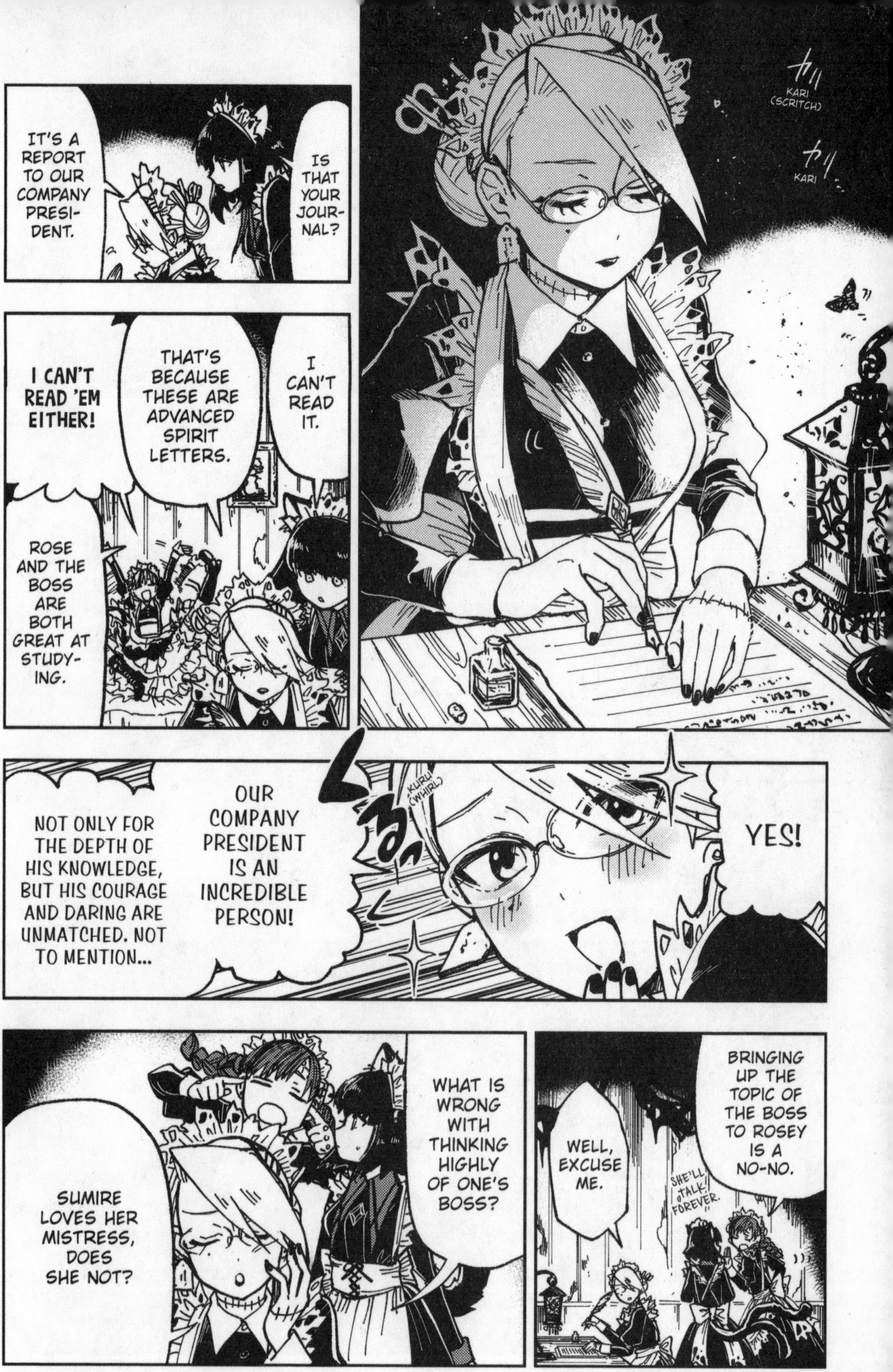
KARI (SCRITCH)
KARI
IS THAT YOUR JOURNAL?
IT'S A REPORT TO OUR COMPANY PRESIDENT.
I CAN'T READ IT.
THAT'S BECAUSE THESE ARE ADVANCED SPIRIT LETTERS.
I CAN'T READ 'EM EITHER!
ROSE AND THE BOSS ARE BOTH GREAT AT STUDYING.
YES!
KURU (WHIRL)
OUR COMPANY PRESIDENT IS AN INCREDIBLE PERSON!
NOT ONLY FOR THE DEPTH OF HIS KNOWLEDGE, BUT HIS COURAGE AND DARING ARE UNMATCHED. NOT TO MENTION...
BRINGING UP THE TOPIC OF THE BOSS TO ROSEY IS A NO-NO.
SHE'LL TALK FOREVER.
WELL, EXCUSE ME.
WHAT IS WRONG WITH THINKING HIGHLY OF ONE'S BOSS?
SUMIRE LOVES HER MISTRESS, DOES SHE NOT?

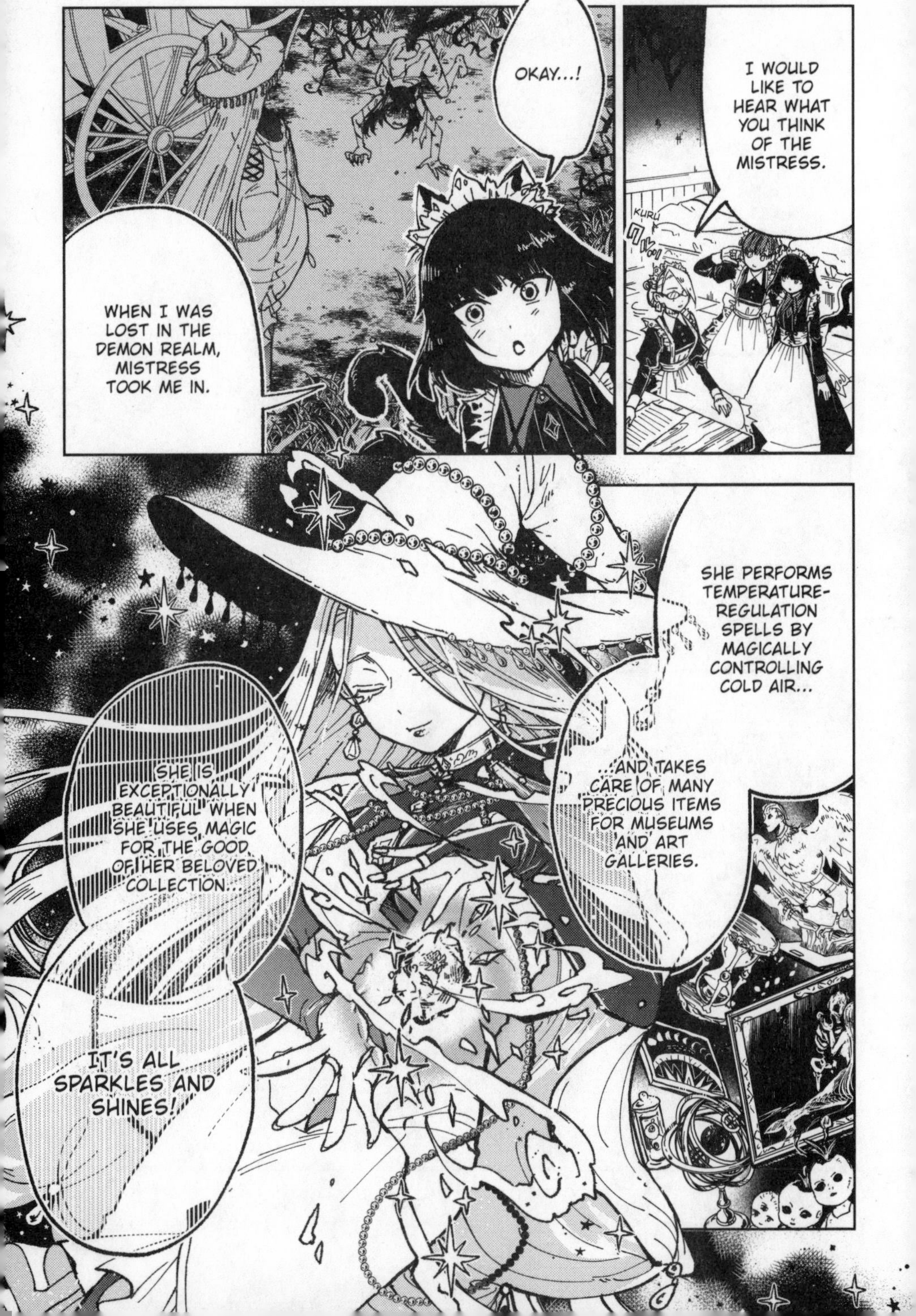
I WOULD LIKE TO HEAR WHAT YOU THINK OF THE MISTRESS.
KURU
OKAY...!
WHEN I WAS LOST IN THE DEMON REALM, MISTRESS TOOK ME IN.
SHE PERFORMS TEMPERATURE-REGULATION SPELLS BY MAGICALLY CONTROLLING COLD AIR...
...AND TAKES CARE OF MANY PRECIOUS ITEMS FOR MUSEUMS AND ART GALLERIES.
SHE IS EXCEPTIONALLY BEAUTIFUL WHEN SHE USES MAGIC FOR THE GOOD OF HER BELOVED COLLECTION...
IT'S ALL SPARKLES AND SHINES!

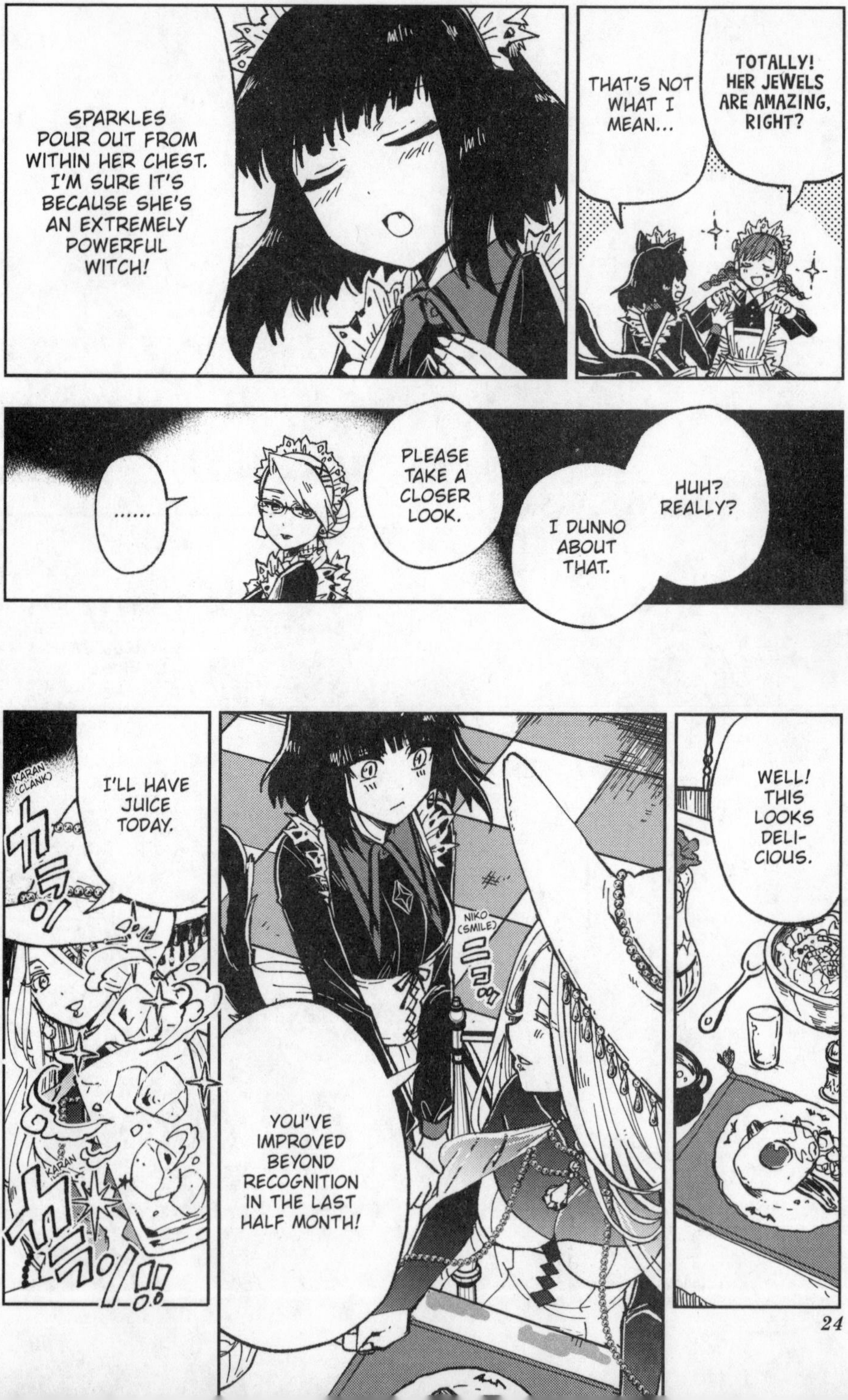
TOTALLY! HER JEWELS ARE AMAZING, RIGHT?
THAT'S NOT WHAT I MEAN...
SPARKLES POUR OUT FROM WITHIN HER CHEST. I'M SURE IT'S BECAUSE SHE'S AN EXTREMELY POWERFUL WITCH!
HUH? REALLY?
I DUNNO ABOUT THAT.
PLEASE TAKE A CLOSER LOOK.
......
WELL! THIS LOOKS DELICIOUS.
NIKO (SMILE)
YOU'VE IMPROVED BEYOND RECOGNITION IN THE LAST HALF MONTH!
KARAN (CLANK)
I'LL HAVE JUICE TODAY.
KARAN

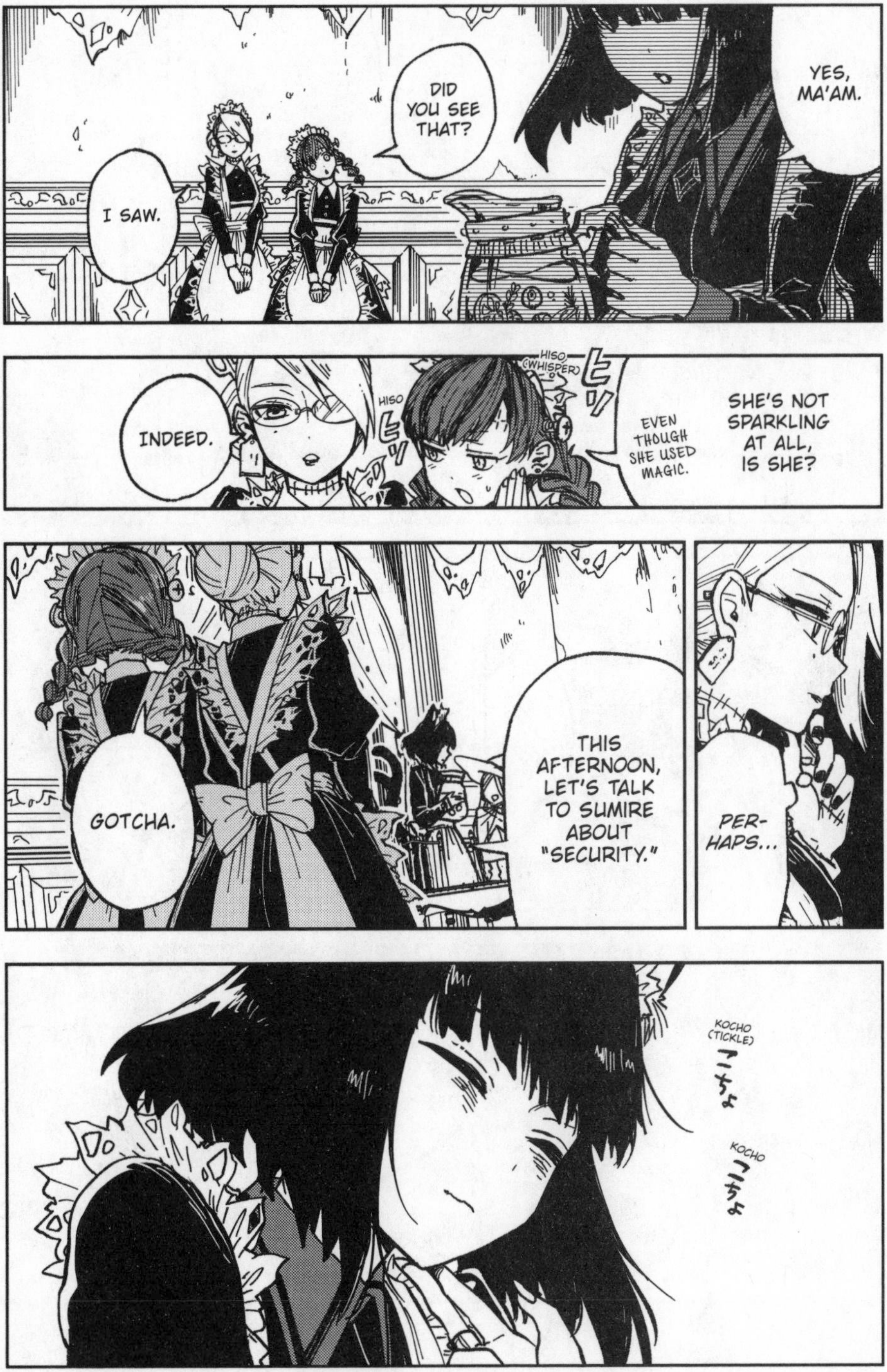
YES, MA'AM.
DID YOU SEE THAT?
I SAW.
SHE'S NOT SPARKLING AT ALL, IS SHE?
HISO (WHISPER)
EVEN THOUGH SHE USED MAGIC.
HISO
INDEED.
PER-HAPS...
THIS AFTERNOON, LET'S TALK TO SUMIRE ABOUT "SECURITY."
GOTCHA.
KOCHO (TICKLE)
こちょ
KOCHO
こちょ

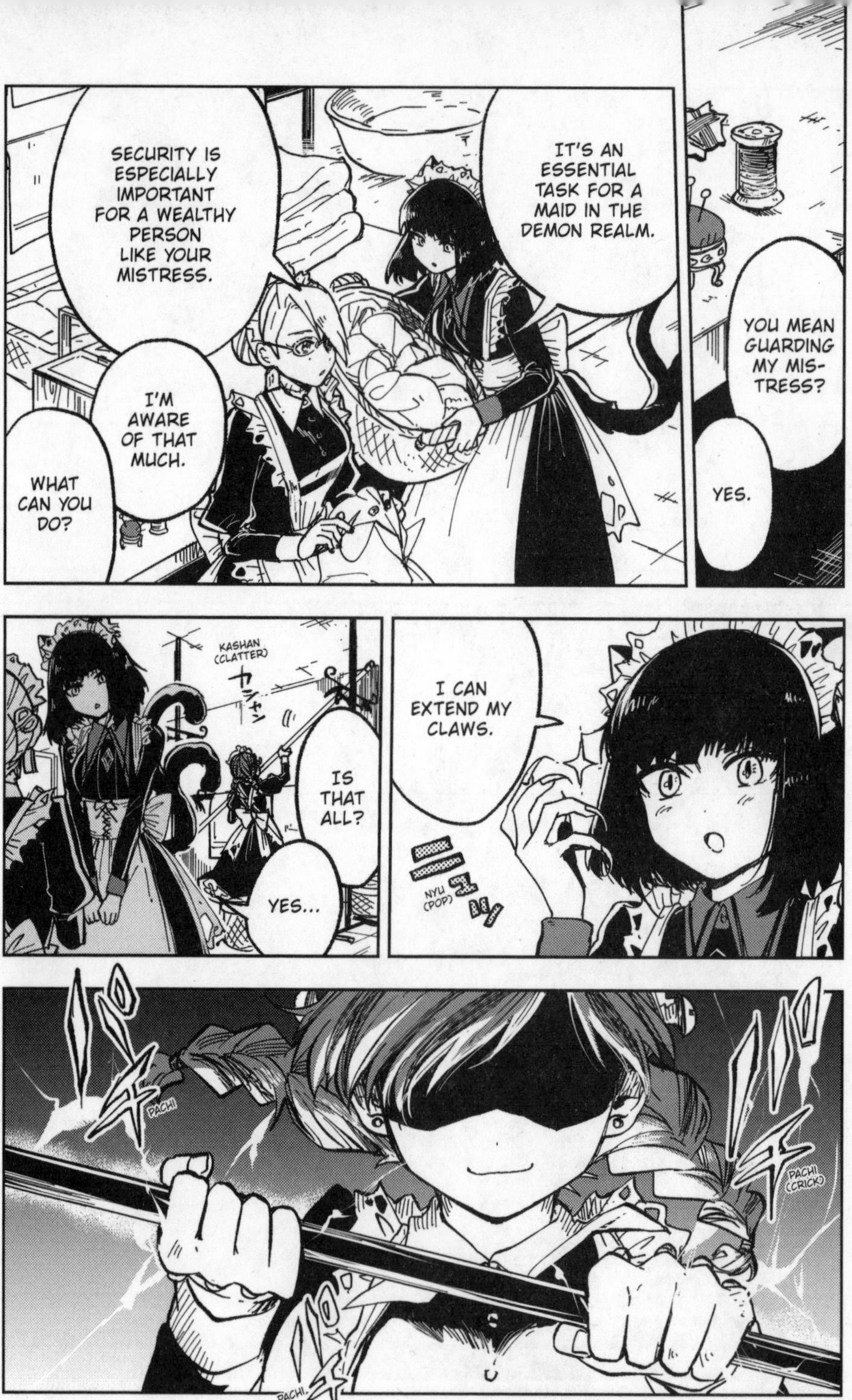
YOU MEAN GUARDING MY MIS-TRESS?
YES.
IT'S AN ESSENTIAL TASK FOR A MAID IN THE DEMON REALM.
SECURITY IS ESPECIALLY IMPORTANT FOR A WEALTHY PERSON LIKE YOUR MISTRESS.
I'M AWARE OF THAT MUCH.
WHAT CAN YOU DO?
I CAN EXTEND MY CLAWS.
NYU (POP)
KASHAN (CLATTER)
IS THAT ALL?
YES...
PACHI (CRICK)
PACHI
PACHI

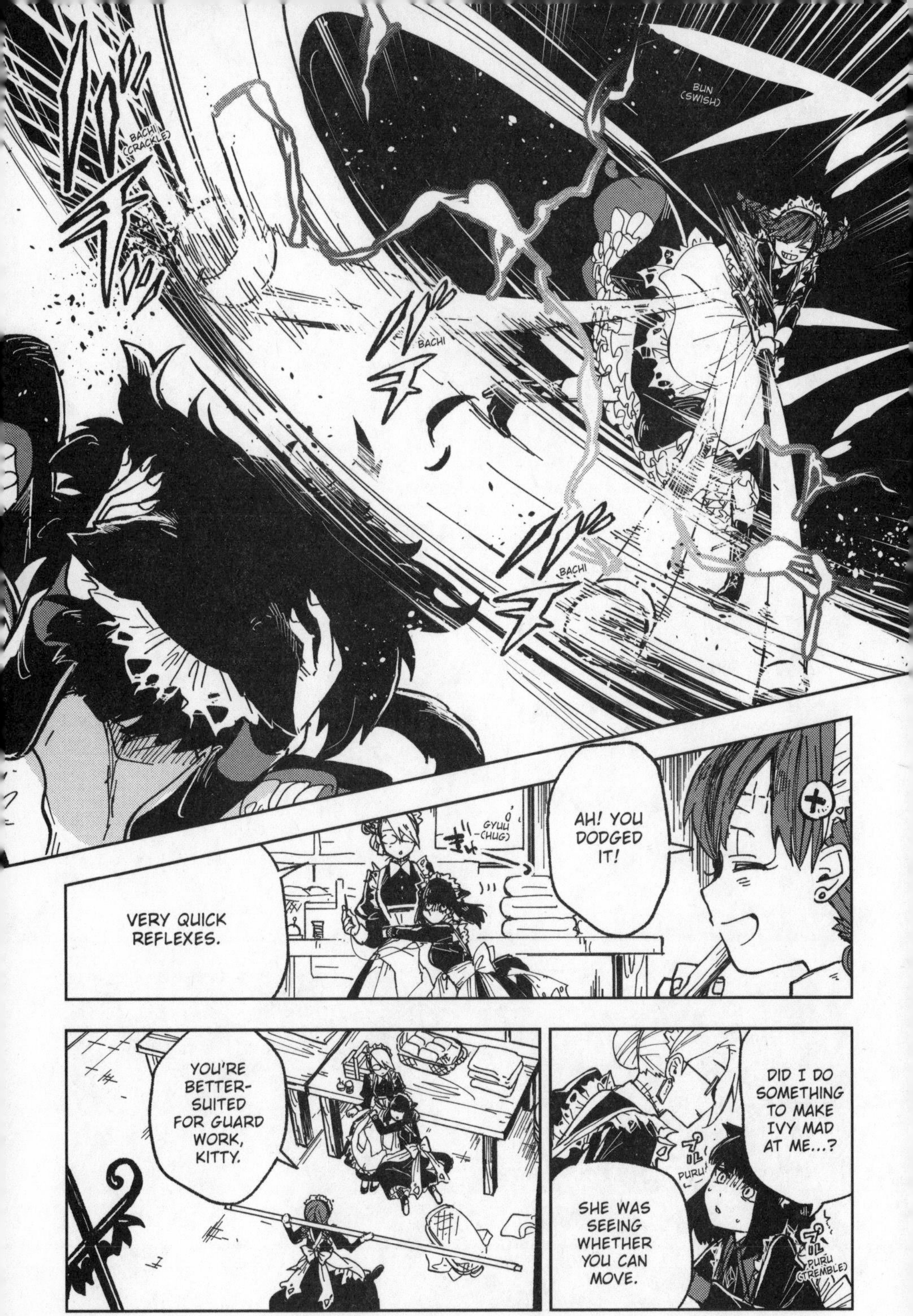
BUN (SWISH)
BACHI (CRACKLE)
BACHI
BACHI
AH! YOU DODGED IT!
GYUU (HUG)
VERY QUICK REFLEXES.
DID I DO SOMETHING TO MAKE IVY MAD AT ME...?
PURU
SHE WAS SEEING WHETHER YOU CAN MOVE.
PURU (TREMBLE)
YOU'RE BETTER-SUITED FOR GUARD WORK, KITTY.

KEYS
...?

...BY
THE
WAY...

...WHAT DO
YOU THINK
WHEN YOU
LOOK AT
THESE KEYS,
SUMIRE?

CHARI
(JINGLE)

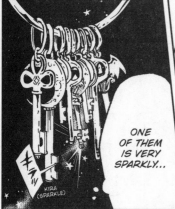

ONE
OF THEM
IS VERY
SPARKLY...

KIRA
(SPARKLE)

HUH...?

CHARI

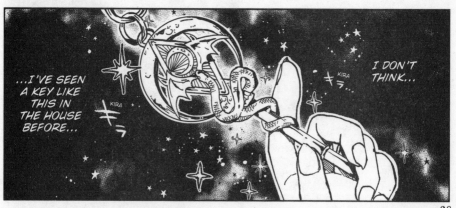

...I'VE SEEN
A KEY LIKE
THIS IN
THE HOUSE
BEFORE...

KIRA

KIRA

I DON'T
THINK...

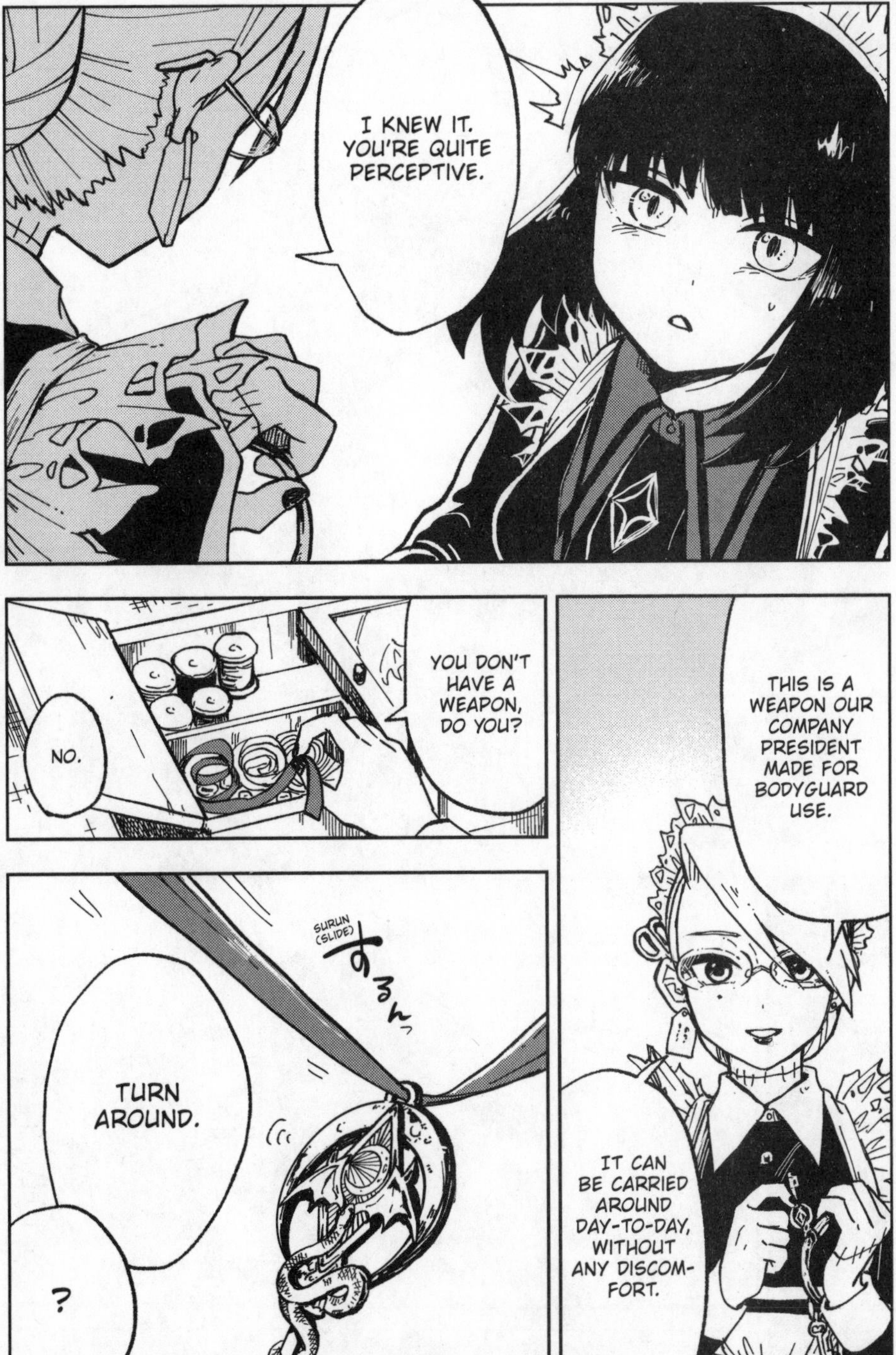
I KNEW IT. YOU'RE QUITE PERCEPTIVE.
THIS IS A WEAPON OUR COMPANY PRESIDENT MADE FOR BODYGUARD USE.
IT CAN BE CARRIED AROUND DAY-TO-DAY, WITHOUT ANY DISCOM-FORT.
YOU DON'T HAVE A WEAPON, DO YOU?
NO.
SURUN (SLIDE)
するん
TURN AROUND.
?

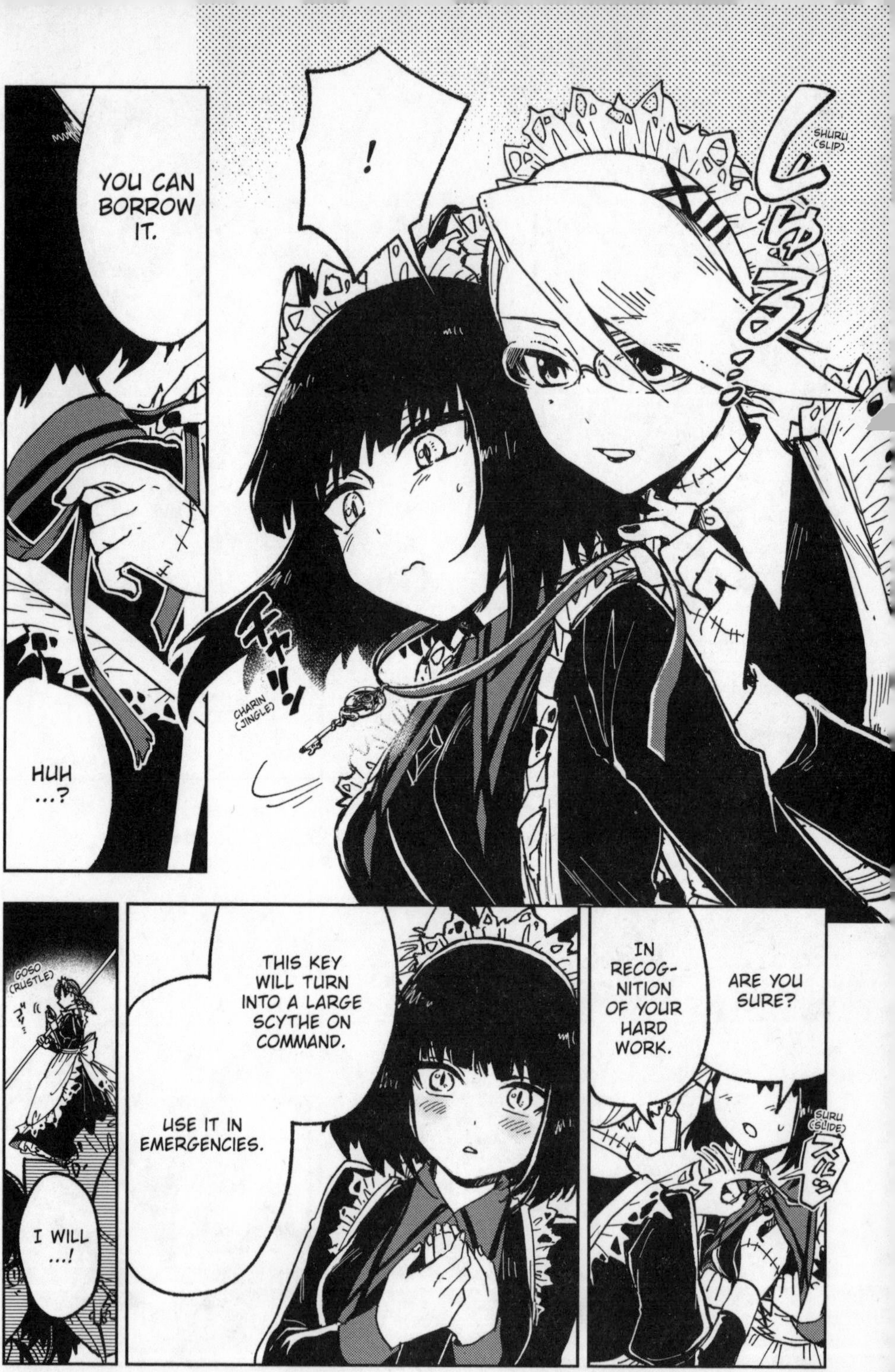
!
SHURU (SLIP)
CHARIN (JINGLE)
YOU CAN BORROW IT.
HUH ...?
ARE YOU SURE?
IN RECOGNITION OF YOUR HARD WORK.
SURU (SLIDE)
THIS KEY WILL TURN INTO A LARGE SCYTHE ON COMMAND.
USE IT IN EMERGENCIES.
GOSO (RUSTLE)
I WILL ...!

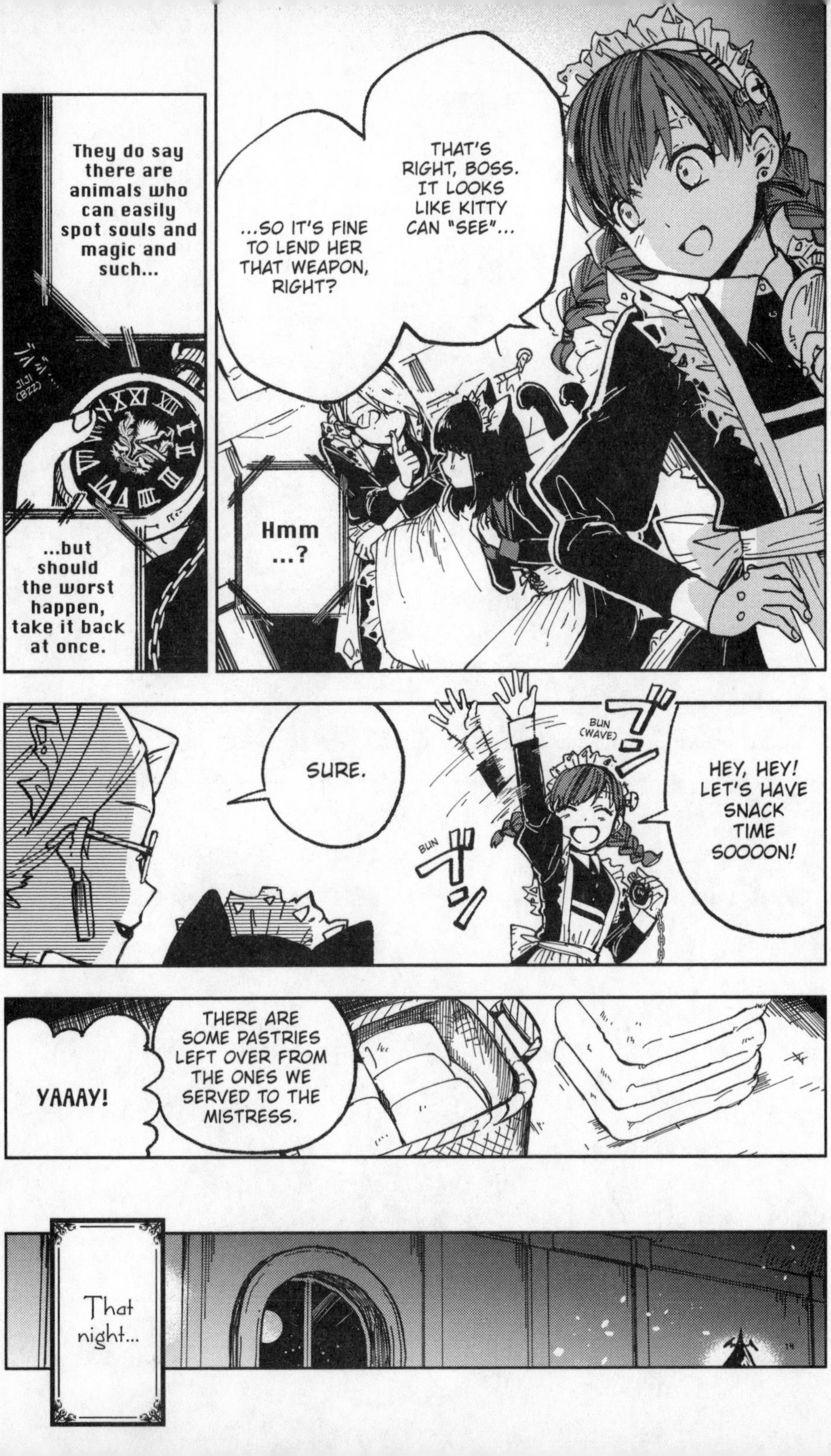
THAT'S RIGHT, BOSS. IT LOOKS LIKE KITTY CAN "SEE"...
...SO IT'S FINE TO LEND HER THAT WEAPON, RIGHT?
Hmm ...?
They do say there are animals who can easily spot souls and magic and such...
JIJI (BZZ)
...but should the worst happen, take it back at once.
HEY, HEY! LET'S HAVE SNACK TIME SOOOON!
BUN (WAVE)
BUN
SURE.
THERE ARE SOME PASTRIES LEFT OVER FROM THE ONES WE SERVED TO THE MISTRESS.
YAAAY!
That night...

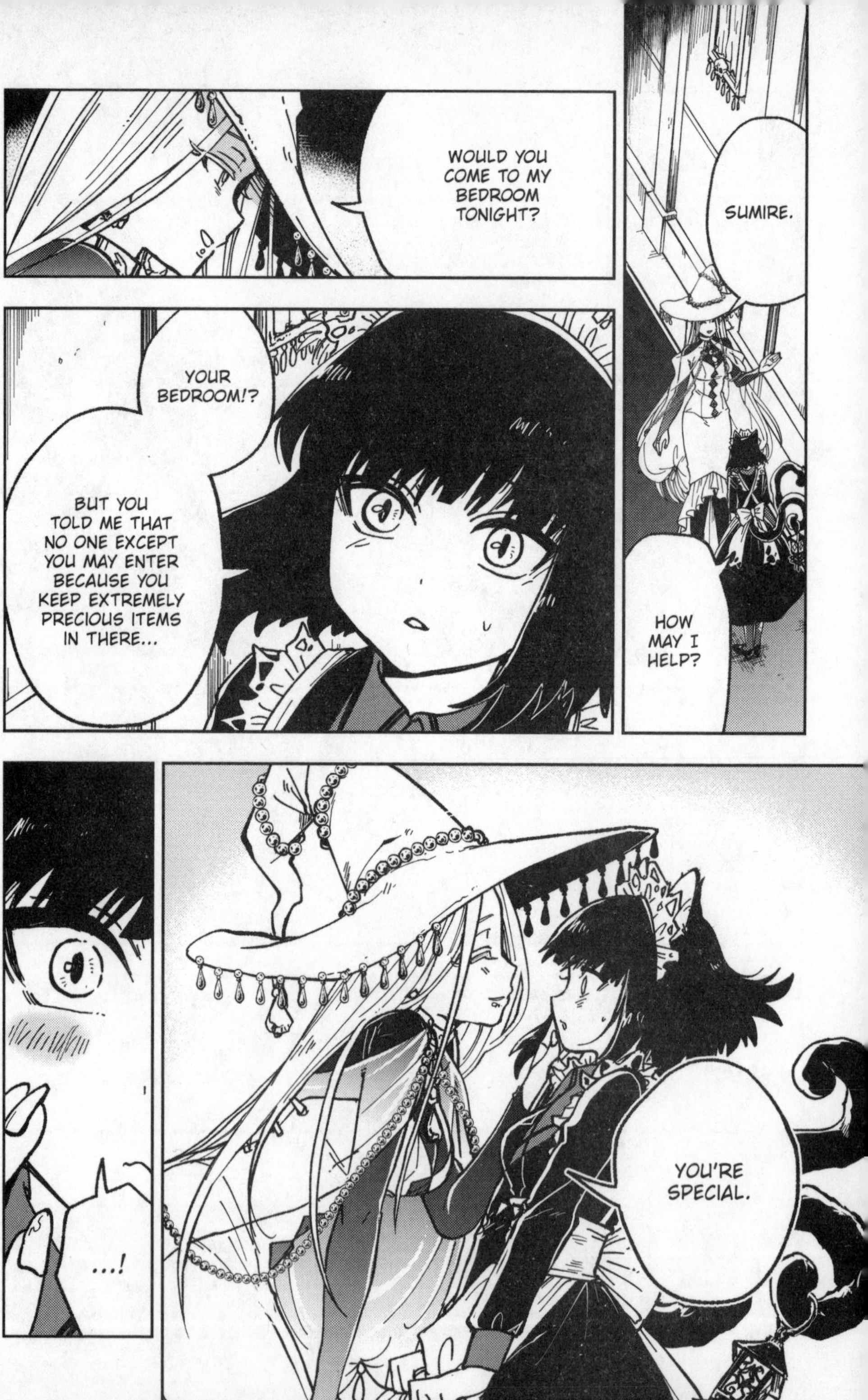
SUMIRE.
HOW MAY I HELP?
WOULD YOU COME TO MY BEDROOM TONIGHT?
YOUR BEDROOM!?
BUT YOU TOLD ME THAT NO ONE EXCEPT YOU MAY ENTER BECAUSE YOU KEEP EXTREMELY PRECIOUS ITEMS IN THERE...
YOU'RE SPECIAL.
...!

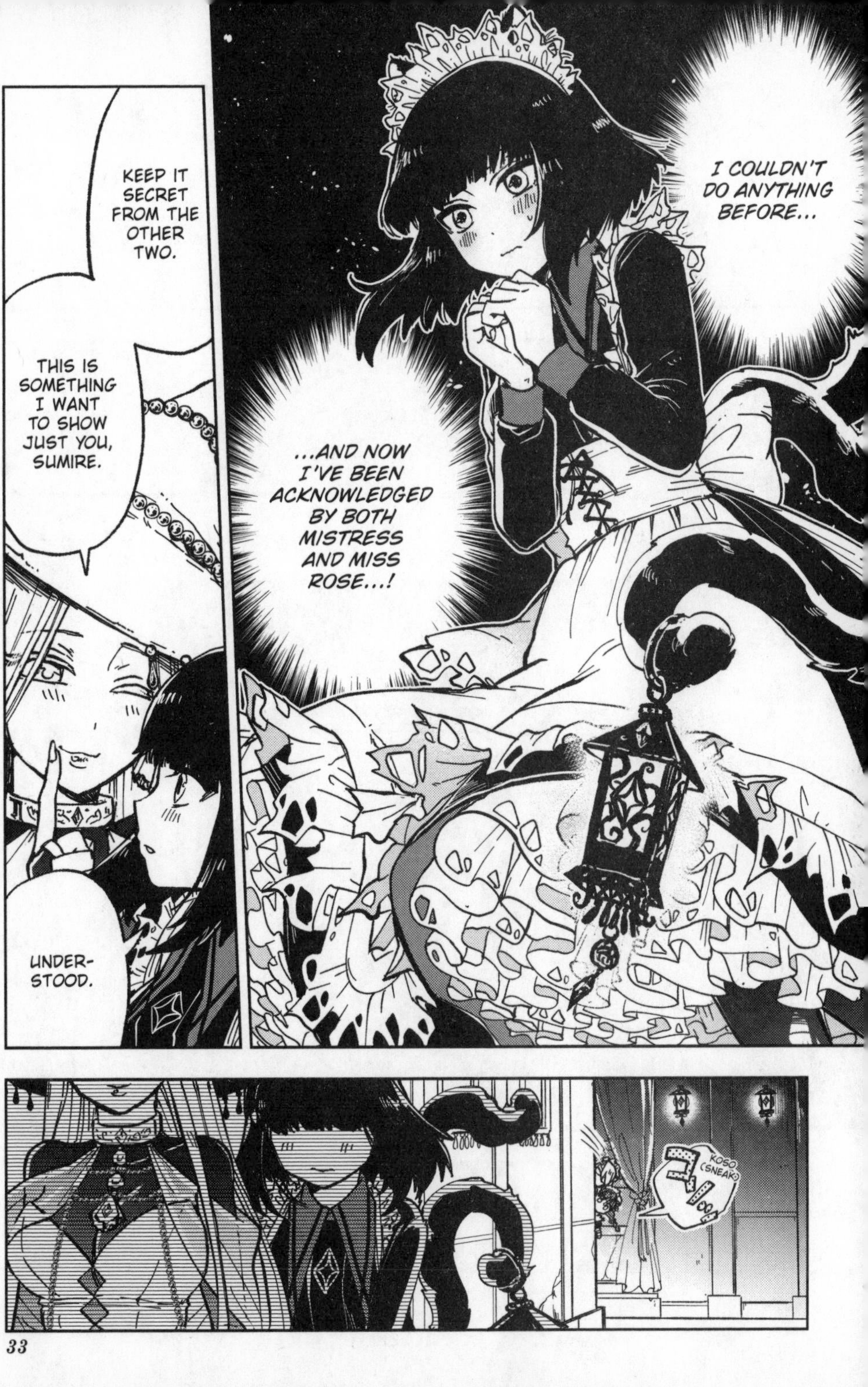

I COULDN'T DO ANYTHING BEFORE...
...AND NOW I'VE BEEN ACKNOWLEDGED BY BOTH MISTRESS AND MISS ROSE...!
KEEP IT SECRET FROM THE OTHER TWO.
THIS IS SOMETHING I WANT TO SHOW JUST YOU, SUMIRE.
UNDER-STOOD.
KOSO (SNEAK)

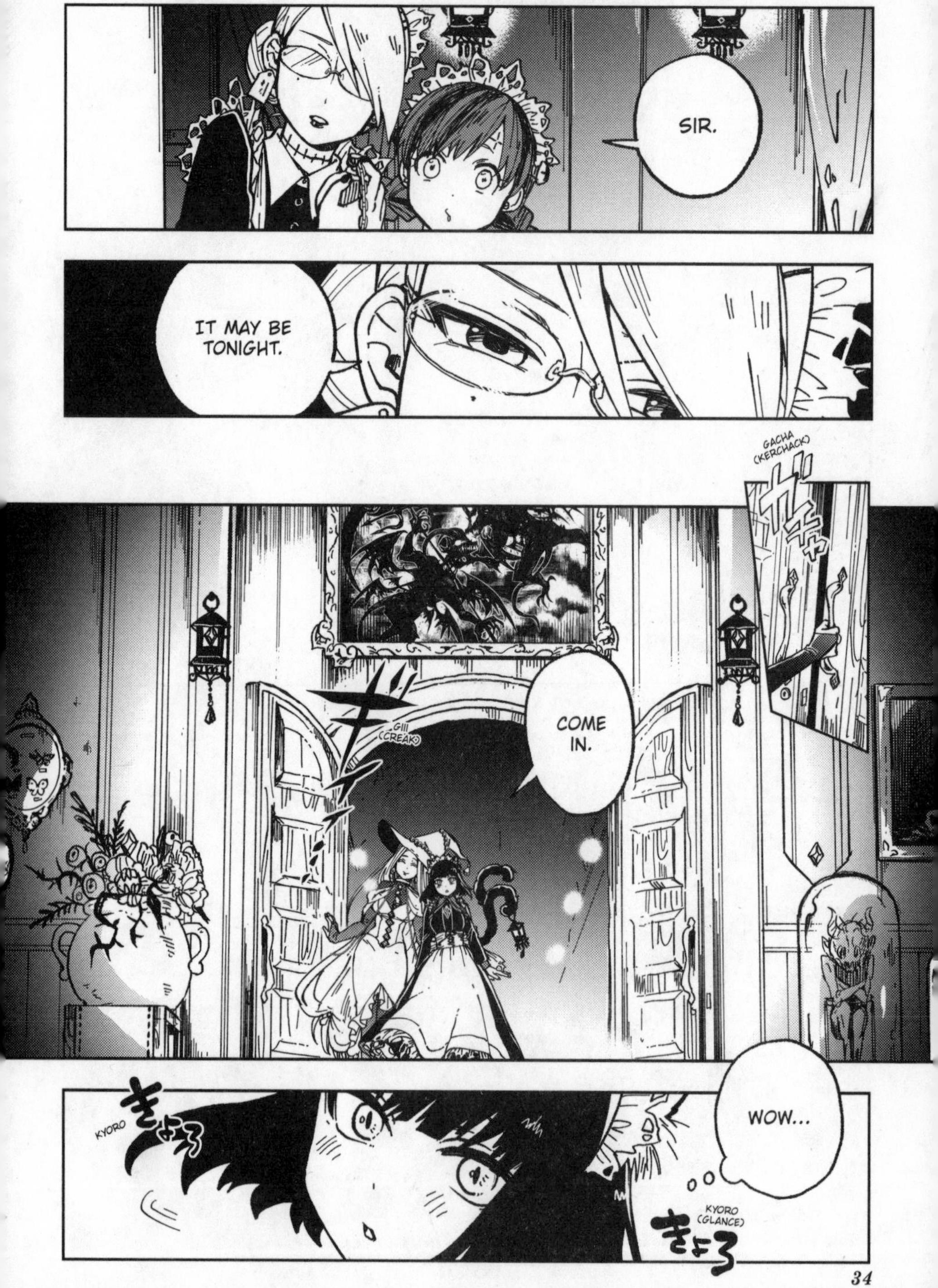
SIR.
IT MAY BE TONIGHT.
GACHA (KERCHACK)
COME IN.
GIII (CREAK)
WOW...
KYORO (GLANCE)
KYORO

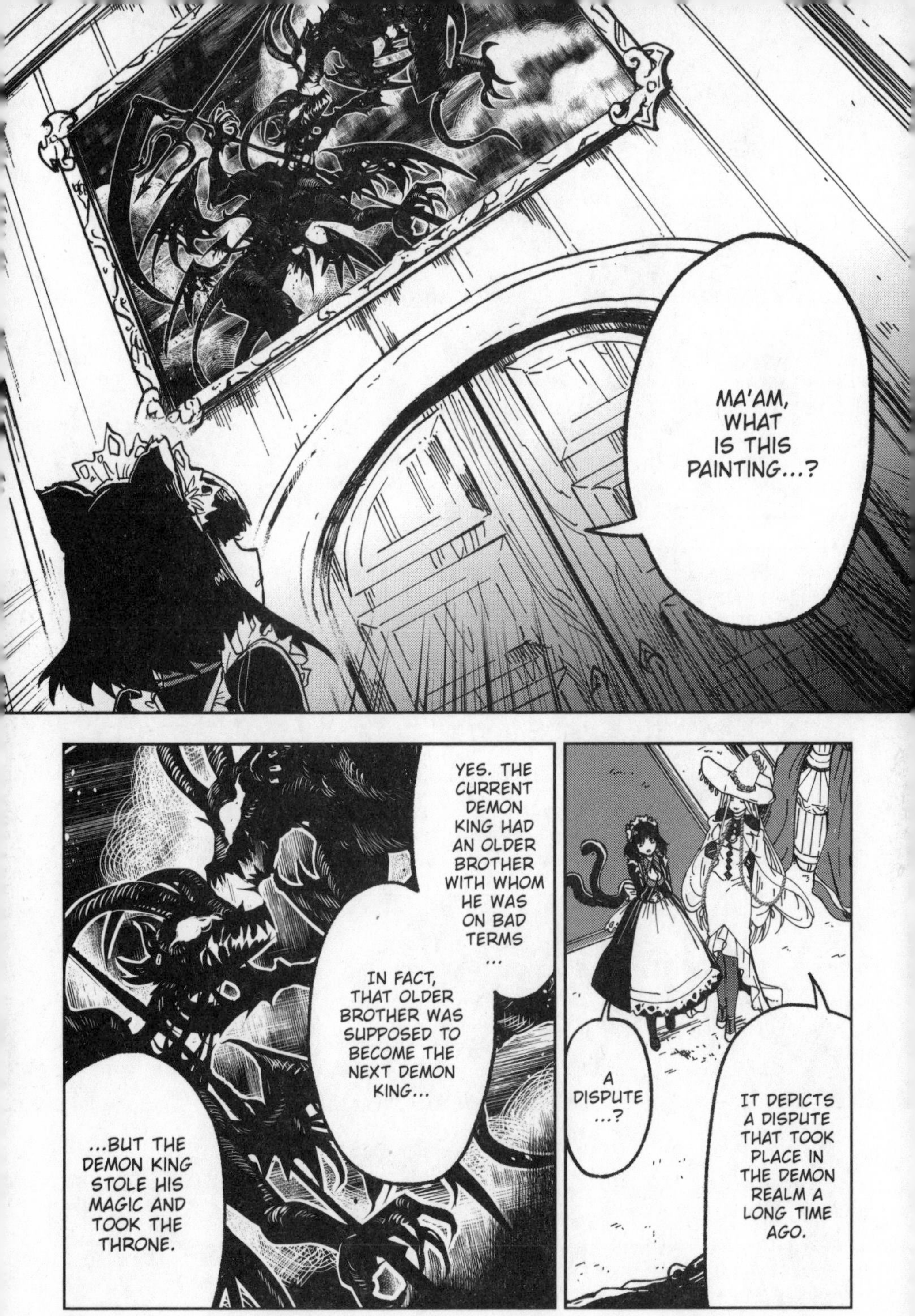
MA'AM, WHAT IS THIS PAINTING...?
IT DEPICTS A DISPUTE THAT TOOK PLACE IN THE DEMON REALM A LONG TIME AGO.
A DISPUTE ...?
YES. THE CURRENT DEMON KING HAD AN OLDER BROTHER WITH WHOM HE WAS ON BAD TERMS ...
IN FACT, THAT OLDER BROTHER WAS SUPPOSED TO BECOME THE NEXT DEMON KING...
...BUT THE DEMON KING STOLE HIS MAGIC AND TOOK THE THRONE.

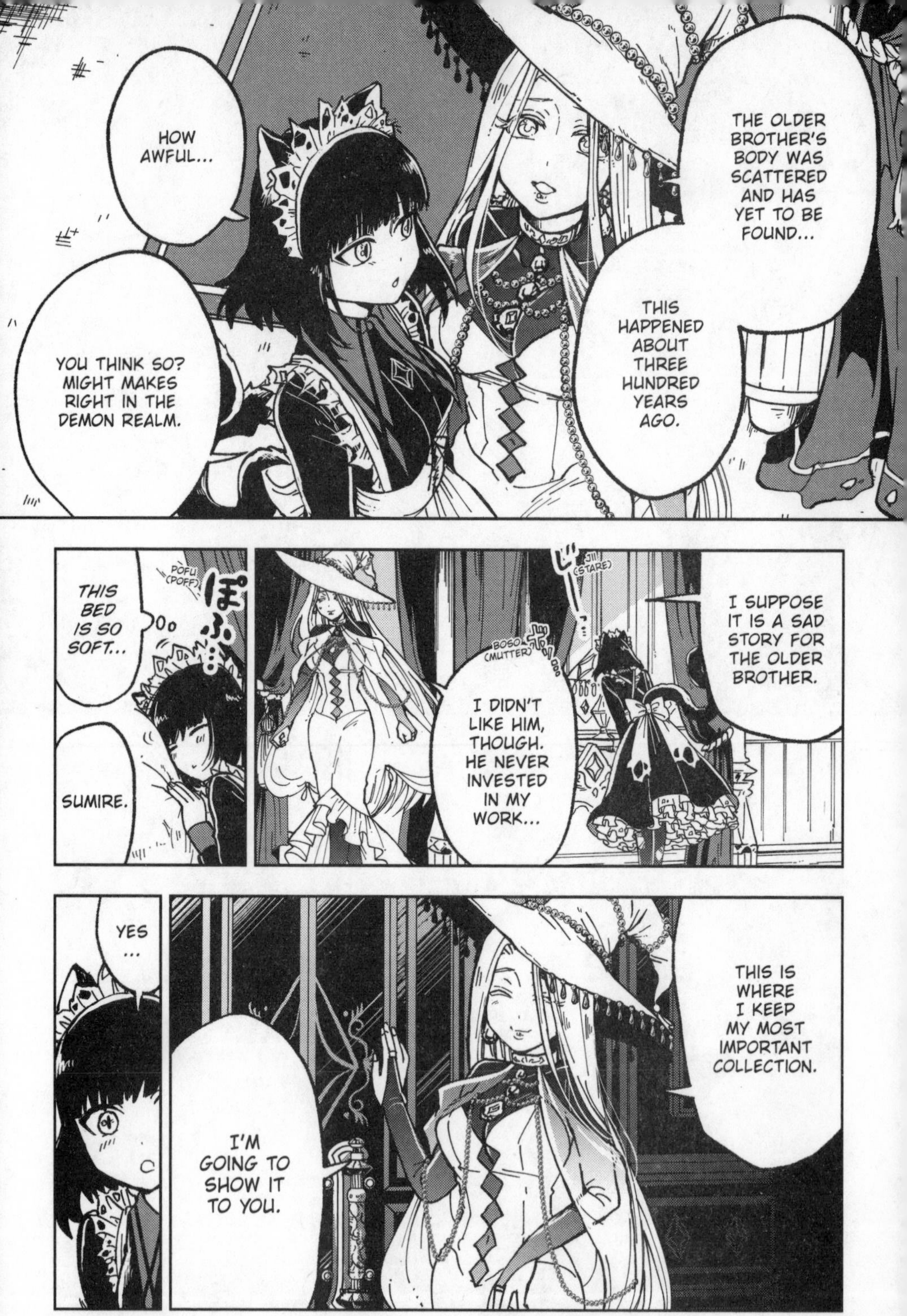
THE OLDER BROTHER'S BODY WAS SCATTERED AND HAS YET TO BE FOUND...
THIS HAPPENED ABOUT THREE HUNDRED YEARS AGO.
HOW AWFUL...
YOU THINK SO? MIGHT MAKES RIGHT IN THE DEMON REALM.
JII (STARE)
I SUPPOSE IT IS A SAD STORY FOR THE OLDER BROTHER.
BOSO (MUTTER)
I DIDN'T LIKE HIM, THOUGH. HE NEVER INVESTED IN MY WORK...
POFU (POFF)
THIS BED IS SO SOFT...
SUMIRE.
THIS IS WHERE I KEEP MY MOST IMPORTANT COLLECTION.
I'M GOING TO SHOW IT TO YOU.
YES...

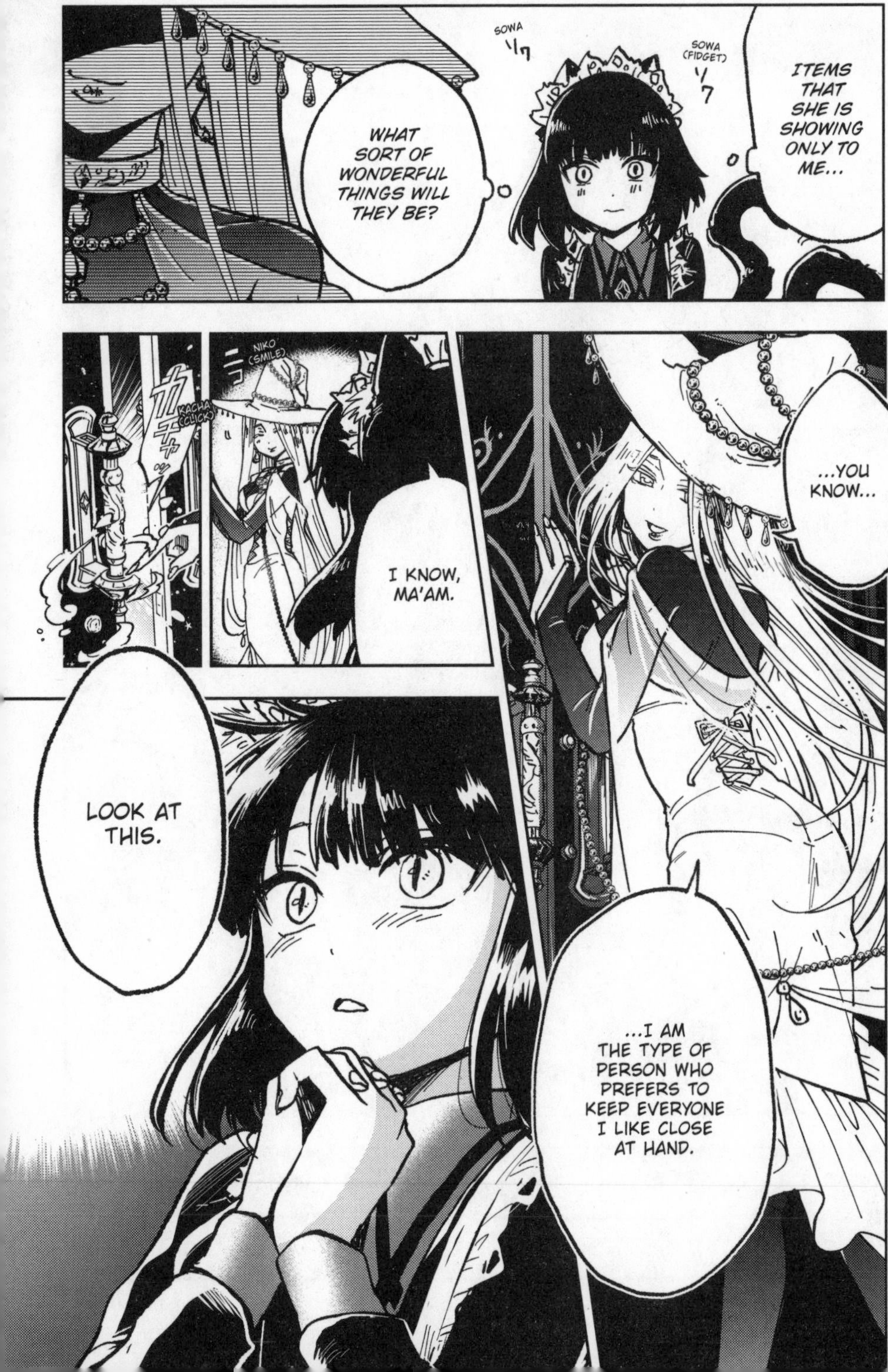
ITEMS THAT SHE IS SHOWING ONLY TO ME...
SOWA (FIDGET)
SOWA
WHAT SORT OF WONDERFUL THINGS WILL THEY BE?
...YOU KNOW...
...I AM THE TYPE OF PERSON WHO PREFERS TO KEEP EVERYONE I LIKE CLOSE AT HAND.
NIKO (SMILE)
I KNOW, MA'AM.
KACHA (CLICK)
LOOK AT THIS.

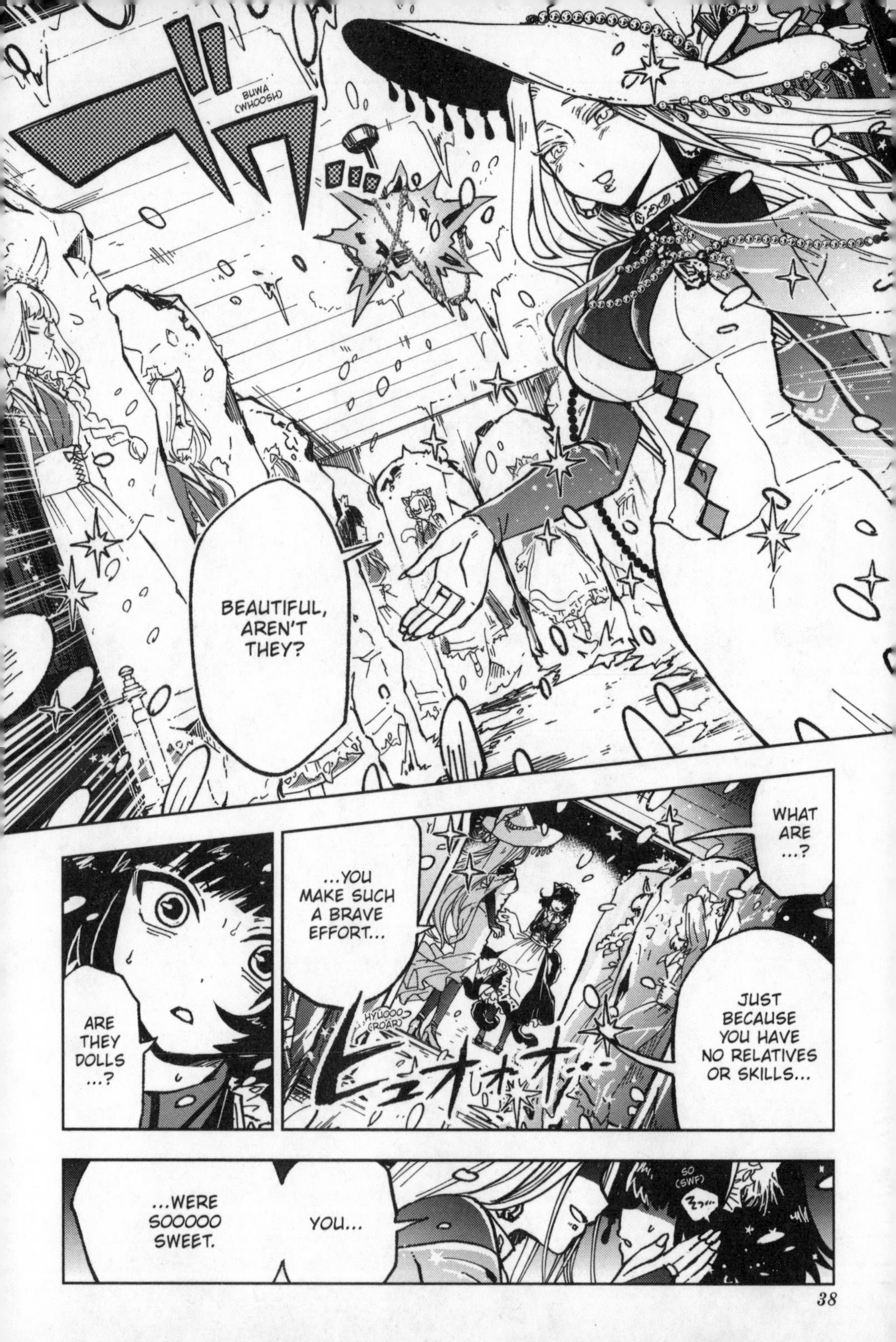
BUWA (WHOOSH)
BEAUTIFUL, AREN'T THEY?
WHAT ARE ...?
...YOU MAKE SUCH A BRAVE EFFORT...
JUST BECAUSE YOU HAVE NO RELATIVES OR SKILLS...
HYUOOO (ROAR)
ARE THEY DOLLS ...?
SO (SWF)
YOU...
...WERE SOOOOO SWEET.

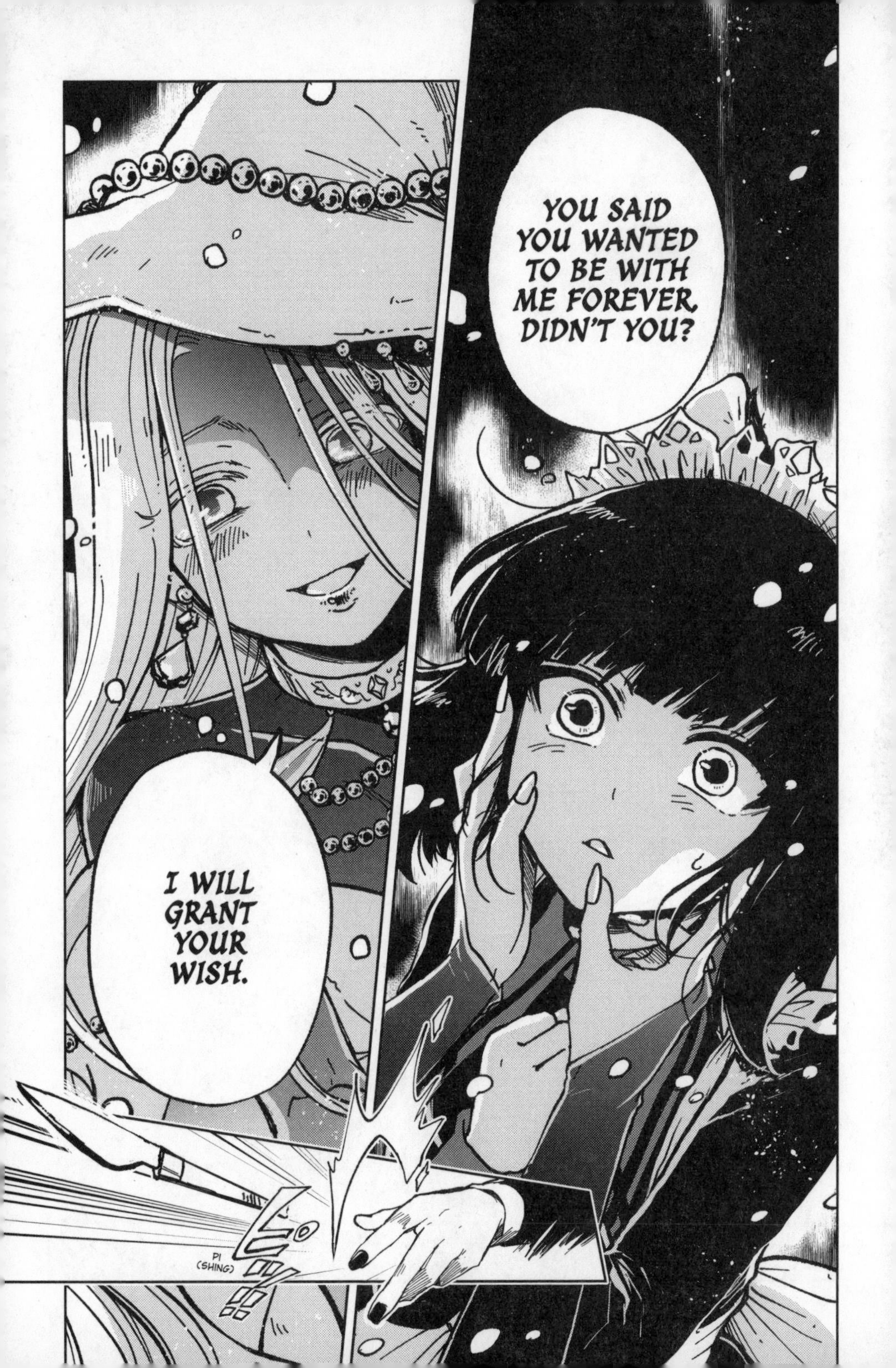
YOU SAID YOU WANTED TO BE WITH ME FOREVER, DIDN'T YOU?
I WILL GRANT YOUR WISH.
PI (SHING)

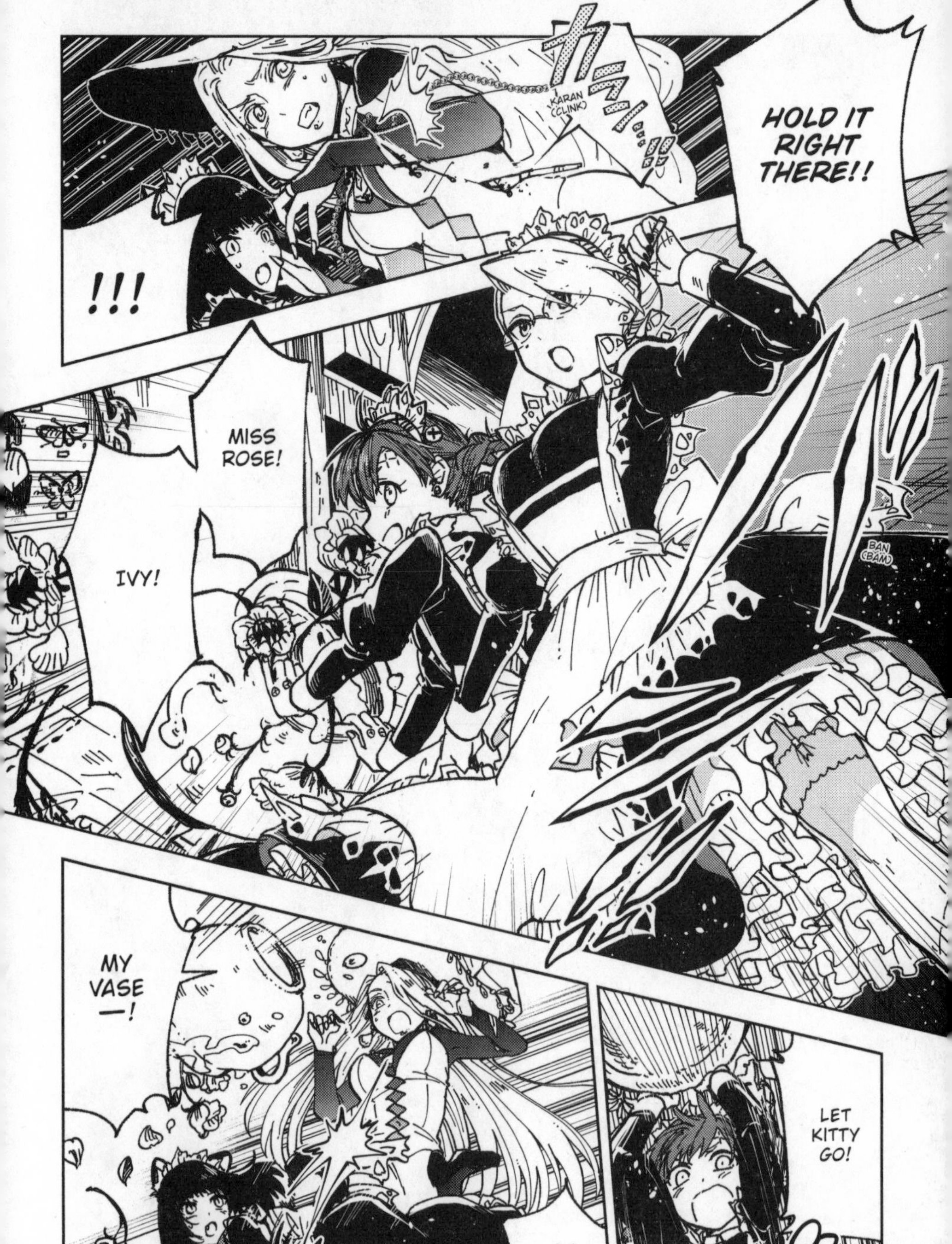
HOLD IT RIGHT THERE!!
KARAN (CLINK)
!!!
BAN (BAM)
MISS ROSE!
IVY!
LET KITTY GO!
BUN (FWISH)
MY VASE—!
!!

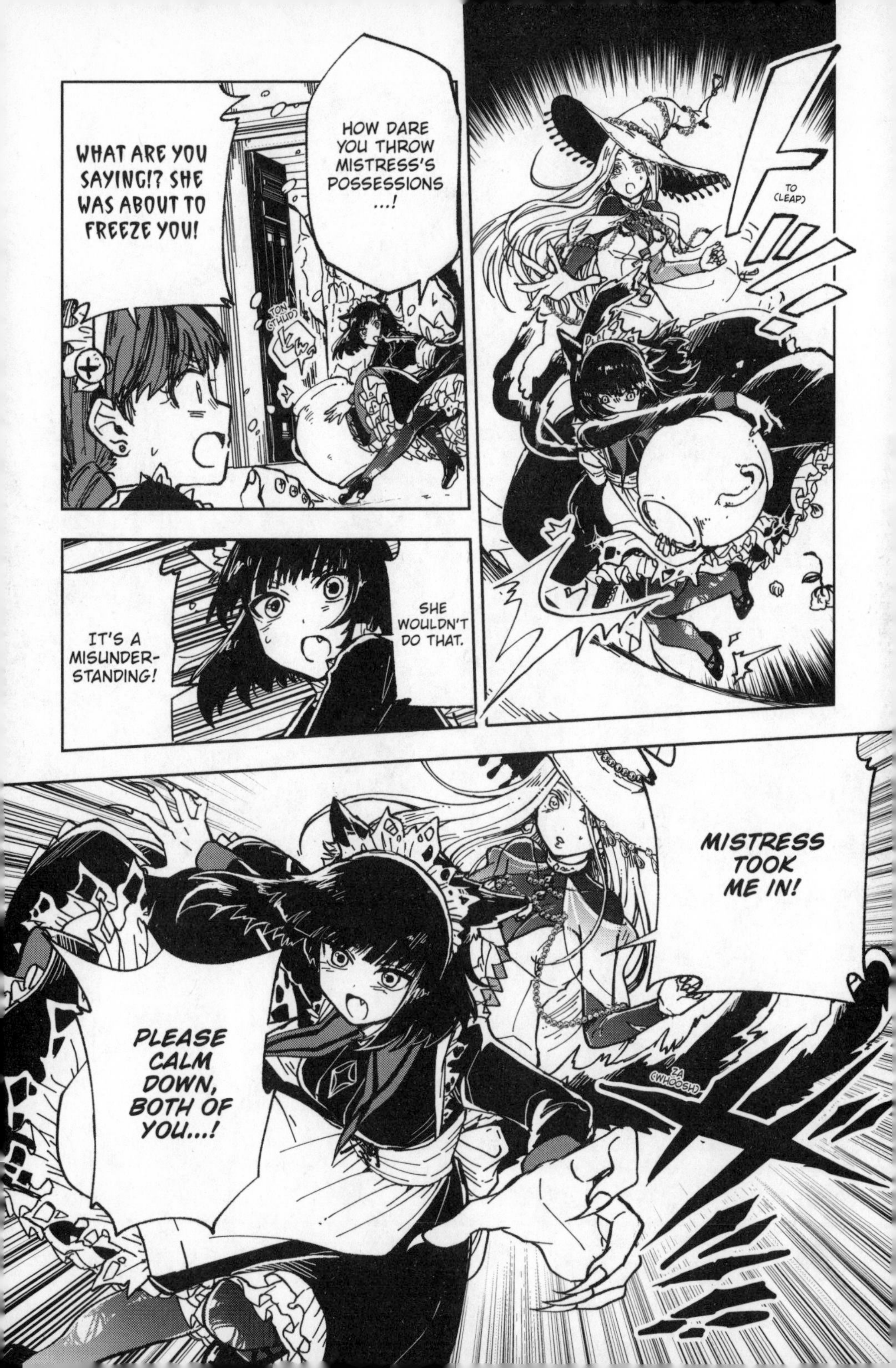
TO (LEAP)
HOW DARE YOU THROW MISTRESS'S POSSESSIONS ...!
WHAT ARE YOU SAYING!? SHE WAS ABOUT TO FREEZE YOU!
TON (THUD)
SHE WOULDN'T DO THAT.
IT'S A MISUNDER-STANDING!
MISTRESS TOOK ME IN!
ZA (WHOOSH)
PLEASE CALM DOWN, BOTH OF YOU...!

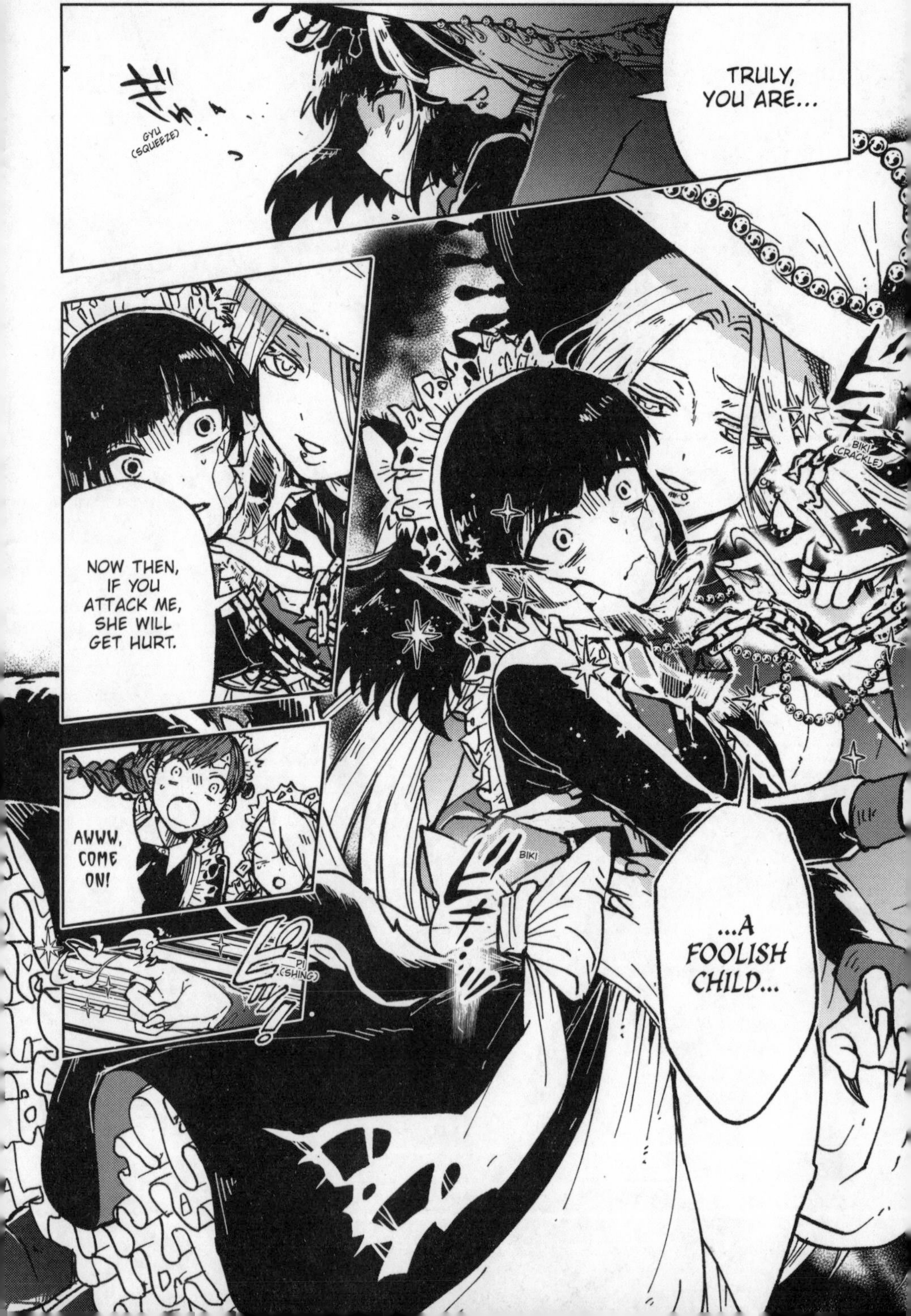
TRULY, YOU ARE...
GYU (SQUEEZE)
BIKI (CRACKLE)
BIKI
...A FOOLISH CHILD...
NOW THEN, IF YOU ATTACK ME, SHE WILL GET HURT.
AWWW, COME ON!
PI (SHING)

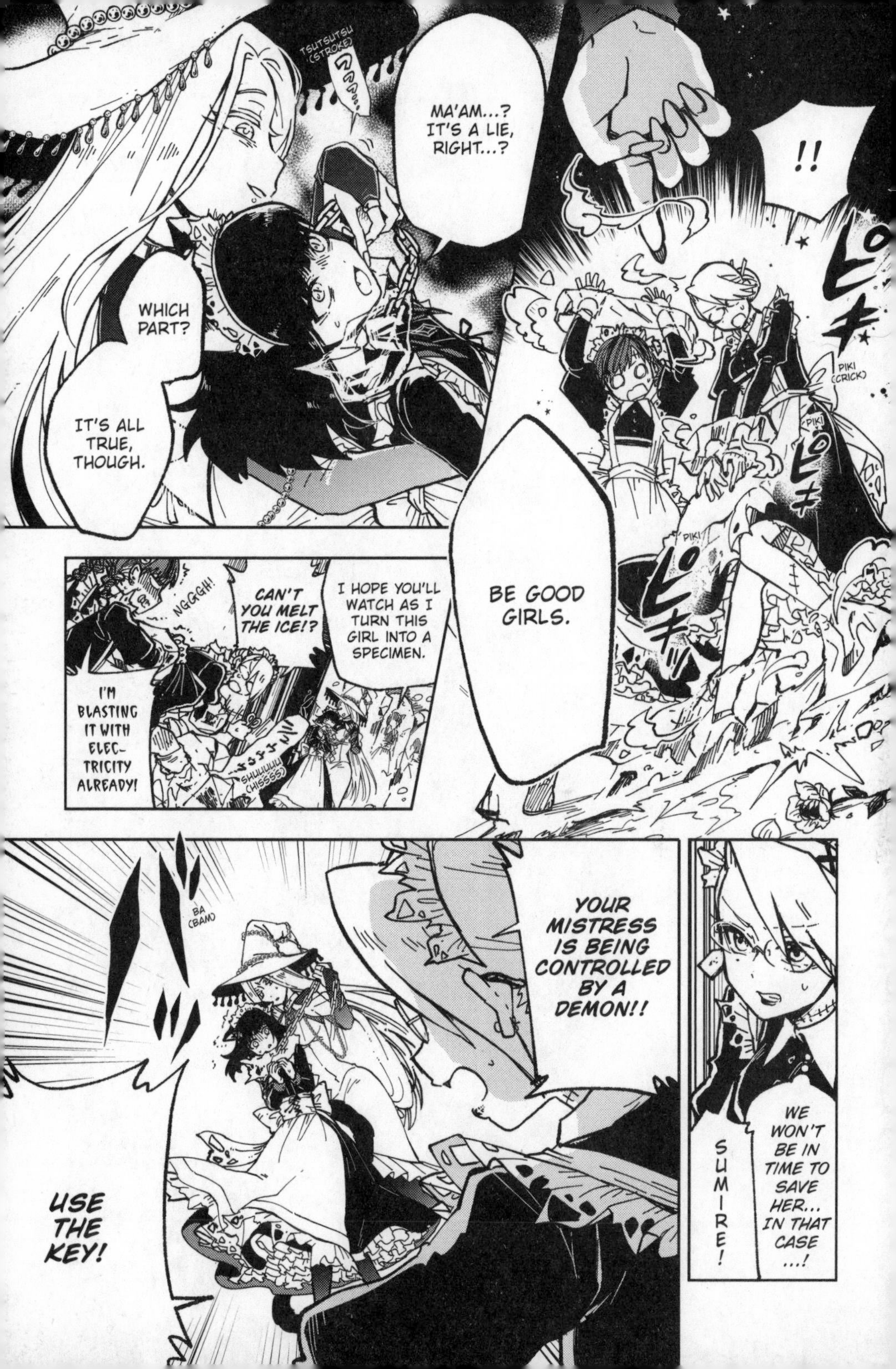
!!
PIKI (CRICK)
PIKI
PIKI
BE GOOD GIRLS.
TSUTSUTSU (STROKE)
MA'AM...? IT'S A LIE, RIGHT...?
WHICH PART?
IT'S ALL TRUE, THOUGH.
I HOPE YOU'LL WATCH AS I TURN THIS GIRL INTO A SPECIMEN.
CAN'T YOU MELT THE ICE!?
NGGGH!
I'M BLASTING IT WITH ELEC-TRICITY ALREADY!
SHUUUUU (HISSSS)
SUMIRE!
WE WON'T BE IN TIME TO SAVE HER... IN THAT CASE ...!
YOUR MISTRESS IS BEING CONTROLLED BY A DEMON!!
BA (BAM)
USE THE KEY!

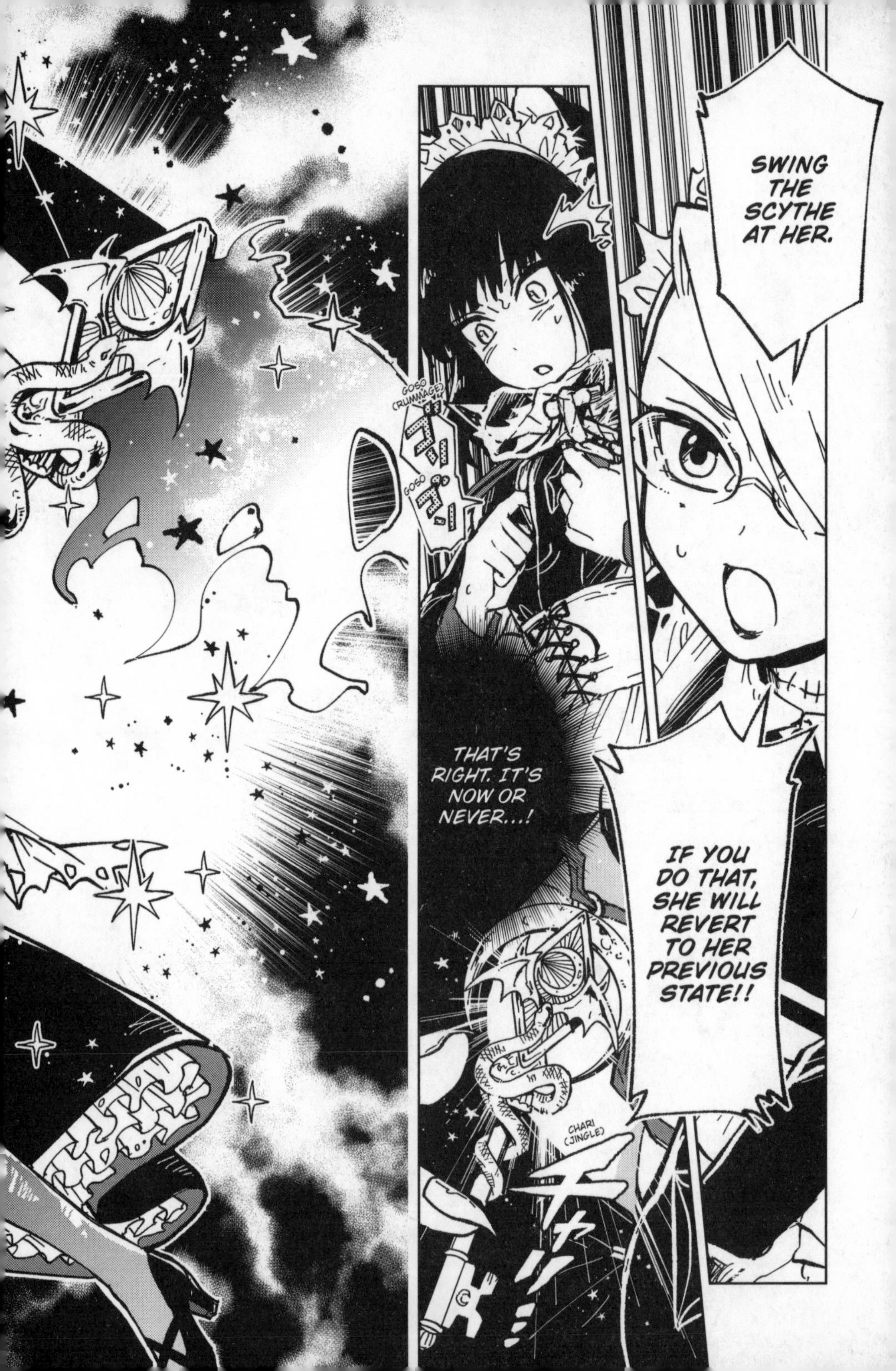
SWING THE SCYTHE AT HER.
GOSO (RUMMAGE)
GOSO
IF YOU DO THAT, SHE WILL REVERT TO HER PREVIOUS STATE!!
THAT'S RIGHT. IT'S NOW OR NEVER...!
CHARI (JINGLE)

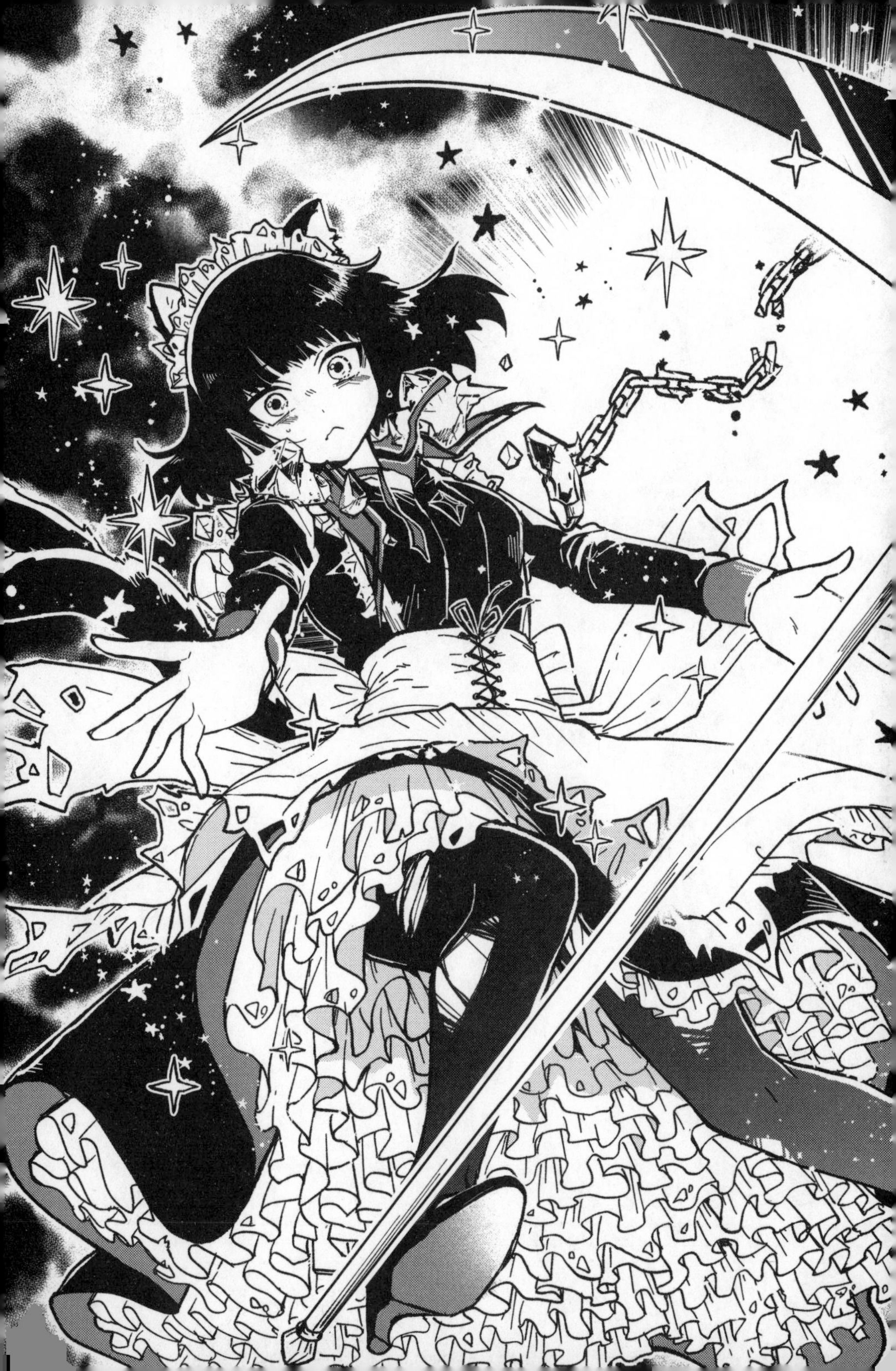

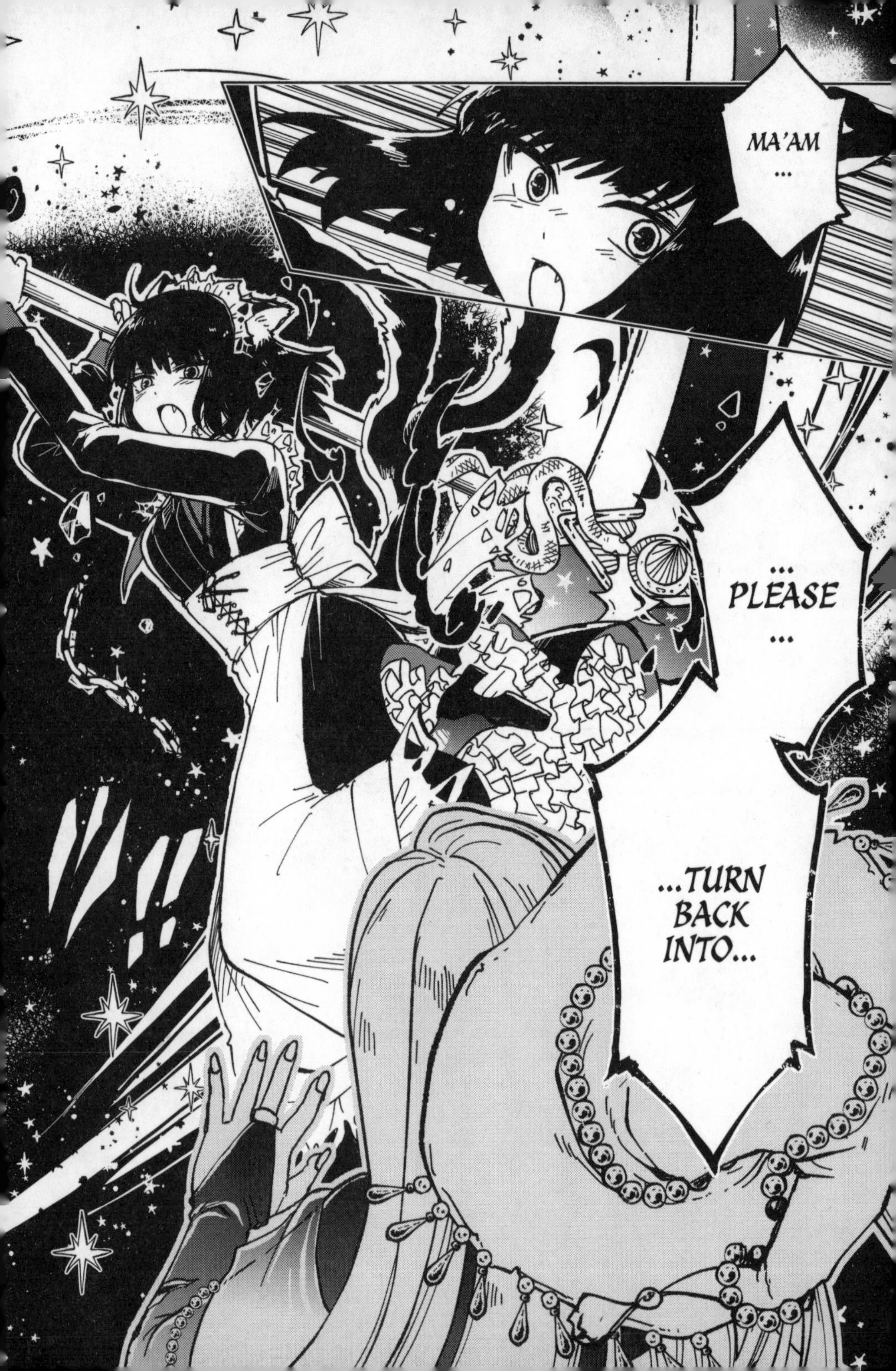
MA'AM ...
... PLEASE ...
...TURN BACK INTO...

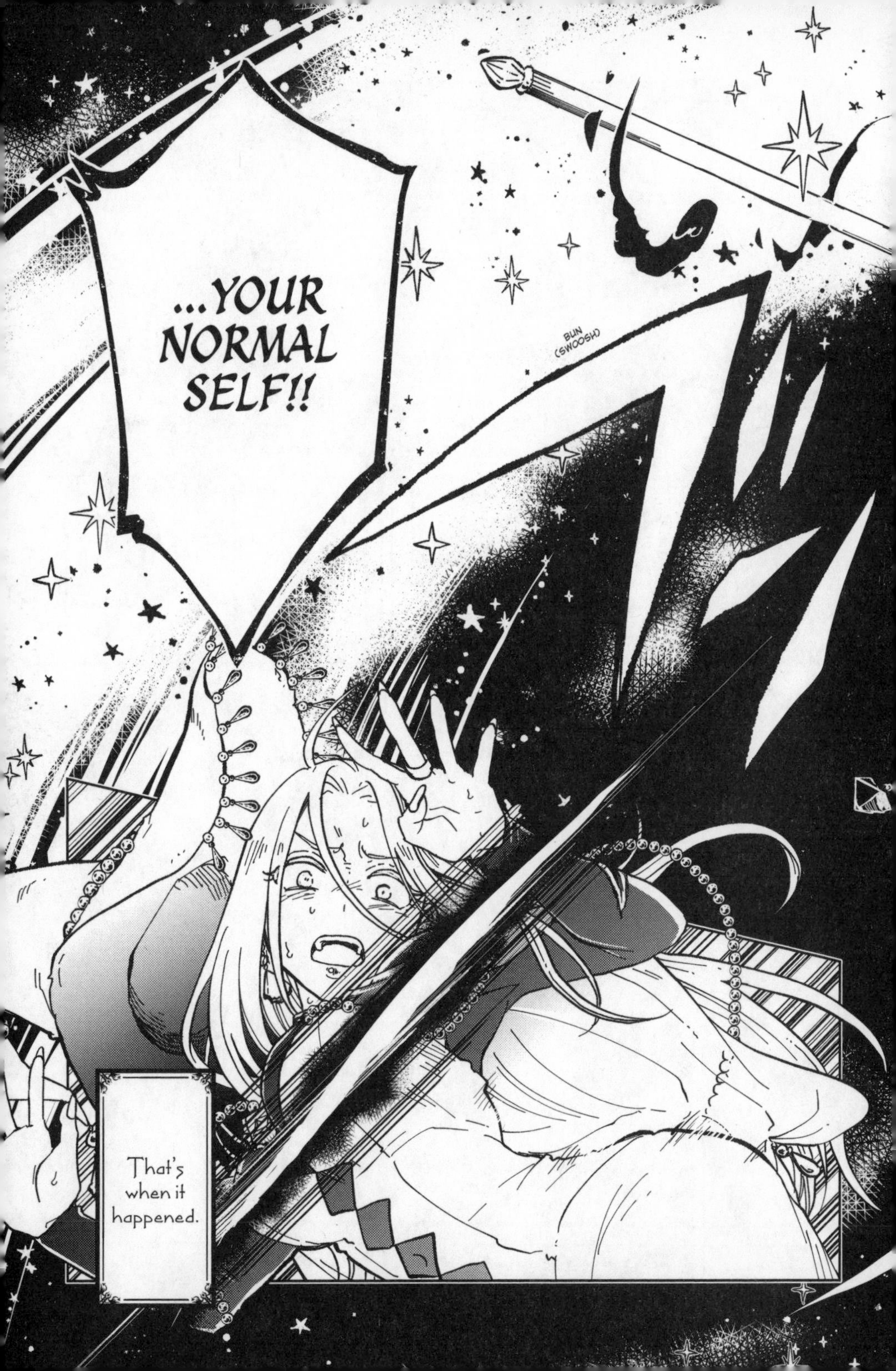
...YOUR NORMAL SELF!!
BUN (SWOOSH)
That's when it happened.

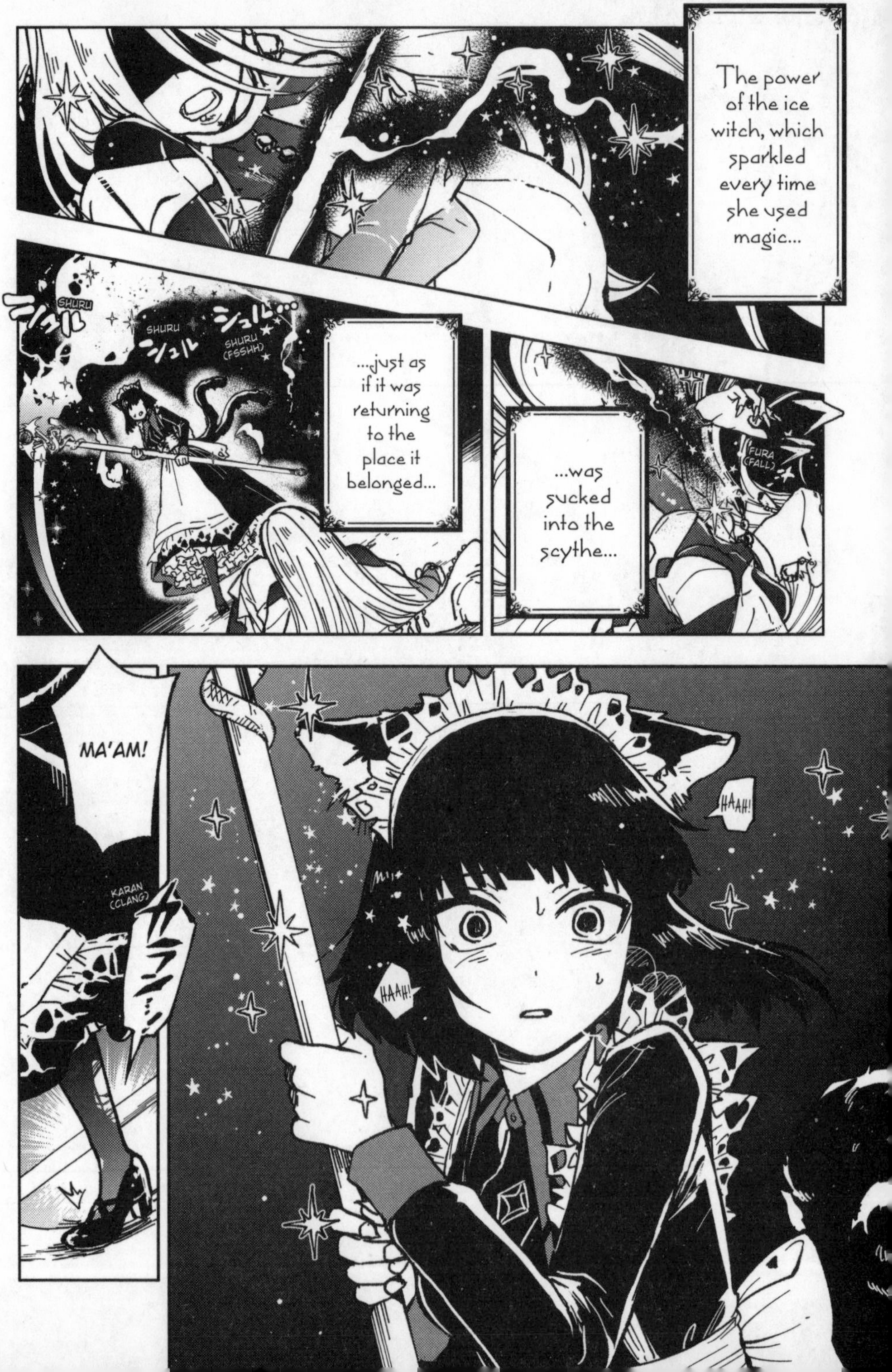

The power of the ice witch, which sparkled every time she used magic...
FURA (FALL)
...was sucked into the scythe...
...just as if it was returning to the place it belonged...
SHURU
SHURU (FSSHH)
SHURU
HAAH!
HAAH!
MA'AM!
KARAN (CLANG)

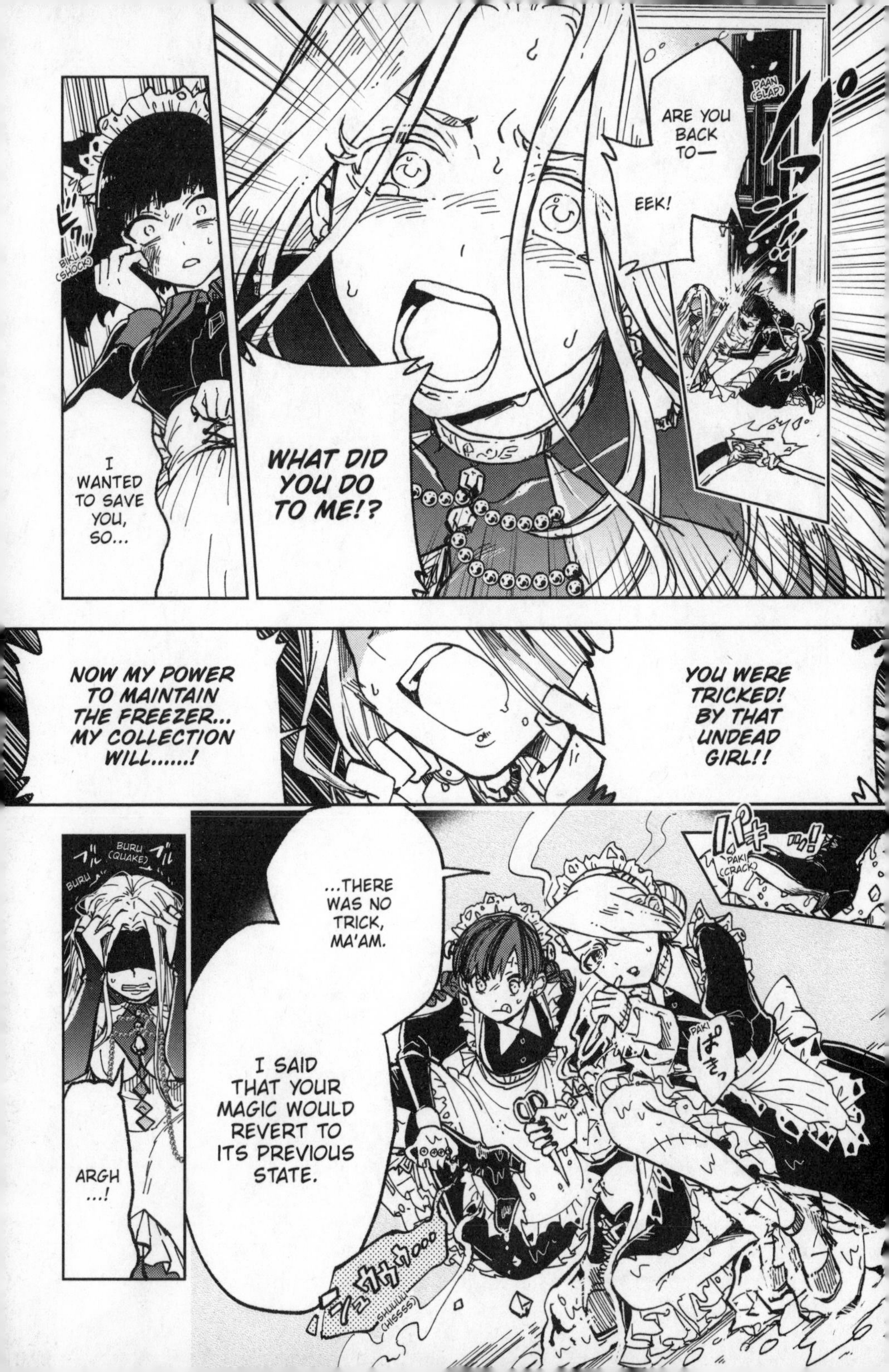
PAAN (SLAP)
ARE YOU BACK TO—
EEK!
WHAT DID YOU DO TO ME!?
BIKU (SHOCK)
I WANTED TO SAVE YOU, SO...
YOU WERE TRICKED! BY THAT UNDEAD GIRL!!
NOW MY POWER TO MAINTAIN THE FREEZER... MY COLLECTION WILL......!
PAKI (CRACK)
PAKI
...THERE WAS NO TRICK, MA'AM.
I SAID THAT YOUR MAGIC WOULD REVERT TO ITS PREVIOUS STATE.
SHUUUU (HISSSS)
BURU (QUAKE) BURU
ARGH ...!

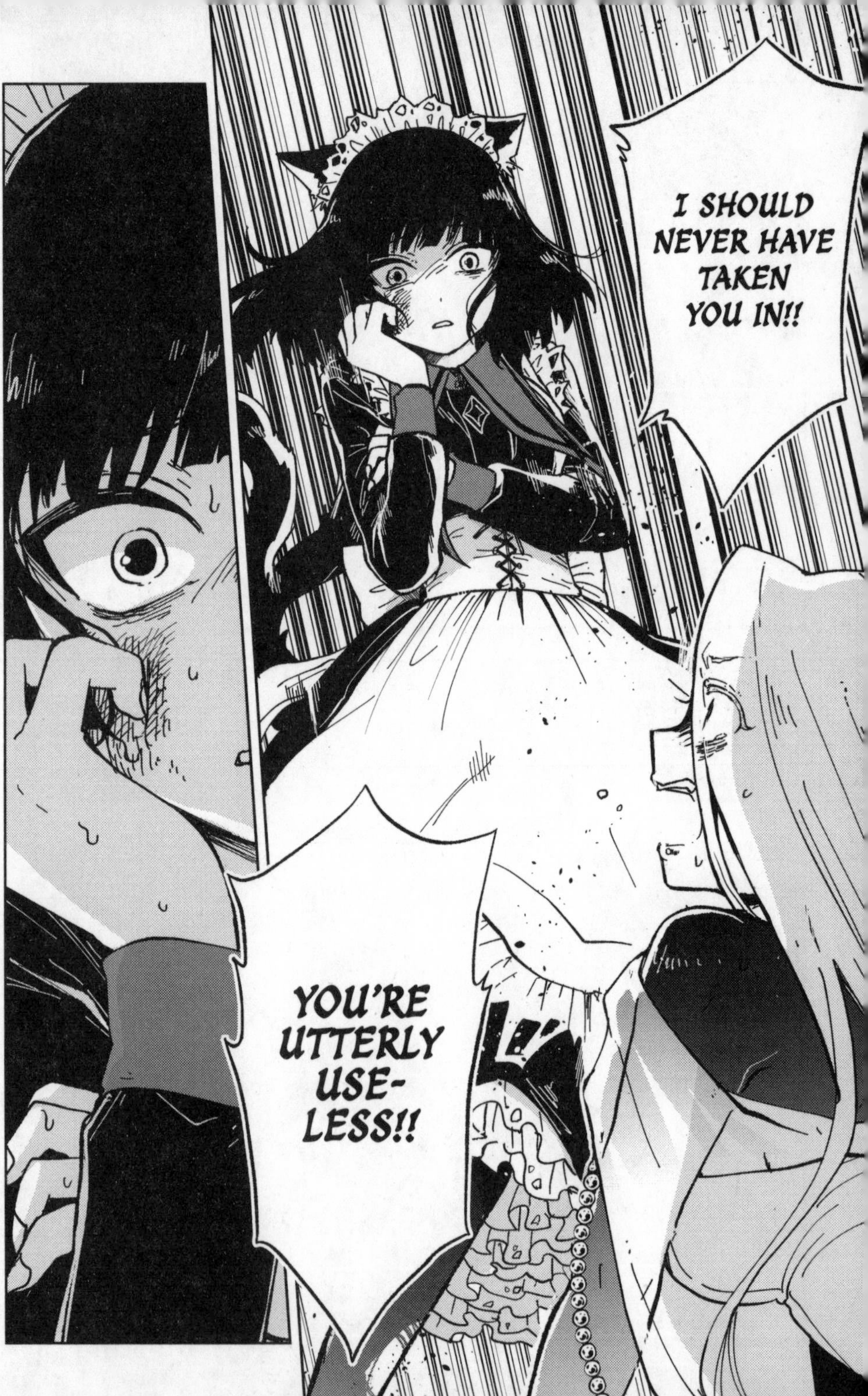
I SHOULD NEVER HAVE TAKEN YOU IN!!
YOU'RE UTTERLY USE-LESS!!

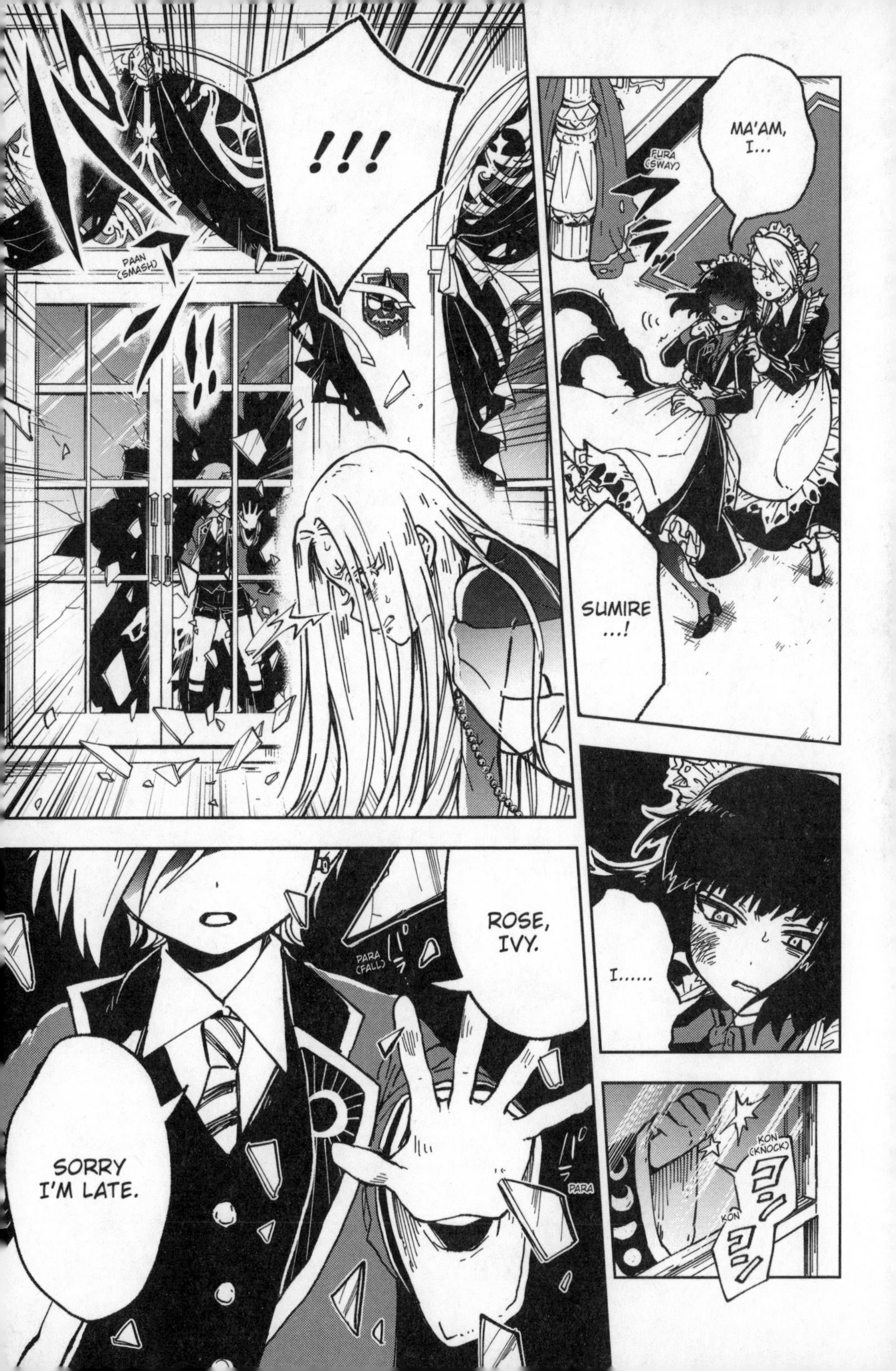
MA'AM, I...
FURA (SWAY)
SUMIRE ...!
I......
KON (KNOCK)
KON
PAAN (SMASH)
!!!
ROSE, IVY.
PARA (FALL)
PARA
SORRY I'M LATE.

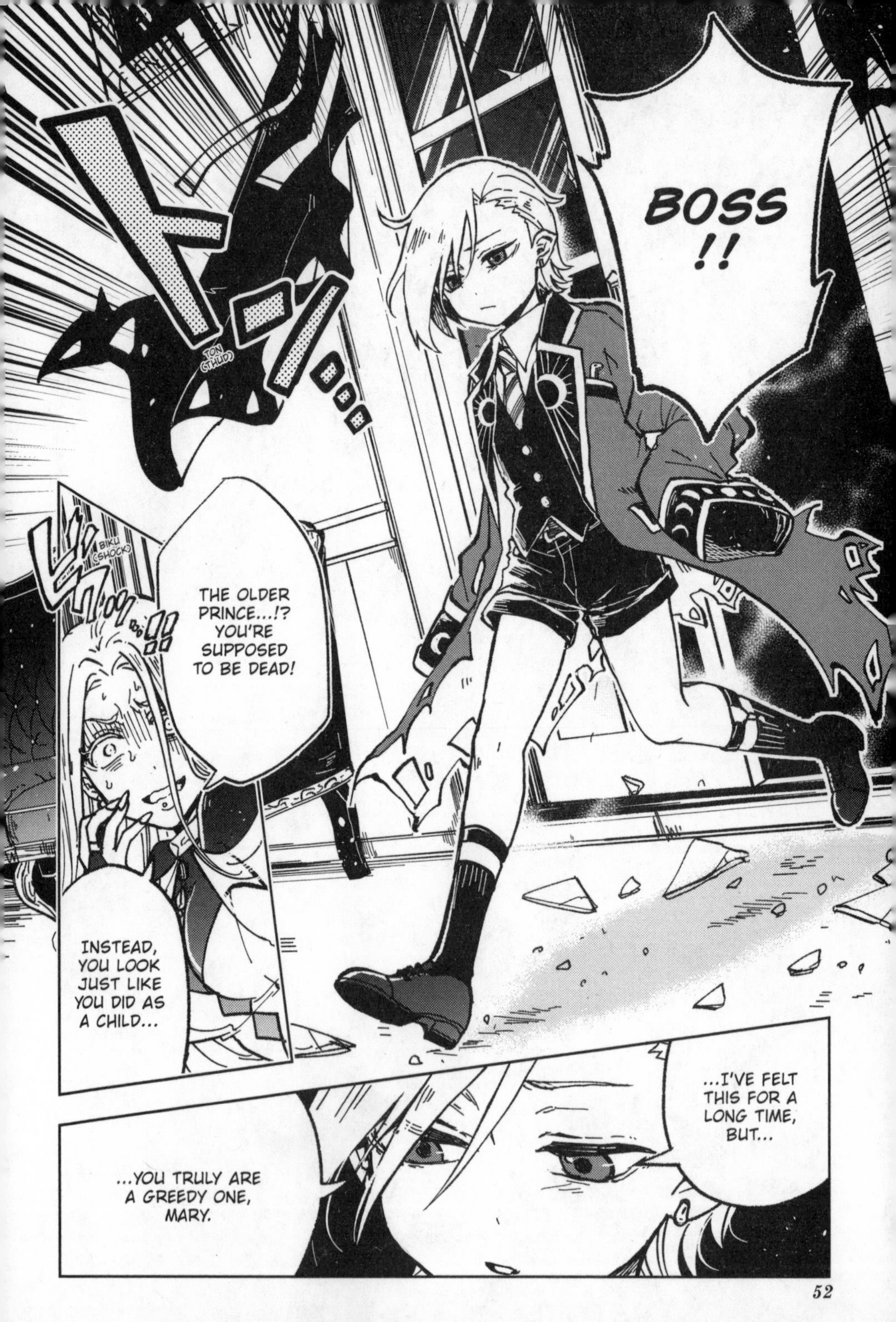
BOSS !!
TON (THUD)
BIKU (SHOCK)
THE OLDER PRINCE...!? YOU'RE SUPPOSED TO BE DEAD!
INSTEAD, YOU LOOK JUST LIKE YOU DID AS A CHILD...
...I'VE FELT THIS FOR A LONG TIME, BUT...
...YOU TRULY ARE A GREEDY ONE, MARY.

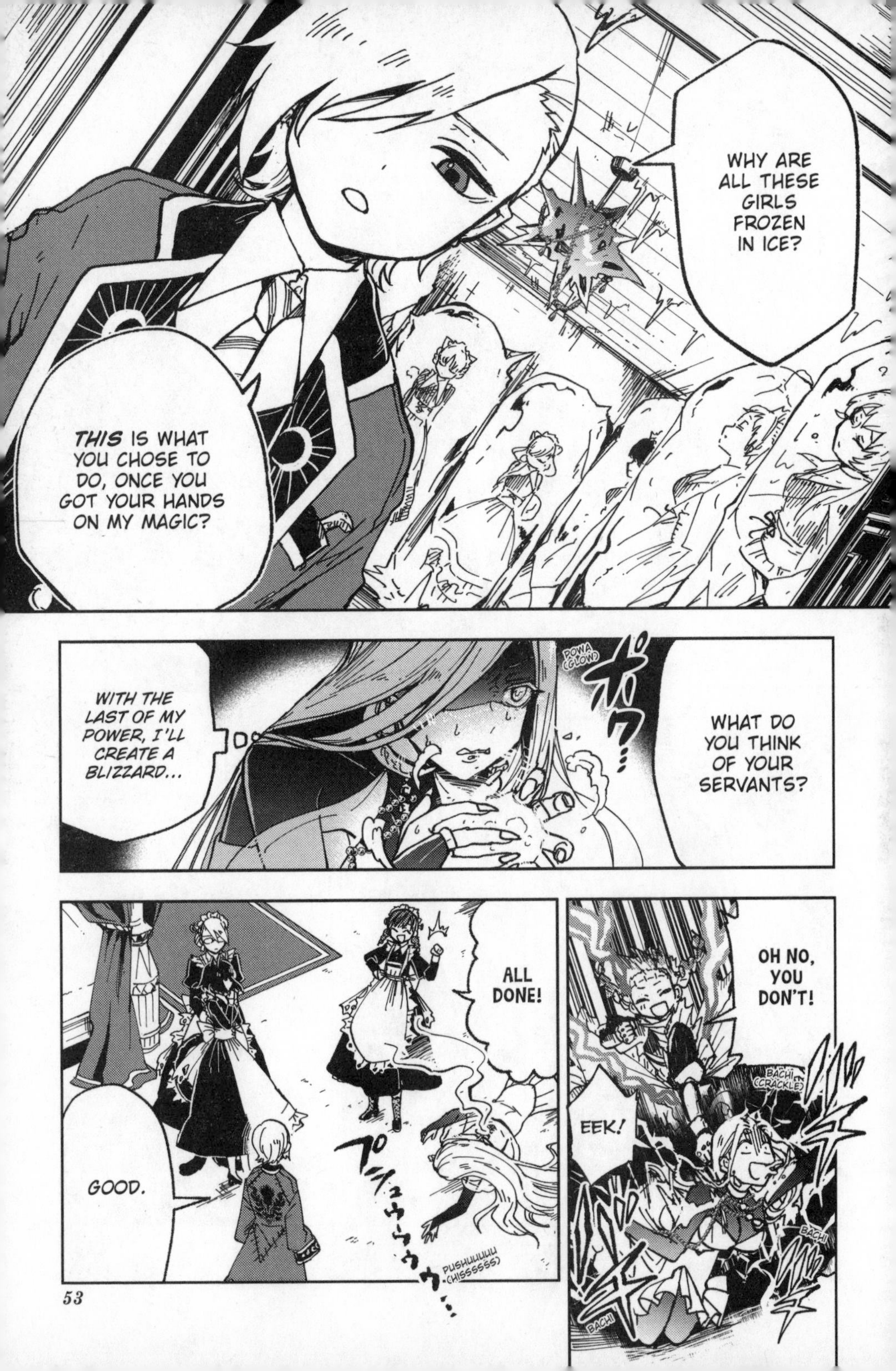
WHY ARE ALL THESE GIRLS FROZEN IN ICE?
THIS IS WHAT YOU CHOSE TO DO, ONCE YOU GOT YOUR HANDS ON MY MAGIC?
POWA (GLOW)
WHAT DO YOU THINK OF YOUR SERVANTS?
WITH THE LAST OF MY POWER, I'LL CREATE A BLIZZARD...
OH NO, YOU DON'T!
BACHI (CRACKLE)
EEK!
BACHI
BACHI
ALL DONE!
GOOD.
PUSHUUUUU (CHISSSSSS)

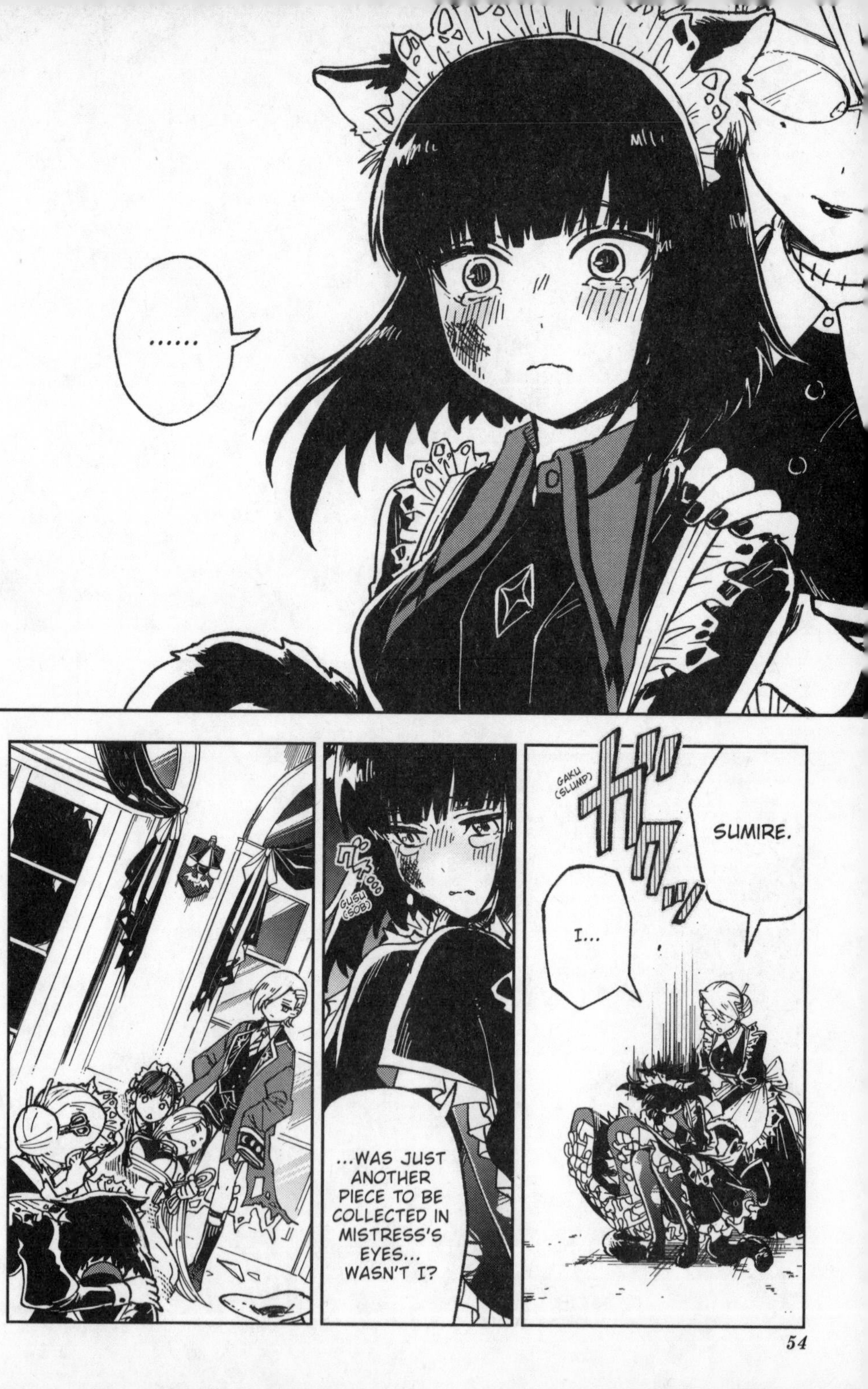
......
GAKU (SLUMP)
SUMIRE.
I...
GUSU (SOB)
...WAS JUST ANOTHER PIECE TO BE COLLECTED IN MISTRESS'S EYES... WASN'T I?

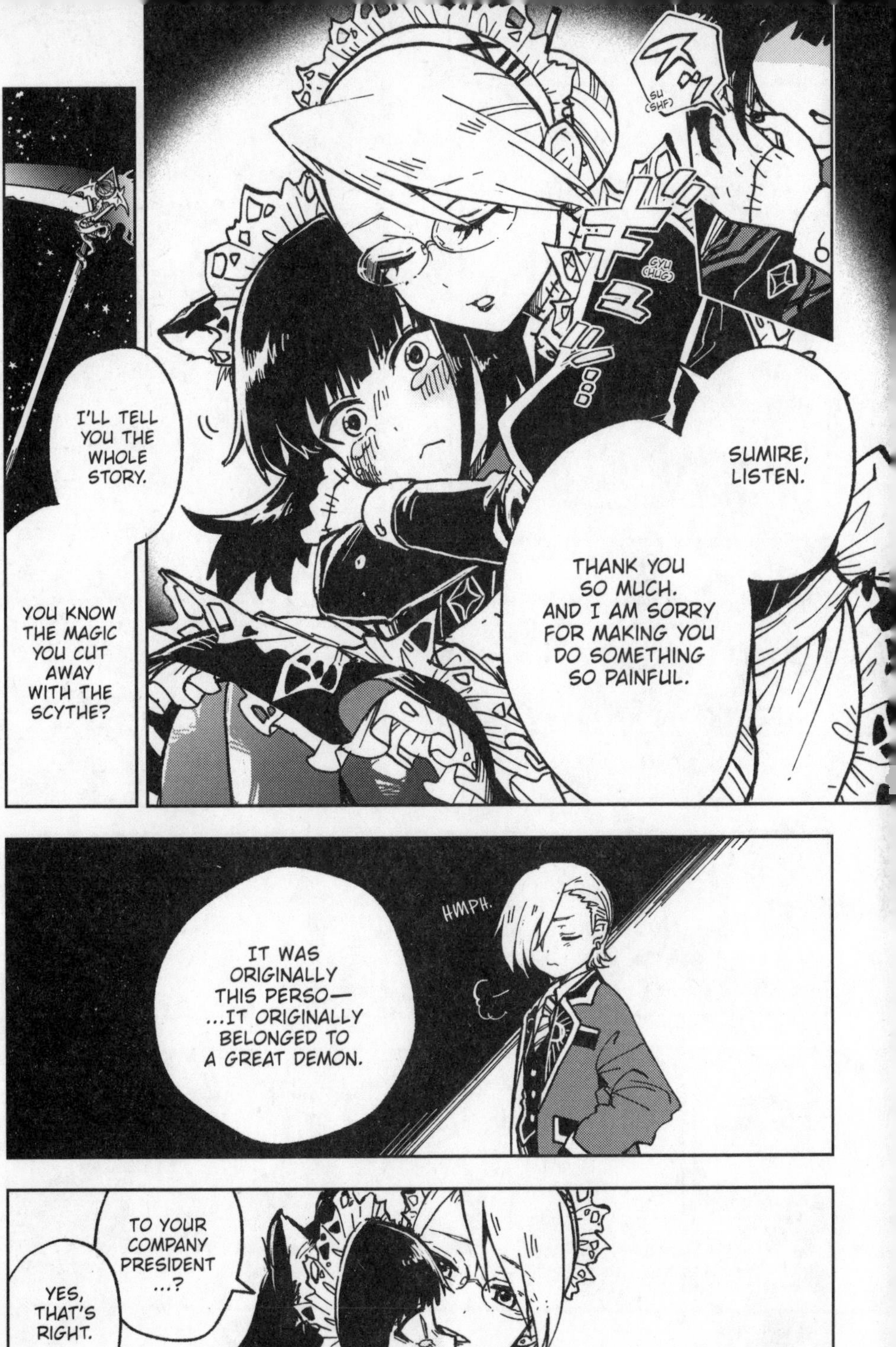
SU (SHF)
GYU (HUG)
SUMIRE, LISTEN.
THANK YOU SO MUCH. AND I AM SORRY FOR MAKING YOU DO SOMETHING SO PAINFUL.
I'LL TELL YOU THE WHOLE STORY.
YOU KNOW THE MAGIC YOU CUT AWAY WITH THE SCYTHE?
HMPH.
IT WAS ORIGINALLY THIS PERSO— ...IT ORIGINALLY BELONGED TO A GREAT DEMON.
TO YOUR COMPANY PRESIDENT ...?
YES, THAT'S RIGHT.

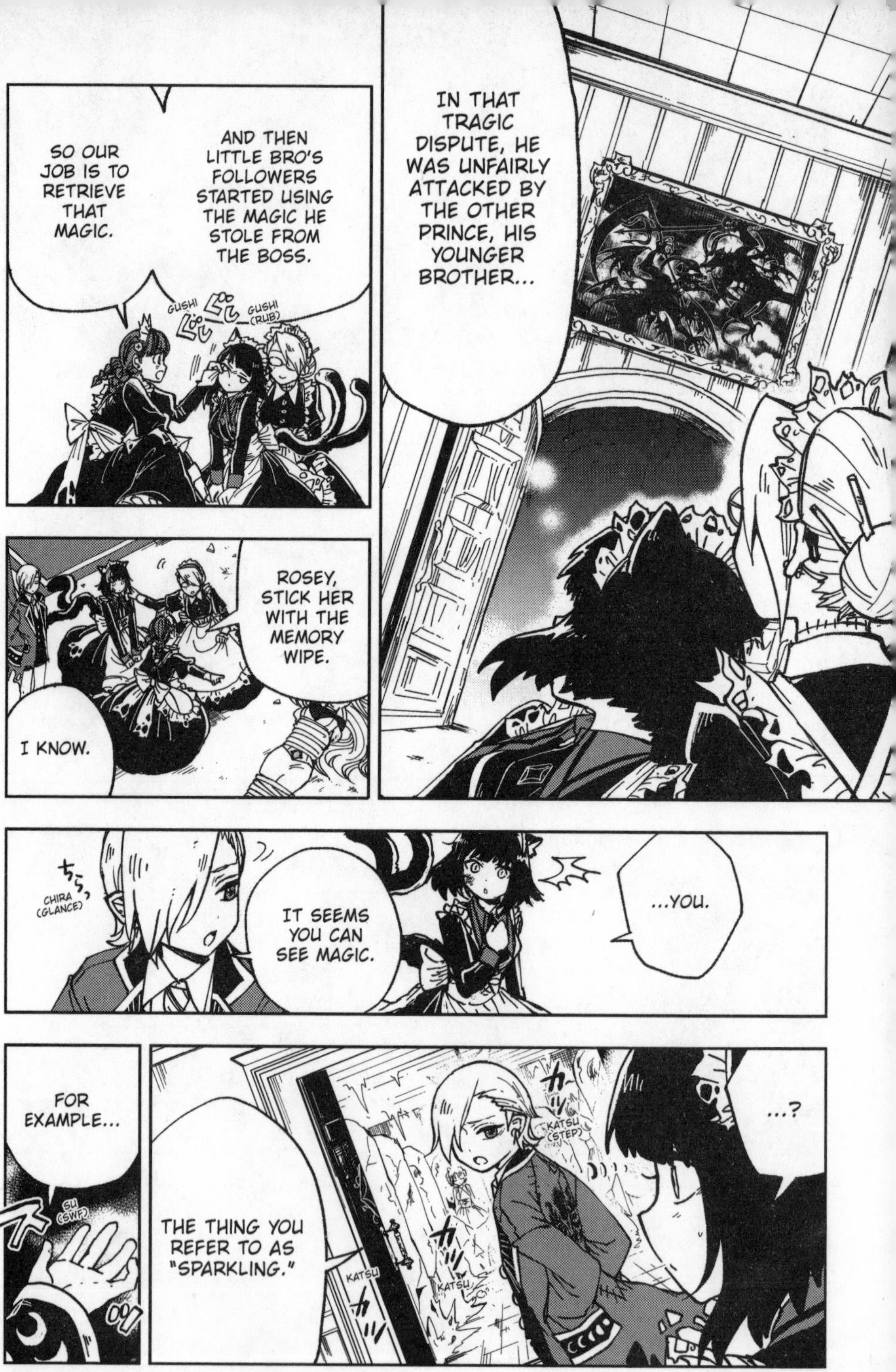
IN THAT TRAGIC DISPUTE, HE WAS UNFAIRLY ATTACKED BY THE OTHER PRINCE, HIS YOUNGER BROTHER...
AND THEN LITTLE BRO'S FOLLOWERS STARTED USING THE MAGIC HE STOLE FROM THE BOSS.
SO OUR JOB IS TO RETRIEVE THAT MAGIC.
GUSHI
GUSHI (RUB)
ROSEY, STICK HER WITH THE MEMORY WIPE.
I KNOW.
...YOU.
IT SEEMS YOU CAN SEE MAGIC.
CHIRA (GLANCE)
...?
KATSU (STEP)
THE THING YOU REFER TO AS "SPARKLING."
KATSU
KATSU
FOR EXAMPLE...
SU (SWF)

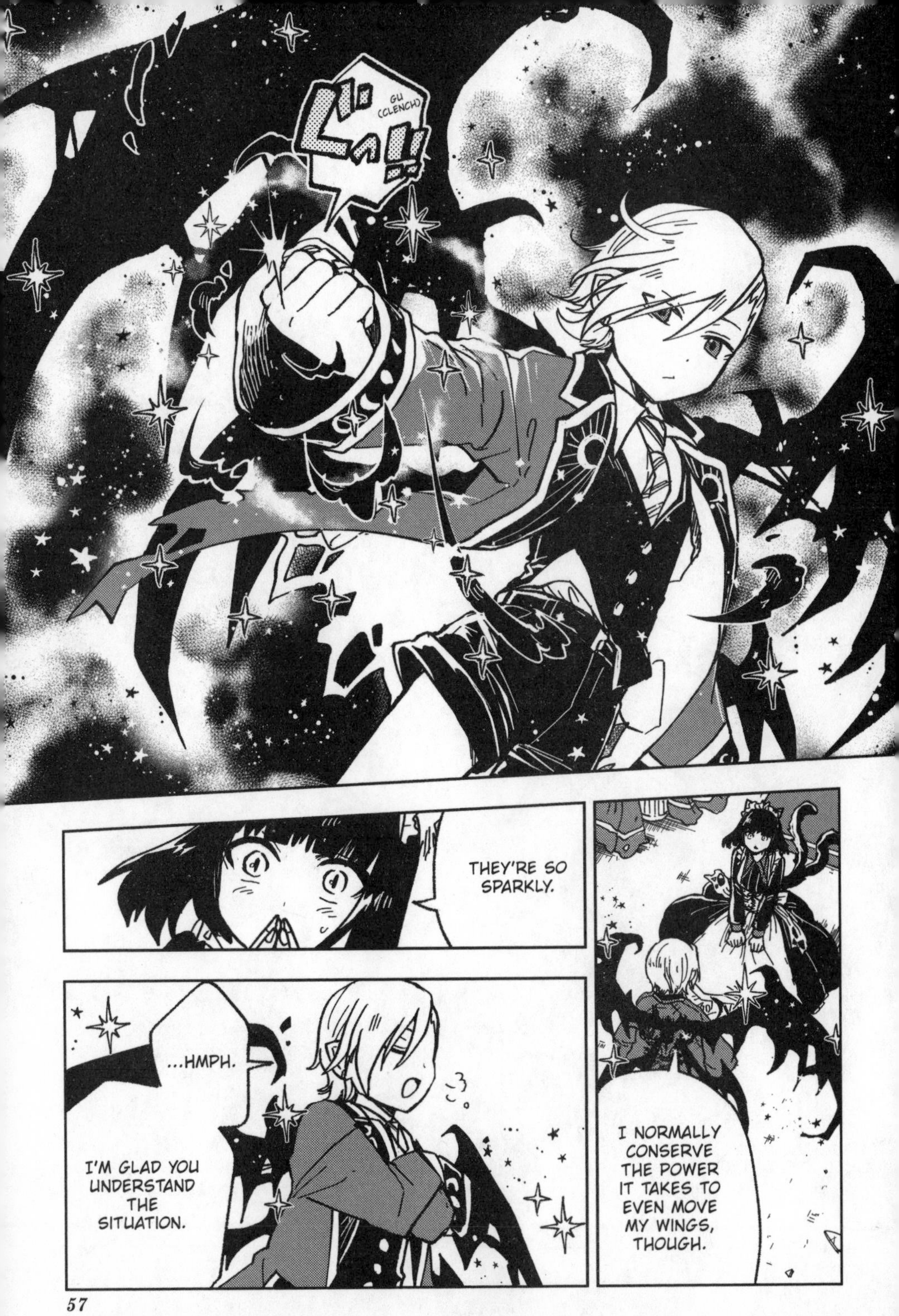
ぐっ!!
GU (CLENCH)
I NORMALLY CONSERVE THE POWER IT TAKES TO EVEN MOVE MY WINGS, THOUGH.
THEY'RE SO SPARKLY.
...HMPH.
I'M GLAD YOU UNDERSTAND THE SITUATION.

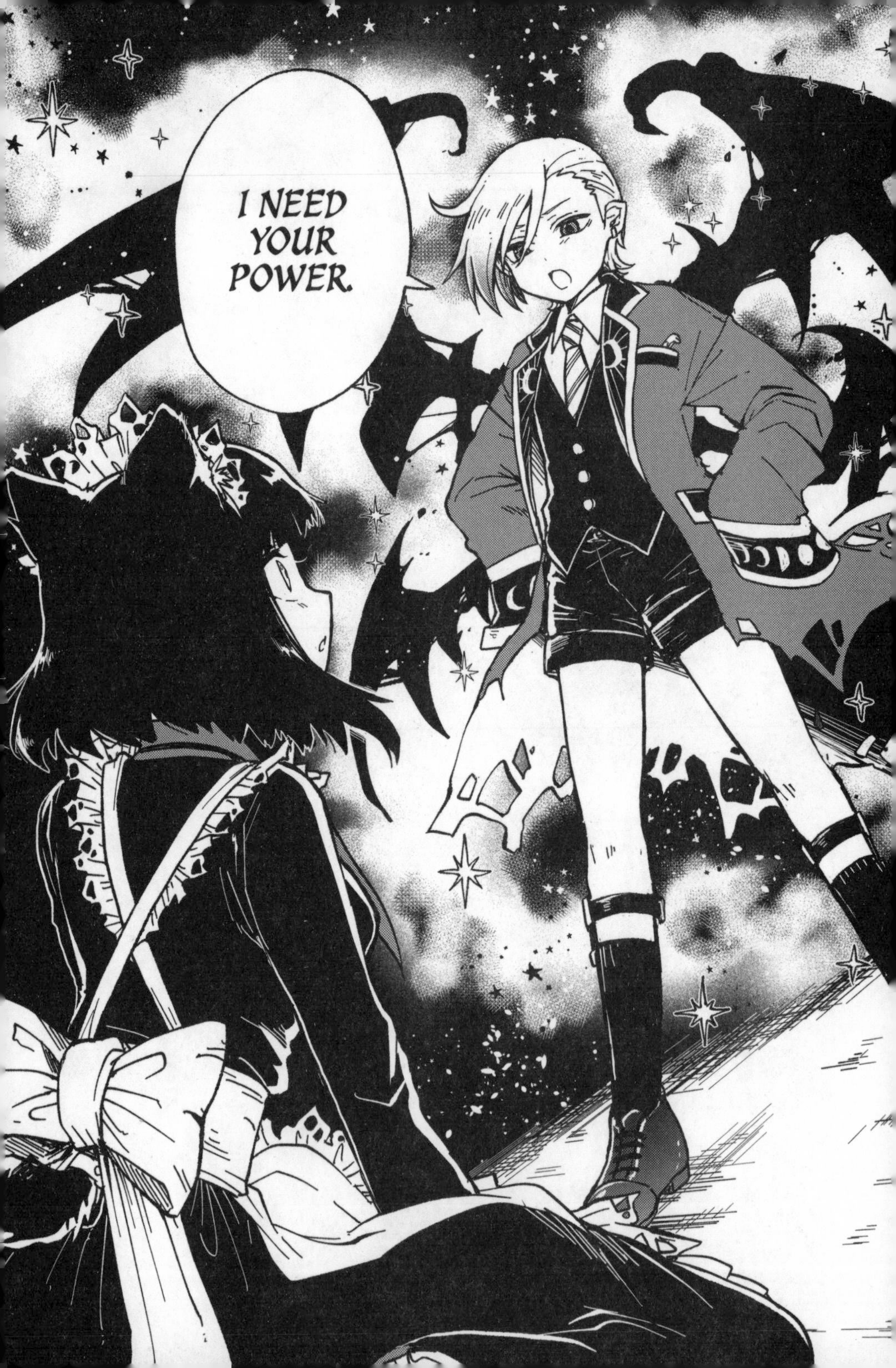
I NEED YOUR POWER.

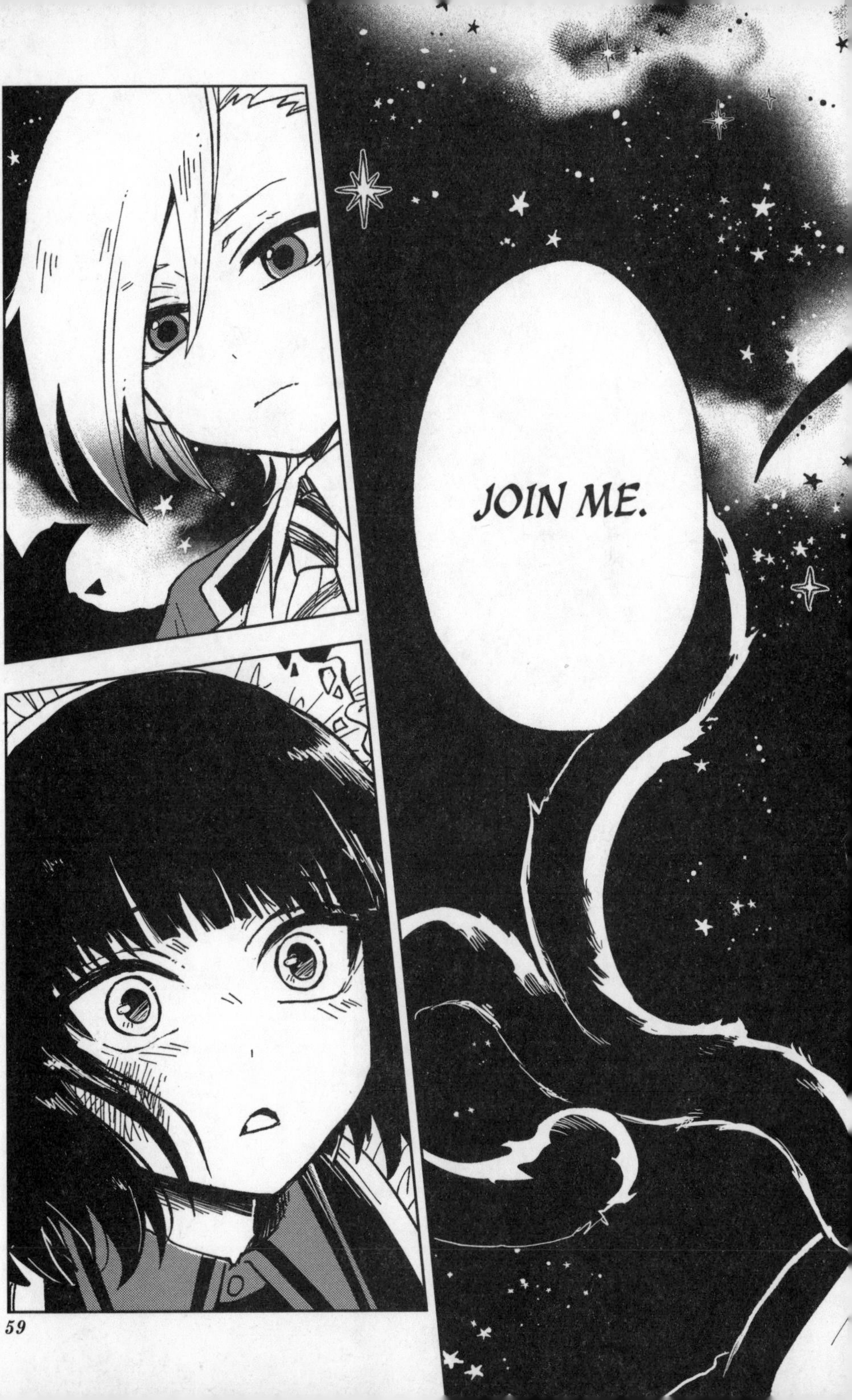
JOIN ME.

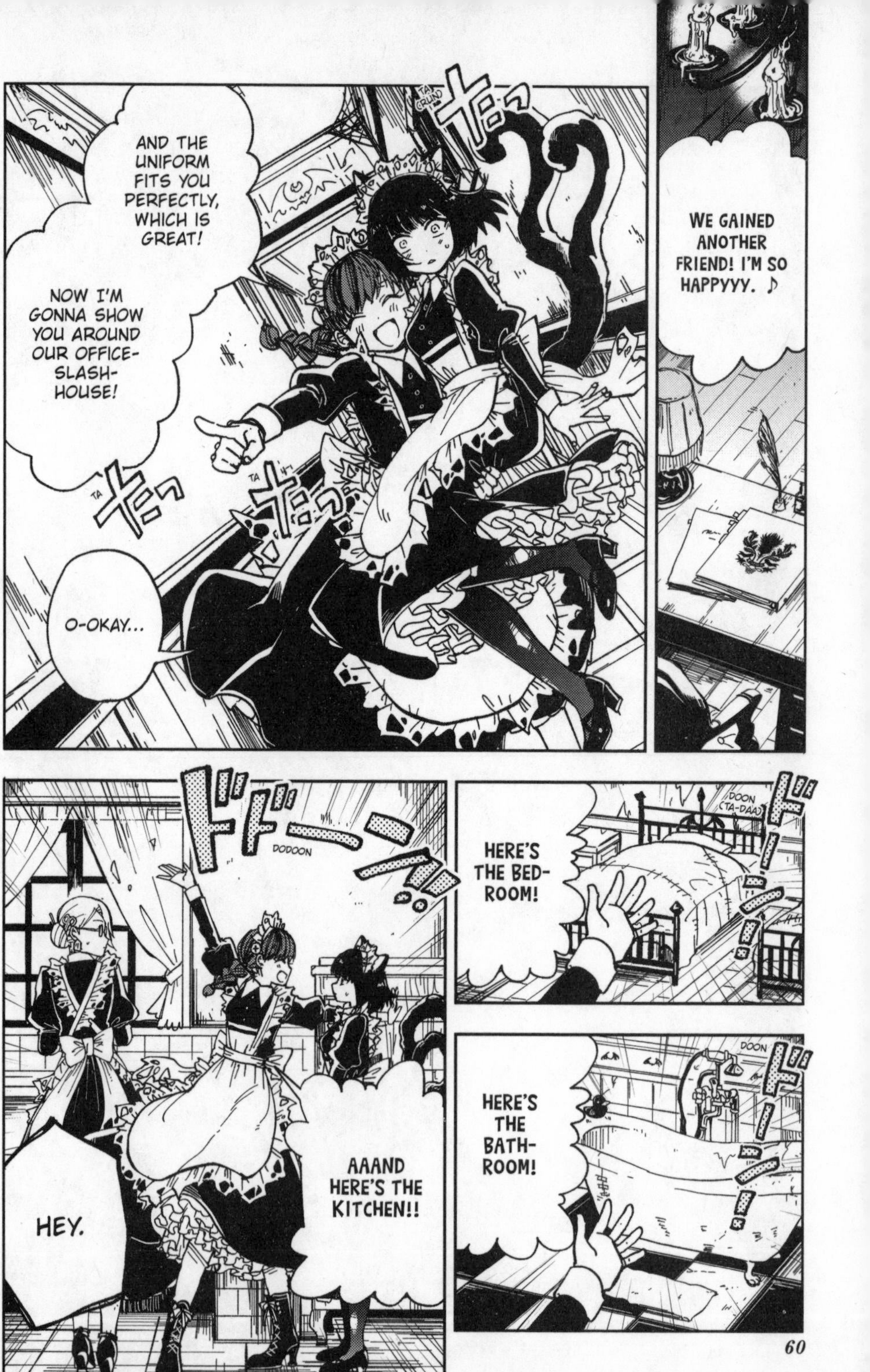
WE GAINED ANOTHER FRIEND! I'M SO HAPPYYY. ♪
TA (RUN)
AND THE UNIFORM FITS YOU PERFECTLY, WHICH IS GREAT!
NOW I'M GONNA SHOW YOU AROUND OUR OFFICE-SLASH-HOUSE!
TA
TA
O-OKAY...
DOON (TA-DAA)
HERE'S THE BED-ROOM!
DOON
HERE'S THE BATH-ROOM!
DODOON
AAAND HERE'S THE KITCHEN!!
HEY.

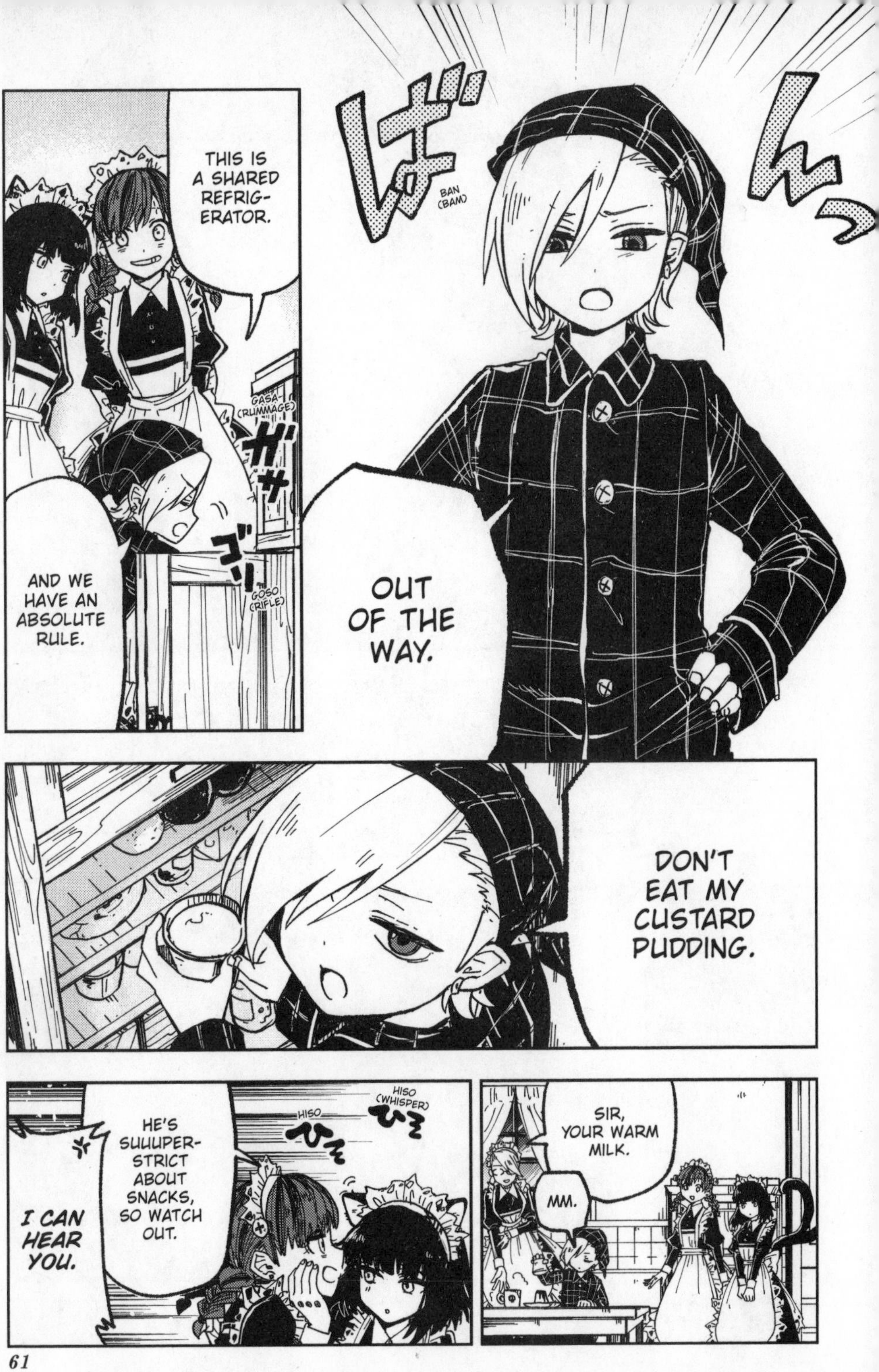
ばんっ
BAN (BAM)
OUT OF THE WAY.
THIS IS A SHARED REFRIGERATOR.
GASA (RUMMAGE)
ガサ
ゴソ
GOSO (RIFLE)
AND WE HAVE AN ABSOLUTE RULE.
DON'T EAT MY CUSTARD PUDDING.
SIR, YOUR WARM MILK.
MM.
HISO (WHISPER)
ひそ
HISO
ひそ
HE'S SUUUPER-STRICT ABOUT SNACKS, SO WATCH OUT.
I CAN HEAR YOU.

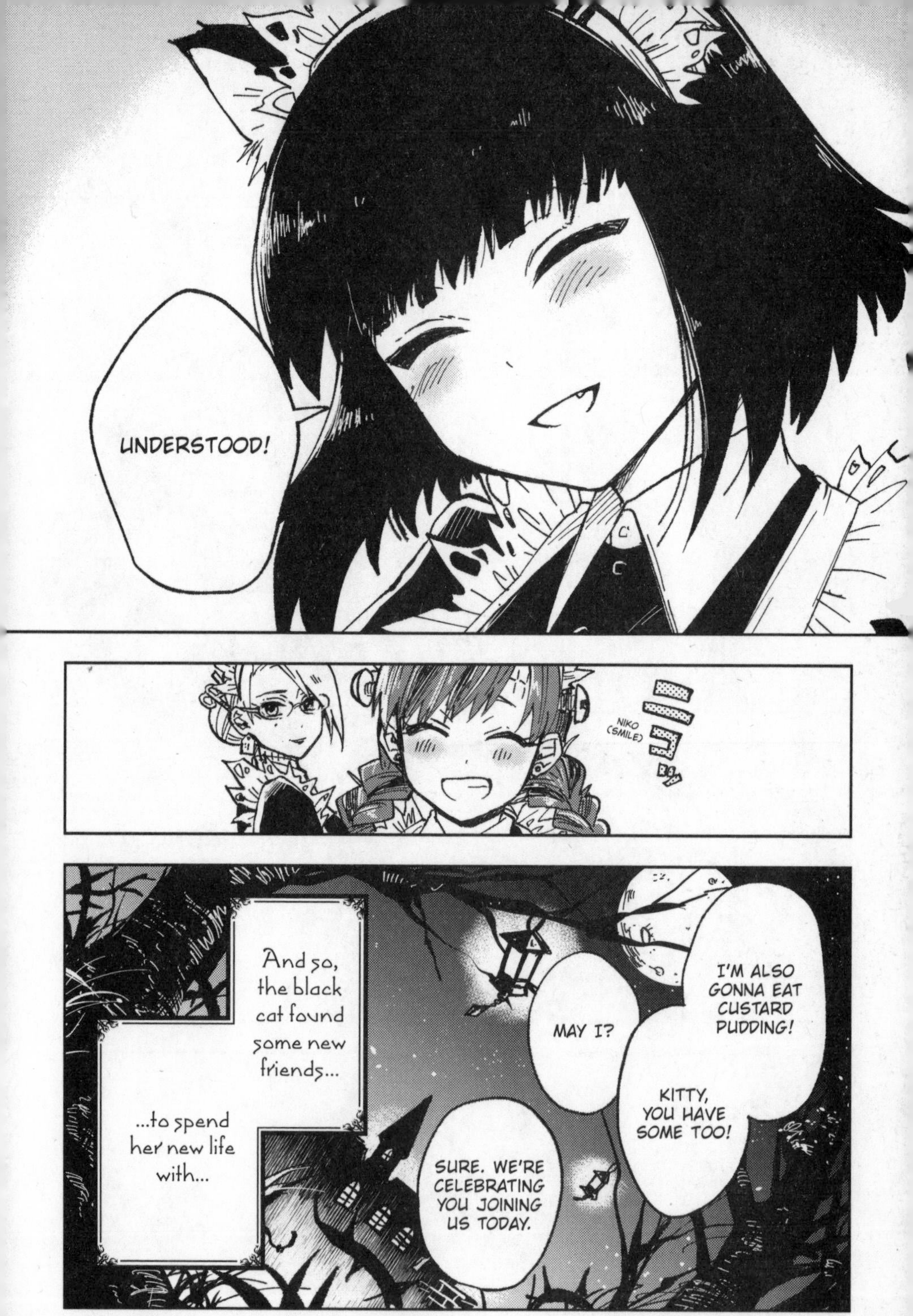
UNDERSTOOD!
NIKO (SMILE)
I'M ALSO GONNA EAT CUSTARD PUDDING!
MAY I?
KITTY, YOU HAVE SOME TOO!
SURE. WE'RE CELEBRATING YOU JOINING US TODAY.
And so, the black cat found some new friends...
...to spend her new life with...

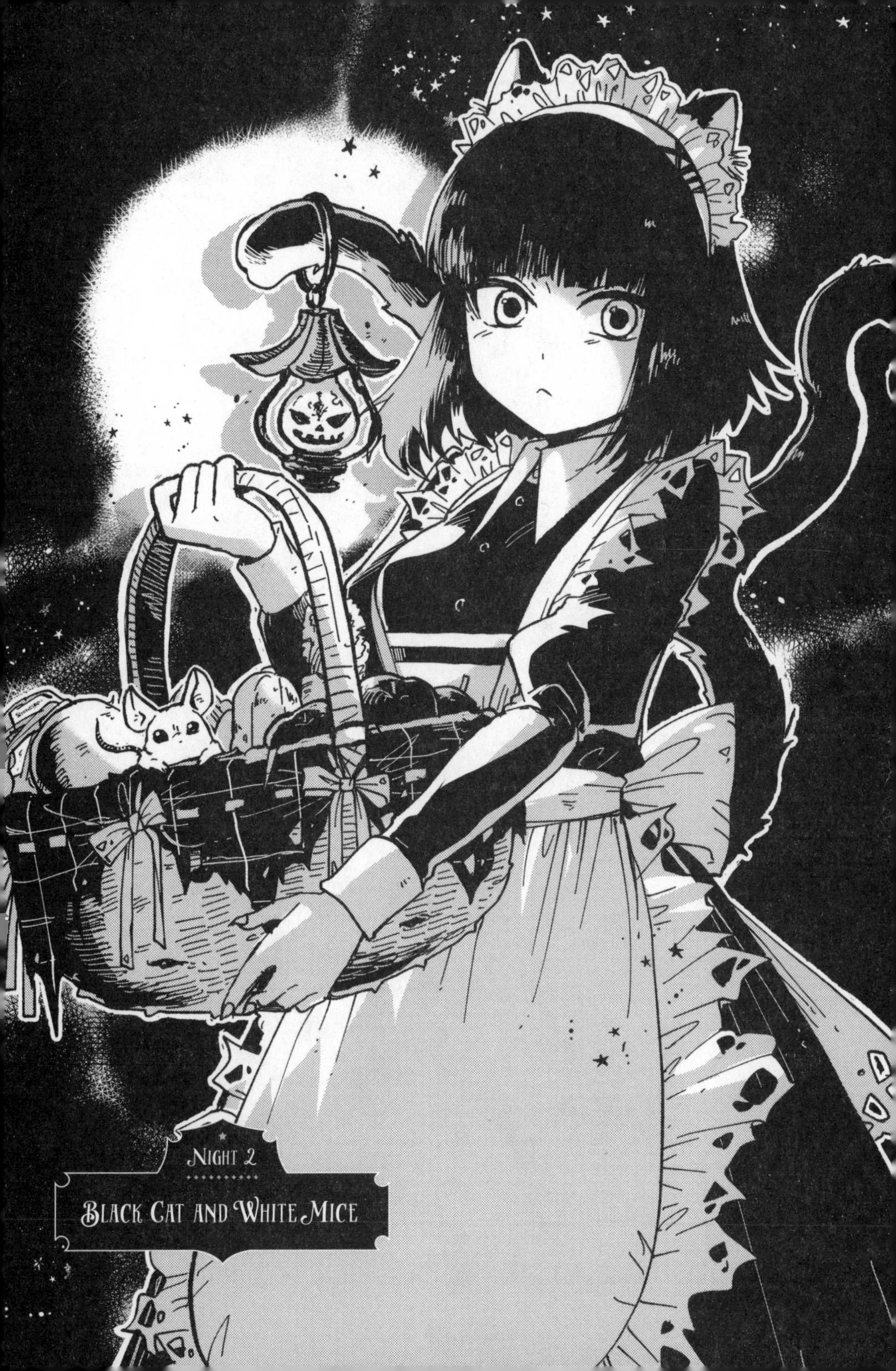
Night 2
Black Cat and White Mice

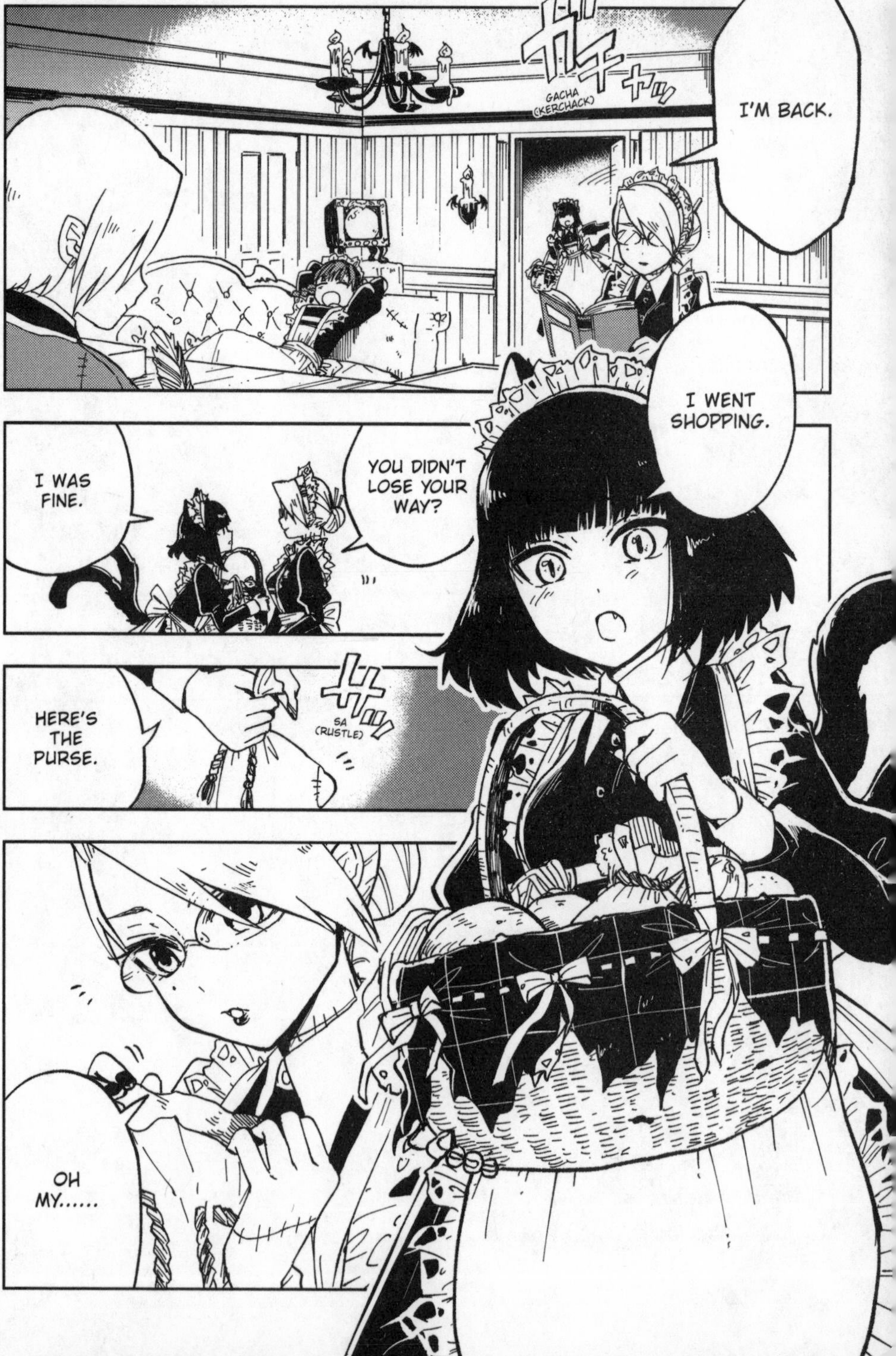

GACHA (KERCHACK)
I'M BACK.
I WENT SHOPPING.
YOU DIDN'T LOSE YOUR WAY?
I WAS FINE.
SA (RUSTLE)
HERE'S THE PURSE.
OH MY......

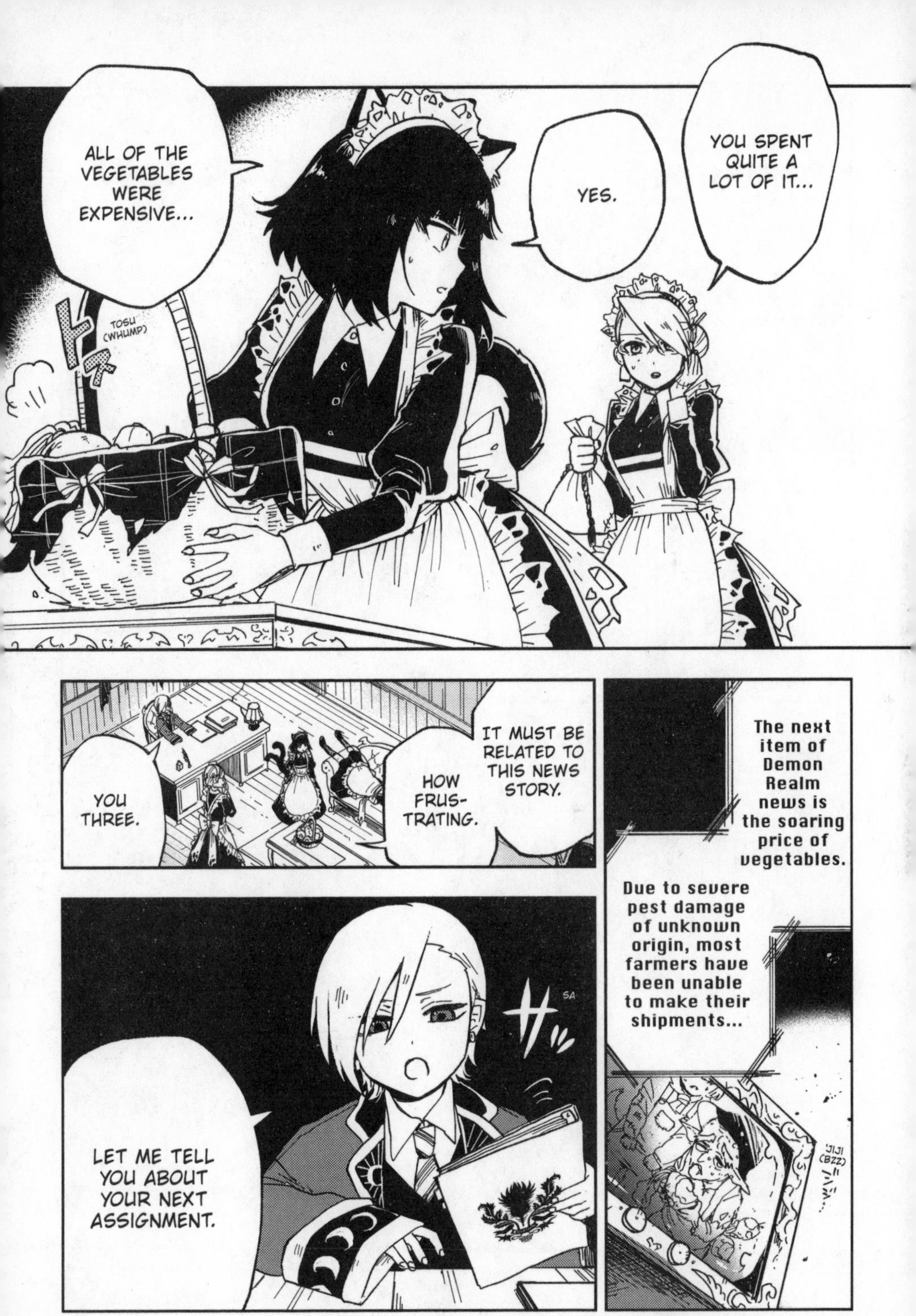
YOU SPENT QUITE A LOT OF IT...
YES.
ALL OF THE VEGETABLES WERE EXPENSIVE...
TOSU (WHUMP)
The next item of Demon Realm news is the soaring price of vegetables.
Due to severe pest damage of unknown origin, most farmers have been unable to make their shipments...
JIJI (BZZ)
IT MUST BE RELATED TO THIS NEWS STORY.
HOW FRUS-TRATING.
YOU THREE.
SA
LET ME TELL YOU ABOUT YOUR NEXT ASSIGNMENT.

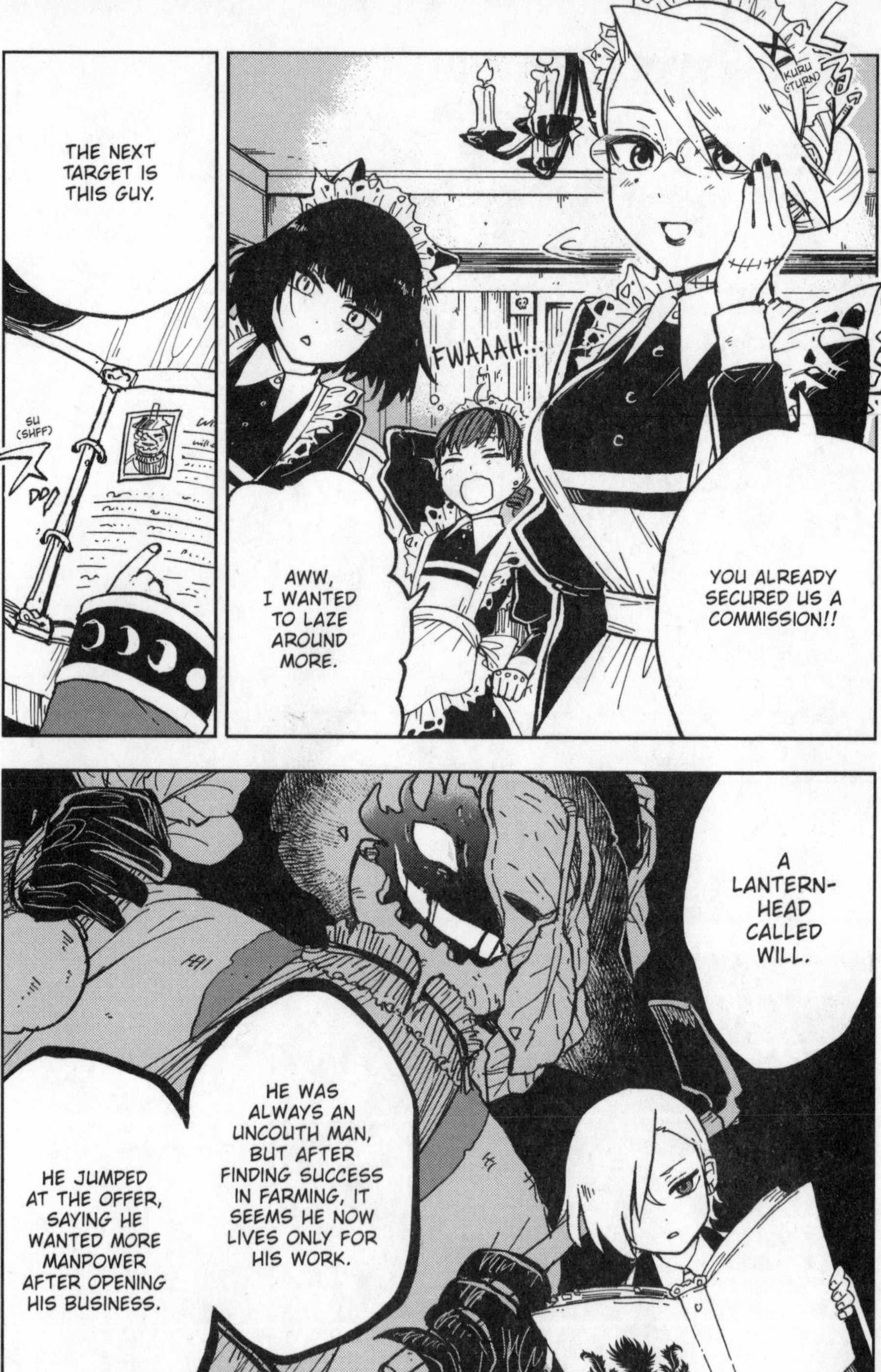
KURU (TURN)
FWAAAH...
YOU ALREADY SECURED US A COMMISSION!!
AWW, I WANTED TO LAZE AROUND MORE.
THE NEXT TARGET IS THIS GUY.
SU (SHFF)
A LANTERN-HEAD CALLED WILL.
HE WAS ALWAYS AN UNCOUTH MAN, BUT AFTER FINDING SUCCESS IN FARMING, IT SEEMS HE NOW LIVES ONLY FOR HIS WORK.
HE JUMPED AT THE OFFER, SAYING HE WANTED MORE MANPOWER AFTER OPENING HIS BUSINESS.

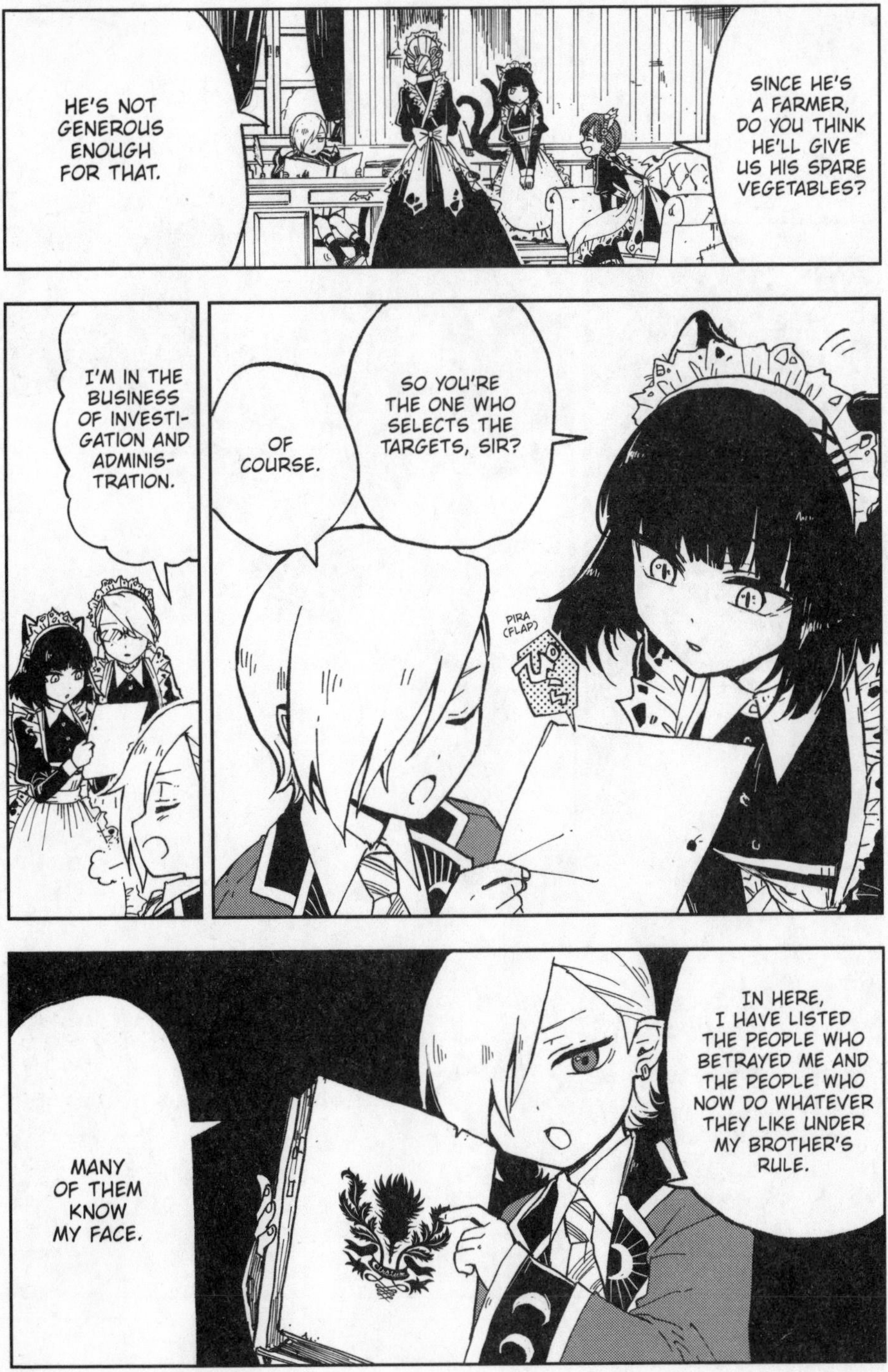
SINCE HE'S A FARMER, DO YOU THINK HE'LL GIVE US HIS SPARE VEGETABLES?
HE'S NOT GENEROUS ENOUGH FOR THAT.
SO YOU'RE THE ONE WHO SELECTS THE TARGETS, SIR?
PIRA (FLAP)
OF COURSE.
I'M IN THE BUSINESS OF INVESTIGATION AND ADMINISTRATION.
IN HERE, I HAVE LISTED THE PEOPLE WHO BETRAYED ME AND THE PEOPLE WHO NOW DO WHATEVER THEY LIKE UNDER MY BROTHER'S RULE.
MANY OF THEM KNOW MY FACE.

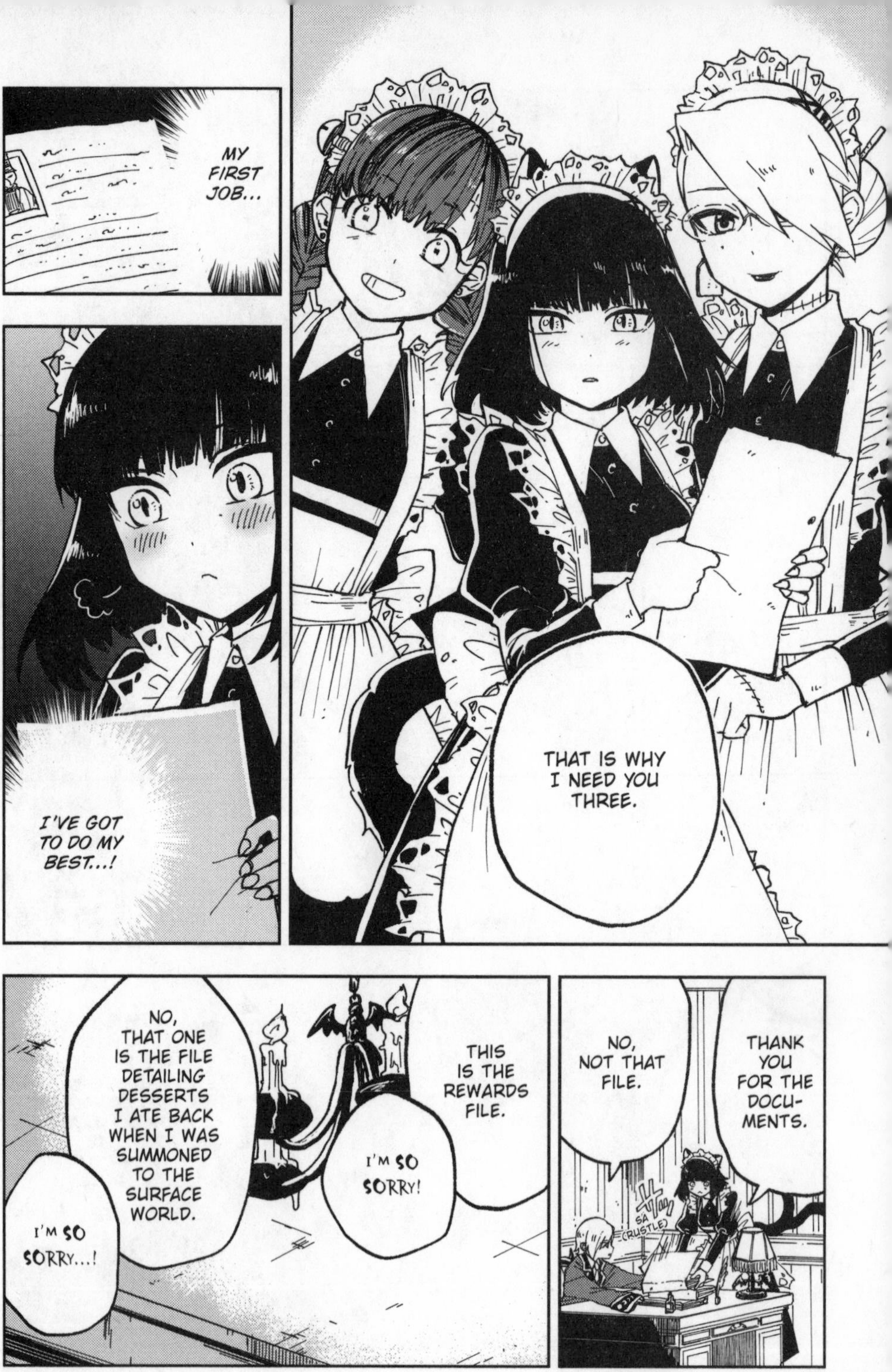
THAT IS WHY I NEED YOU THREE.
MY FIRST JOB...
I'VE GOT TO DO MY BEST...!
THANK YOU FOR THE DOCU-MENTS.
NO, NOT THAT FILE.
SA (RUSTLE)
THIS IS THE REWARDS FILE.
I'M SO SORRY!
NO, THAT ONE IS THE FILE DETAILING DESSERTS I ATE BACK WHEN I WAS SUMMONED TO THE SURFACE WORLD.
I'M SO SORRY...!

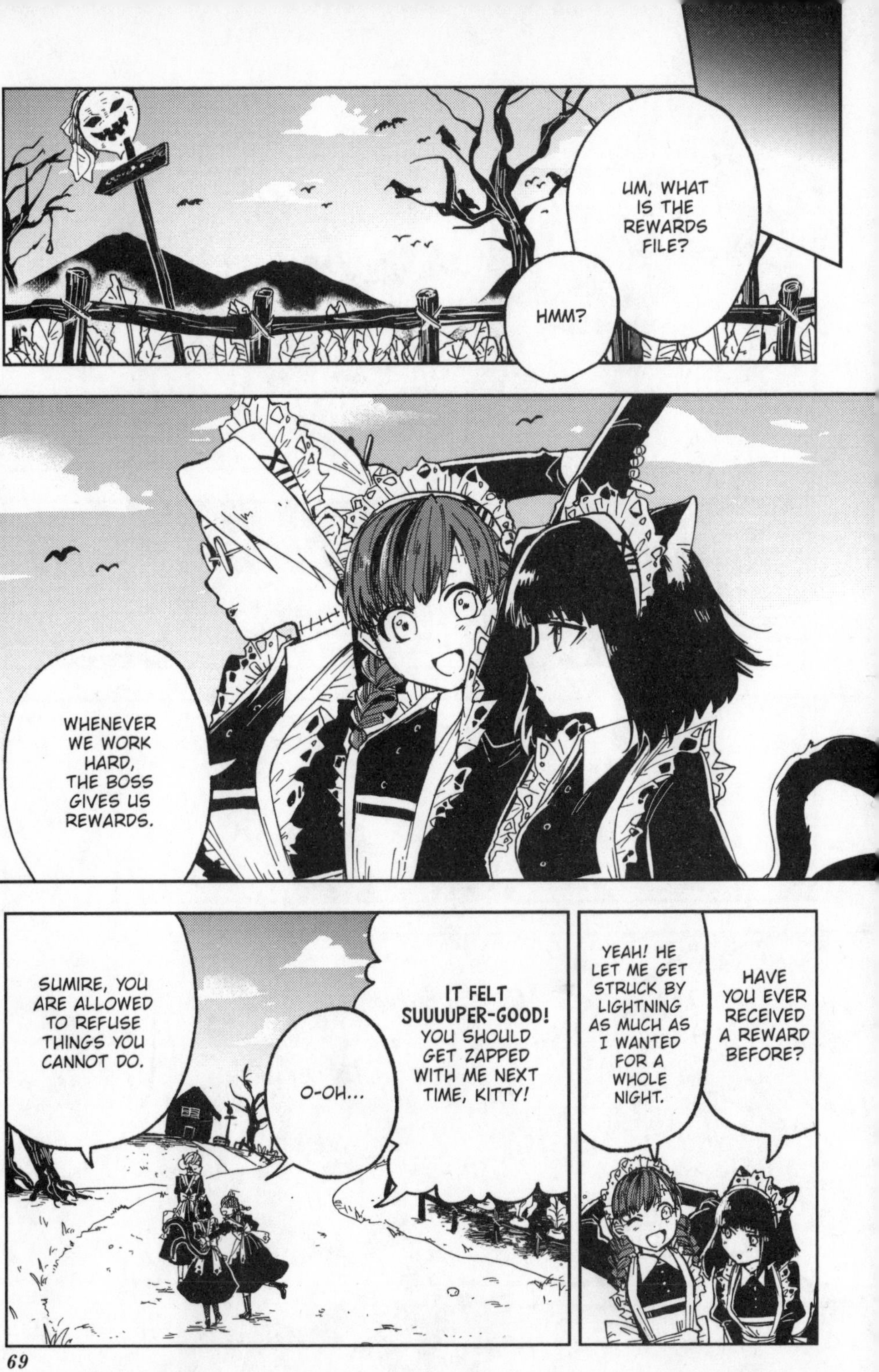
UM, WHAT IS THE REWARDS FILE?
HMM?
WHENEVER WE WORK HARD, THE BOSS GIVES US REWARDS.
HAVE YOU EVER RECEIVED A REWARD BEFORE?
YEAH! HE LET ME GET STRUCK BY LIGHTNING AS MUCH AS I WANTED FOR A WHOLE NIGHT.
IT FELT SUUUUPER-GOOD! YOU SHOULD GET ZAPPED WITH ME NEXT TIME, KITTY!
O-OH...
SUMIRE, YOU ARE ALLOWED TO REFUSE THINGS YOU CANNOT DO.

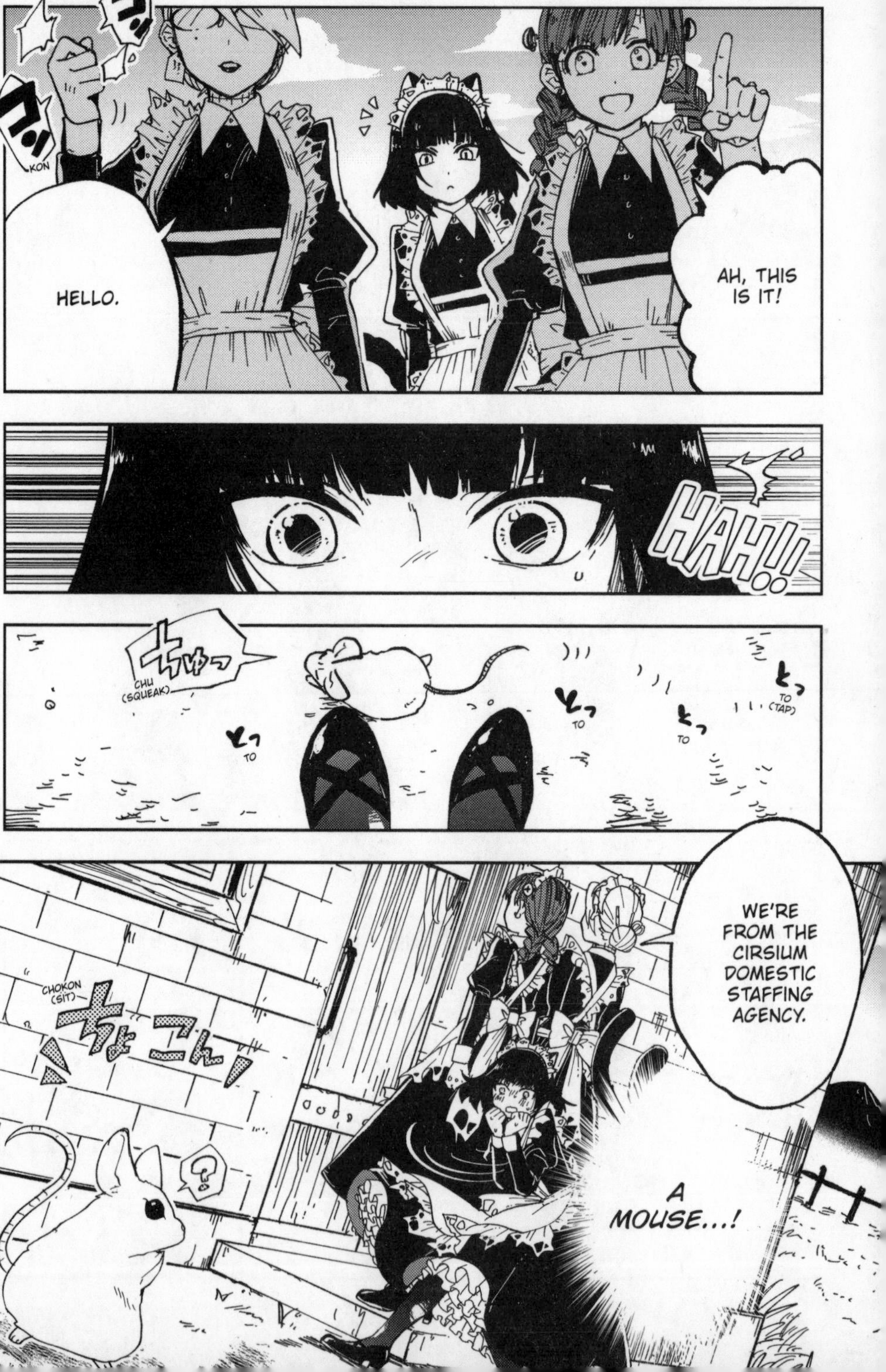

AH, THIS IS IT!
KON (KNOCK)
KON
HELLO.
HAH!!
TO (TAP)
TO
TO
TO
CHU (SQUEAK)
WE'RE FROM THE CIRSIUM DOMESTIC STAFFING AGENCY.
A MOUSE...!
CHOKON (SIT)
?

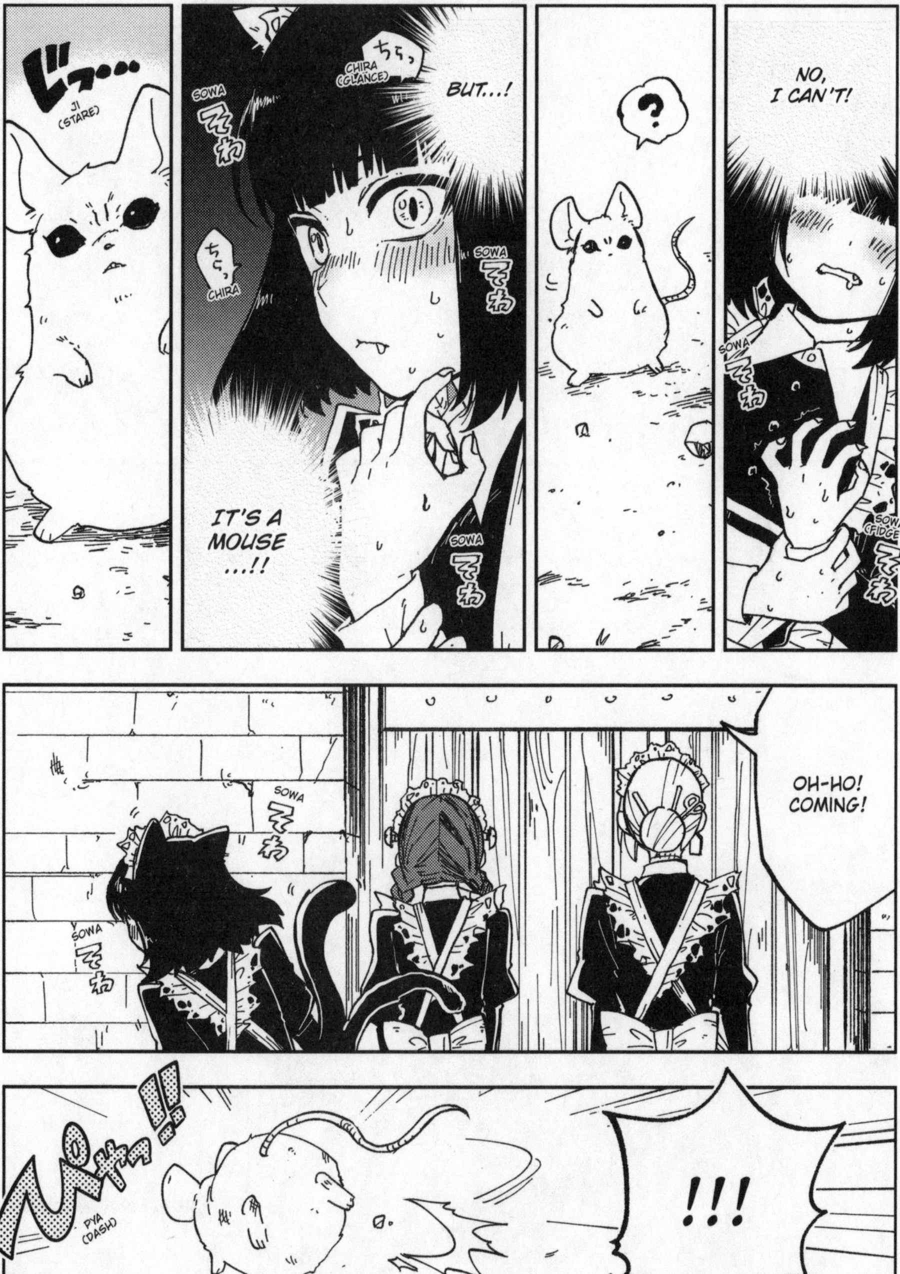
NO, I CAN'T!
SOWA そわ
SOWA (FIDGET) そわ
?
CHIRA (GLANCE) ちらっ
BUT...!
SOWA そわ
ちらっ CHIRA
SOWA そわ
IT'S A MOUSE ...!!
SOWA そわ
ジッ...
JI (STARE)
OH-HO! COMING!
SOWA そわ
SOWA そわ
!!!
ぴゃっ!!
PYA (DASH)

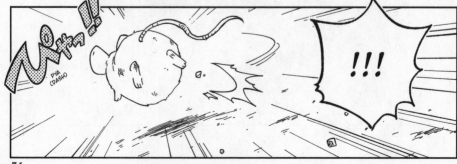

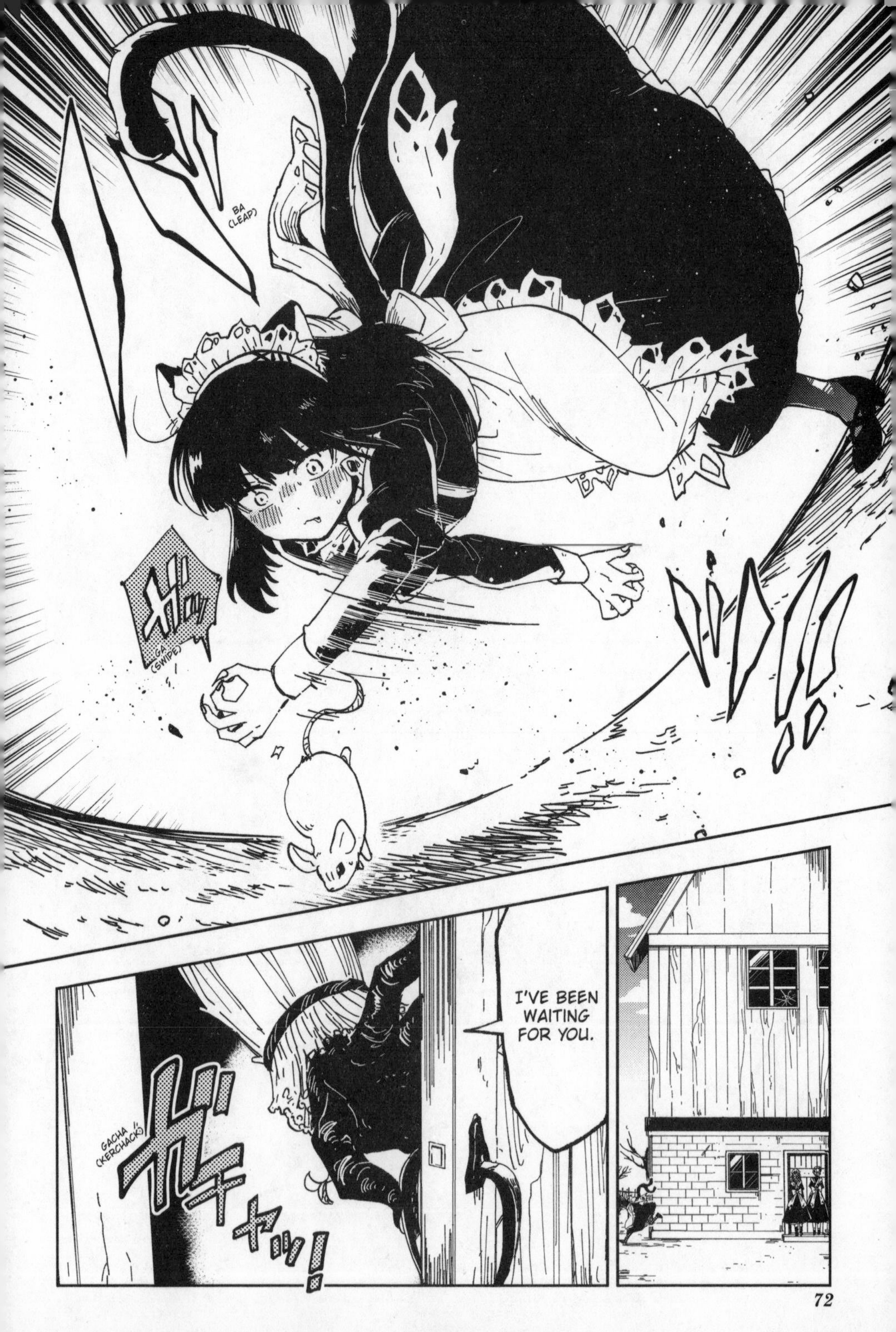
BA (LEAP)
GA (SWIPE)
I'VE BEEN WAITING FOR YOU.
GACHA (KERCHACK)

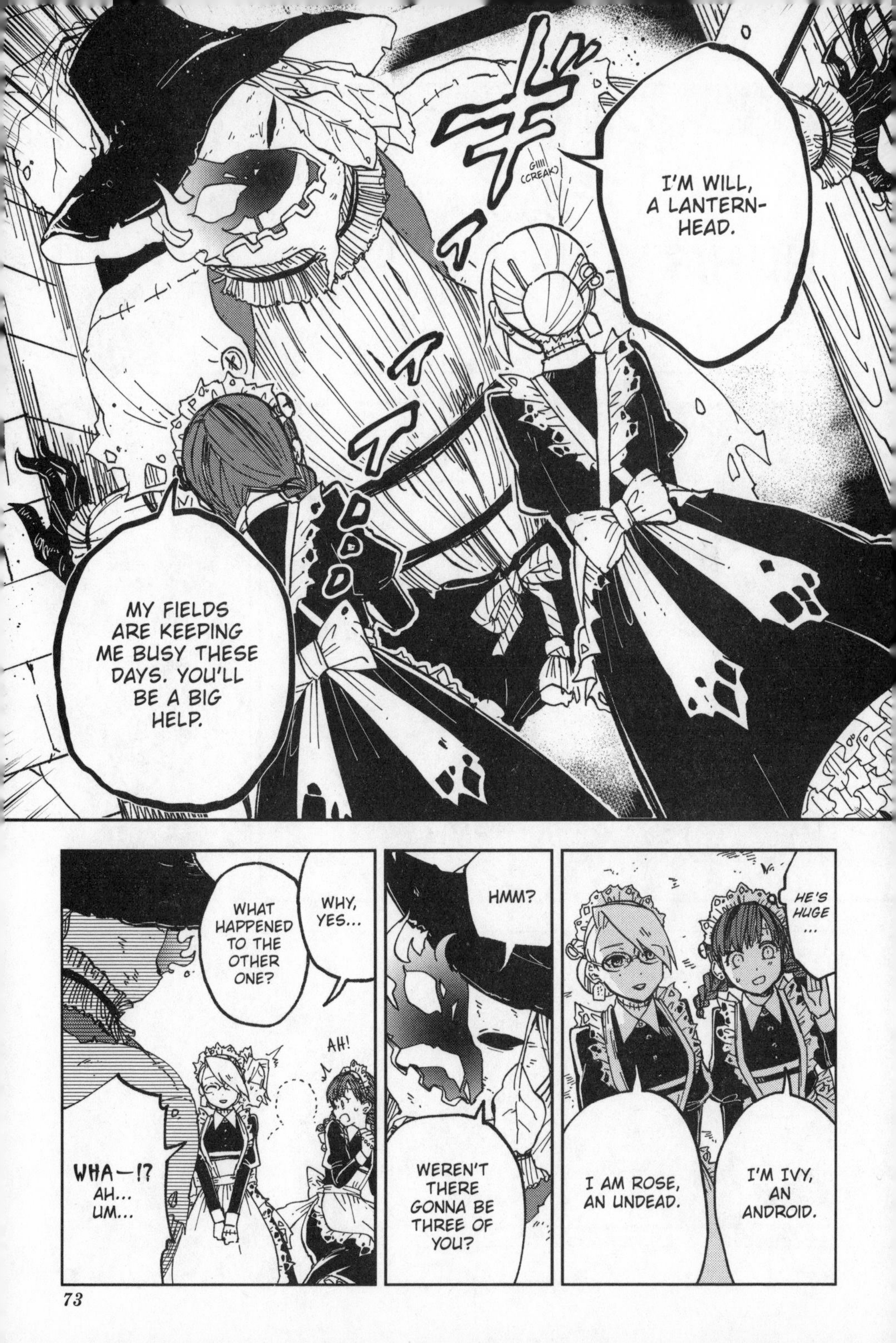
I'M WILL, A LANTERN-HEAD.
GIIII (CREAK)
MY FIELDS ARE KEEPING ME BUSY THESE DAYS. YOU'LL BE A BIG HELP.
HE'S HUGE ...
I'M IVY, AN ANDROID.
I AM ROSE, AN UNDEAD.
HMM?
WEREN'T THERE GONNA BE THREE OF YOU?
WHY, YES...
WHAT HAPPENED TO THE OTHER ONE?
AH!
WHA—!? AH... UM...

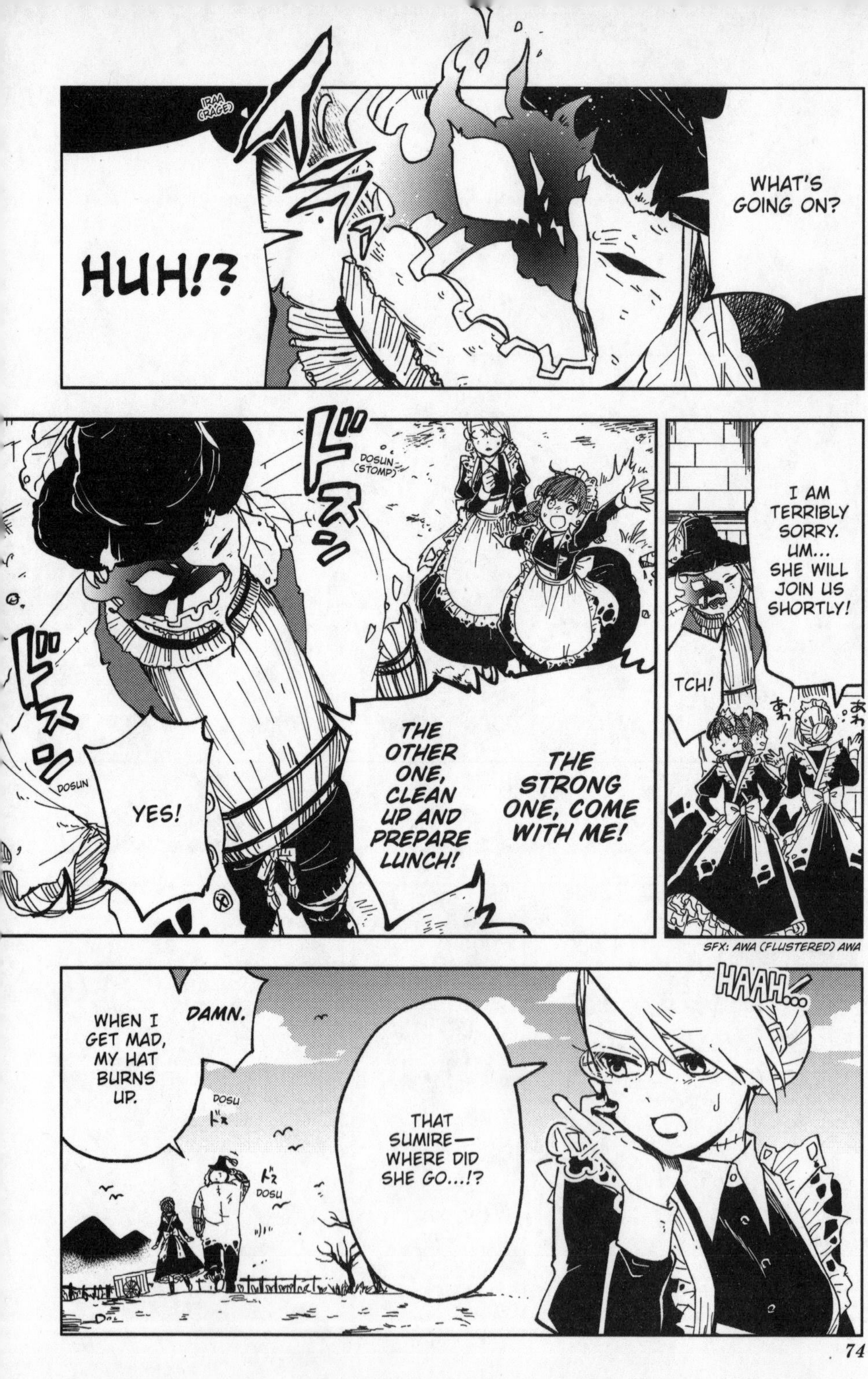
WHAT'S GOING ON?
IRAA (RAGE)
HUH!?
I AM TERRIBLY SORRY. UM... SHE WILL JOIN US SHORTLY!
TCH!
DOSUN (STOMP)
THE STRONG ONE, COME WITH ME!
THE OTHER ONE, CLEAN UP AND PREPARE LUNCH!
YES!
DOSUN
SFX: AWA (FLUSTERED) AWA
HAAH...
THAT SUMIRE— WHERE DID SHE GO...!?
DAMN.
WHEN I GET MAD, MY HAT BURNS UP.
DOSU
DOSU

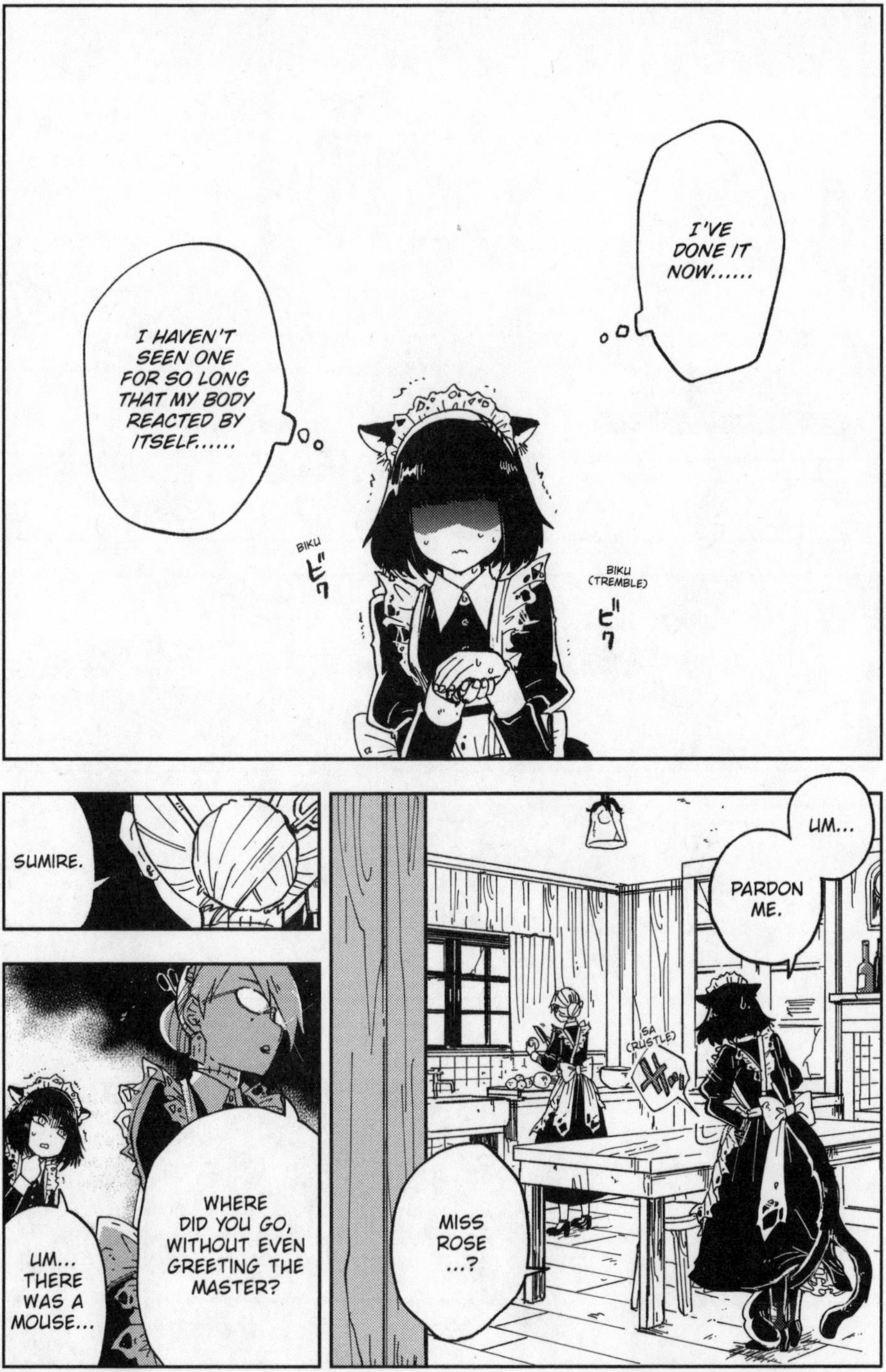
I'VE DONE IT NOW......
BIKU (TREMBLE)
I HAVEN'T SEEN ONE FOR SO LONG THAT MY BODY REACTED BY ITSELF......
BIKU
UM... PARDON ME.
SA (RUSTLE)
MISS ROSE ...?
SUMIRE.
WHERE DID YOU GO, WITHOUT EVEN GREETING THE MASTER?
UM... THERE WAS A MOUSE...

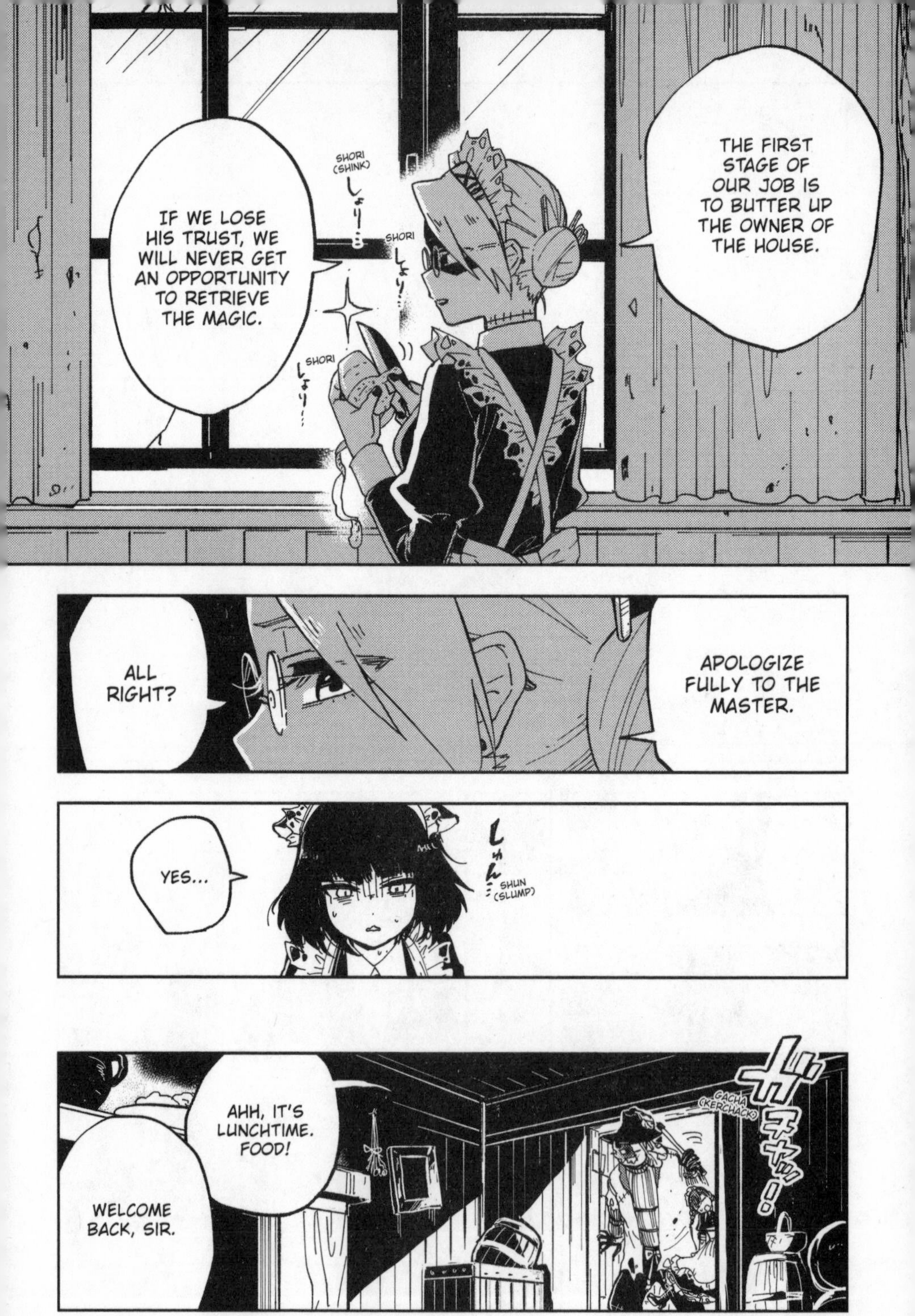
THE FIRST STAGE OF OUR JOB IS TO BUTTER UP THE OWNER OF THE HOUSE.
しょり
SHORI
しょり
SHORI (SHINK)
しょり
SHORI
IF WE LOSE HIS TRUST, WE WILL NEVER GET AN OPPORTUNITY TO RETRIEVE THE MAGIC.
APOLOGIZE FULLY TO THE MASTER.
ALL RIGHT?
しゅん
SHUN (SLUMP)
YES...
ガチャッ!
GACHA (KERCHACK)
AHH, IT'S LUNCHTIME. FOOD!
WELCOME BACK, SIR.

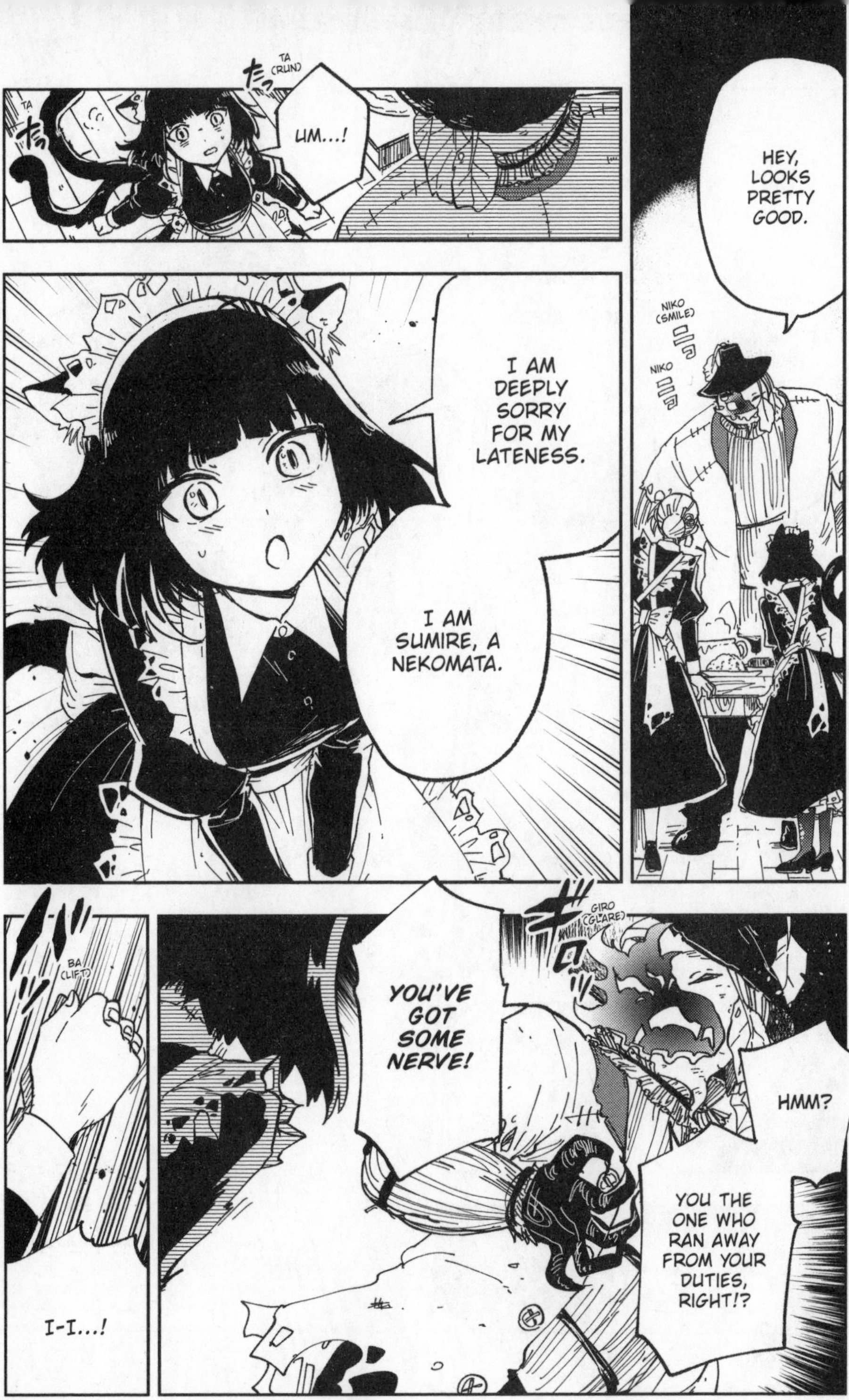
HEY, LOOKS PRETTY GOOD.
NIKO (SMILE)
NIKO
TA (RUN)
TA
UM...!
I AM DEEPLY SORRY FOR MY LATENESS.
I AM SUMIRE, A NEKOMATA.
GIRO (GLARE)
HMM?
YOU THE ONE WHO RAN AWAY FROM YOUR DUTIES, RIGHT!?
YOU'VE GOT SOME NERVE!
BA (LIFT)
I-I...!

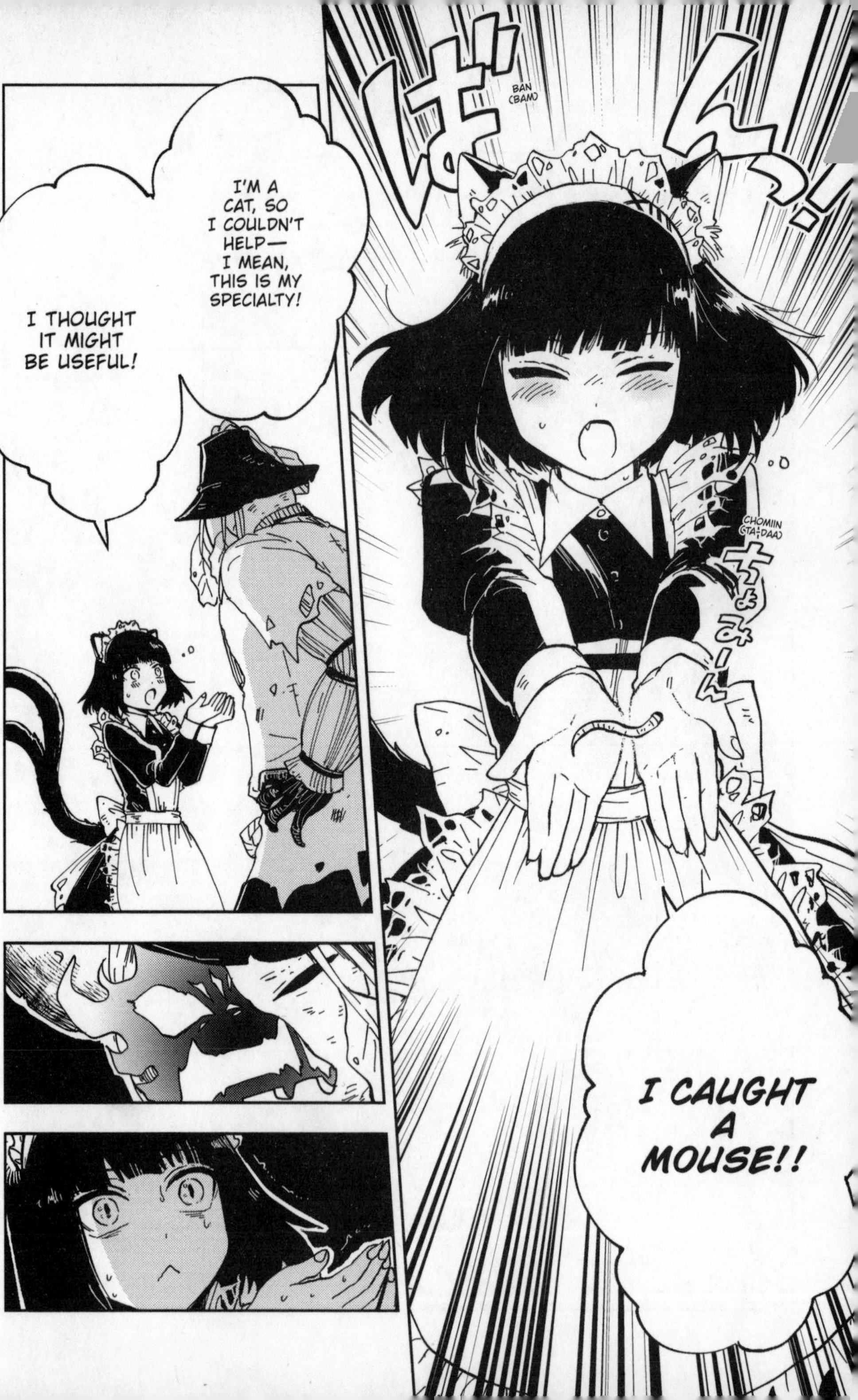
BAN (BAM)
CHOMIIN (TA-DAA)
I CAUGHT A MOUSE!!
I'M A CAT, SO I COULDN'T HELP— I MEAN, THIS IS MY SPECIALTY!
I THOUGHT IT MIGHT BE USEFUL!

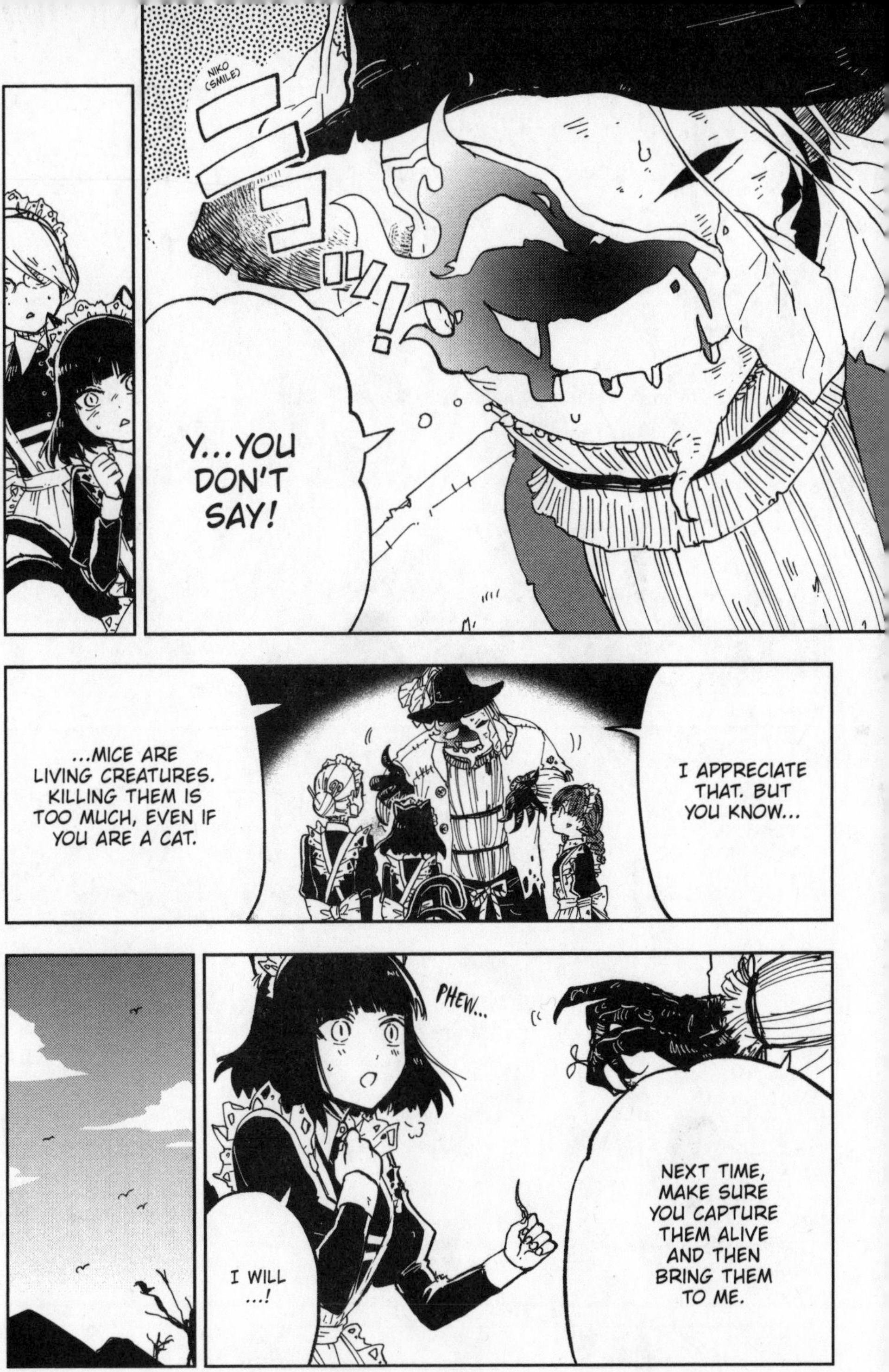
NIKO (SMILE)
ニコッ!
Y...YOU DON'T SAY!
I APPRECIATE THAT. BUT YOU KNOW...
...MICE ARE LIVING CREATURES. KILLING THEM IS TOO MUCH, EVEN IF YOU ARE A CAT.
PHEW...
NEXT TIME, MAKE SURE YOU CAPTURE THEM ALIVE AND THEN BRING THEM TO ME.
I WILL ...!

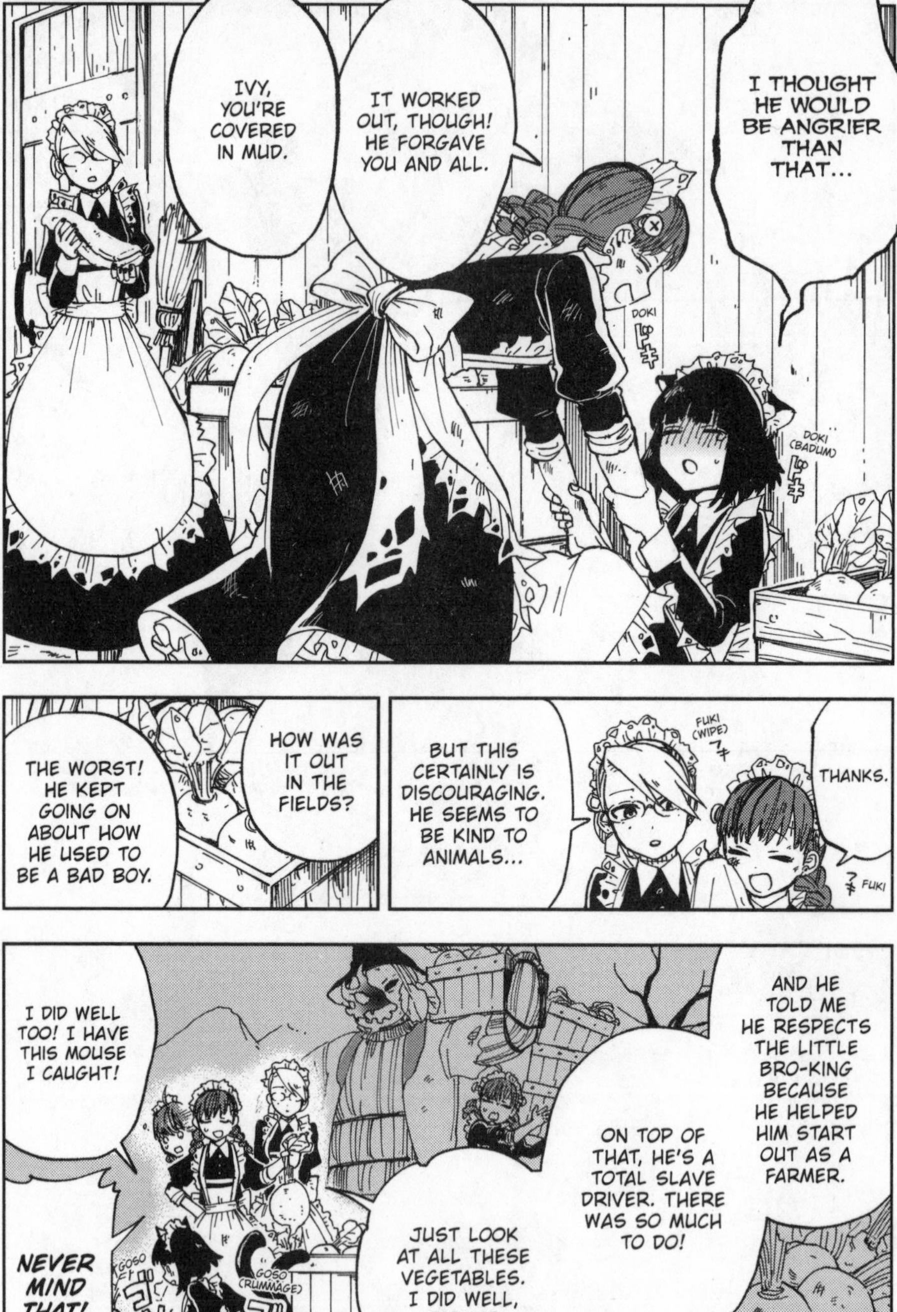
I THOUGHT HE WOULD BE ANGRIER THAN THAT...
IT WORKED OUT, THOUGH! HE FORGAVE YOU AND ALL.
IVY, YOU'RE COVERED IN MUD.
DOKI
DOKI (BADUM)
THANKS.
FUKI (WIPE)
FUKI
BUT THIS CERTAINLY IS DISCOURAGING. HE SEEMS TO BE KIND TO ANIMALS...
HOW WAS IT OUT IN THE FIELDS?
THE WORST! HE KEPT GOING ON ABOUT HOW HE USED TO BE A BAD BOY.
AND HE TOLD ME HE RESPECTS THE LITTLE BRO-KING BECAUSE HE HELPED HIM START OUT AS A FARMER.
ON TOP OF THAT, HE'S A TOTAL SLAVE DRIVER. THERE WAS SO MUCH TO DO!
JUST LOOK AT ALL THESE VEGETABLES. I DID WELL, RIGHT?
I DID WELL TOO! I HAVE THIS MOUSE I CAUGHT!
NEVER MIND THAT!
GOSO
GOSO (RUMMAGE)

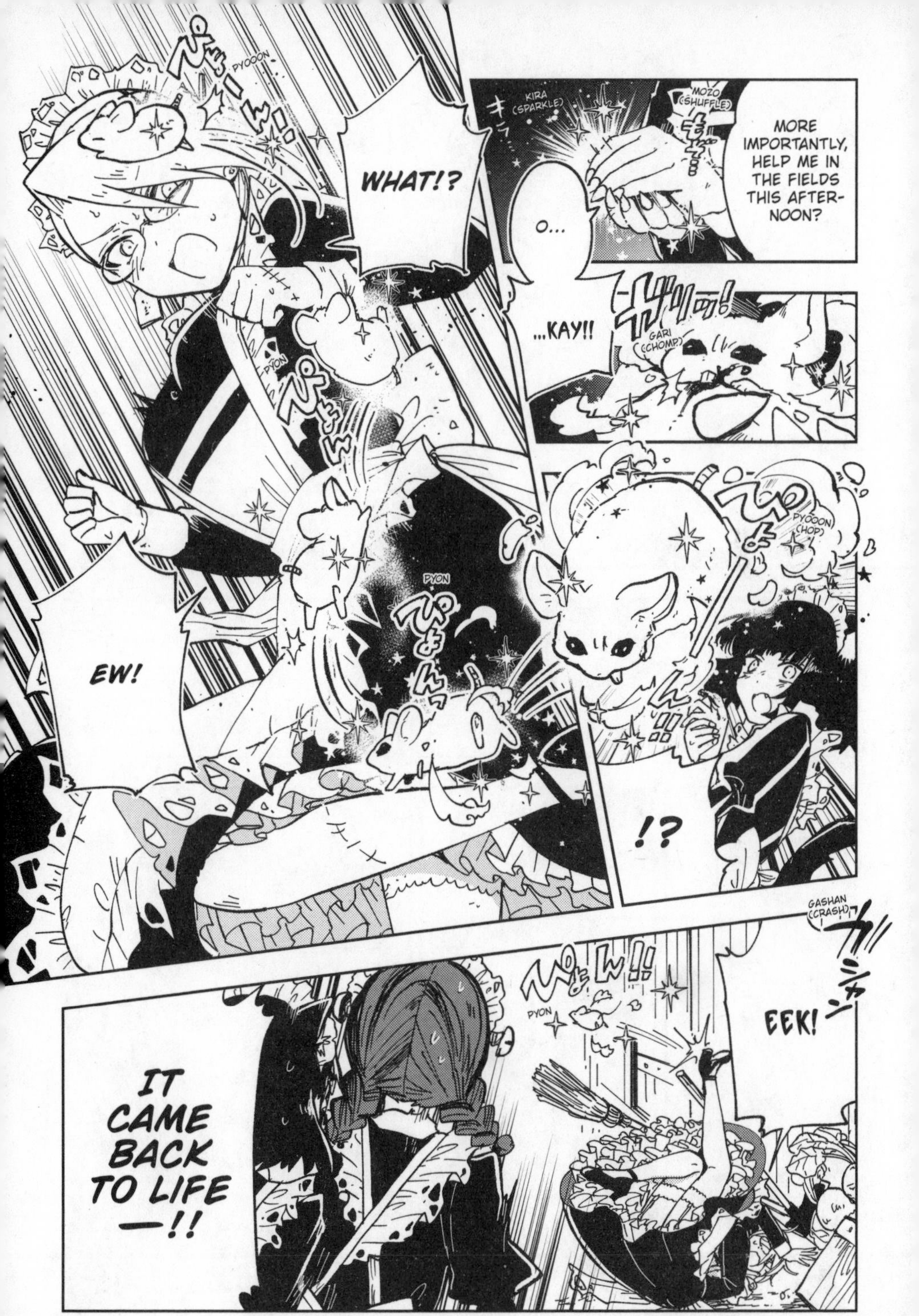

MORE IMPORTANTLY, HELP ME IN THE FIELDS THIS AFTERNOON?
MOZO (SHUFFLE)
KIRA (SPARKLE)
O...
...KAY!!
GARI (CHOMP)
PYOOON (HOP)
!?
PYOOON
WHAT!?
PYON
PYON
EW!
EEK!
GASHAN (CRASH)
PYON
IT CAME BACK TO LIFE —!!

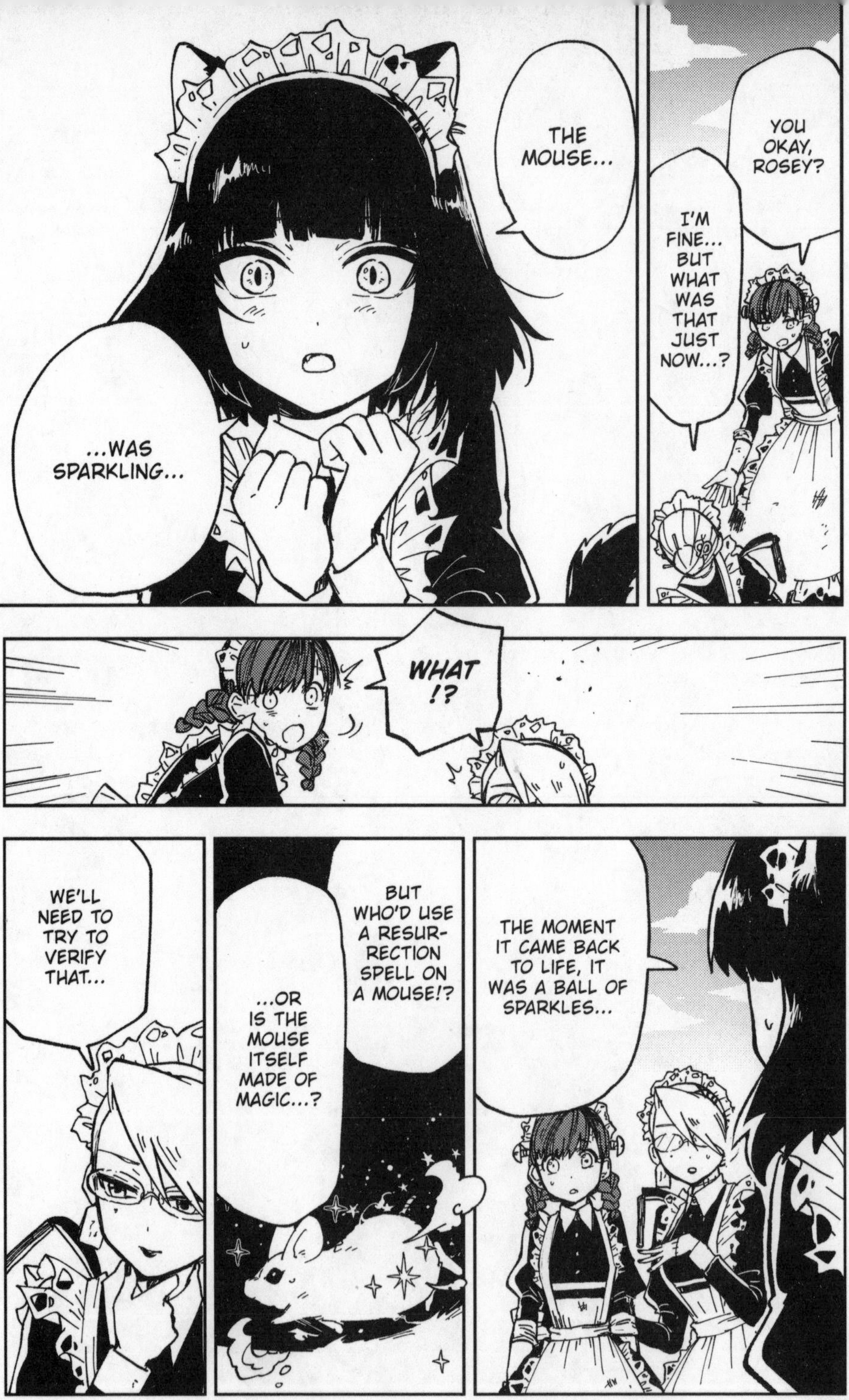
YOU OKAY, ROSEY?
I'M FINE... BUT WHAT WAS THAT JUST NOW...?
THE MOUSE...
...WAS SPARKLING...
WHAT!?
THE MOMENT IT CAME BACK TO LIFE, IT WAS A BALL OF SPARKLES...
BUT WHO'D USE A RESURRECTION SPELL ON A MOUSE!?
...OR IS THE MOUSE ITSELF MADE OF MAGIC...?
WE'LL NEED TO TRY TO VERIFY THAT...

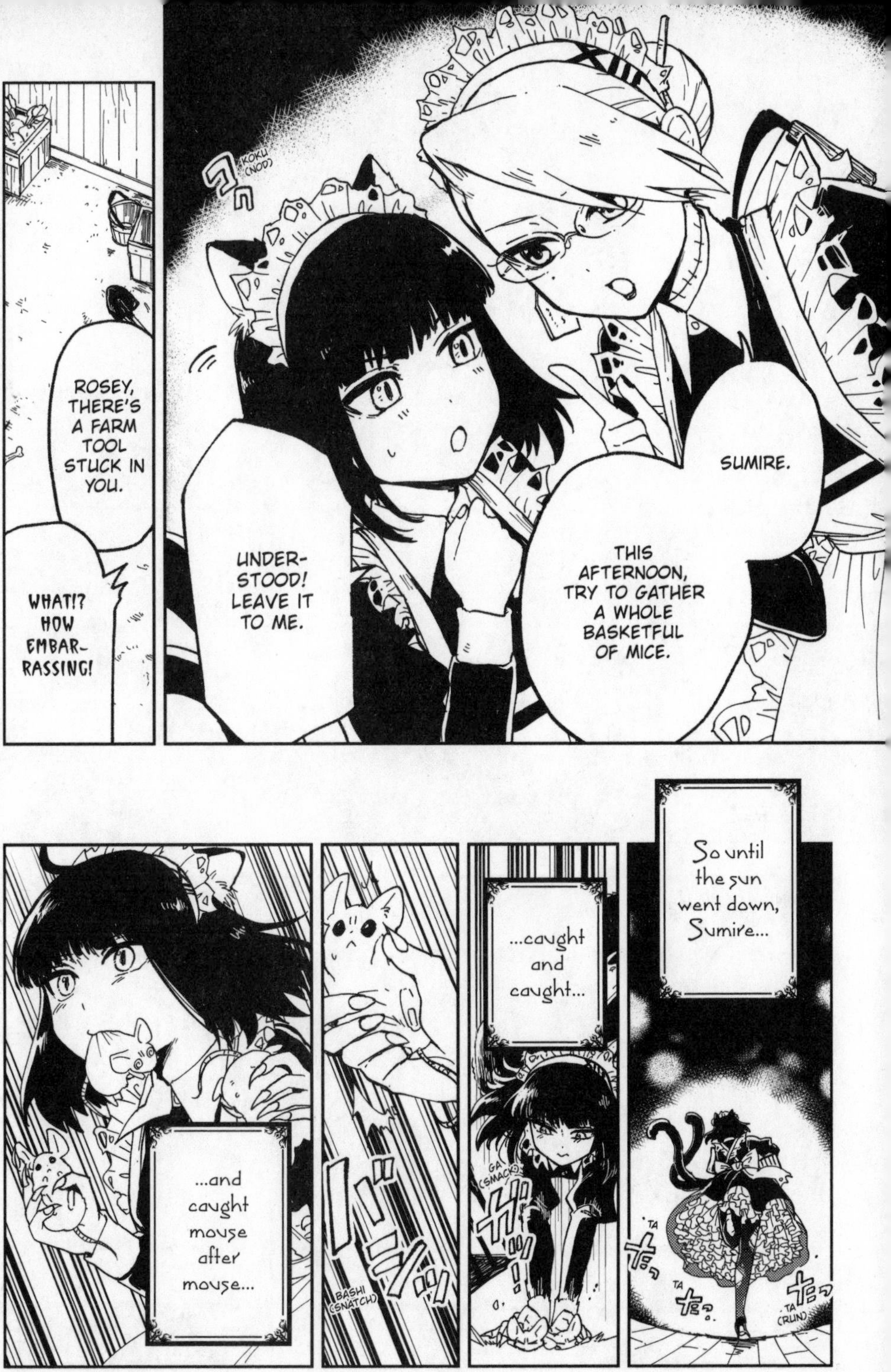
SUMIRE.
THIS AFTERNOON, TRY TO GATHER A WHOLE BASKETFUL OF MICE.
KOKU (NOD)
UNDER-STOOD! LEAVE IT TO ME.
ROSEY, THERE'S A FARM TOOL STUCK IN YOU.
WHAT!? HOW EMBAR-RASSING!
So until the sun went down, Sumire...
TA TA TA (RUN)
...caught and caught...
GA (SMACK)
BASHI (SNATCH)
...and caught mouse after mouse...

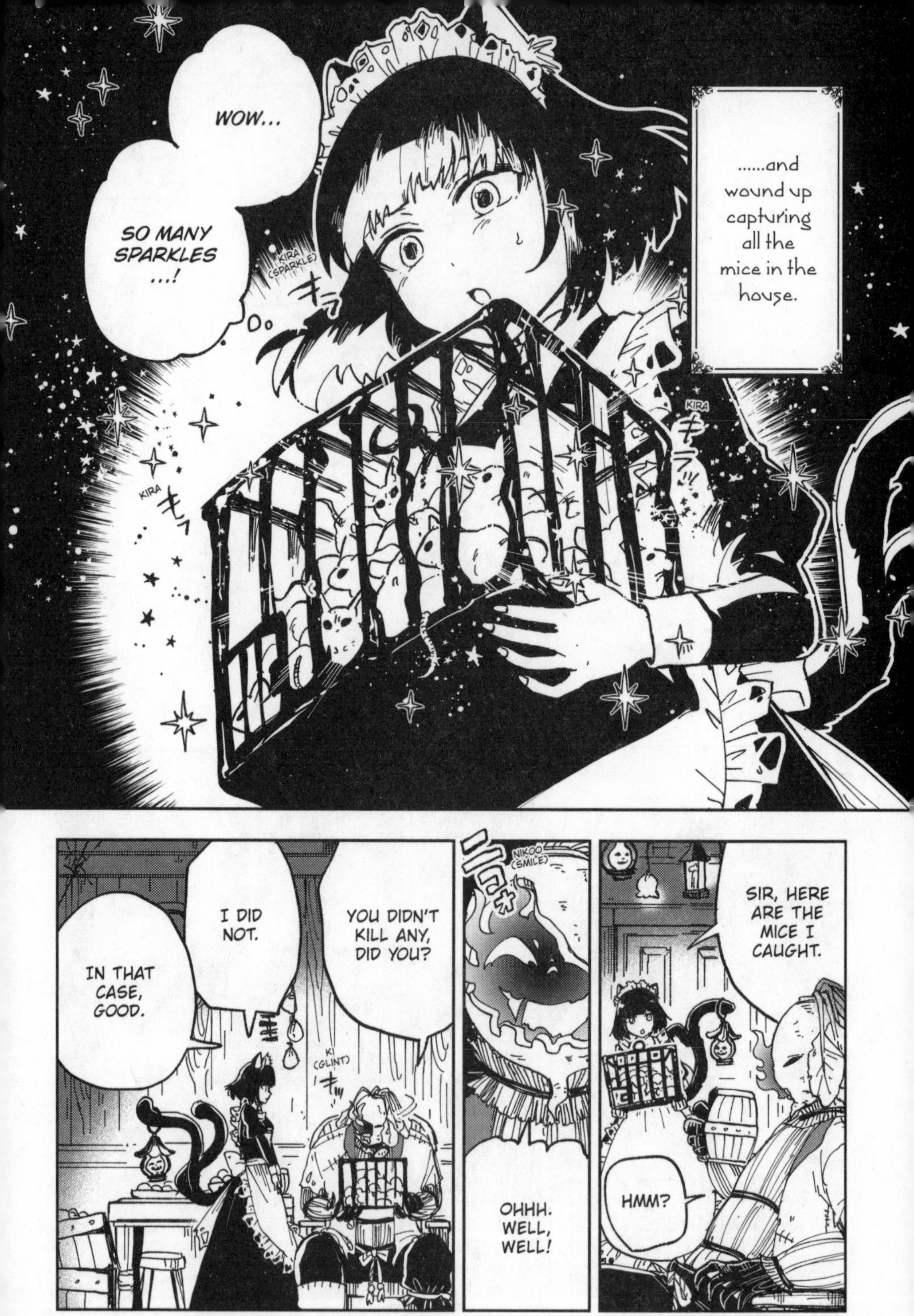
......and wound up capturing all the mice in the house.
KIRA
WOW...
SO MANY SPARKLES ...!
KIRA (SPARKLE)
KIRA
SIR, HERE ARE THE MICE I CAUGHT.
HMM?
NIKOO (SMILE)
OHHH. WELL, WELL!
YOU DIDN'T KILL ANY, DID YOU?
KI (GLINT)
I DID NOT.
IN THAT CASE, GOOD.

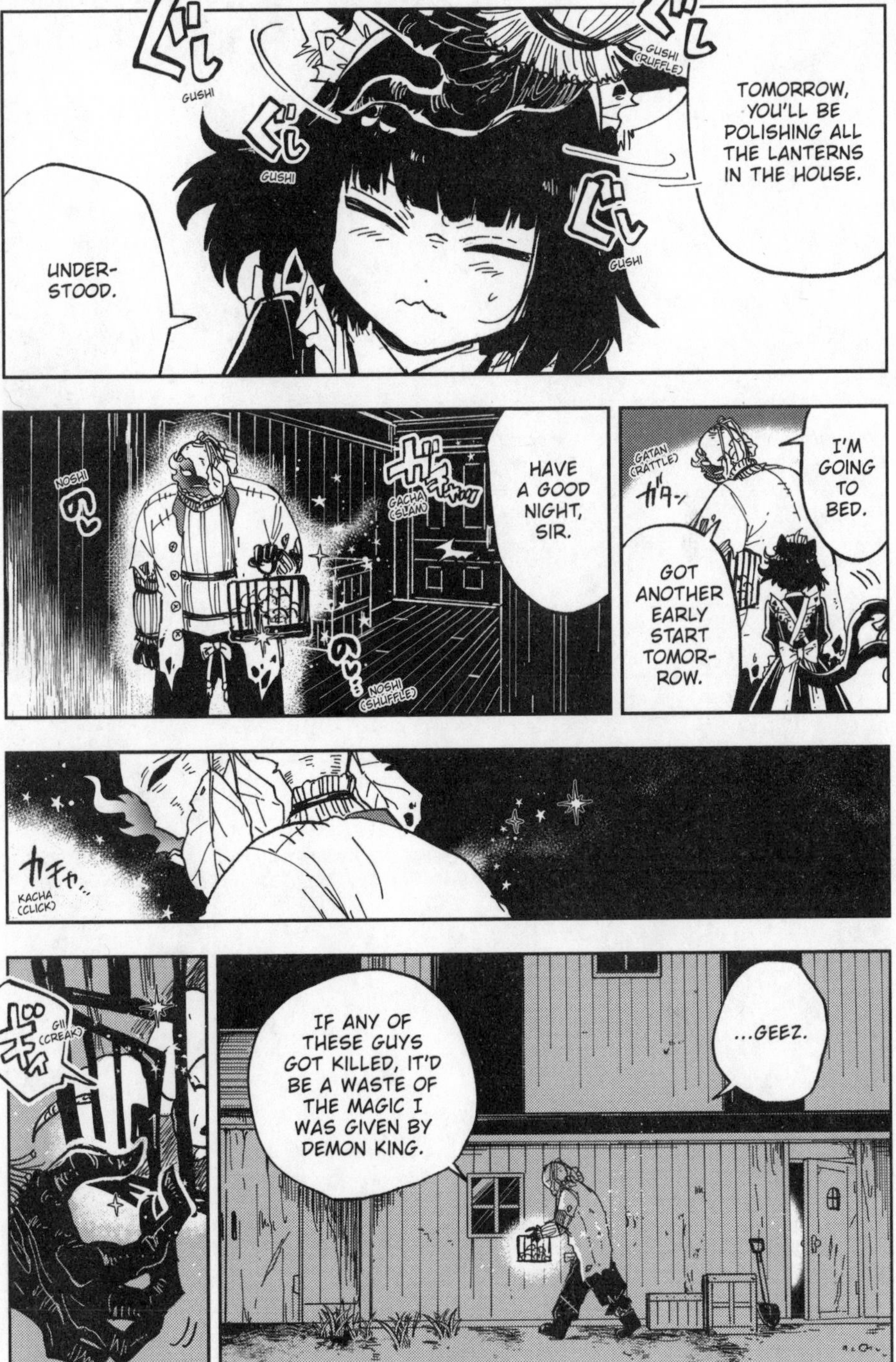
GUSHI (RUFFLE)
TOMORROW, YOU'LL BE POLISHING ALL THE LANTERNS IN THE HOUSE.
GUSHI
GUSHI
GUSHI
UNDER-STOOD.
I'M GOING TO BED.
GATAN (RATTLE)
GOT ANOTHER EARLY START TOMORROW.
HAVE A GOOD NIGHT, SIR.
GACHA (SLAM)
NOSHI
NOSHI (SHUFFLE)
KACHA (CLICK)
...GEEZ.
IF ANY OF THESE GUYS GOT KILLED, IT'D BE A WASTE OF THE MAGIC I WAS GIVEN BY DEMON KING.
GII (CREAK)

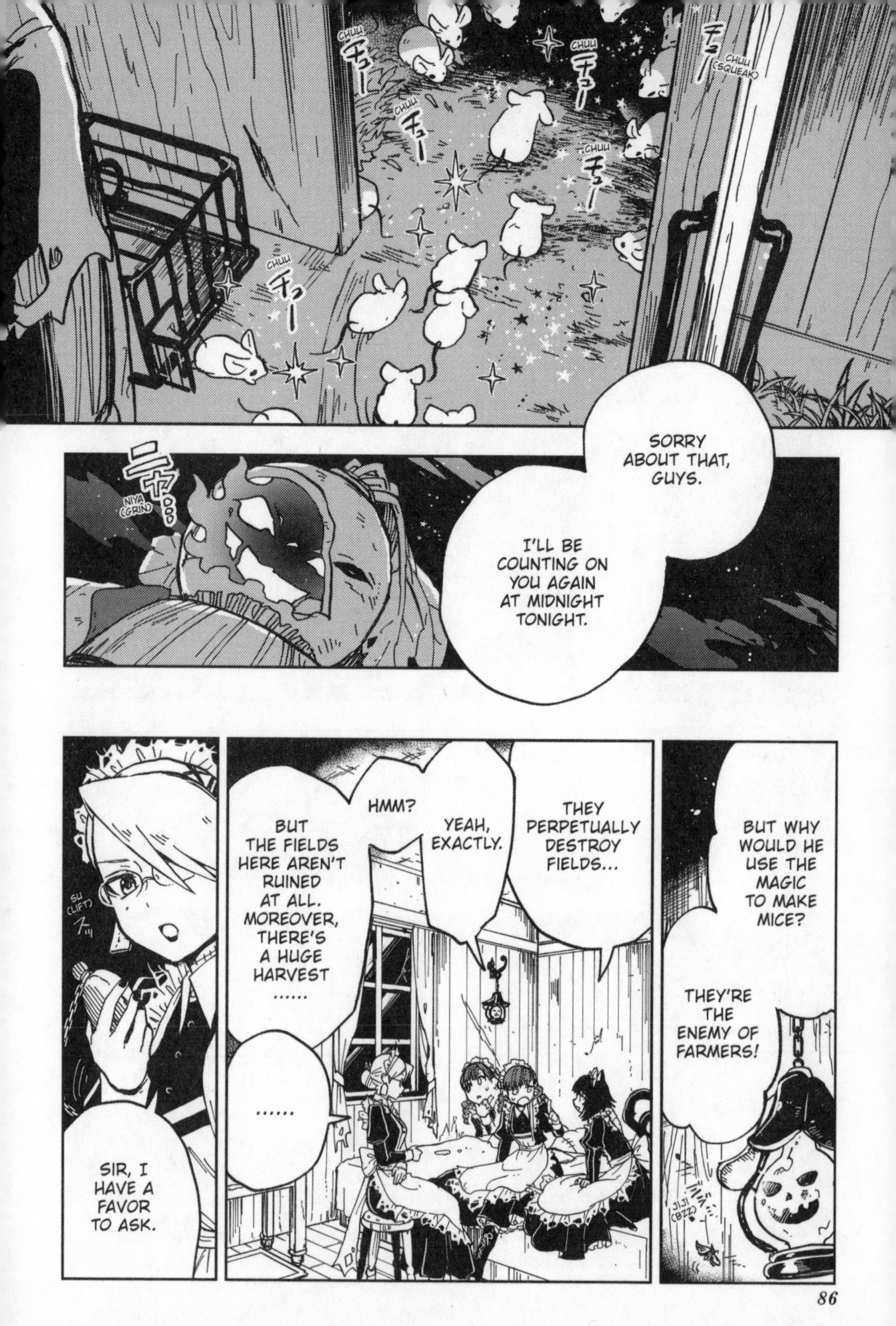
CHUU (SQUEAK)
CHUU
CHUU
CHUU
CHUU
CHUU
SORRY ABOUT THAT, GUYS.
I'LL BE COUNTING ON YOU AGAIN AT MIDNIGHT TONIGHT.
NIYA (GRIN)
BUT WHY WOULD HE USE THE MAGIC TO MAKE MICE?
THEY'RE THE ENEMY OF FARMERS!
JIJI (BZZ)
THEY PERPETUALLY DESTROY FIELDS...
YEAH, EXACTLY.
HMM?
BUT THE FIELDS HERE AREN'T RUINED AT ALL. MOREOVER, THERE'S A HUGE HARVEST ......
......
SU (LIFT)
SIR, I HAVE A FAVOR TO ASK.

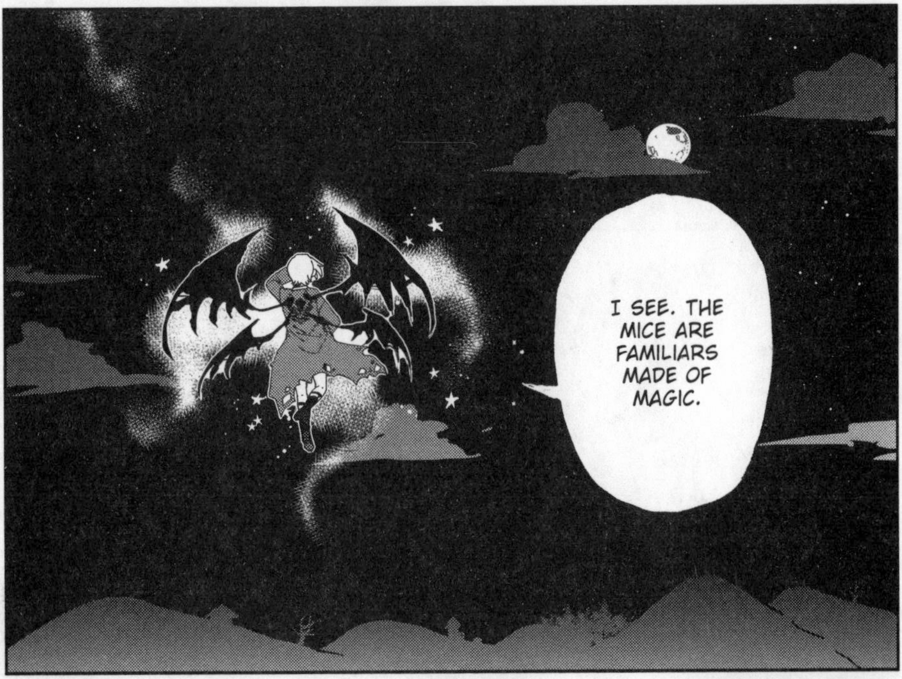
I SEE. THE MICE ARE FAMILIARS MADE OF MAGIC.
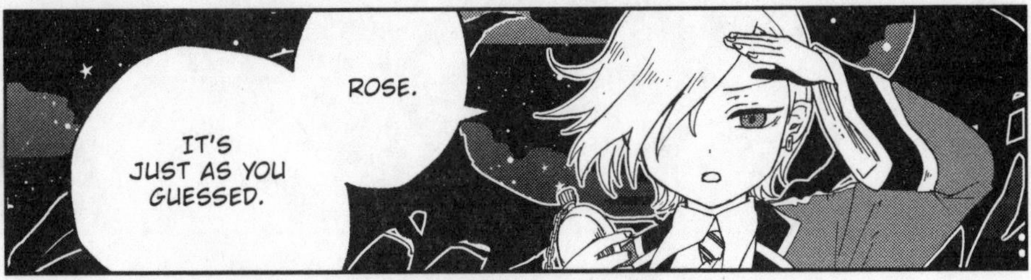
ROSE.
IT'S JUST AS YOU GUESSED.
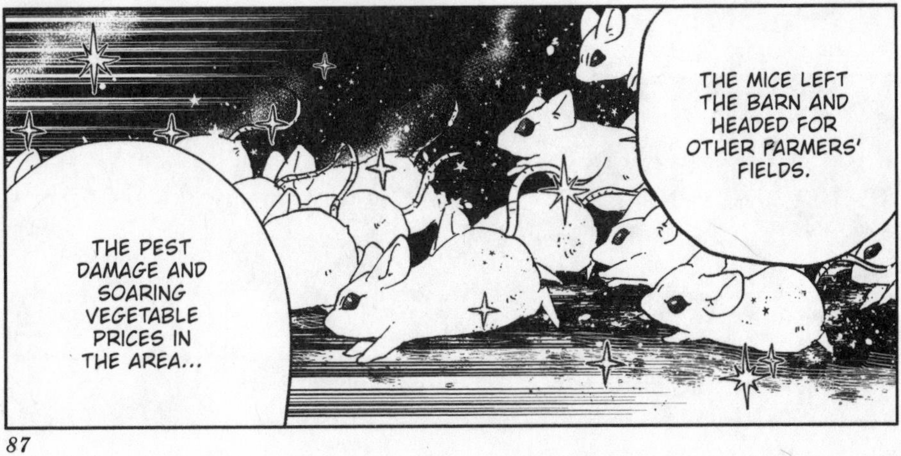
THE MICE LEFT THE BARN AND HEADED FOR OTHER PARMERS' FIELDS.
THE PEST DAMAGE AND SOARING VEGETABLE PRICES IN THE AREA...

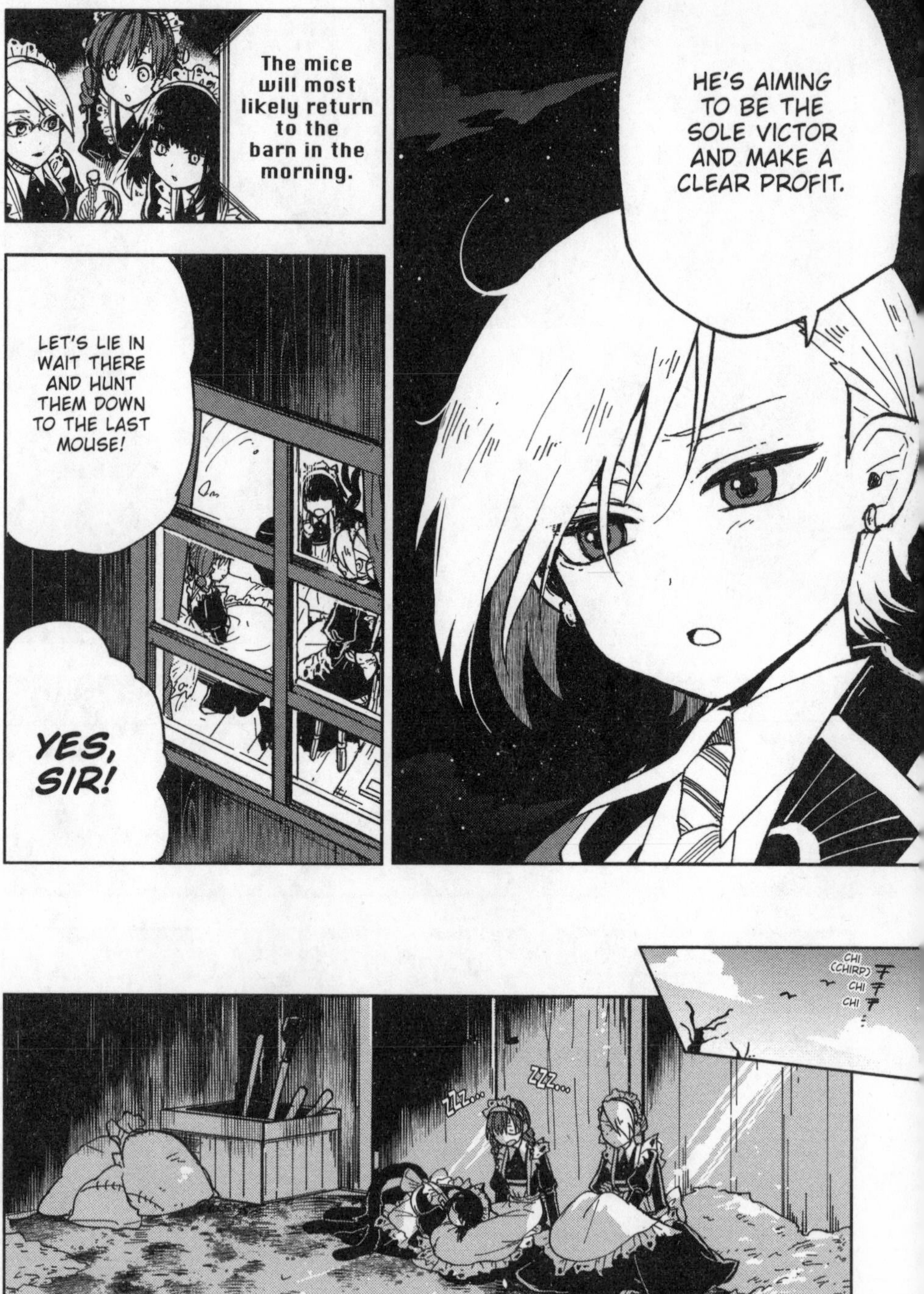
HE'S AIMING TO BE THE SOLE VICTOR AND MAKE A CLEAR PROFIT.
The mice will most likely return to the barn in the morning.
LET'S LIE IN WAIT THERE AND HUNT THEM DOWN TO THE LAST MOUSE!
YES, SIR!
CHI (CHIRP)
CHI
CHI
ZZZ...
ZZZ...

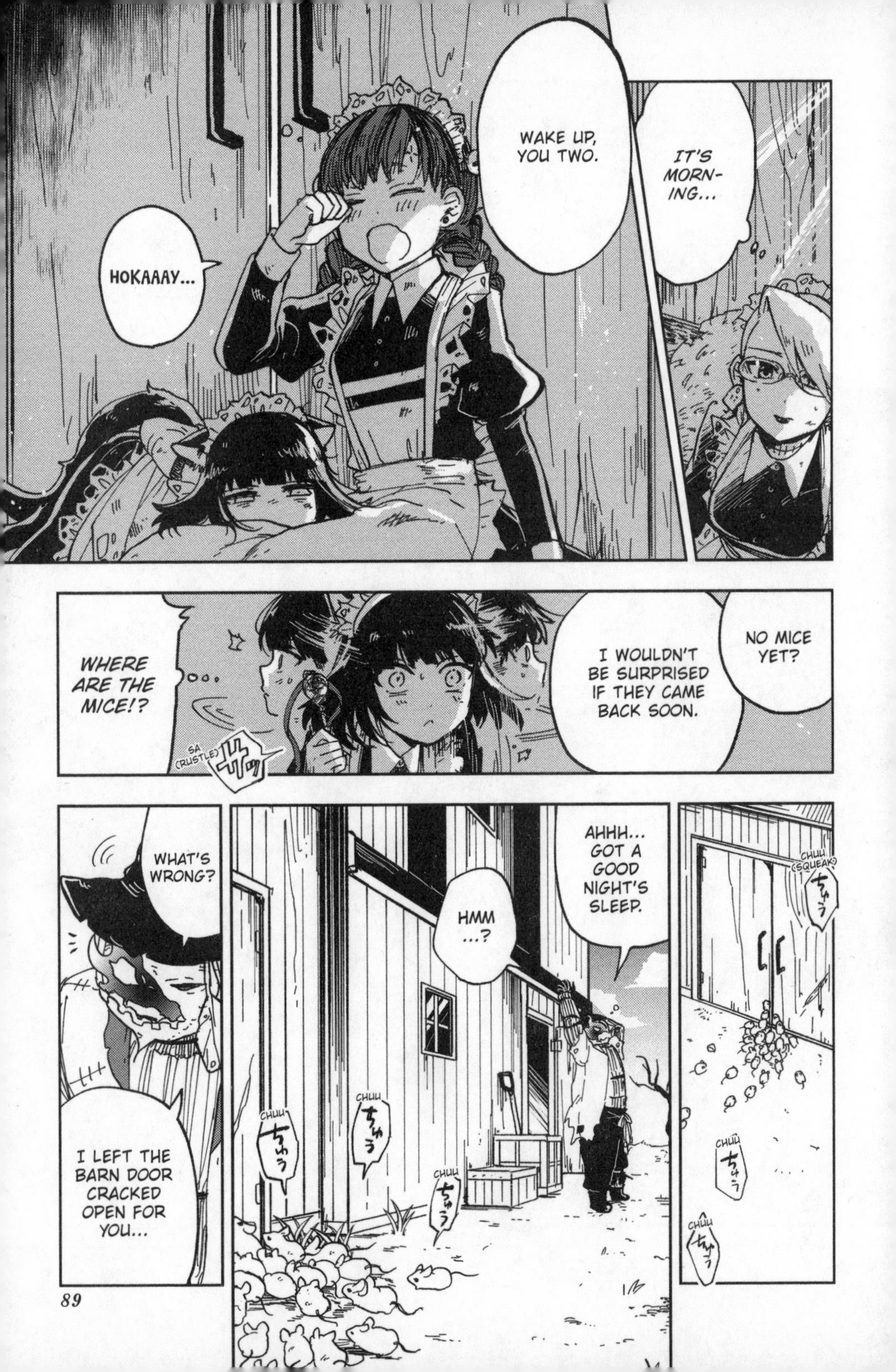
WAKE UP, YOU TWO.
IT'S MORNING-ING...
HOKAAAY...
NO MICE YET?
I WOULDN'T BE SURPRISED IF THEY CAME BACK SOON.
WHERE ARE THE MICE!?
SA (RUSTLE) サッ
CHUU (SQUEAK) ちゅう
CHUU ちゅう
CHUU ちゅう
AHHH... GOT A GOOD NIGHT'S SLEEP.
HMM ...?
CHUU ちゅう
CHUU ちゅう
CHUU ちゅう
WHAT'S WRONG?
I LEFT THE BARN DOOR CRACKED OPEN FOR YOU...

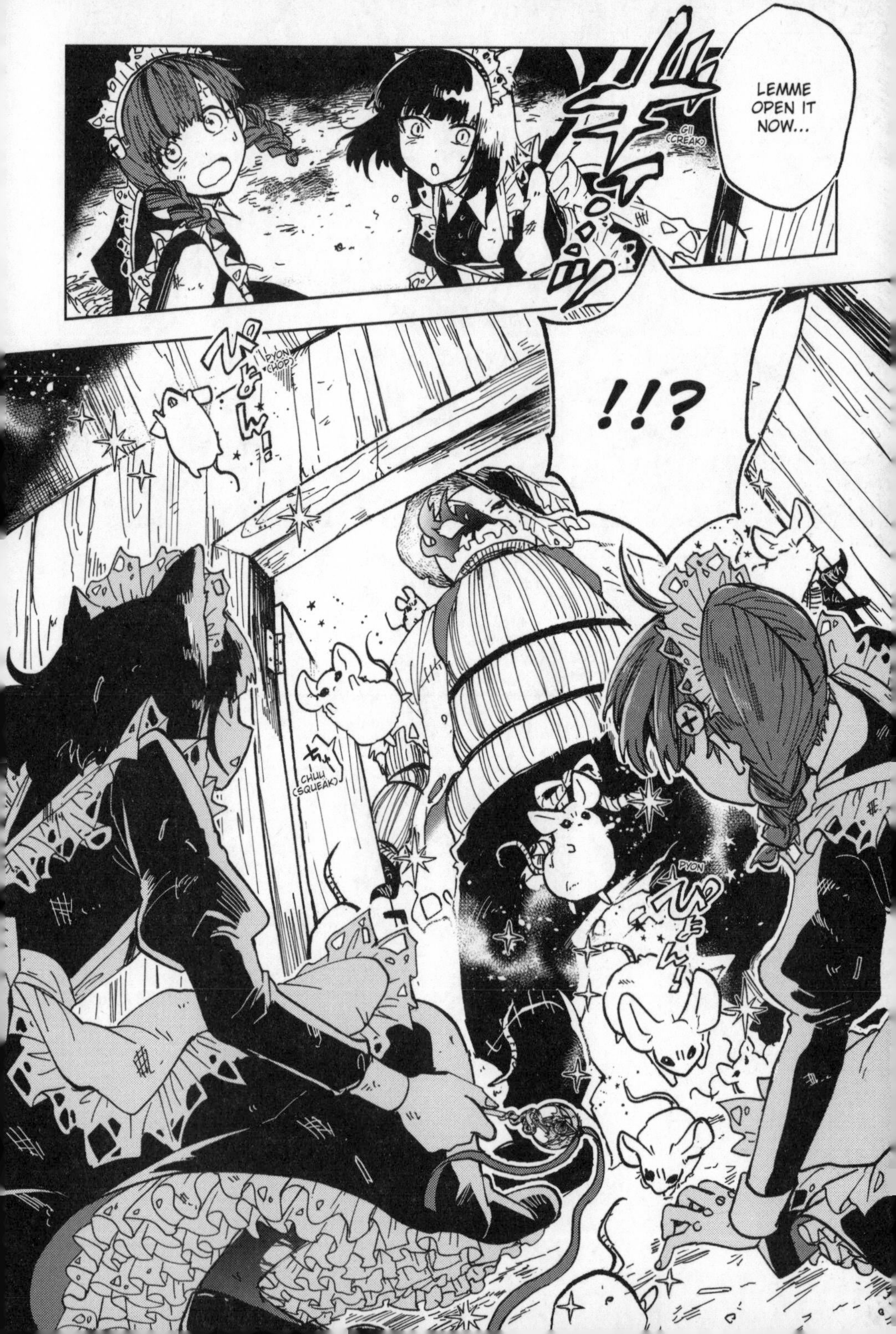
LEMME OPEN IT NOW...
GII (CREAK)
!!?
PYON (HOP)
CHUU (SQUEAK)
PYON

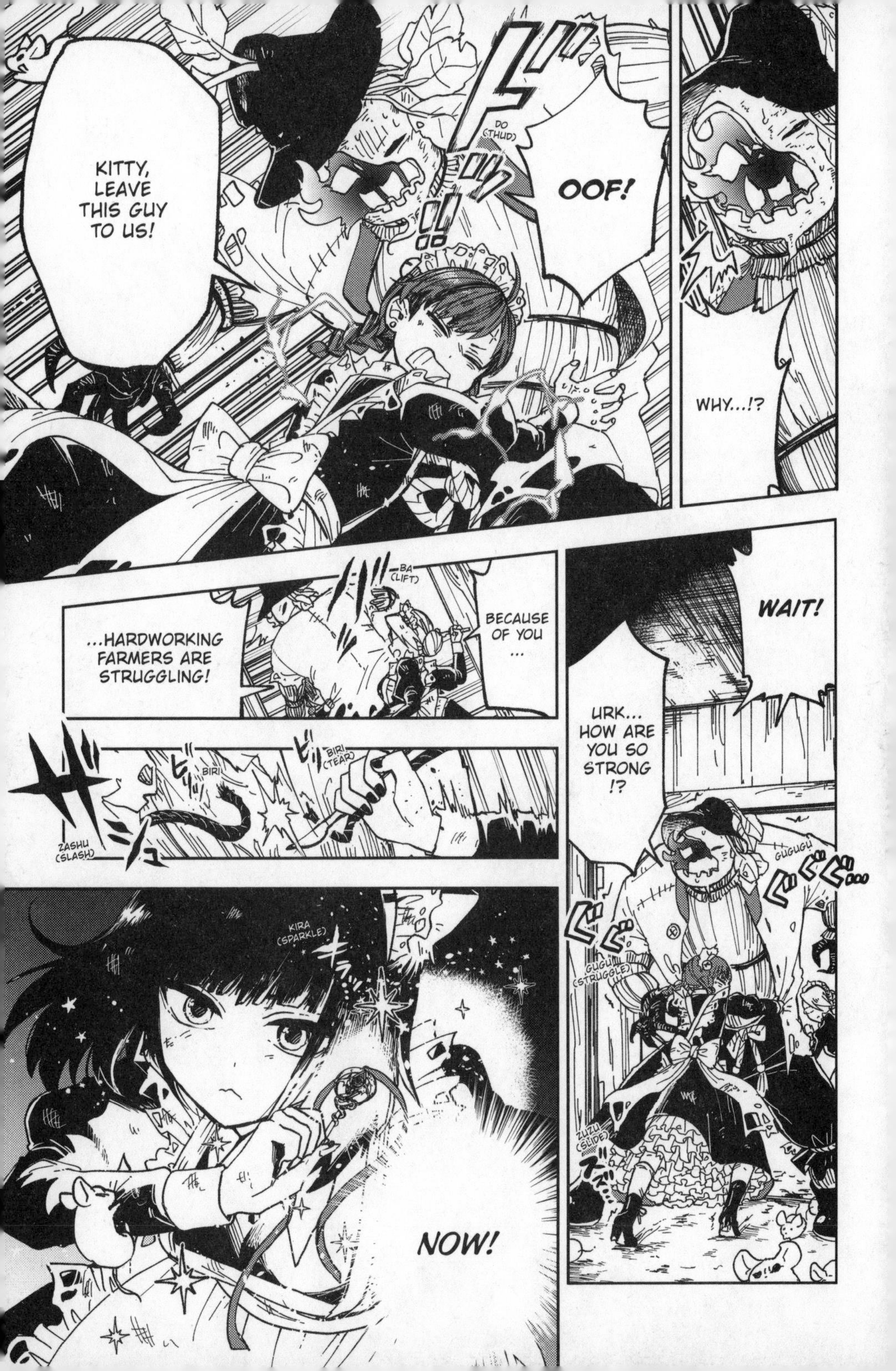
WHY...!?
DO (THUD)
OOF!
KITTY, LEAVE THIS GUY TO US!
WAIT!
URK... HOW ARE YOU SO STRONG !?
GUGUGU
GUGU (STRUGGLE)
ZUZU (SLIDE)
BA (LIFT)
BECAUSE OF YOU ...
...HARDWORKING FARMERS ARE STRUGGLING!
BIRI (TEAR)
BIRI
ZASHU (SLASH)
KIRA (SPARKLE)
NOW!

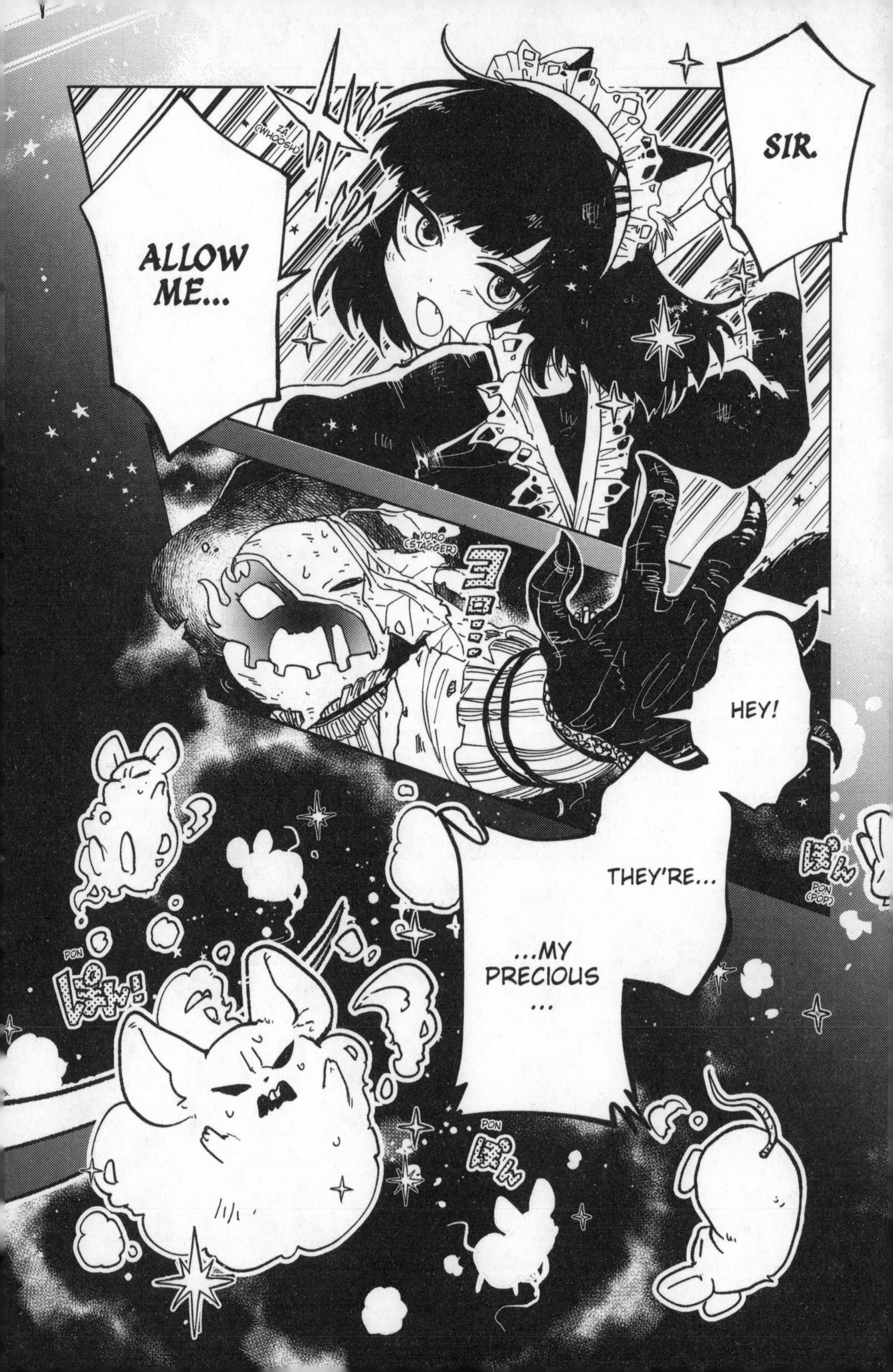
SIR.
ZA (WHOOSH)
ALLOW ME...
YORO (STAGGER)
HEY!
PON (POP)
THEY'RE...
...MY PRECIOUS ...
PON
PON

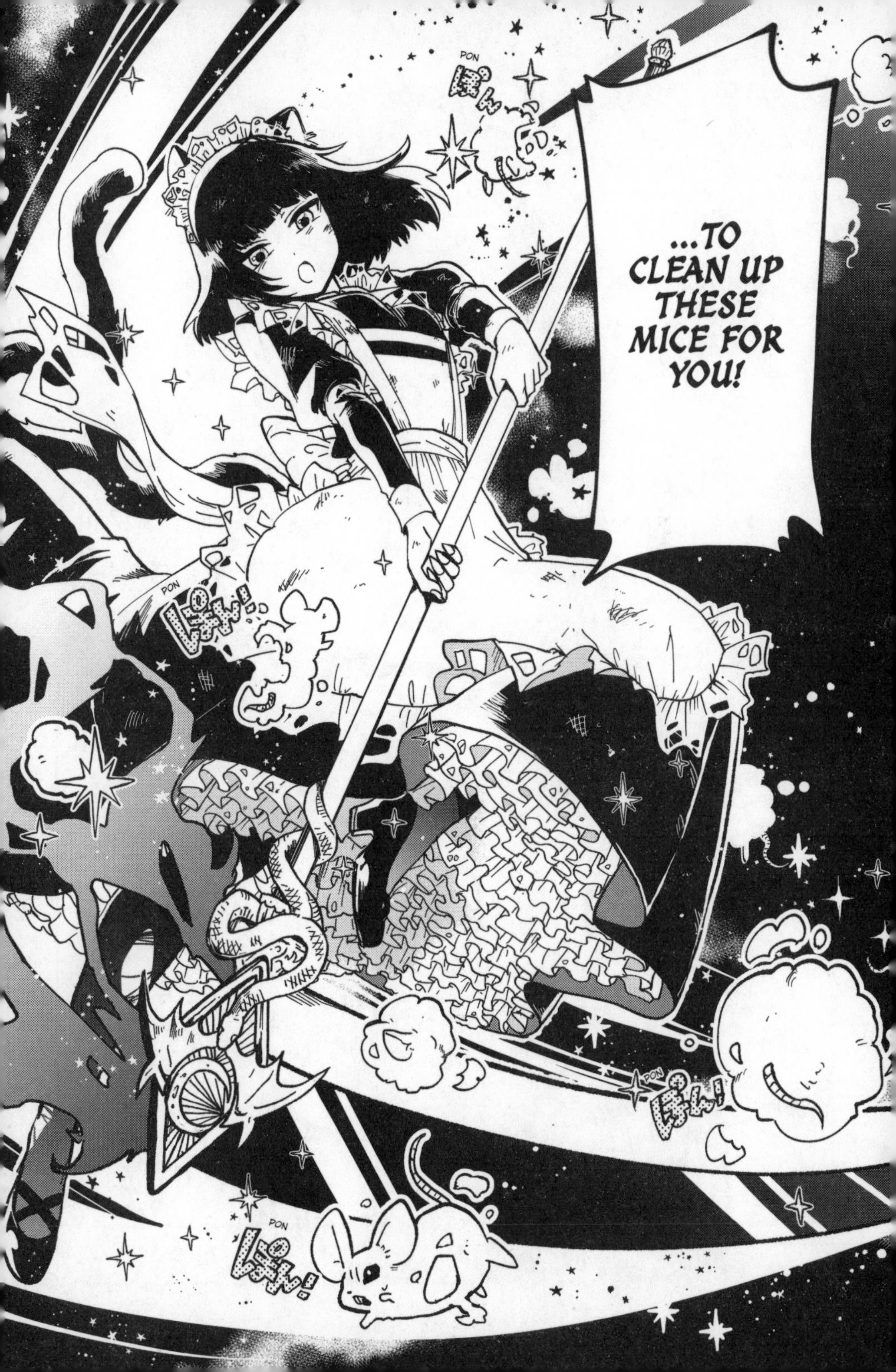
PON
...TO CLEAN UP THESE MICE FOR YOU!
PON
PON
PON

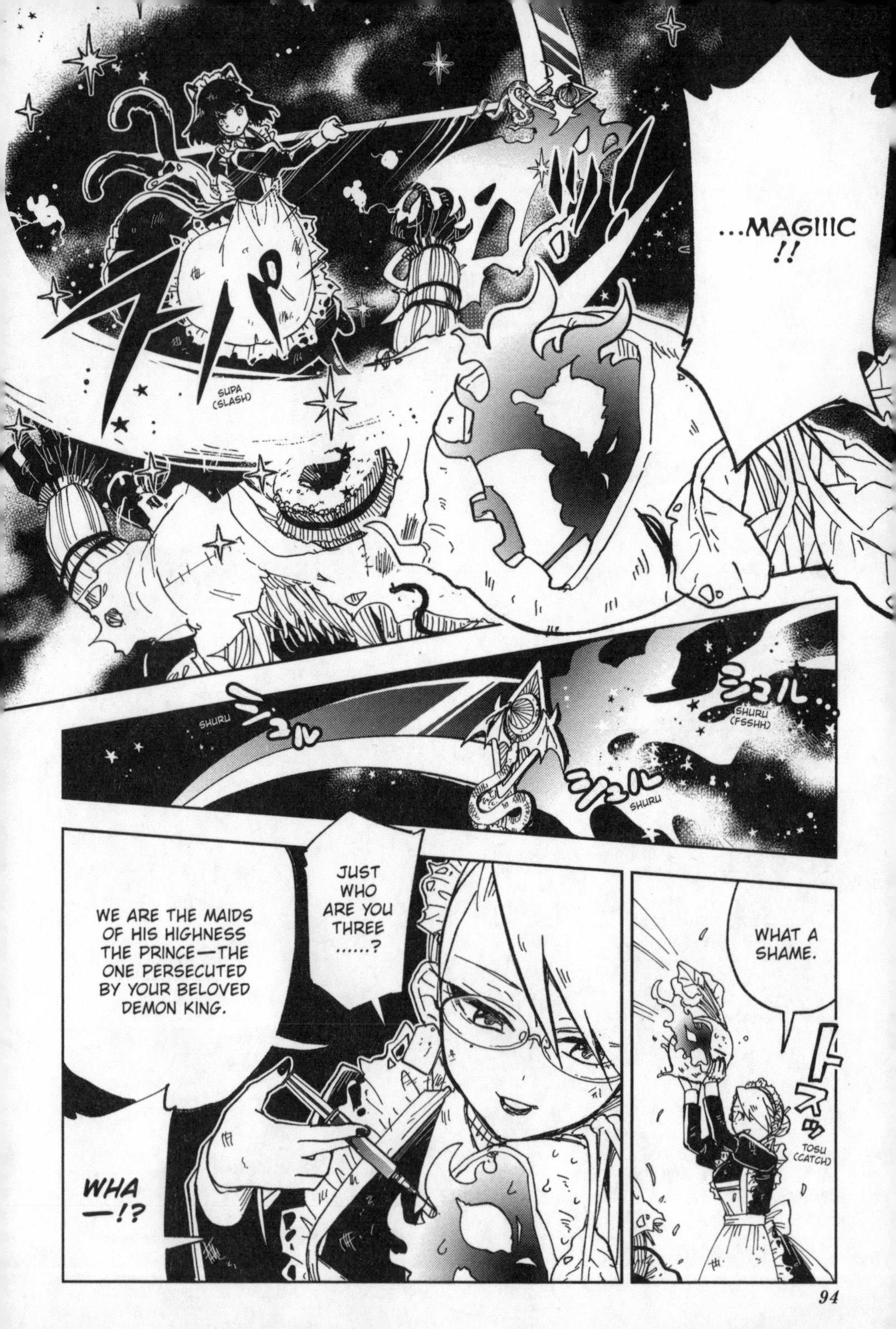
...MAGIIIC !!
SUPA (SLASH)
シュル...
SHURU (FSSHH)
シュル
SHURU
シュル
SHURU
WHAT A SHAME.
トスッ
TOSU (CATCH)
JUST WHO ARE YOU THREE ......?
WE ARE THE MAIDS OF HIS HIGHNESS THE PRINCE—THE ONE PERSECUTED BY YOUR BELOVED DEMON KING.
WHA—!?

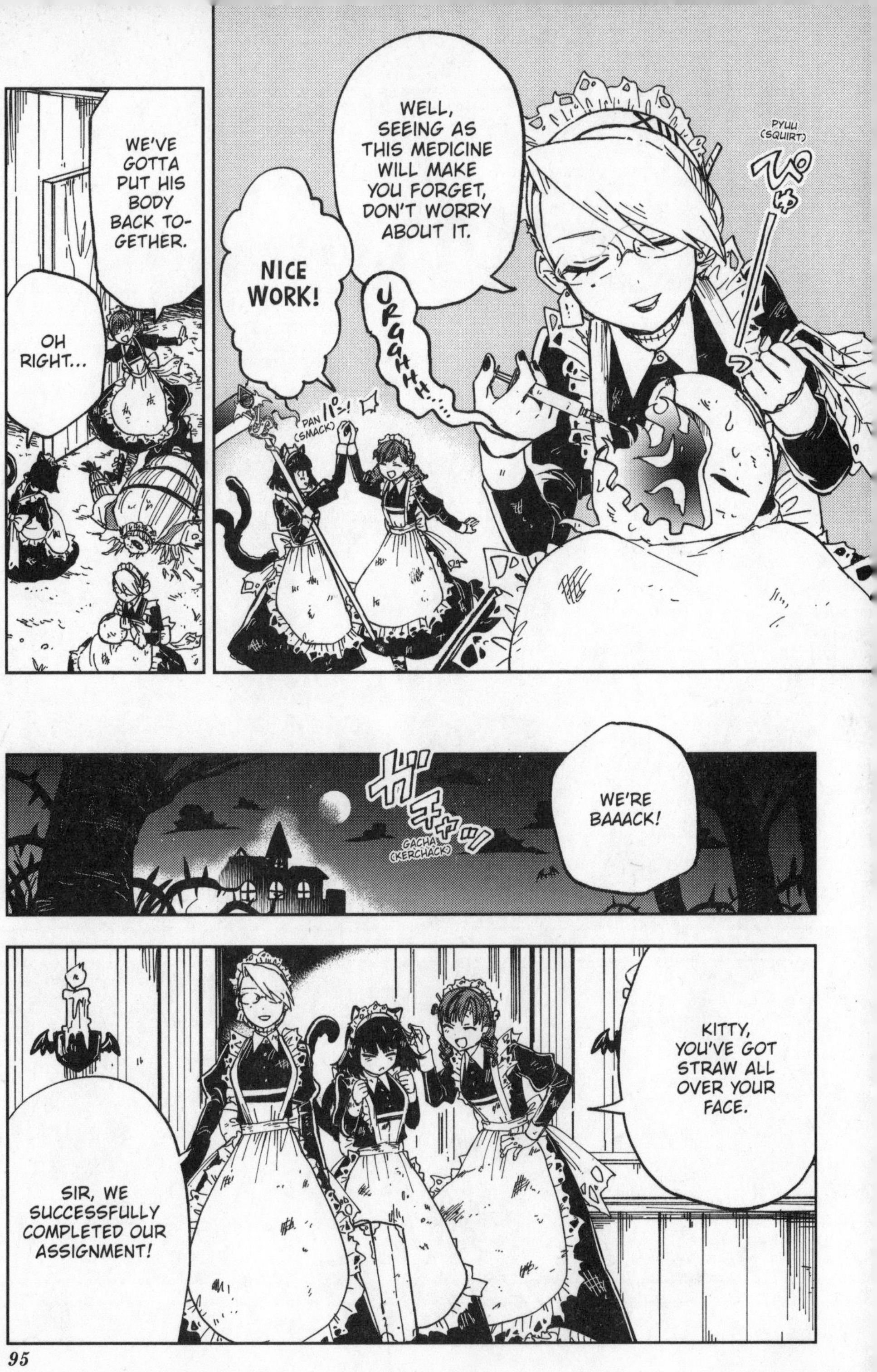
PYUU (SQUIRT)
ぴゅ
WELL, SEEING AS THIS MEDICINE WILL MAKE YOU FORGET, DON'T WORRY ABOUT IT.
URGAHHH...
NICE WORK!
PAN (SMACK)
WE'VE GOTTA PUT HIS BODY BACK TO-GETHER.
OH RIGHT...
WE'RE BAAACK!
ガチャッ
GACHA (KERCHACK)
KITTY, YOU'VE GOT STRAW ALL OVER YOUR FACE.
SIR, WE SUCCESSFULLY COMPLETED OUR ASSIGNMENT!

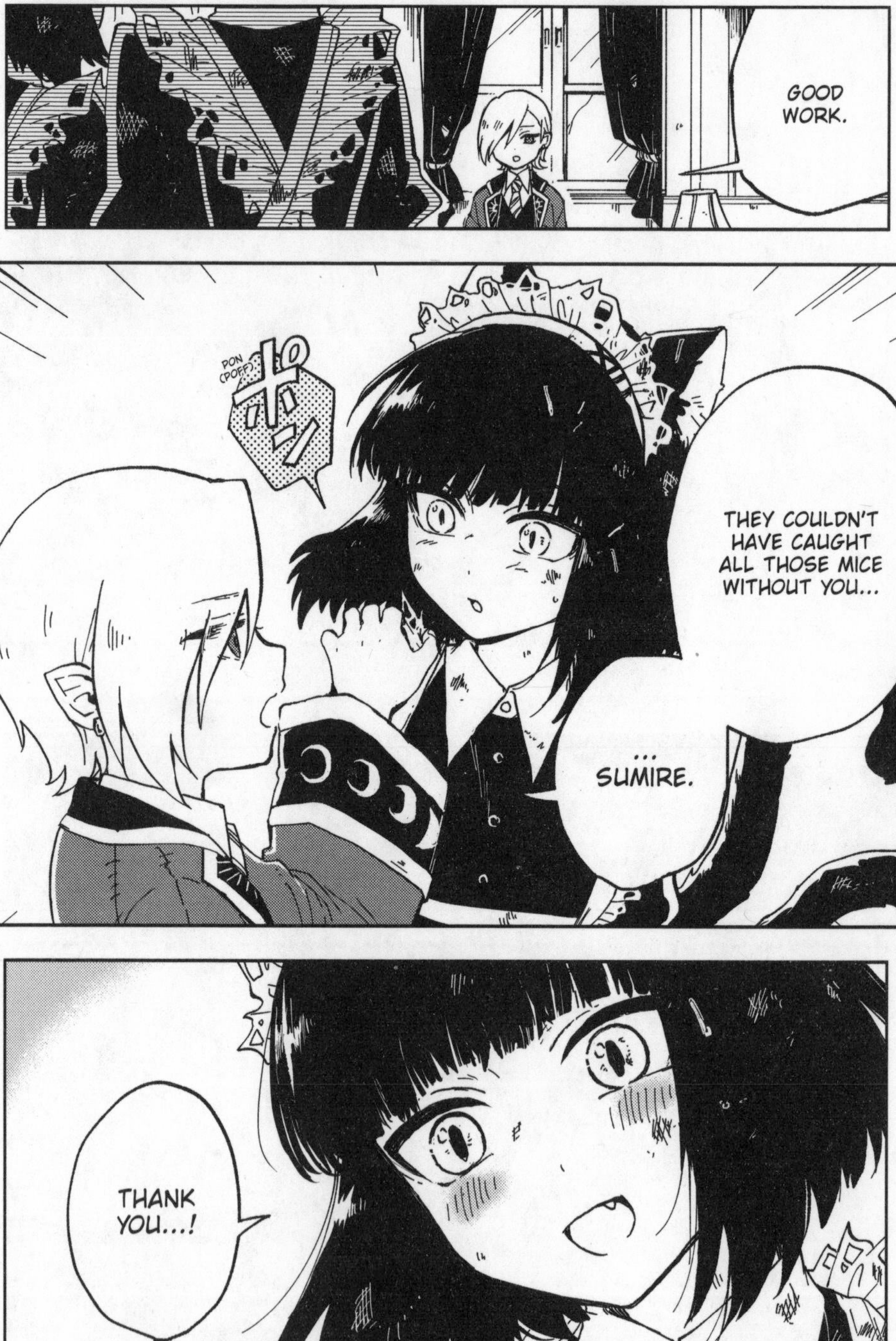
GOOD WORK.
THEY COULDN'T HAVE CAUGHT ALL THOSE MICE WITHOUT YOU...
... SUMIRE.
ポン
PON (POFF)
THANK YOU...!

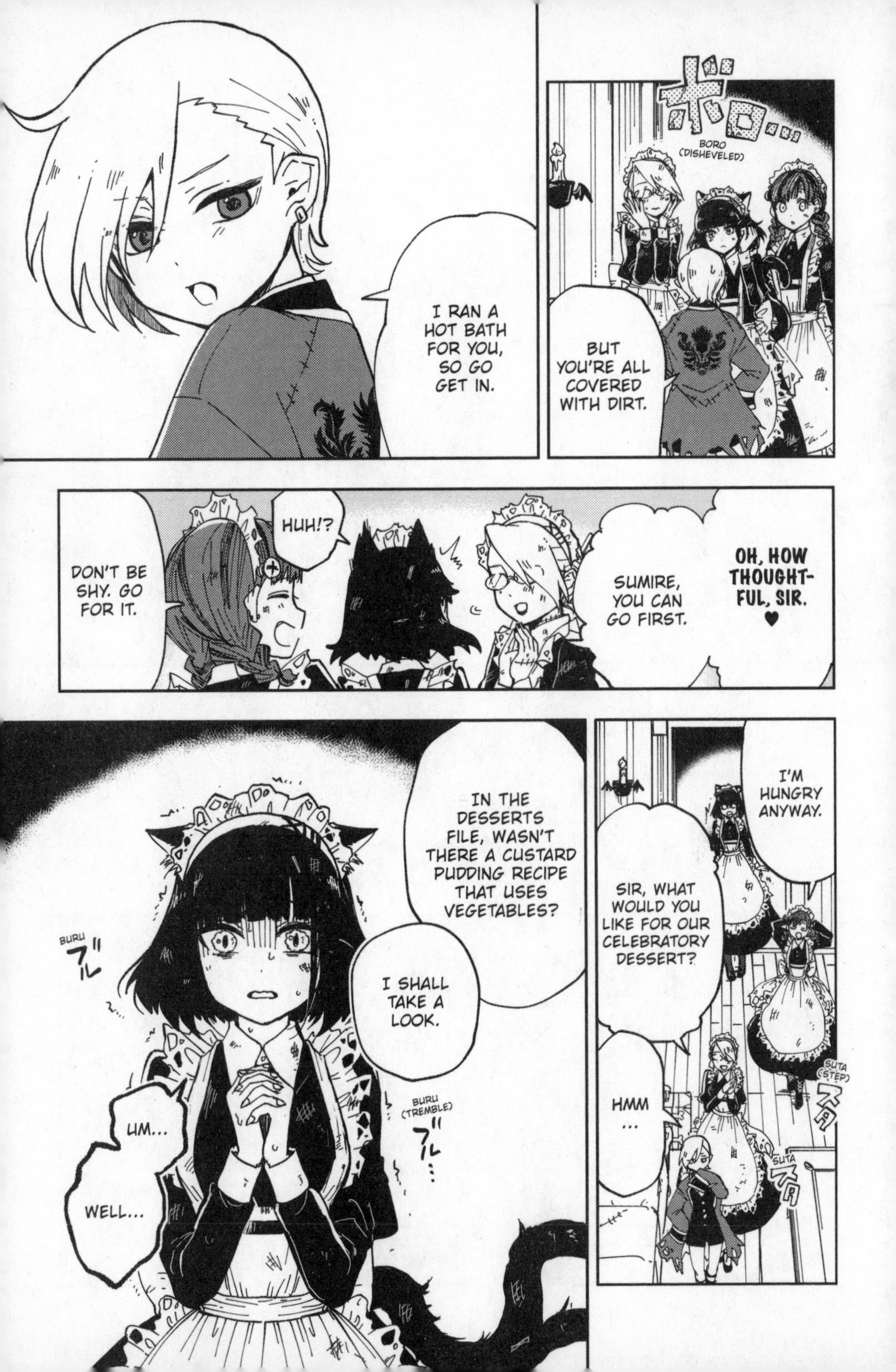
ボロ…
BORO (DISHEVELED)
BUT YOU'RE ALL COVERED WITH DIRT.
I RAN A HOT BATH FOR YOU, SO GO GET IN.
OH, HOW THOUGHTFUL, SIR. ♥
SUMIRE, YOU CAN GO FIRST.
HUH!?
DON'T BE SHY. GO FOR IT.
I'M HUNGRY ANYWAY.
SIR, WHAT WOULD YOU LIKE FOR OUR CELEBRATORY DESSERT?
SUTA (STEP)
SUTA
HMM...
IN THE DESSERTS FILE, WASN'T THERE A CUSTARD PUDDING RECIPE THAT USES VEGETABLES?
I SHALL TAKE A LOOK.
BURU (TREMBLE)
BURU
UM...
WELL...

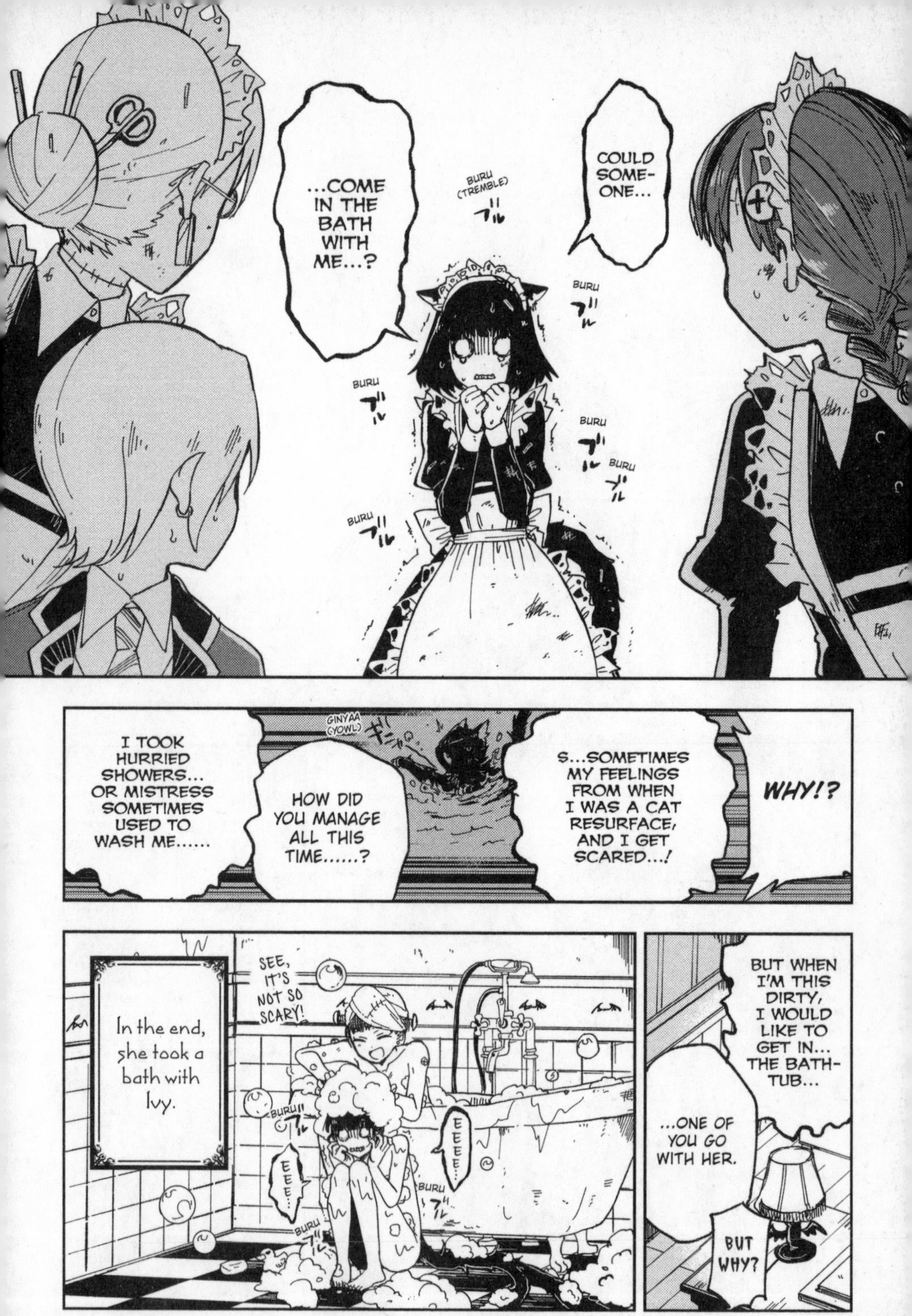
COULD SOME-ONE...
BURU (TREMBLE)
...COME IN THE BATH WITH ME...?
BURU
BURU
BURU
BURU
BURU
WHY!?
S...SOMETIMES MY FEELINGS FROM WHEN I WAS A CAT RESURFACE, AND I GET SCARED...!
GINYAA (YOWL)
HOW DID YOU MANAGE ALL THIS TIME......?
I TOOK HURRIED SHOWERS... OR MISTRESS SOMETIMES USED TO WASH ME......
BUT WHEN I'M THIS DIRTY, I WOULD LIKE TO GET IN... THE BATH-TUB...
...ONE OF YOU GO WITH HER.
BUT WHY?
SEE, IT'S NOT SO SCARY!
EEEE...
BURU!!
EEE...
BURU
BURU
In the end, she took a bath with Ivy.

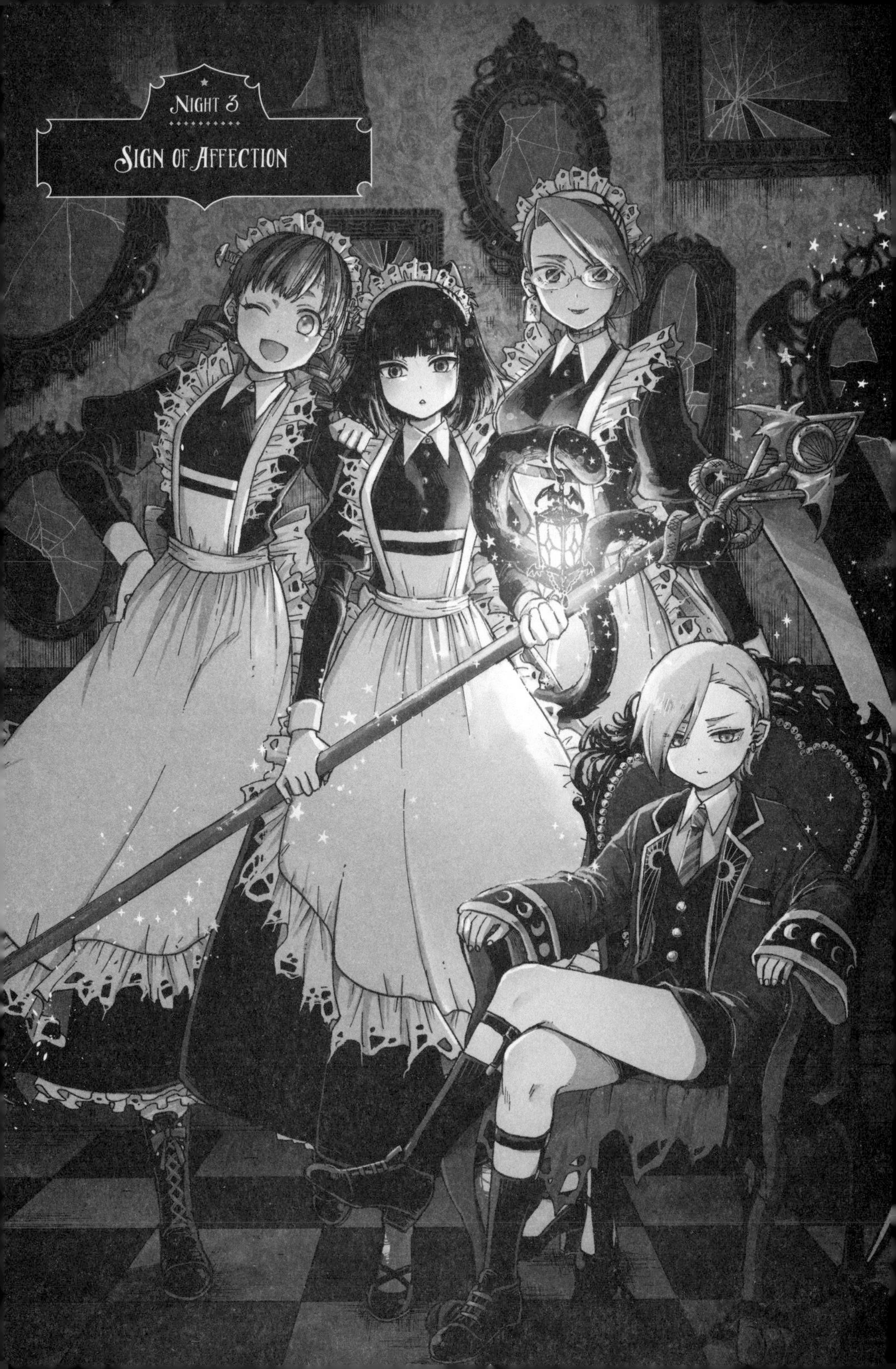
Night 3
Sign of Affection

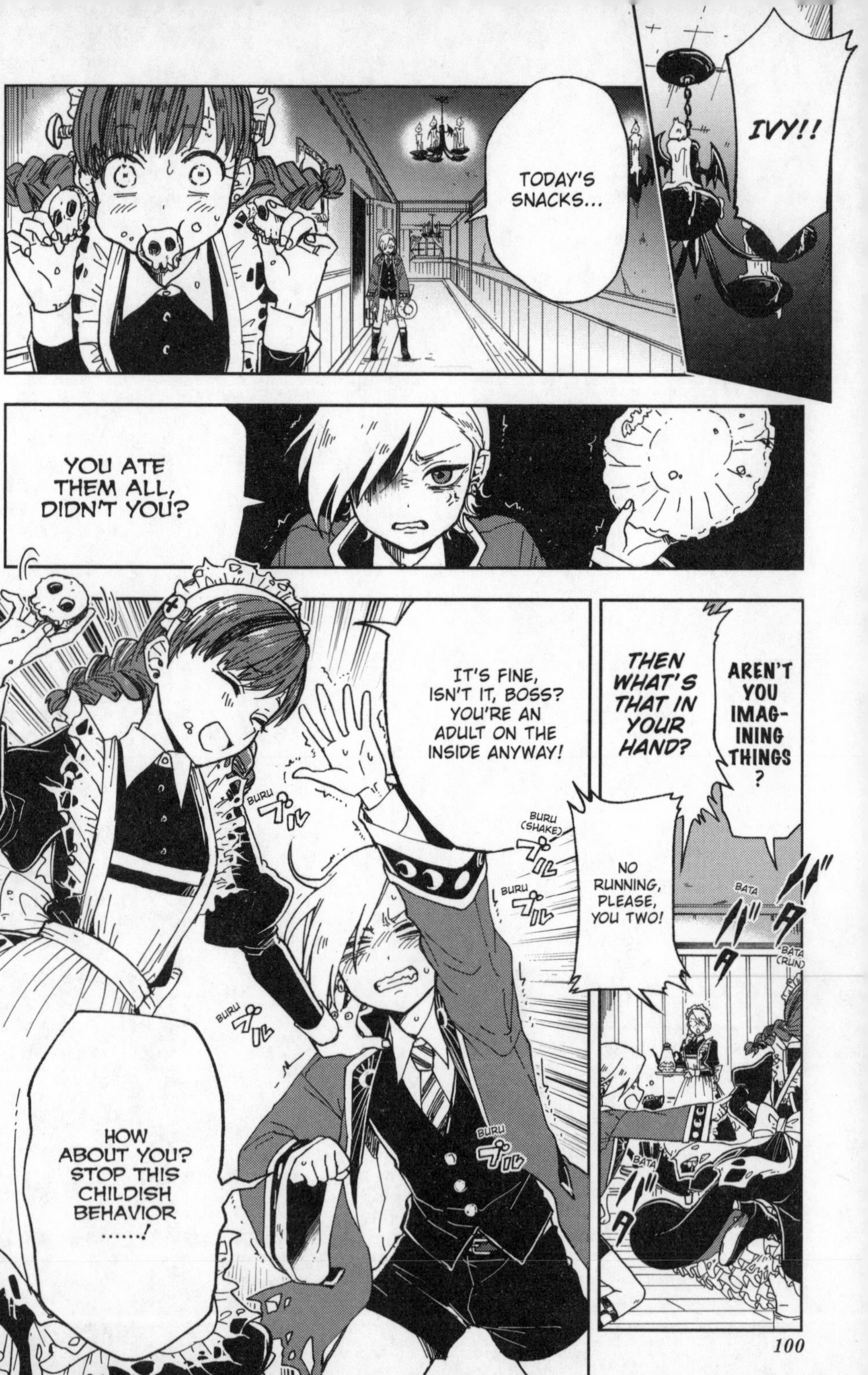
IVY!!
TODAY'S SNACKS...
YOU ATE THEM ALL, DIDN'T YOU?
AREN'T YOU IMAGINING THINGS?
THEN WHAT'S THAT IN YOUR HAND?
BATA
BATA (RUN)
NO RUNNING, PLEASE, YOU TWO!
BATA
IT'S FINE, ISN'T IT, BOSS? YOU'RE AN ADULT ON THE INSIDE ANYWAY!
BURU
BURU (SHAKE)
BURU
BURU
BURU
HOW ABOUT YOU? STOP THIS CHILDISH BEHAVIOR ......!

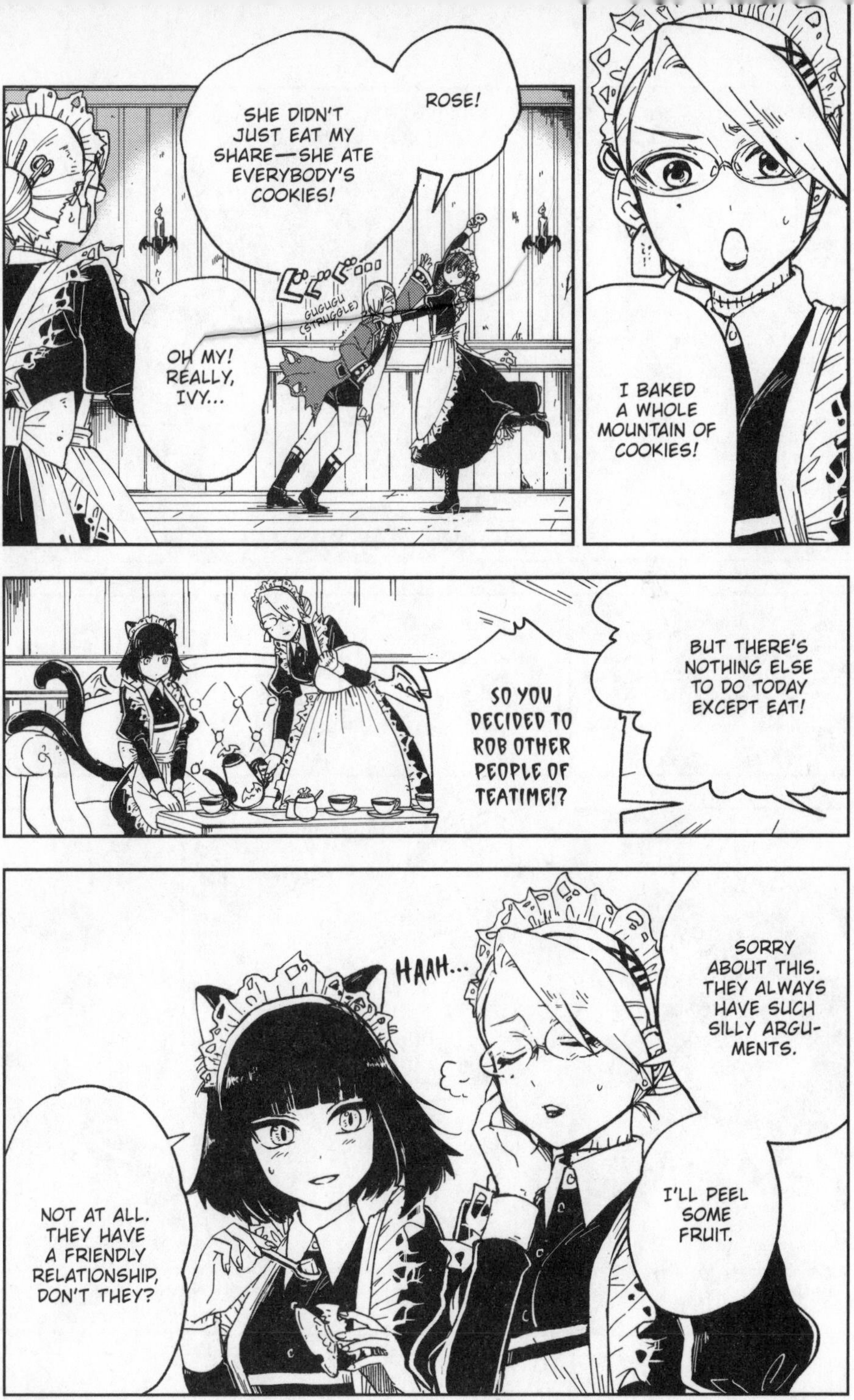
I BAKED A WHOLE MOUNTAIN OF COOKIES!
ROSE!
SHE DIDN'T JUST EAT MY SHARE—SHE ATE EVERYBODY'S COOKIES!
GUGUGU (STRUGGLE)
OH MY! REALLY, IVY...
BUT THERE'S NOTHING ELSE TO DO TODAY EXCEPT EAT!
SO YOU DECIDED TO ROB OTHER PEOPLE OF TEATIME!?
SORRY ABOUT THIS. THEY ALWAYS HAVE SUCH SILLY ARGU-MENTS.
HAAH...
I'LL PEEL SOME FRUIT.
NOT AT ALL. THEY HAVE A FRIENDLY RELATIONSHIP, DON'T THEY?

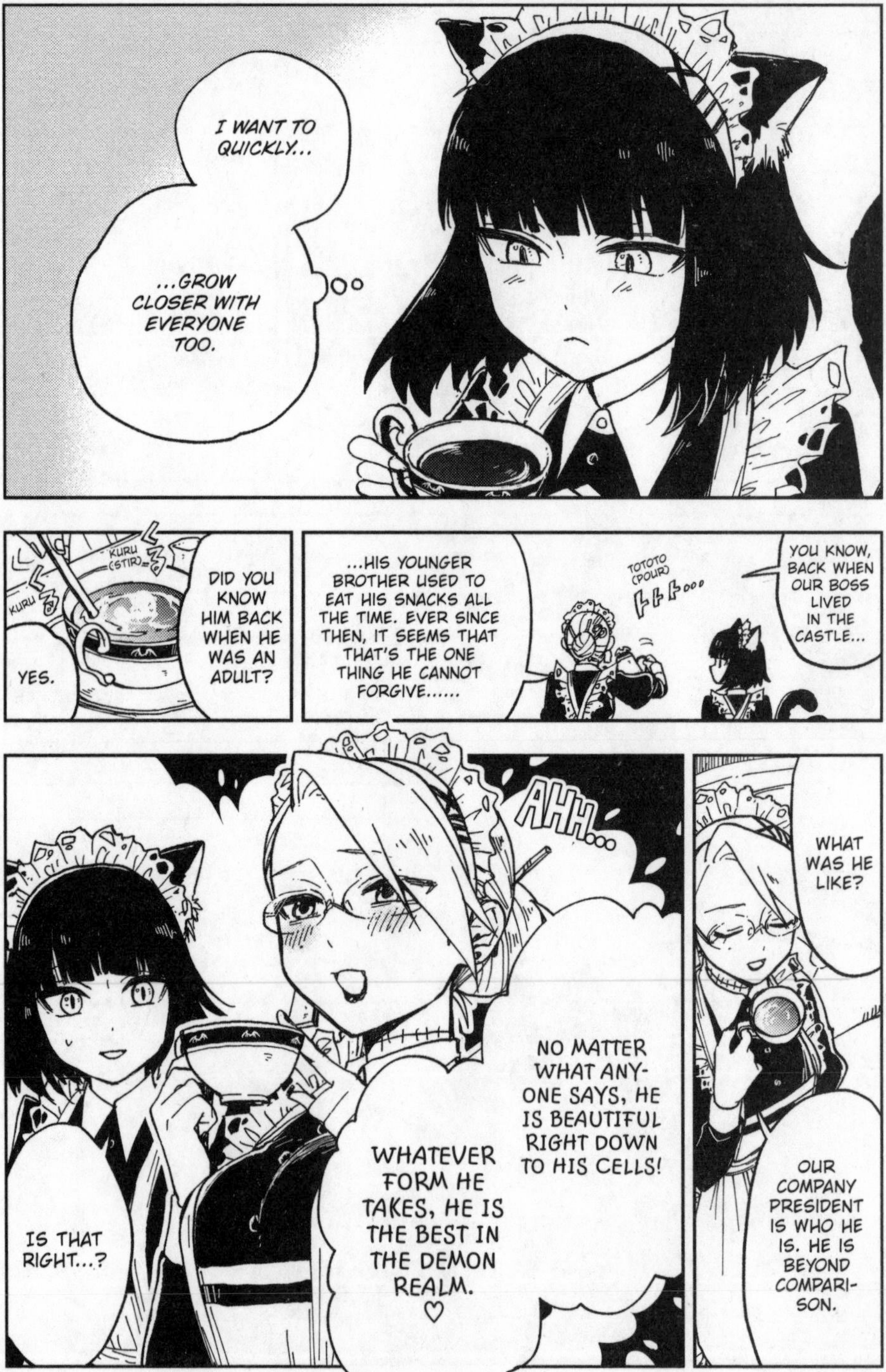

I WANT TO QUICKLY...
...GROW CLOSER WITH EVERYONE TOO.
YOU KNOW, BACK WHEN OUR BOSS LIVED IN THE CASTLE...
TOTOTO (POUR)
...HIS YOUNGER BROTHER USED TO EAT HIS SNACKS ALL THE TIME. EVER SINCE THEN, IT SEEMS THAT THAT'S THE ONE THING HE CANNOT FORGIVE......
DID YOU KNOW HIM BACK WHEN HE WAS AN ADULT?
KURU (STIR)
KURU
YES.
WHAT WAS HE LIKE?
OUR COMPANY PRESIDENT IS WHO HE IS. HE IS BEYOND COMPARI-SON.
AHH...
NO MATTER WHAT ANY-ONE SAYS, HE IS BEAUTIFUL RIGHT DOWN TO HIS CELLS!
WHATEVER FORM HE TAKES, HE IS THE BEST IN THE DEMON REALM. ♡
IS THAT RIGHT...?

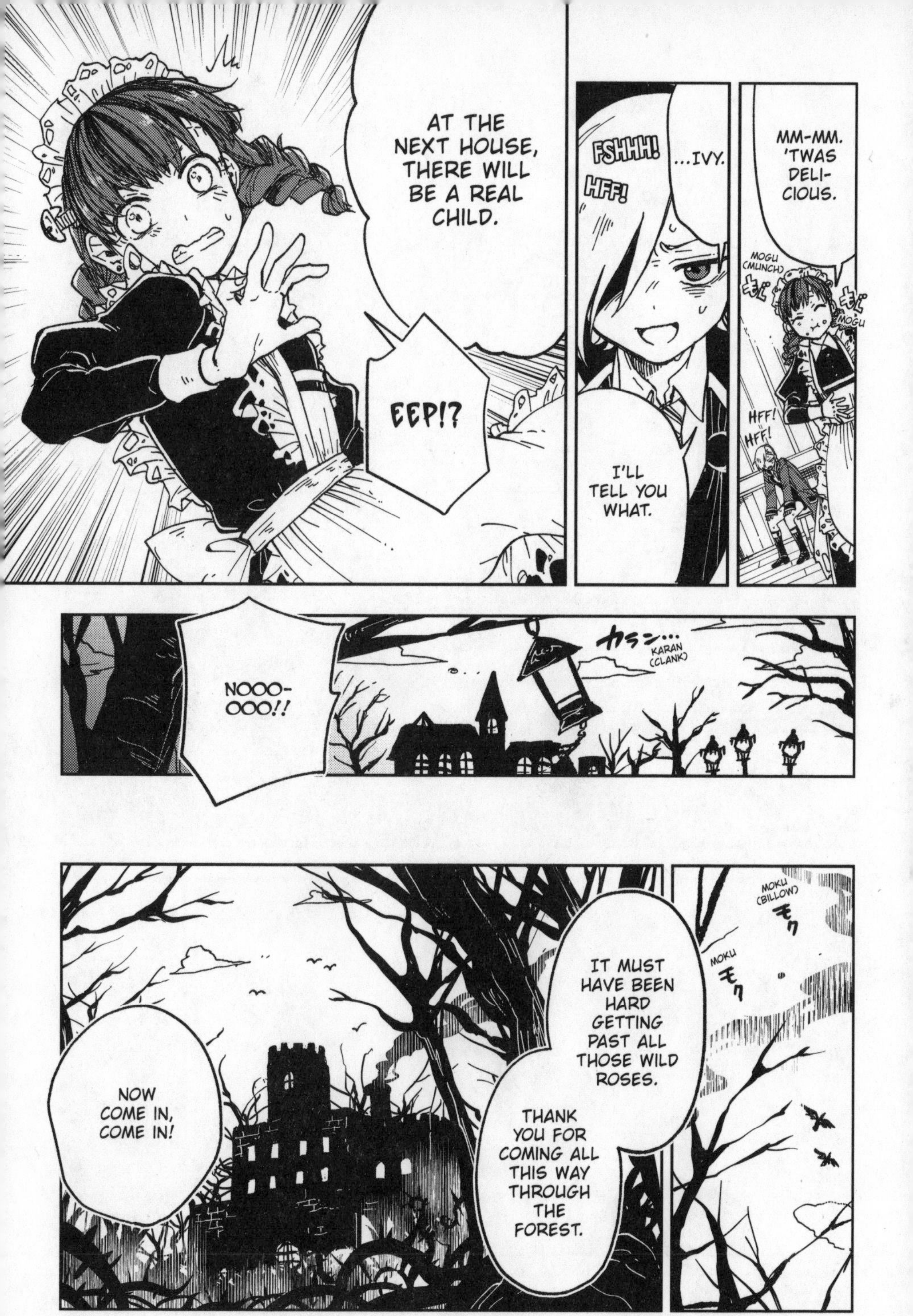
MM-MM. 'TWAS DELICIOUS.
MOGU (MUNCH)
MOGU
HFF! HFF!
FSHHH!
HFF!
...IVY.
I'LL TELL YOU WHAT.
AT THE NEXT HOUSE, THERE WILL BE A REAL CHILD.
EEP!?
カラン…
KARAN (CLANK)
NOOOOOO!!
MOKU (BILLOW)
モク
MOKU
モク
IT MUST HAVE BEEN HARD GETTING PAST ALL THOSE WILD ROSES.
THANK YOU FOR COMING ALL THIS WAY THROUGH THE FOREST.
NOW COME IN, COME IN!

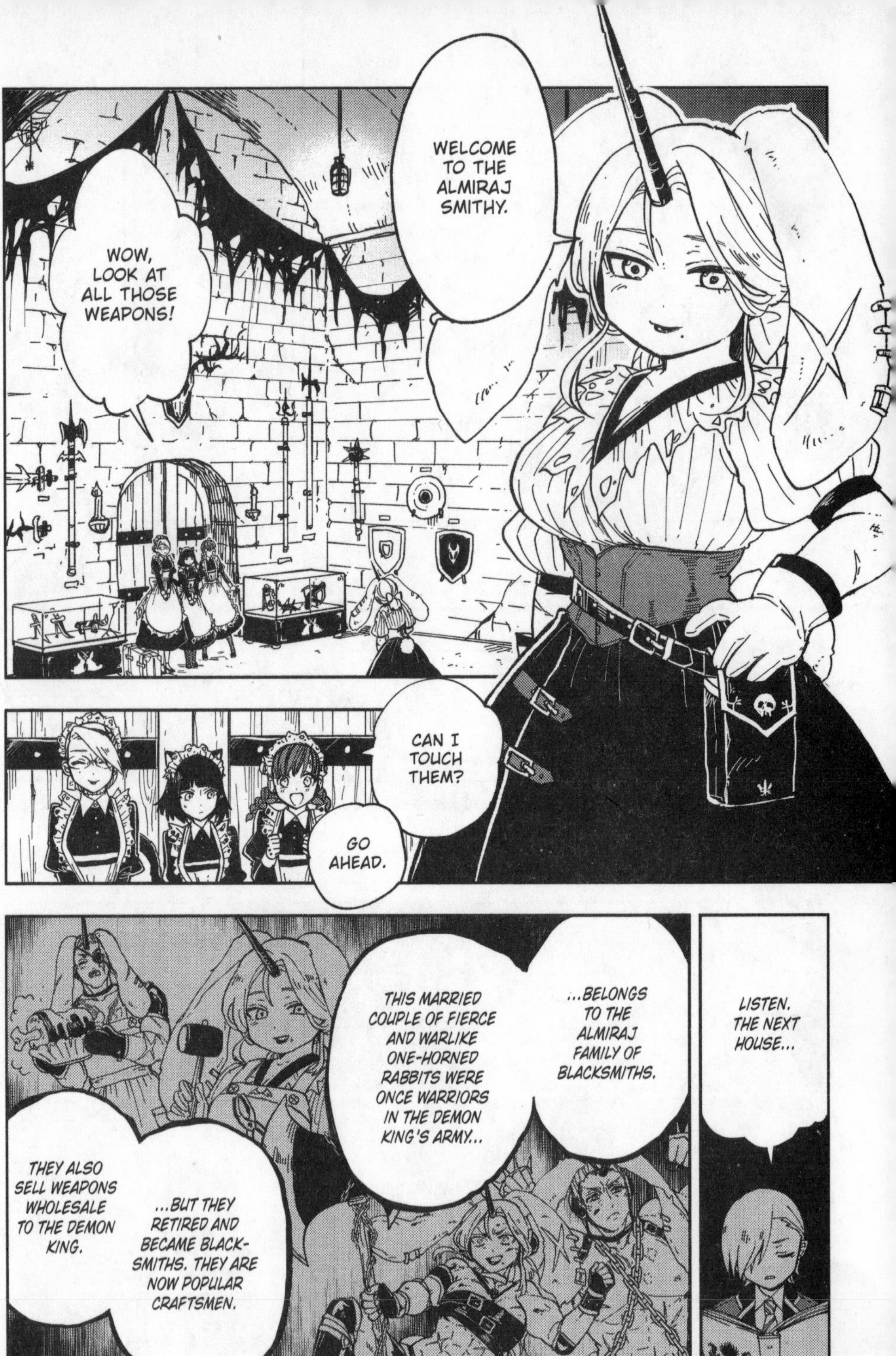
WELCOME TO THE ALMIRAJ SMITHY.
WOW, LOOK AT ALL THOSE WEAPONS!
CAN I TOUCH THEM?
GO AHEAD.
LISTEN. THE NEXT HOUSE...
...BELONGS TO THE ALMIRAJ FAMILY OF BLACKSMITHS.
THIS MARRIED COUPLE OF FIERCE AND WARLIKE ONE-HORNED RABBITS WERE ONCE WARRIORS IN THE DEMON KING'S ARMY...
...BUT THEY RETIRED AND BECAME BLACK-SMITHS. THEY ARE NOW POPULAR CRAFTSMEN.
THEY ALSO SELL WEAPONS WHOLESALE TO THE DEMON KING.

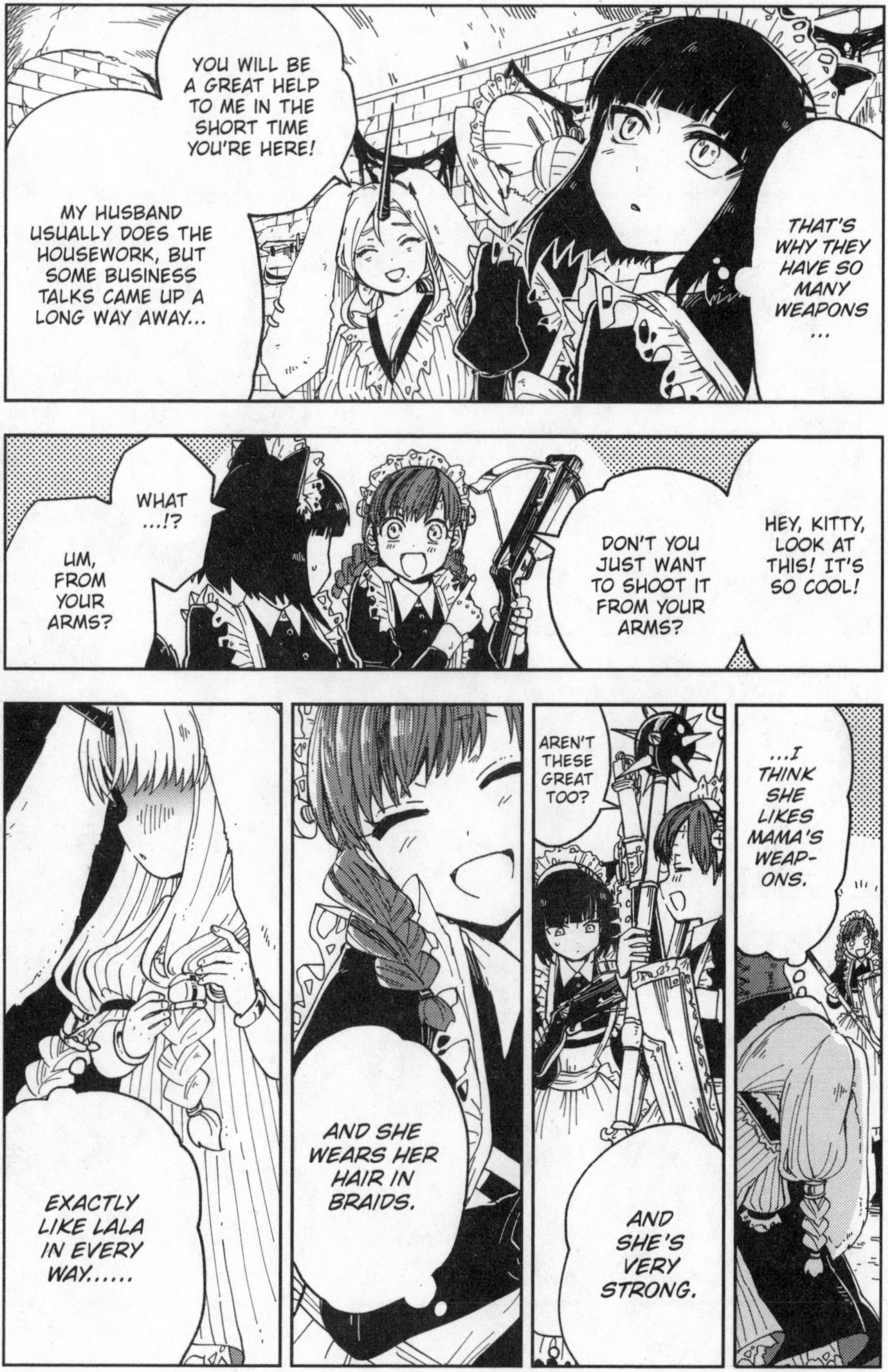
YOU WILL BE A GREAT HELP TO ME IN THE SHORT TIME YOU'RE HERE!
MY HUSBAND USUALLY DOES THE HOUSEWORK, BUT SOME BUSINESS TALKS CAME UP A LONG WAY AWAY...
THAT'S WHY THEY HAVE SO MANY WEAPONS...
HEY, KITTY, LOOK AT THIS! IT'S SO COOL!
DON'T YOU JUST WANT TO SHOOT IT FROM YOUR ARMS?
WHAT...!?
UM, FROM YOUR ARMS?
...I THINK SHE LIKES MAMA'S WEAP-ONS.
AREN'T THESE GREAT TOO?
AND SHE'S VERY STRONG.
AND SHE WEARS HER HAIR IN BRAIDS.
EXACTLY LIKE LALA IN EVERY WAY......

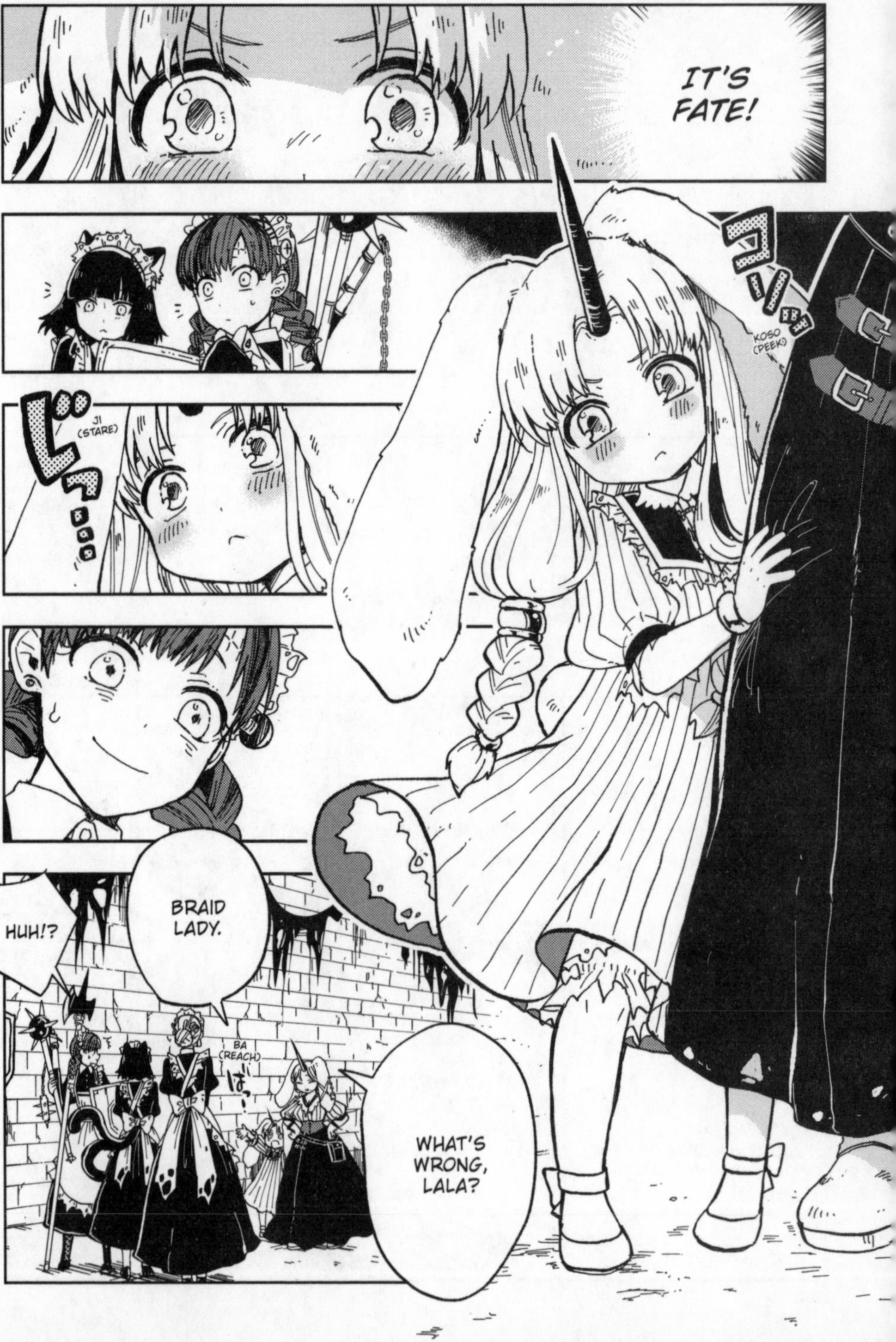
IT'S FATE!
コソッ
KOSO (PEEK)
ジッ
JI (STARE)
BRAID LADY.
HUH!?
はっ
BA (REACH)
WHAT'S WRONG, LALA?

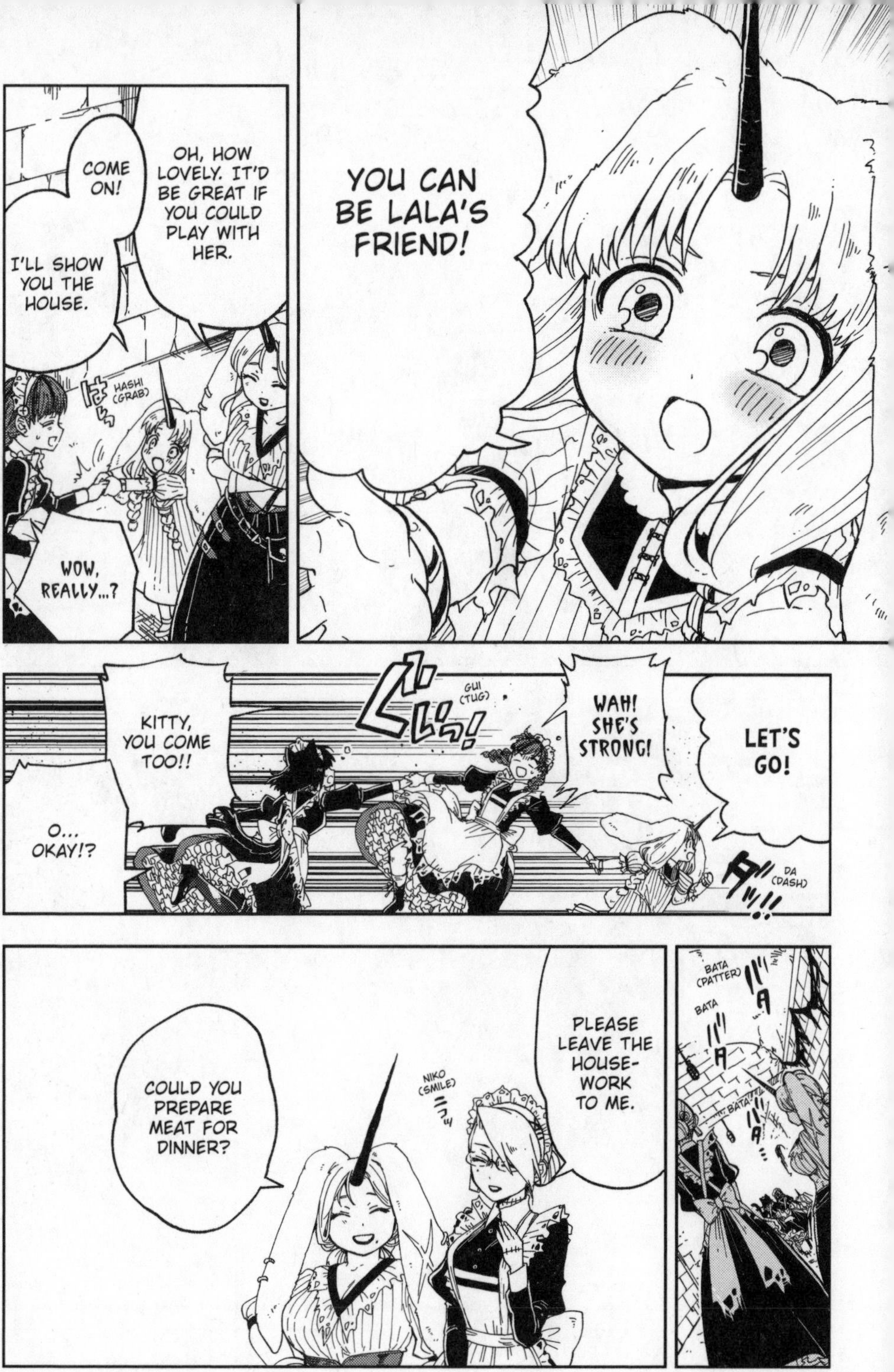
YOU CAN BE LALA'S FRIEND!
OH, HOW LOVELY. IT'D BE GREAT IF YOU COULD PLAY WITH HER.
COME ON!
I'LL SHOW YOU THE HOUSE.
HASHI (GRAB)
WOW, REALLY...?
LET'S GO!
WAH! SHE'S STRONG!
GUI (TUG)
KITTY, YOU COME TOO!!
O... OKAY!?
DA (DASH)
BATA (PATTER)
BATA
BATA
PLEASE LEAVE THE HOUSE-WORK TO ME.
NIKO (SMILE)
COULD YOU PREPARE MEAT FOR DINNER?

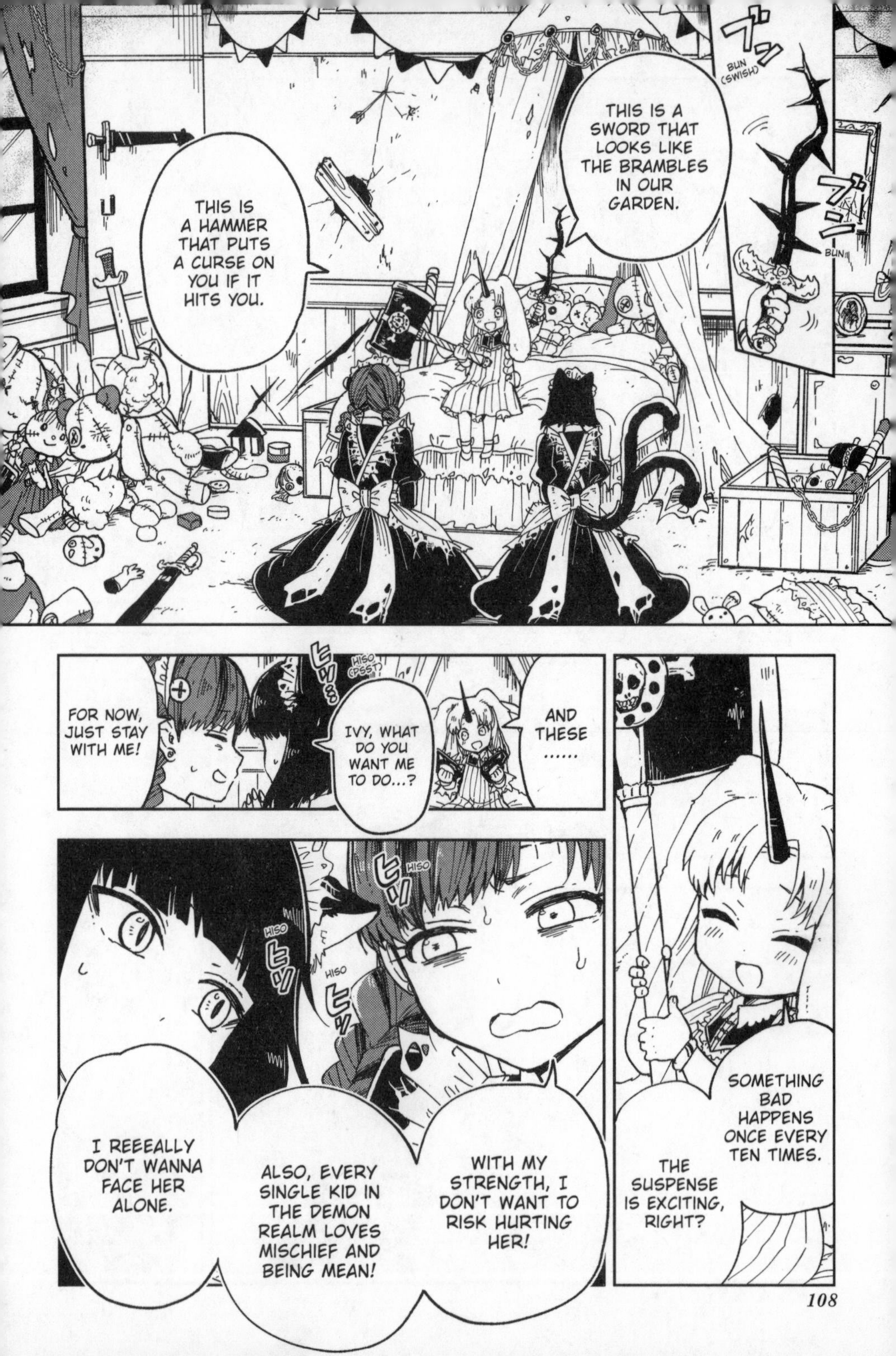
BUN (SWISH)
THIS IS A SWORD THAT LOOKS LIKE THE BRAMBLES IN OUR GARDEN.
BUN
THIS IS A HAMMER THAT PUTS A CURSE ON YOU IF IT HITS YOU.
AND THESE ......
SOMETHING BAD HAPPENS ONCE EVERY TEN TIMES.
THE SUSPENSE IS EXCITING, RIGHT?
HISO (PSST)
IVY, WHAT DO YOU WANT ME TO DO...?
FOR NOW, JUST STAY WITH ME!
HISO
HISO
HISO
WITH MY STRENGTH, I DON'T WANT TO RISK HURTING HER!
ALSO, EVERY SINGLE KID IN THE DEMON REALM LOVES MISCHIEF AND BEING MEAN!
I REEEALLY DON'T WANNA FACE HER ALONE.

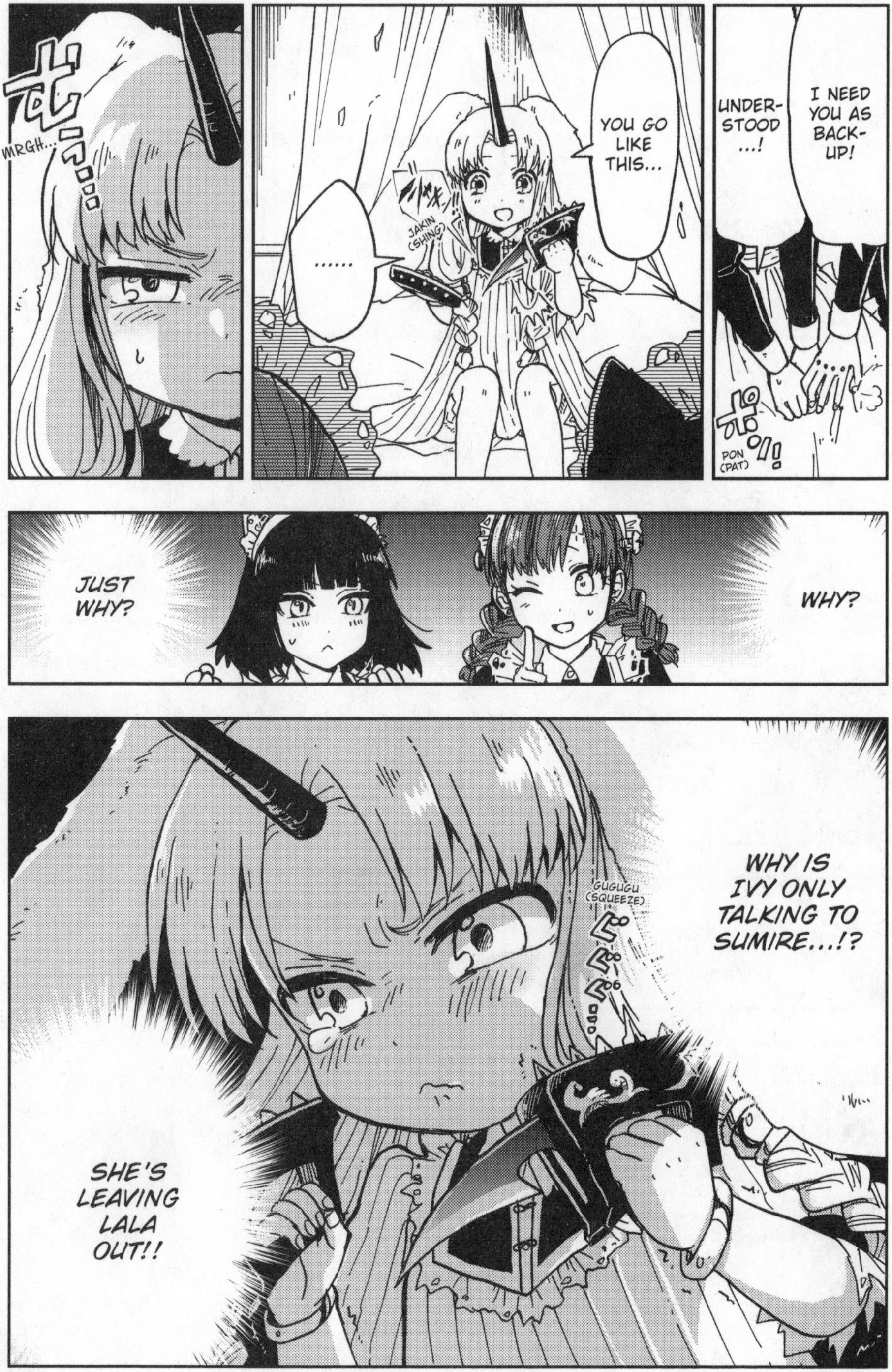
I NEED YOU AS BACK-UP!
UNDER-STOOD...!
PON (PAT)
YOU GO LIKE THIS...
JAKIN (SHING)
......
MRGH...
WHY?
JUST WHY?
WHY IS IVY ONLY TALKING TO SUMIRE...!?
GUGUGU (SQUEEZE)
SHE'S LEAVING LALA OUT!!

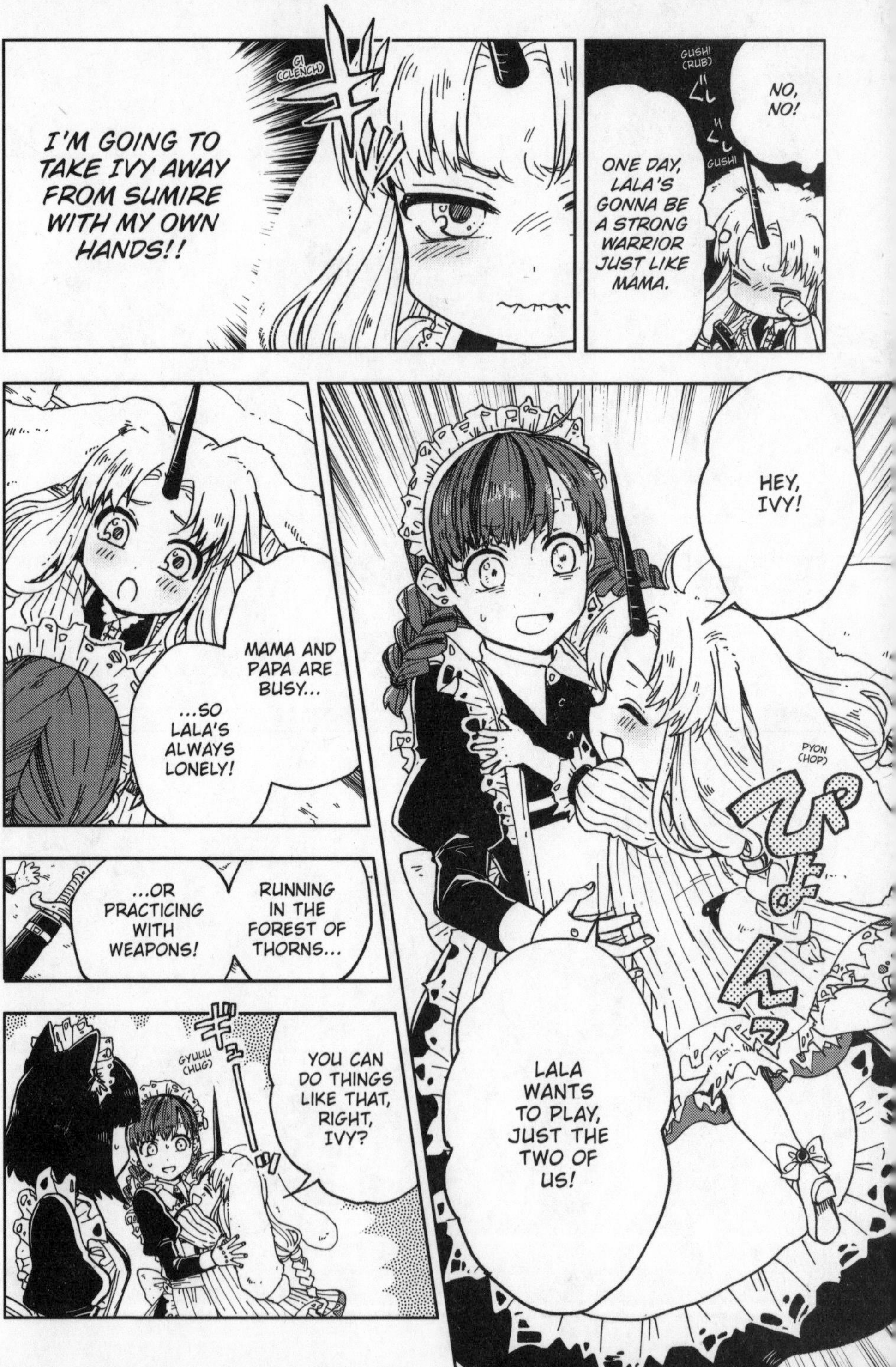
GUSHI (RUB)
NO, NO!
GUSHI
ONE DAY, LALA'S GONNA BE A STRONG WARRIOR JUST LIKE MAMA.
GI (CLENCH)
I'M GOING TO TAKE IVY AWAY FROM SUMIRE WITH MY OWN HANDS!!
HEY, IVY!
PYON (HOP)
LALA WANTS TO PLAY, JUST THE TWO OF US!
MAMA AND PAPA ARE BUSY...
...SO LALA'S ALWAYS LONELY!
RUNNING IN THE FOREST OF THORNS...
...OR PRACTICING WITH WEAPONS!
GYUUU (HUG)
YOU CAN DO THINGS LIKE THAT, RIGHT, IVY?

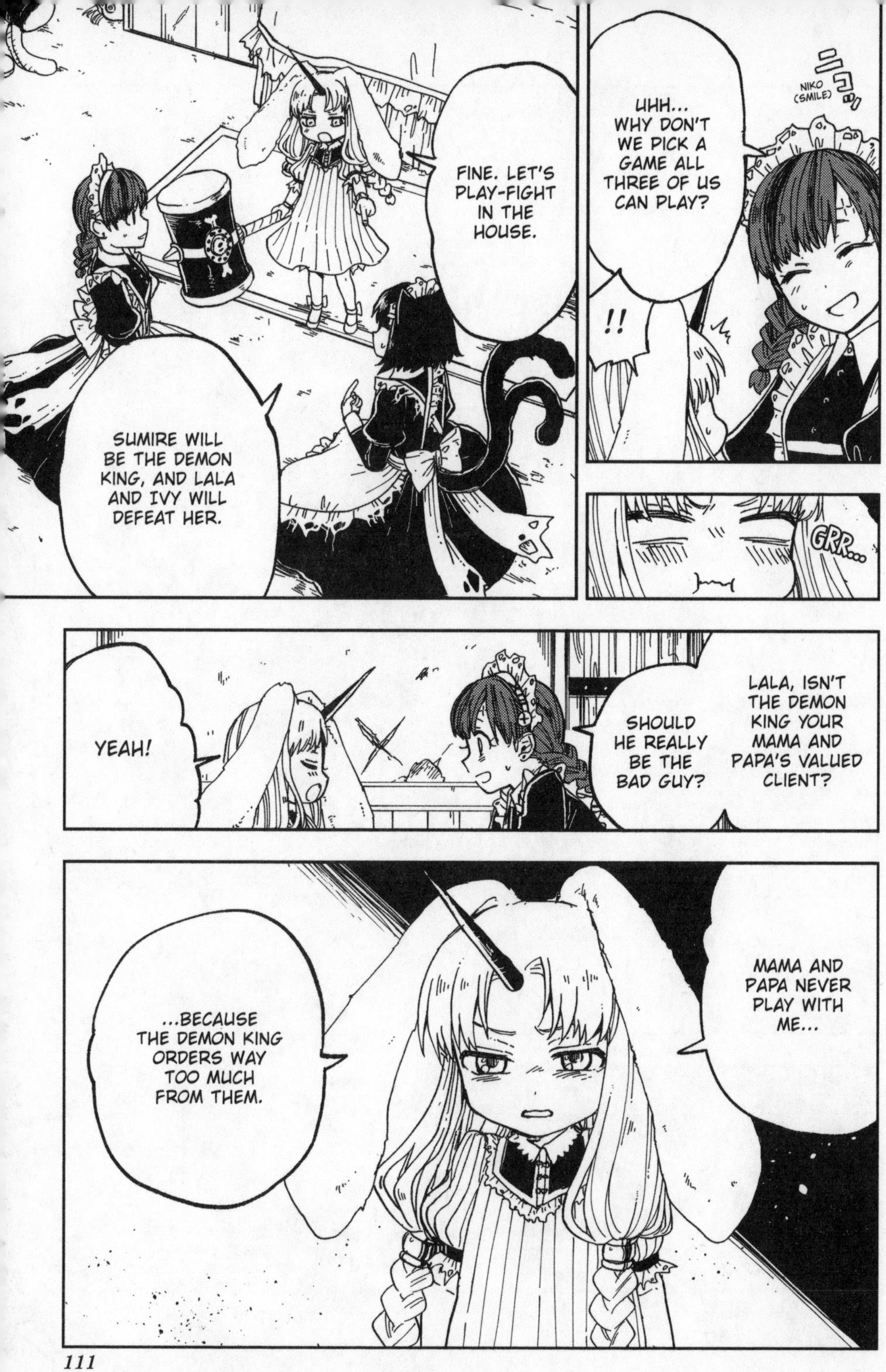

NIKO (SMILE)
UHH... WHY DON'T WE PICK A GAME ALL THREE OF US CAN PLAY?
!!
GRR...
FINE. LET'S PLAY-FIGHT IN THE HOUSE.
SUMIRE WILL BE THE DEMON KING, AND LALA AND IVY WILL DEFEAT HER.
LALA, ISN'T THE DEMON KING YOUR MAMA AND PAPA'S VALUED CLIENT?
SHOULD HE REALLY BE THE BAD GUY?
YEAH!
MAMA AND PAPA NEVER PLAY WITH ME...
...BECAUSE THE DEMON KING ORDERS WAY TOO MUCH FROM THEM.

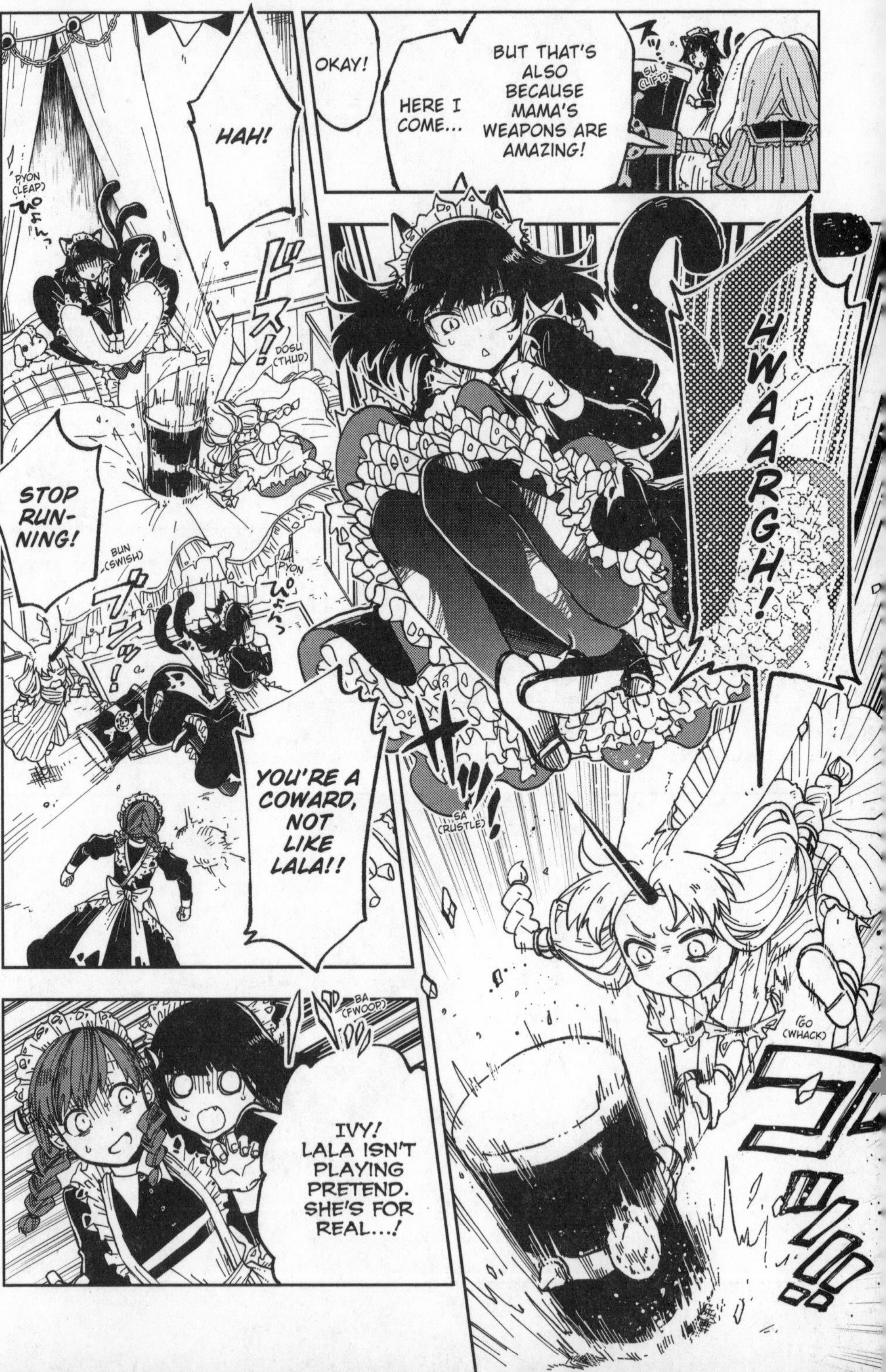
SU (LIFT)
BUT THAT'S ALSO BECAUSE MAMA'S WEAPONS ARE AMAZING!
HERE I COME...
OKAY!
HWAARGH!
SA (RUSTLE)
GO (WHACK)
HAH!
PYON (LEAP)
DOSU (THUD)
STOP RUN-NING!
BUN (SWISH)
PYON
YOU'RE A COWARD, NOT LIKE LALA!!
BA (FWOOP)
IVY! LALA ISN'T PLAYING PRETEND. SHE'S FOR REAL...!

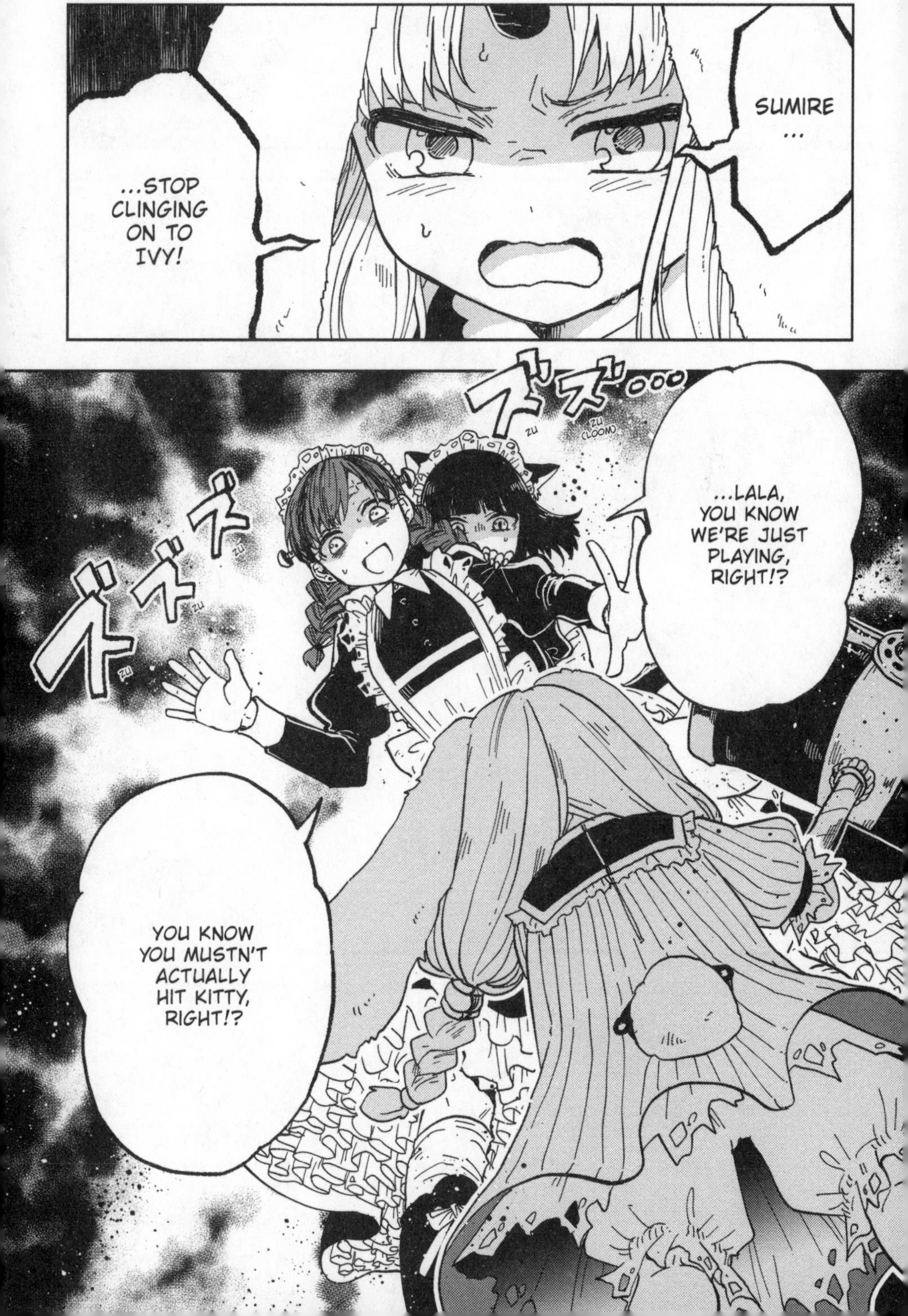
SUMIRE ...
...STOP CLINGING ON TO IVY!
ズズ...
ZU
ZU (LOOM)
...LALA, YOU KNOW WE'RE JUST PLAYING, RIGHT!?
ズズズズ
ZU
ZU
ZU
ZU
YOU KNOW YOU MUSTN'T ACTUALLY HIT KITTY, RIGHT!?

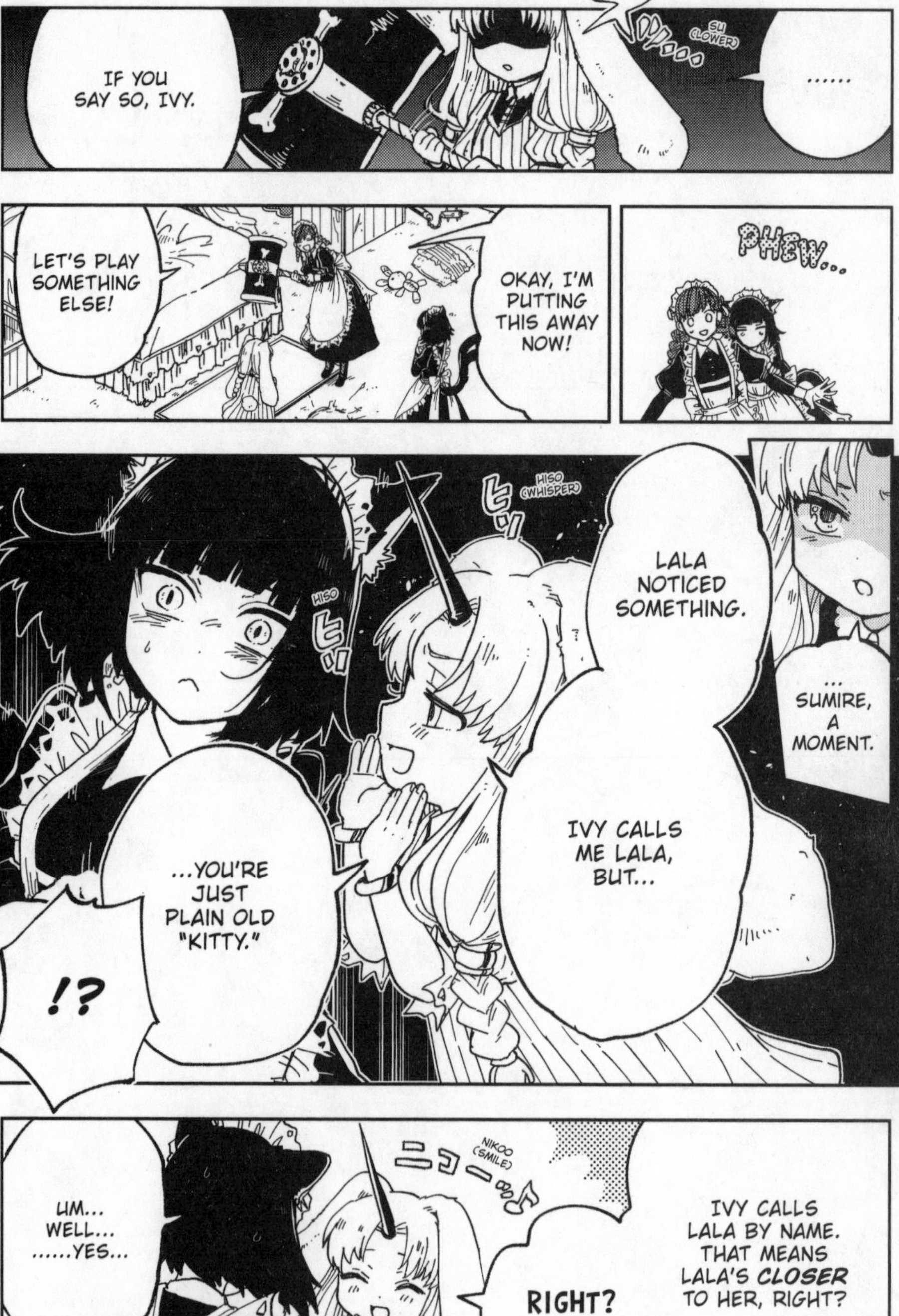
......
SU (LOWER)
IF YOU SAY SO, IVY.
PHEW...
OKAY, I'M PUTTING THIS AWAY NOW!
LET'S PLAY SOMETHING ELSE!
... SUMIRE, A MOMENT.
LALA NOTICED SOMETHING.
HISO (WHISPER)
IVY CALLS ME LALA, BUT...
HISO
...YOU'RE JUST PLAIN OLD "KITTY."
!?
IVY CALLS LALA BY NAME. THAT MEANS LALA'S CLOSER TO HER, RIGHT?
RIGHT?
NIKOO (SMILE)
UM... WELL... ......YES...

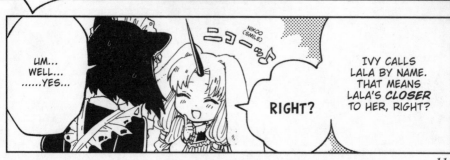

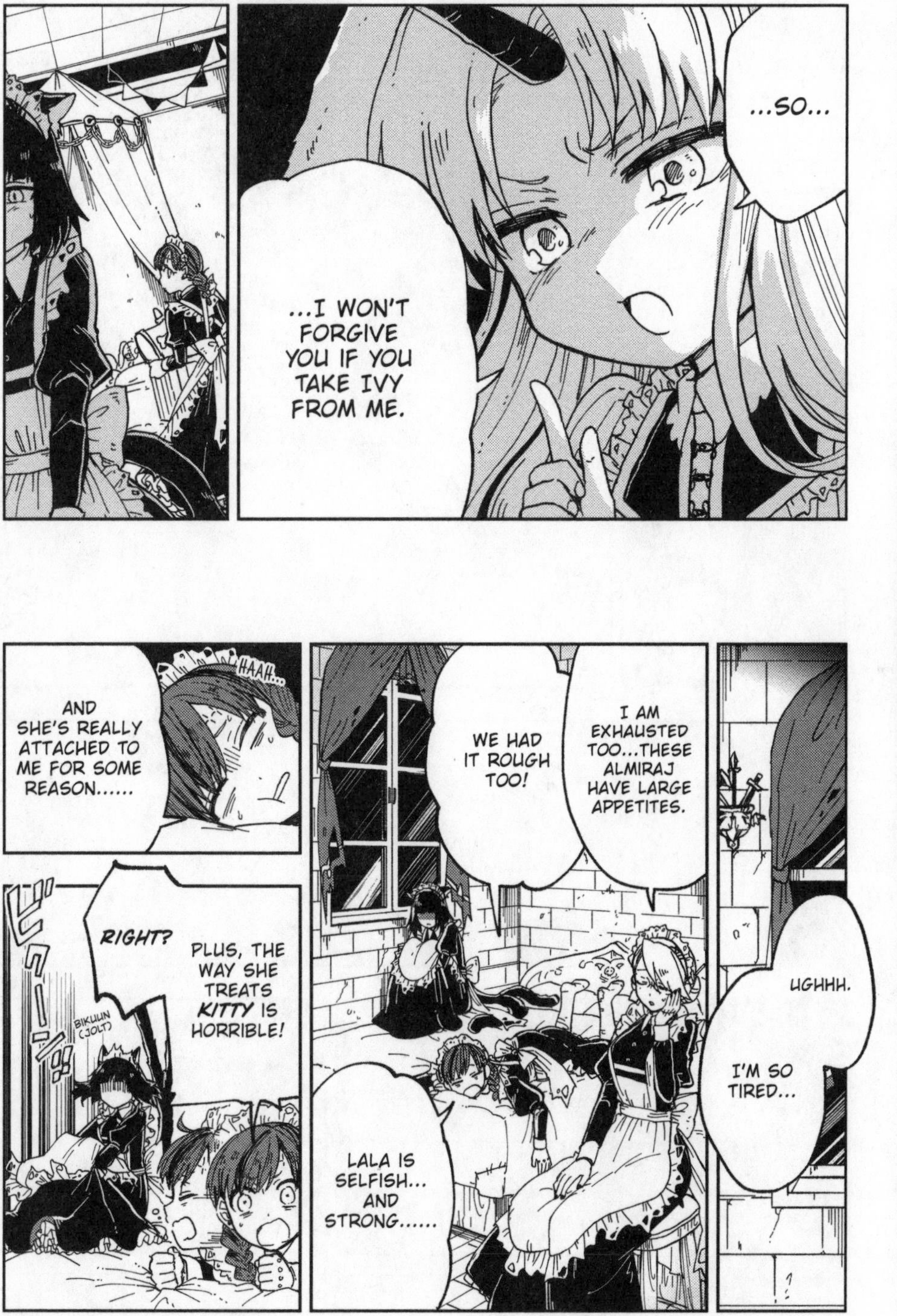

...SO...
...I WON'T FORGIVE YOU IF YOU TAKE IVY FROM ME.
UGHHH.
I'M SO TIRED...
?!
I AM EXHAUSTED TOO...THESE ALMIRAJ HAVE LARGE APPETITES.
WE HAD IT ROUGH TOO!
LALA IS SELFISH... AND STRONG......
HAAAH...
AND SHE'S REALLY ATTACHED TO ME FOR SOME REASON......
RIGHT?
PLUS, THE WAY SHE TREATS *KITTY* IS HORRIBLE!
ビクーン!!
BIKUUN (JOLT)

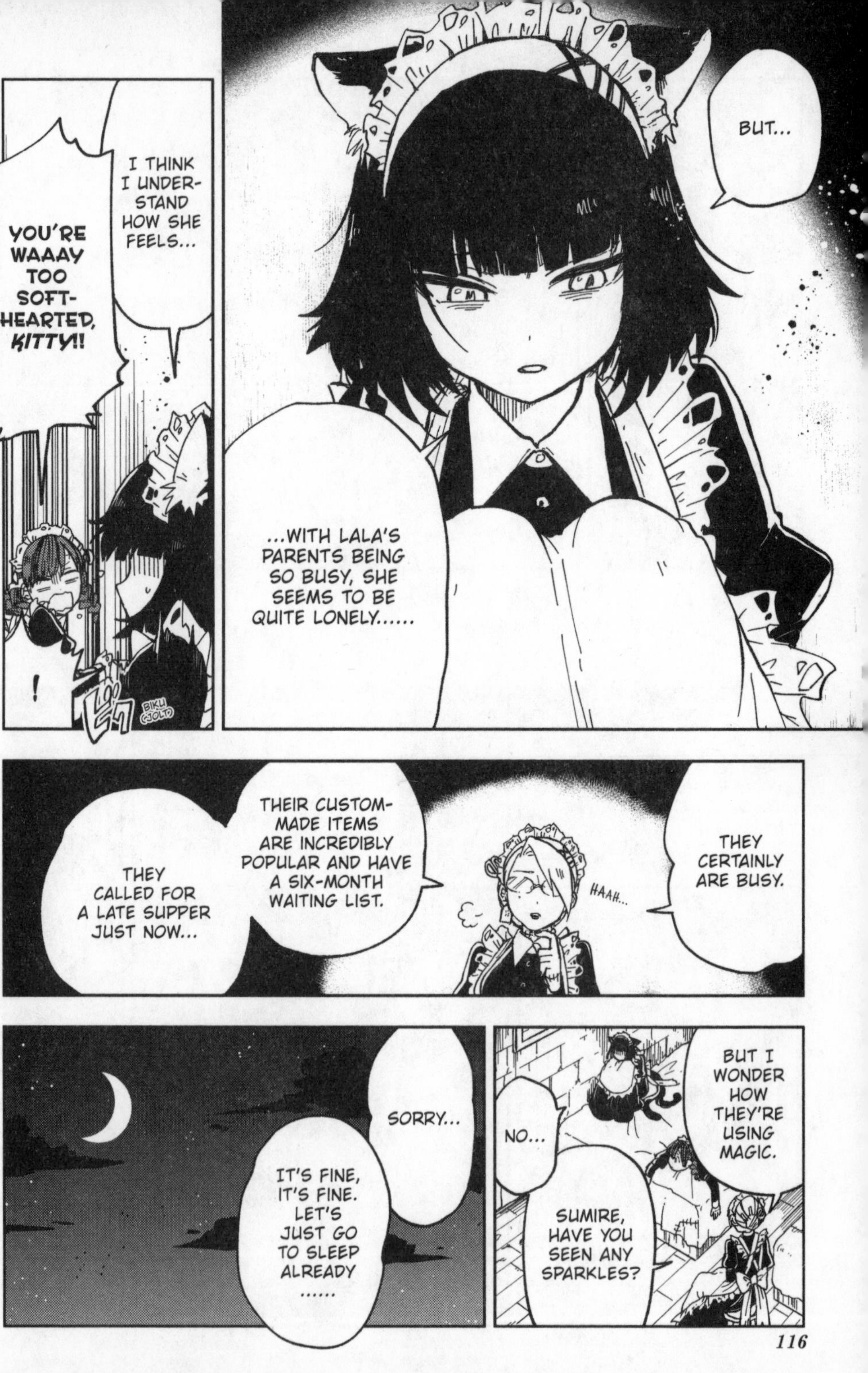
BUT...
...WITH LALA'S PARENTS BEING SO BUSY, SHE SEEMS TO BE QUITE LONELY......
I THINK I UNDERSTAND HOW SHE FEELS...
YOU'RE WAAAY TOO SOFT-HEARTED, KITTY!!
!
BIKU (JOLT)
THEY CERTAINLY ARE BUSY.
HAAH...
THEIR CUSTOM-MADE ITEMS ARE INCREDIBLY POPULAR AND HAVE A SIX-MONTH WAITING LIST.
THEY CALLED FOR A LATE SUPPER JUST NOW...
BUT I WONDER HOW THEY'RE USING MAGIC.
NO...
SUMIRE, HAVE YOU SEEN ANY SPARKLES?
SORRY...
IT'S FINE, IT'S FINE. LET'S JUST GO TO SLEEP ALREADY ......

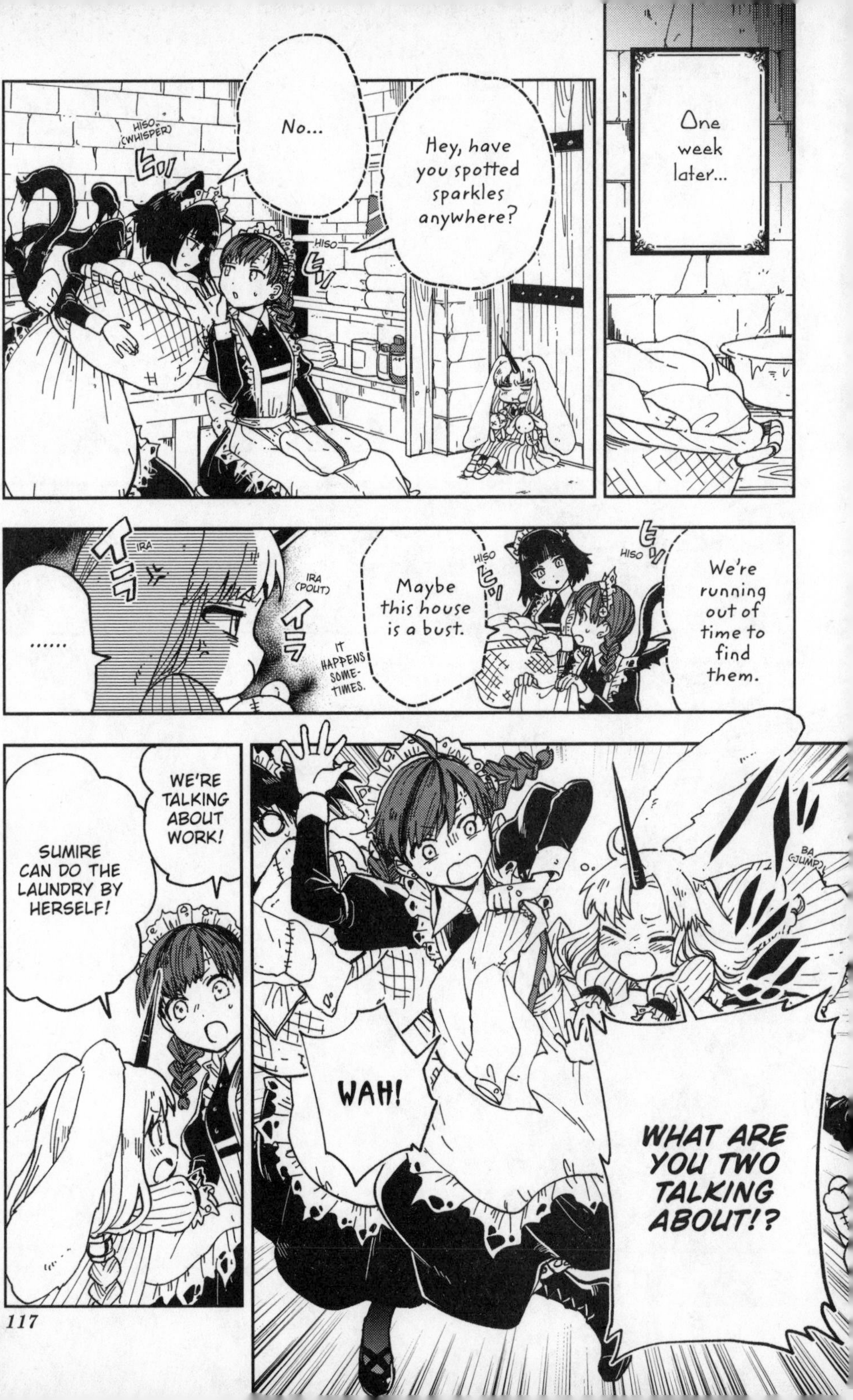

One week later...
Hey, have you spotted sparkles anywhere?
HISO
No...
HISO (WHISPER)
We're running out of time to find them.
HISO
Maybe this house is a bust.
HISO
IRA (POUT)
IT HAPPENS SOMETIMES.
IRA
......
BA (JUMP)
WHAT ARE YOU TWO TALKING ABOUT!?
WAH!
WE'RE TALKING ABOUT WORK!
SUMIRE CAN DO THE LAUNDRY BY HERSELF!

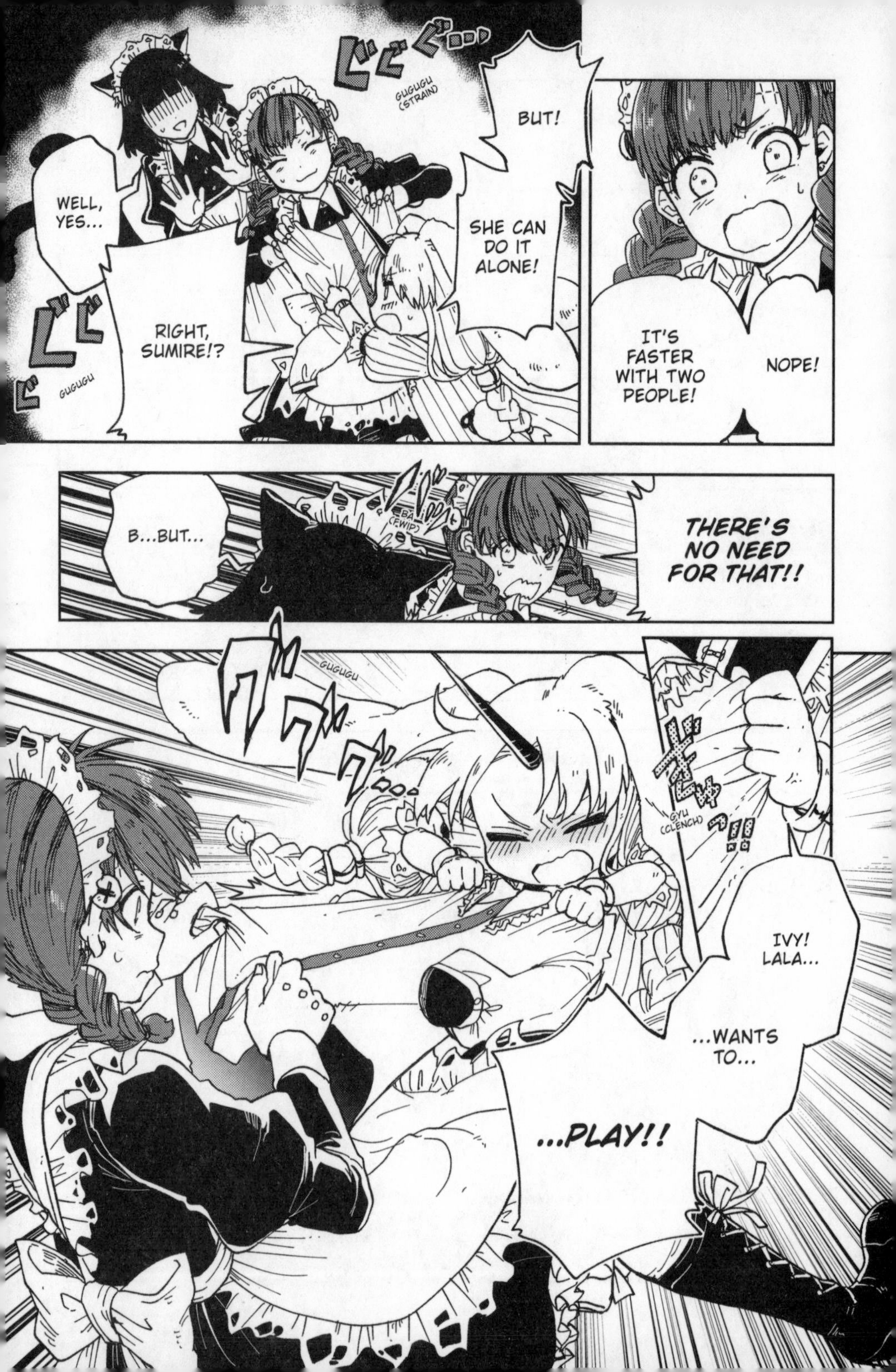
NOPE!
IT'S FASTER WITH TWO PEOPLE!
BUT!
SHE CAN DO IT ALONE!
GUGUGU (STRAIN)
WELL, YES...
RIGHT, SUMIRE!?
GUGUGU
THERE'S NO NEED FOR THAT!!
BA (FWIP)
B...BUT...
GUGUGU
GYU (CLENCH)
IVY! LALA...
...WANTS TO...
...PLAY!!

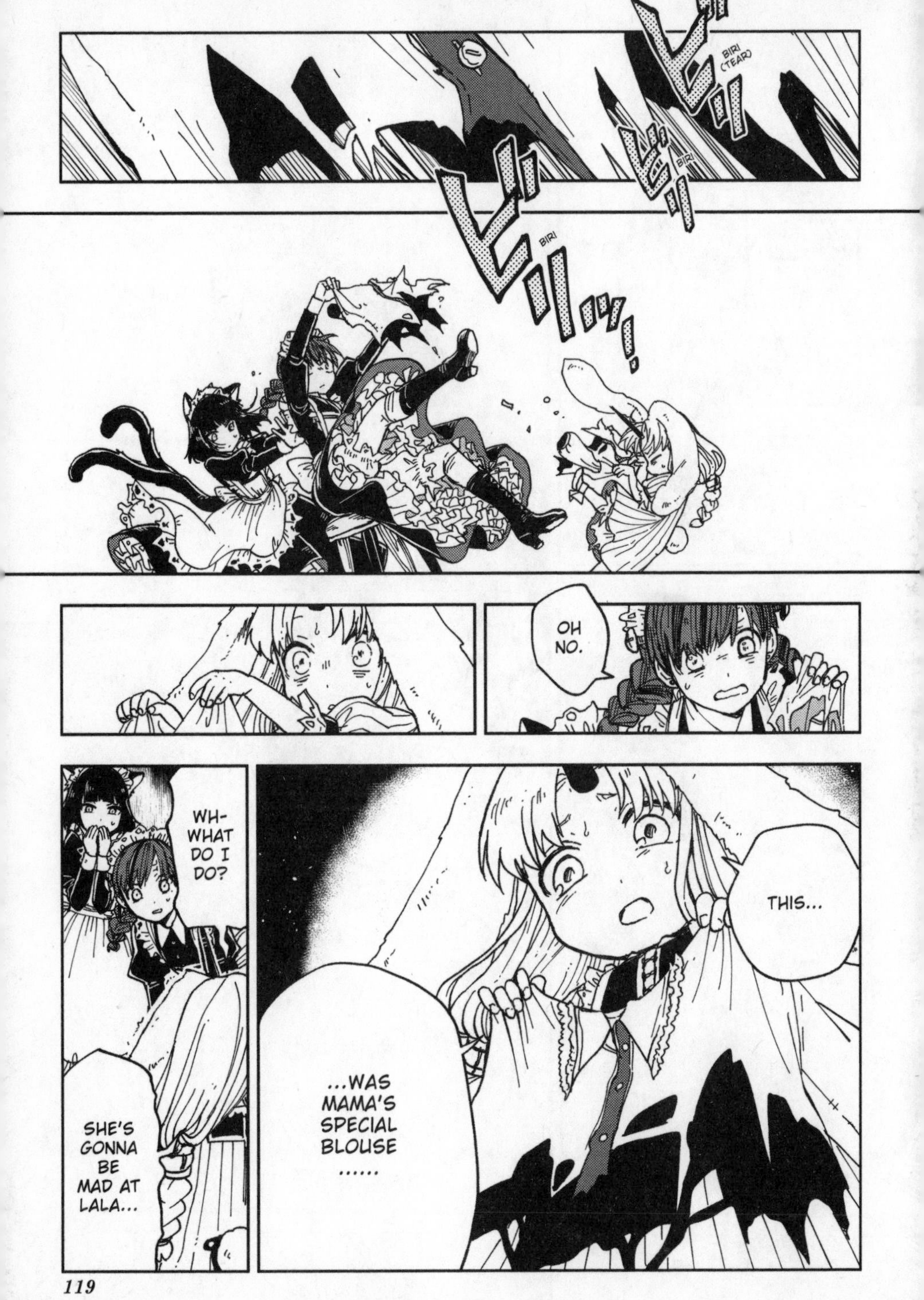

BIRI (TEAR)
BIRI
BIRI
OH NO.
THIS...
...WAS MAMA'S SPECIAL BLOUSE......
WH-WHAT DO I DO?
SHE'S GONNA BE MAD AT LALA...

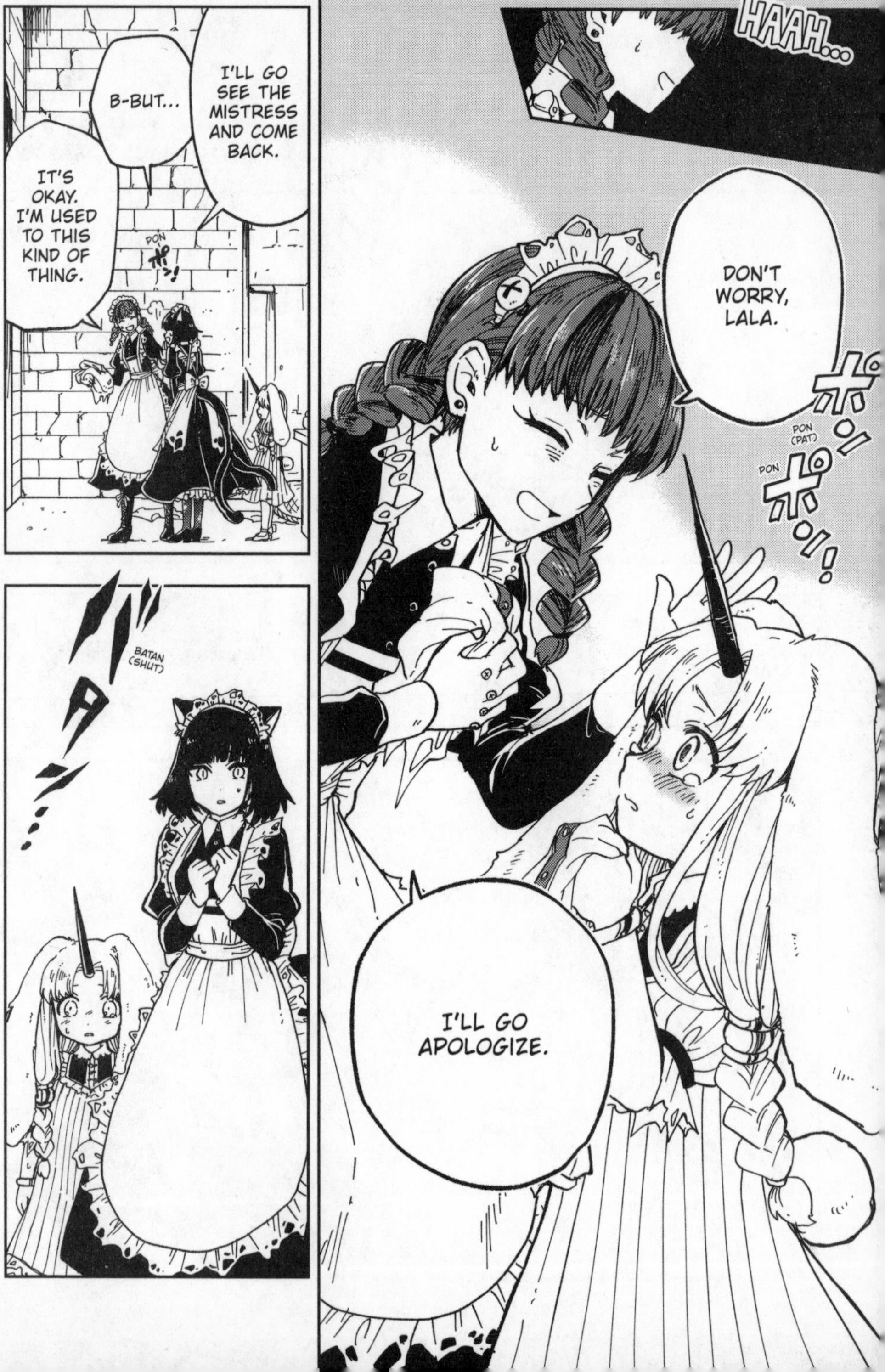
HAAH...
DON'T WORRY, LALA.
PON (PAT)
PON
I'LL GO APOLOGIZE.
I'LL GO SEE THE MISTRESS AND COME BACK.
B-BUT...
IT'S OKAY. I'M USED TO THIS KIND OF THING.
PON
BATAN (SHUT)

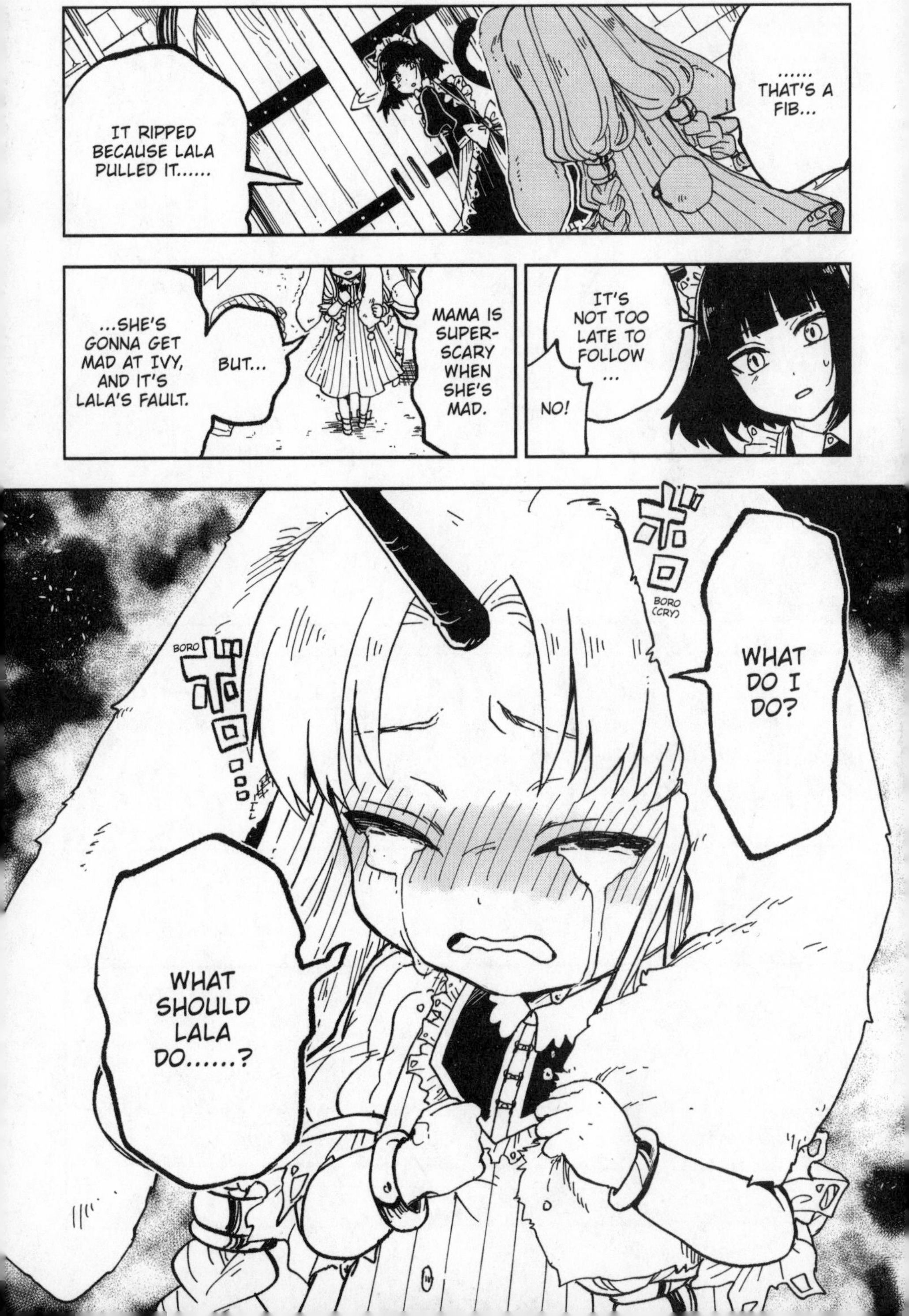
......
THAT'S A FIB...
IT RIPPED BECAUSE LALA PULLED IT......
IT'S NOT TOO LATE TO FOLLOW ...
NO!
MAMA IS SUPER-SCARY WHEN SHE'S MAD.
BUT...
...SHE'S GONNA GET MAD AT IVY, AND IT'S LALA'S FAULT.
ボロ
BORO (CRY)
WHAT DO I DO?
BORO
ボロ...
WHAT SHOULD LALA DO......?

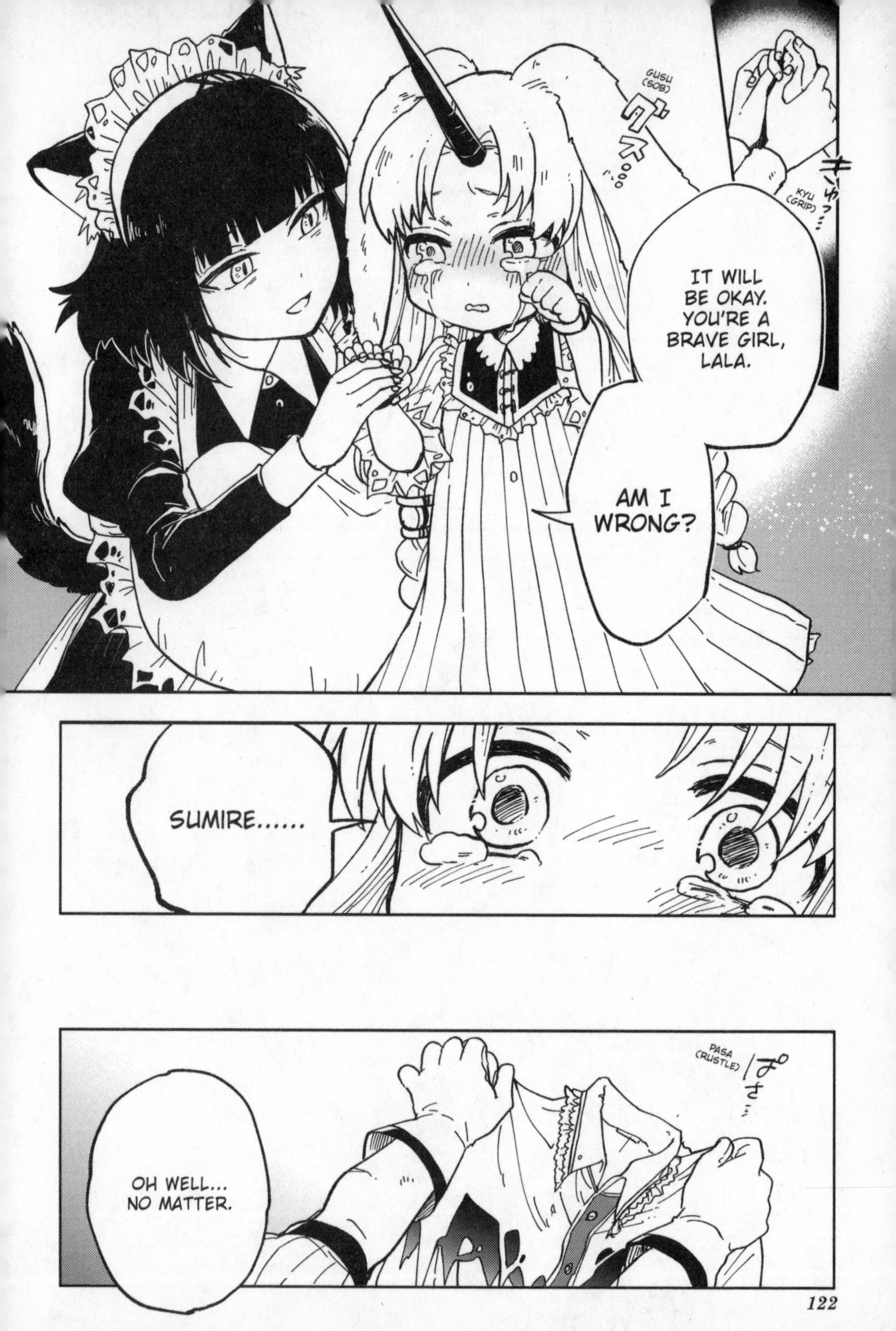

KYU (GRIP)
GUSU (SOB)
IT WILL BE OKAY. YOU'RE A BRAVE GIRL, LALA.
AM I WRONG?
SUMIRE......
PASA (RUSTLE)
OH WELL... NO MATTER.

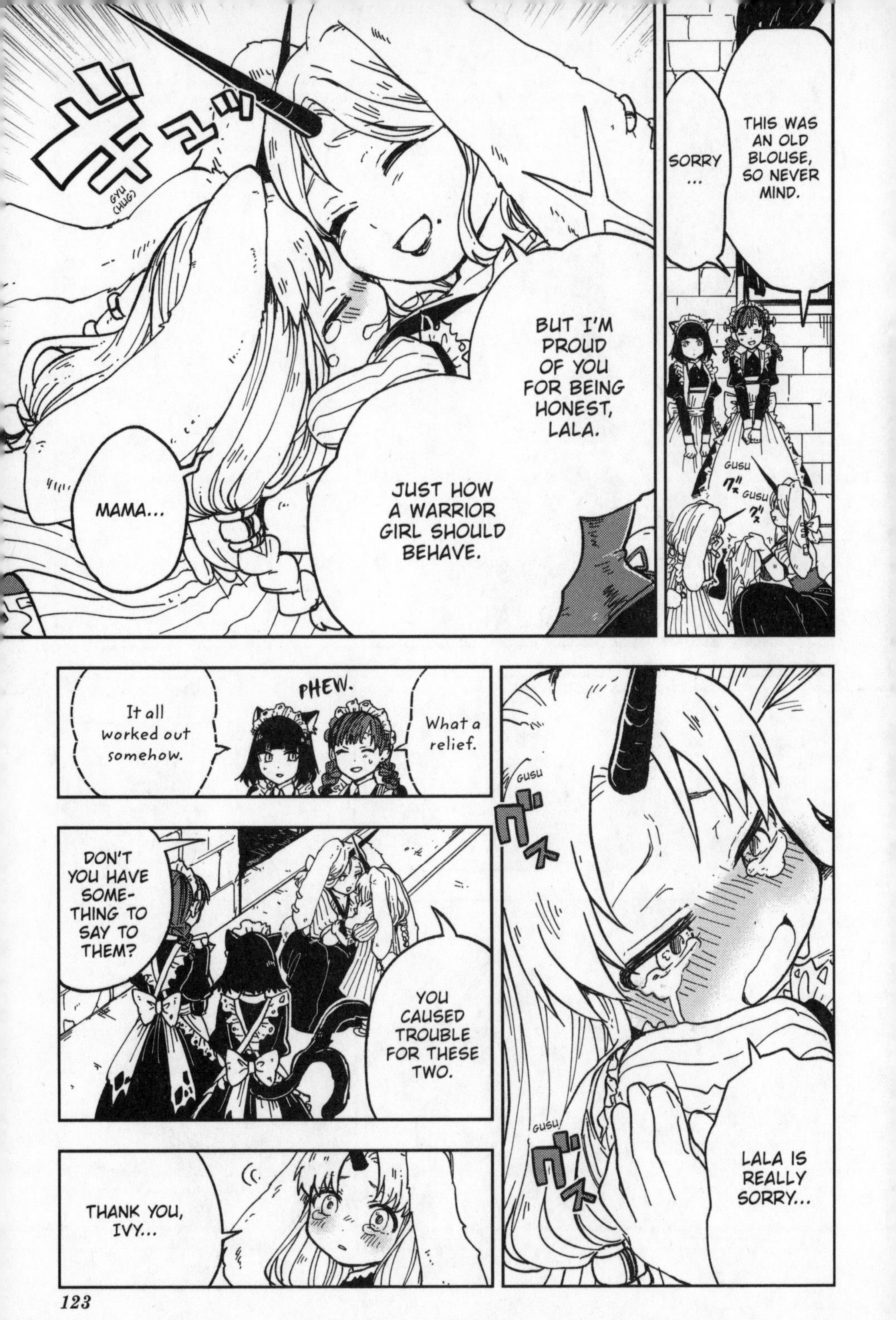
THIS WAS AN OLD BLOUSE, SO NEVER MIND.
SORRY...
GUSU
GUSU
GYU (HUG)
BUT I'M PROUD OF YOU FOR BEING HONEST, LALA.
JUST HOW A WARRIOR GIRL SHOULD BEHAVE.
MAMA...
GUSU
LALA IS REALLY SORRY...
GUSU
What a relief.
PHEW.
It all worked out somehow.
YOU CAUSED TROUBLE FOR THESE TWO.
DON'T YOU HAVE SOME-THING TO SAY TO THEM?
THANK YOU, IVY...

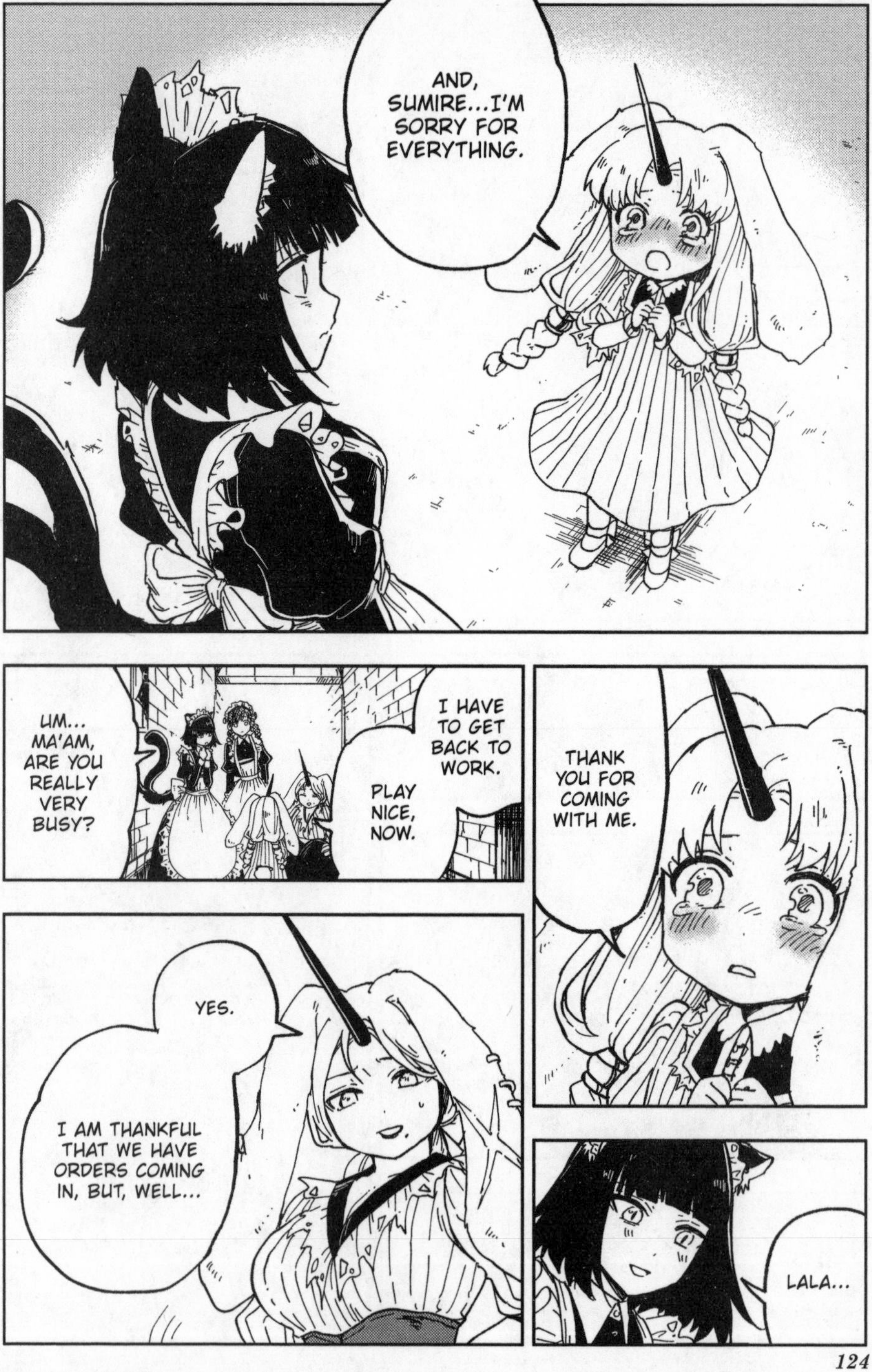
AND, SUMIRE...I'M SORRY FOR EVERYTHING.
THANK YOU FOR COMING WITH ME.
I HAVE TO GET BACK TO WORK.
PLAY NICE, NOW.
UM... MA'AM, ARE YOU REALLY VERY BUSY?
YES.
I AM THANKFUL THAT WE HAVE ORDERS COMING IN, BUT, WELL...
LALA...

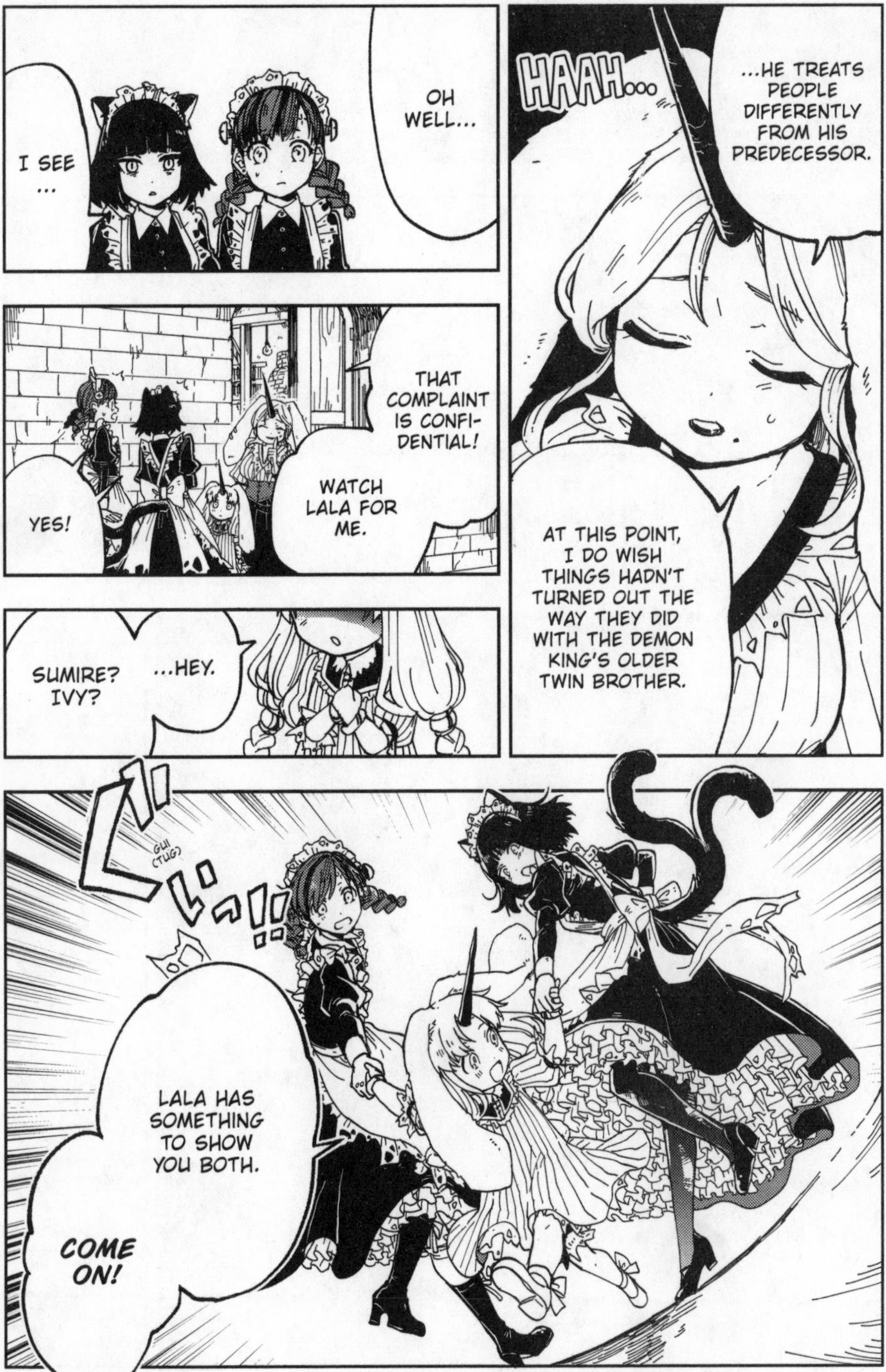
...HE TREATS PEOPLE DIFFERENTLY FROM HIS PREDECESSOR.
HAAH...
AT THIS POINT, I DO WISH THINGS HADN'T TURNED OUT THE WAY THEY DID WITH THE DEMON KING'S OLDER TWIN BROTHER.
OH WELL...
I SEE...
THAT COMPLAINT IS CONFIDENTIAL!
WATCH LALA FOR ME.
YES!
...HEY.
SUMIRE? IVY?
ぐいっ!!
GUI (TUG)
LALA HAS SOMETHING TO SHOW YOU BOTH.
COME ON!

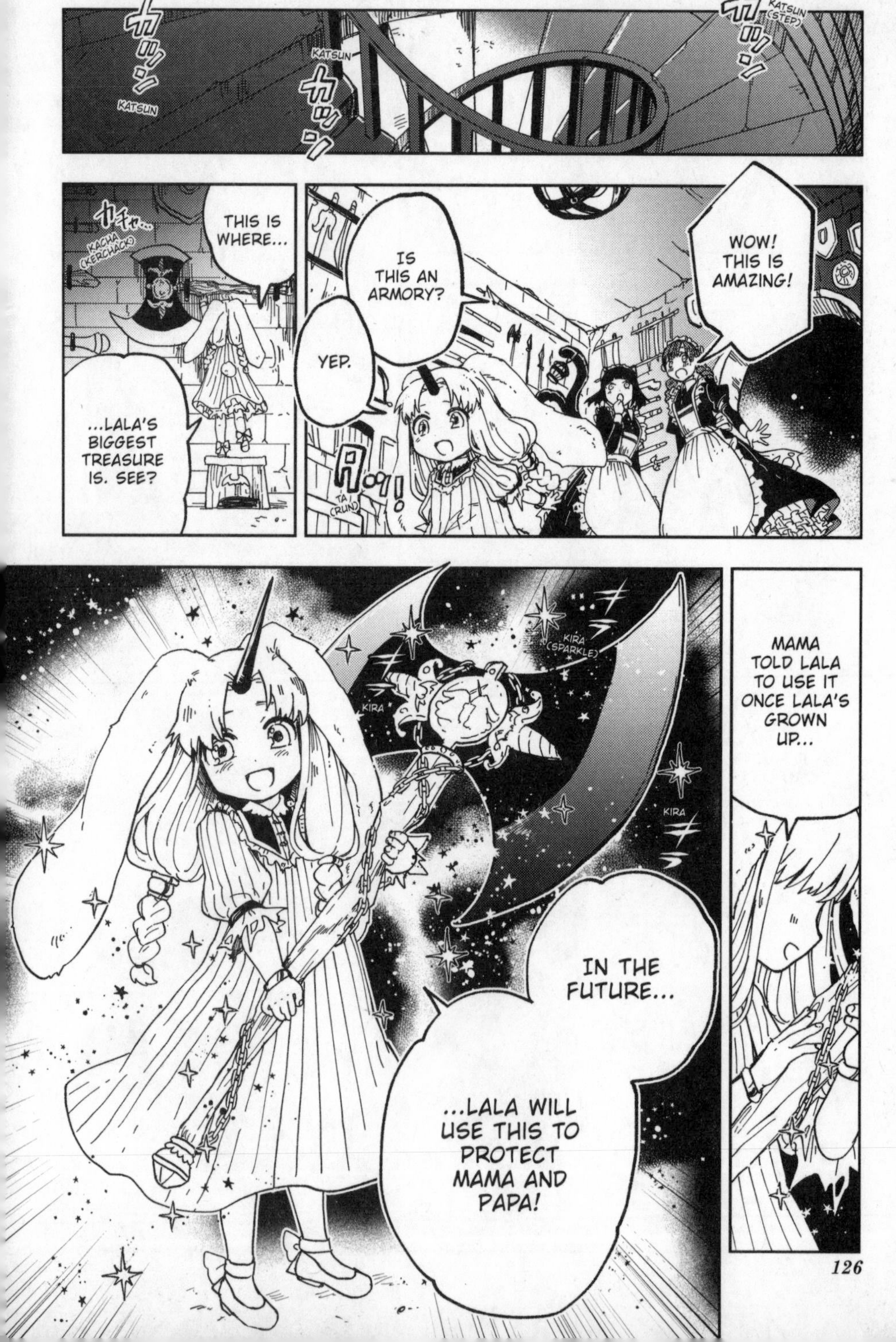
KATSUN (STEP)
KATSUN
KATSUN
WOW! THIS IS AMAZING!
IS THIS AN ARMORY?
YEP.
TA (RUN)
KACHA (KERCHACK)
THIS IS WHERE...
...LALA'S BIGGEST TREASURE IS. SEE?
MAMA TOLD LALA TO USE IT ONCE LALA'S GROWN UP...
KIRA (SPARKLE)
KIRA
KIRA
IN THE FUTURE...
...LALA WILL USE THIS TO PROTECT MAMA AND PAPA!

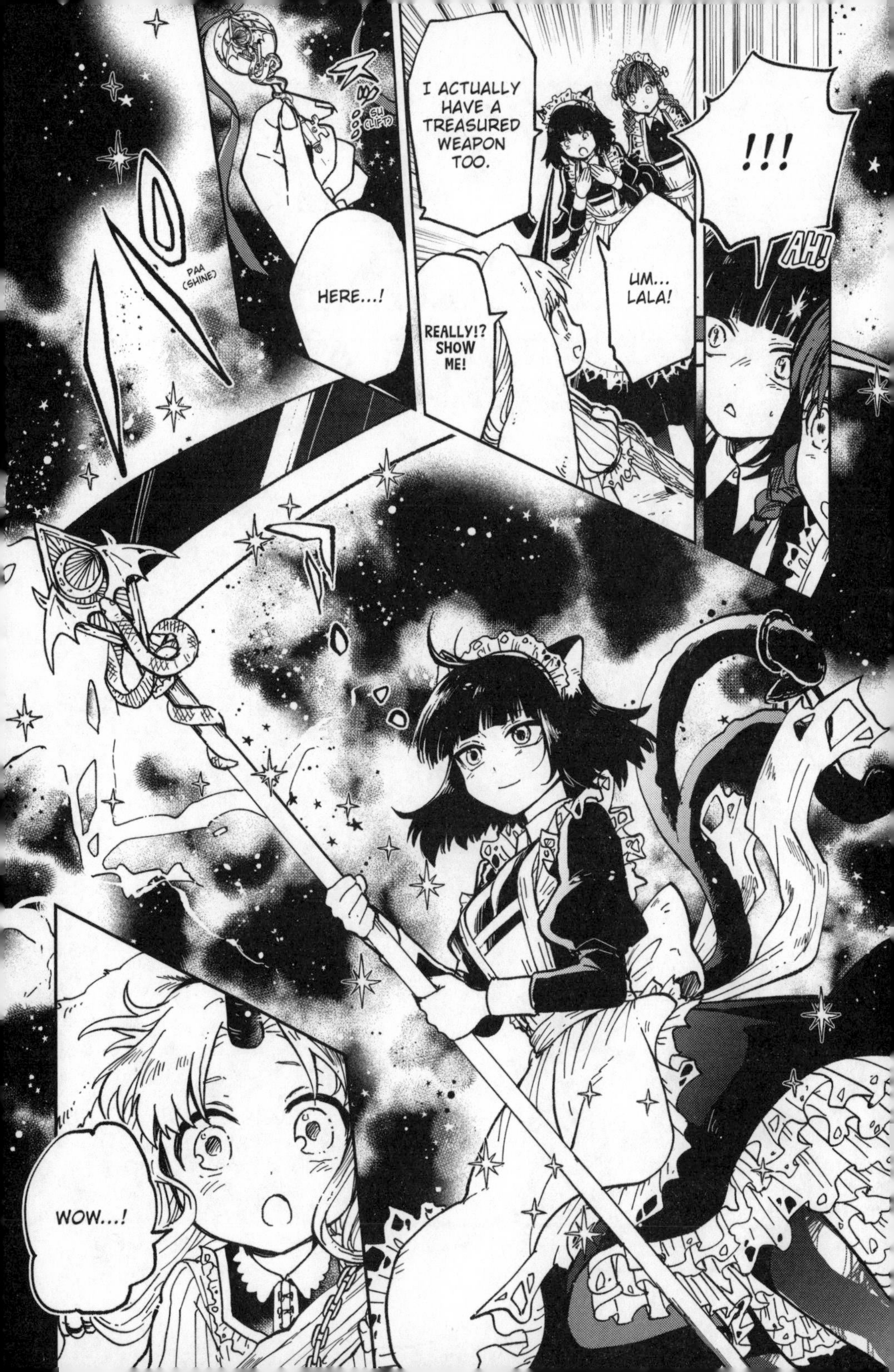
!!!
AH!
UM... LALA!
I ACTUALLY HAVE A TREASURED WEAPON TOO.
REALLY!? SHOW ME!
SU (LIFT)
HERE...!
PAA (SHINE)
WOW...!

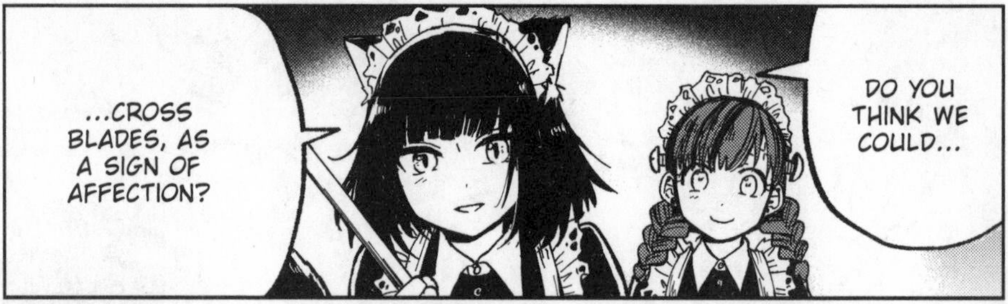
DO YOU THINK WE COULD...
...CROSS BLADES, AS A SIGN OF AFFECTION?

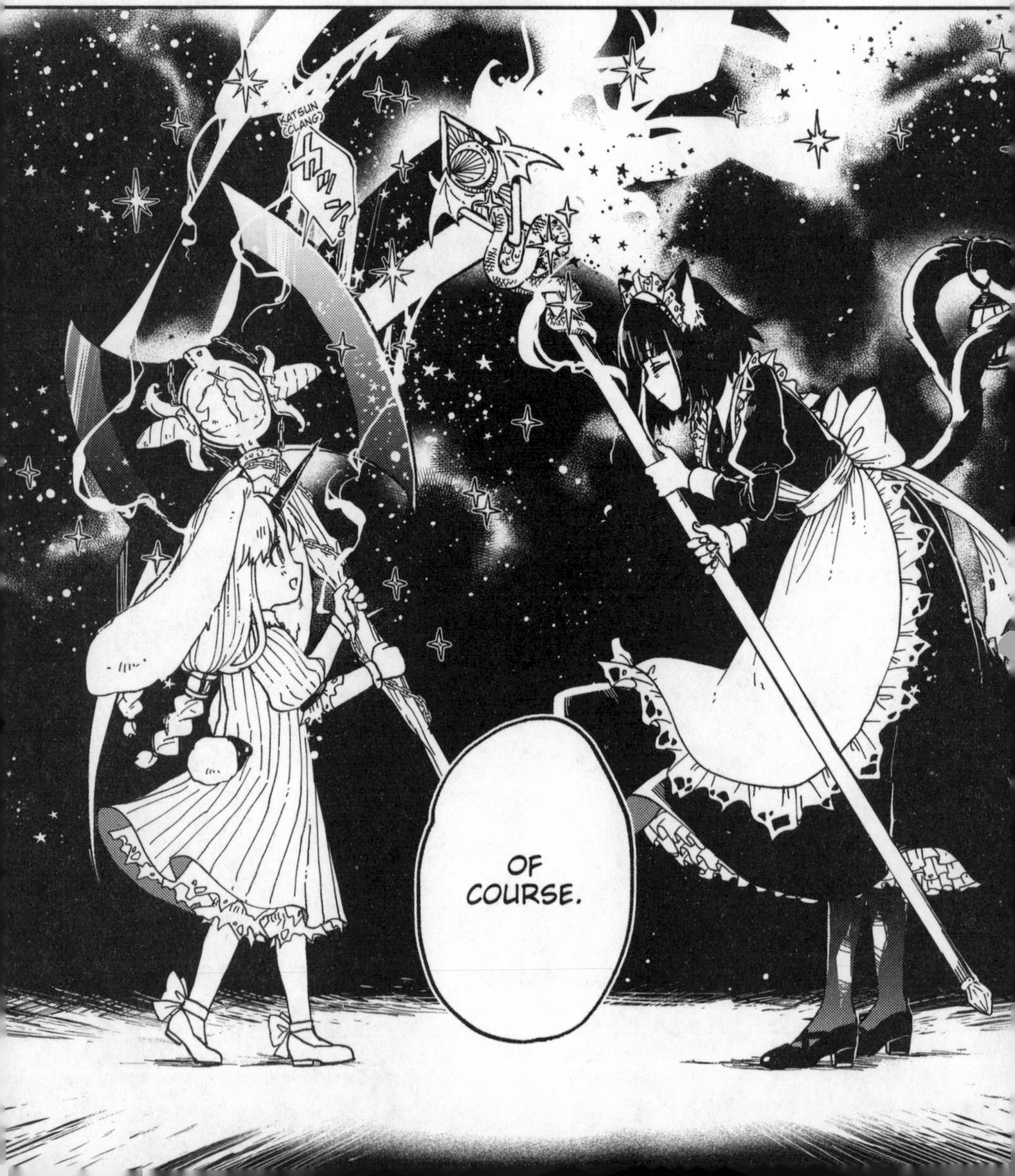
KATSUN (CLANG)
OF COURSE.

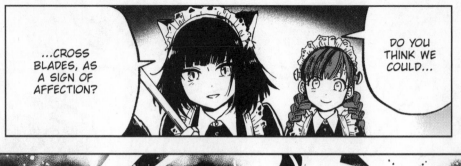

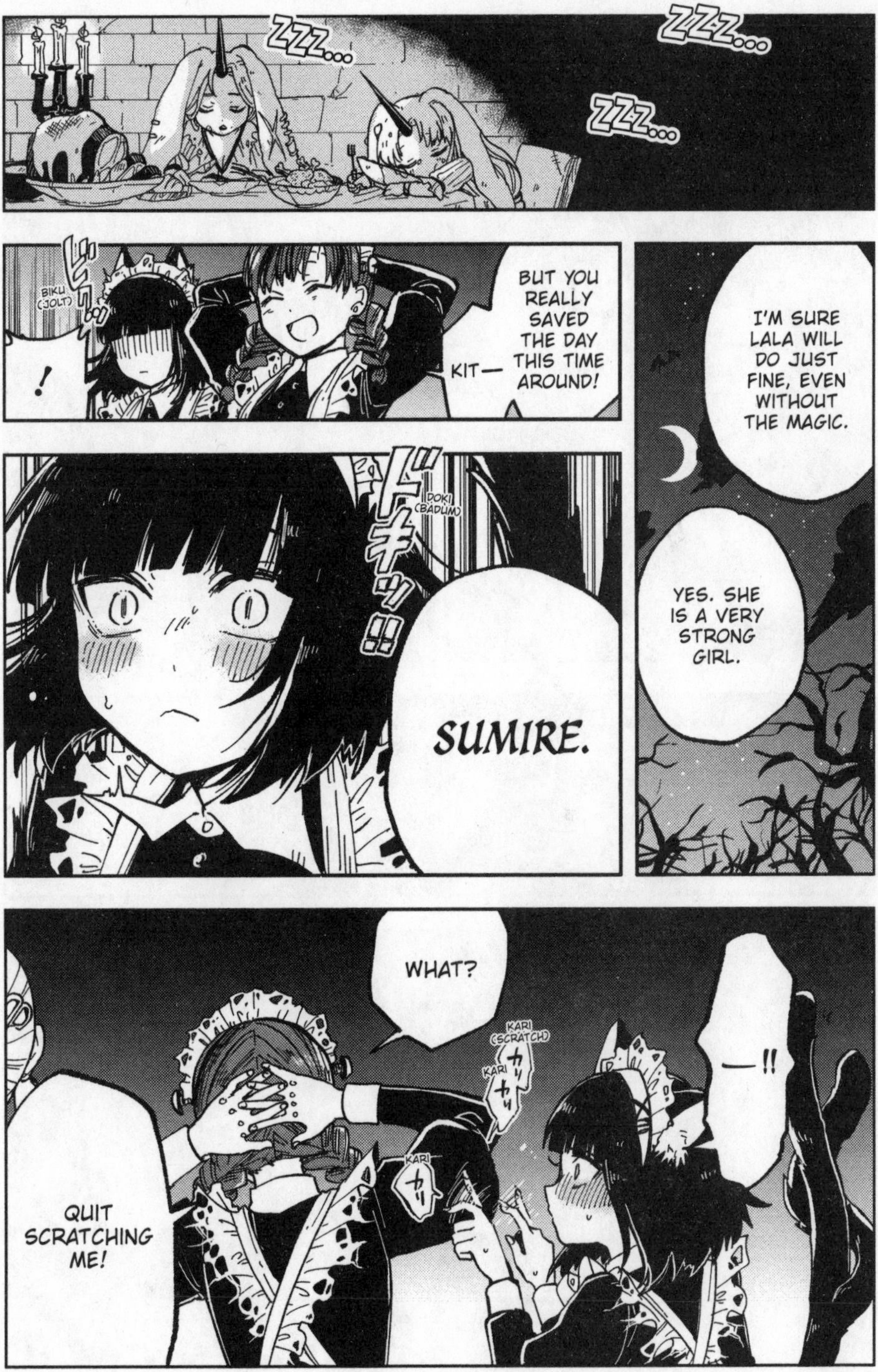
ZZZ...
ZZZ...
ZZZ...
I'M SURE LALA WILL DO JUST FINE, EVEN WITHOUT THE MAGIC.
YES. SHE IS A VERY STRONG GIRL.
BUT YOU REALLY SAVED THE DAY THIS TIME AROUND!
KIT—
BIKU (JOLT)
!
DOKI (BADUM)
SUMIRE.
WHAT?
—!!
KARI (SCRATCH)
KARI
KARI
QUIT SCRATCHING ME!

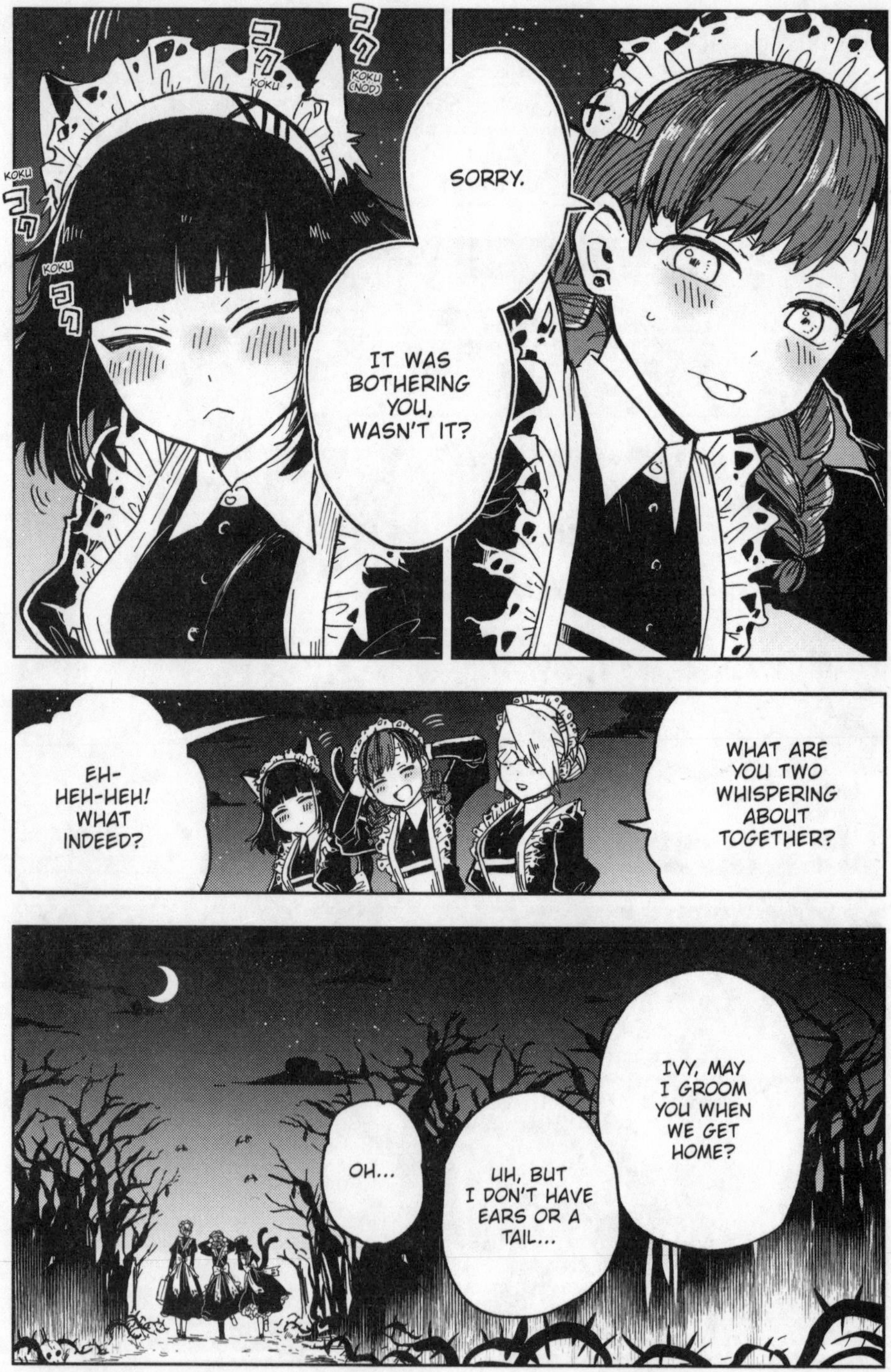
SORRY.
IT WAS BOTHERING YOU, WASN'T IT?
KOKU (NOD)
KOKU
KOKU
KOKU
WHAT ARE YOU TWO WHISPERING ABOUT TOGETHER?
EH-HEH-HEH! WHAT INDEED?
IVY, MAY I GROOM YOU WHEN WE GET HOME?
UH, BUT I DON'T HAVE EARS OR A TAIL...
OH...

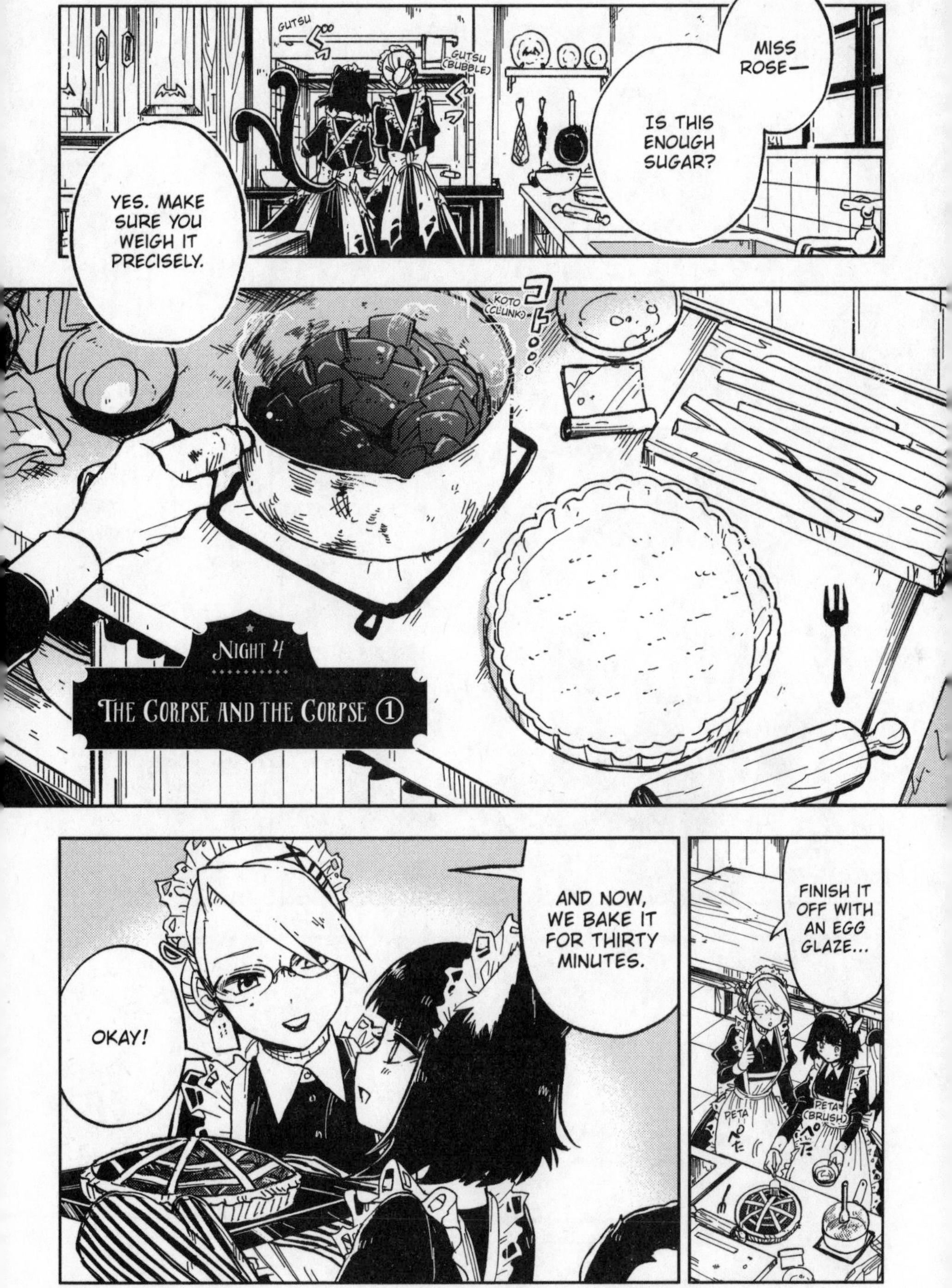
MISS ROSE—
IS THIS ENOUGH SUGAR?
GUTSU
GUTSU (BUBBLE)
YES. MAKE SURE YOU WEIGH IT PRECISELY.
KOTO (CLUNK)
NIGHT 4
THE CORPSE AND THE CORPSE ①
FINISH IT OFF WITH AN EGG GLAZE...
PETA
PETA (BRUSH)
AND NOW, WE BAKE IT FOR THIRTY MINUTES.
OKAY!

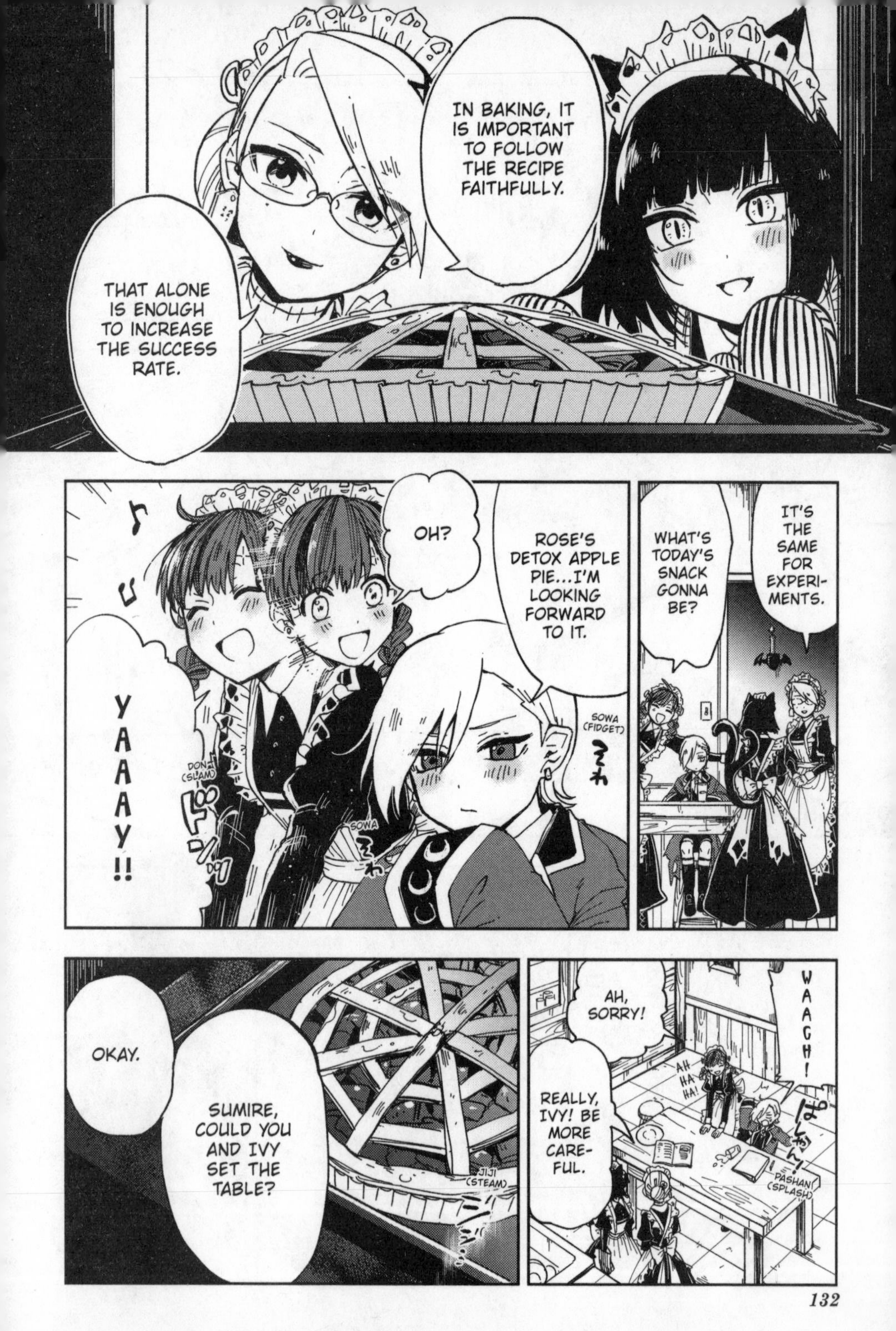
IN BAKING, IT IS IMPORTANT TO FOLLOW THE RECIPE FAITHFULLY.
THAT ALONE IS ENOUGH TO INCREASE THE SUCCESS RATE.
IT'S THE SAME FOR EXPERIMENTS.
WHAT'S TODAY'S SNACK GONNA BE?
ROSE'S DETOX APPLE PIE...I'M LOOKING FORWARD TO IT.
SOWA (FIDGET)
OH?
YAAAAY!!
DON! (SLAM)
SOWA
WAAGH!
AH, SORRY!
AH HA HA!
REALLY, IVY! BE MORE CAREFUL.
PASHAN! (SPLASH)
OKAY.
SUMIRE, COULD YOU AND IVY SET THE TABLE?
JIJI (STEAM)

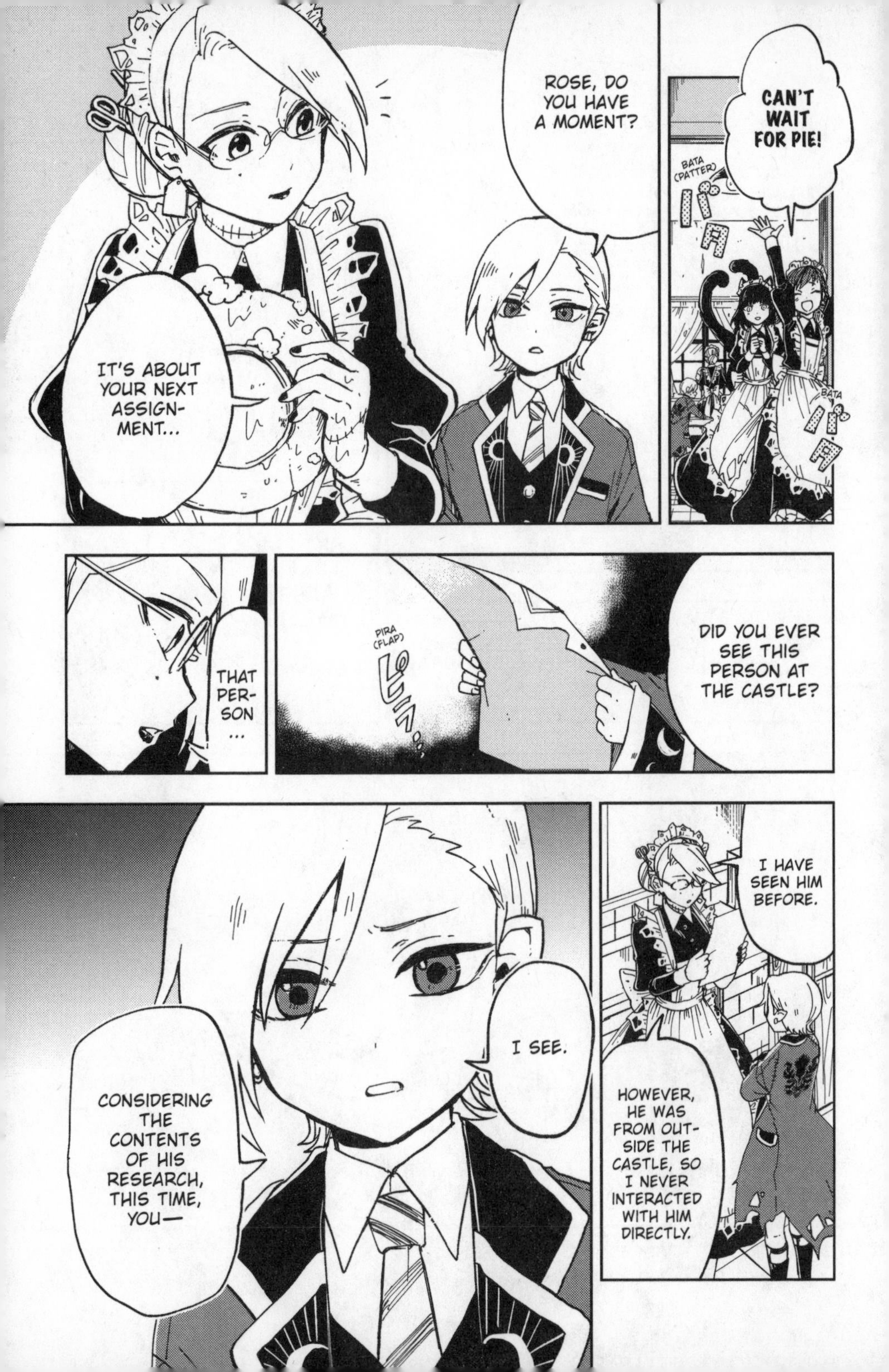
CAN'T WAIT FOR PIE!
BATA (PATTER)
BATA
ROSE, DO YOU HAVE A MOMENT?
IT'S ABOUT YOUR NEXT ASSIGN-MENT...
DID YOU EVER SEE THIS PERSON AT THE CASTLE?
PIRA (FLAP)
THAT PER-SON...
I HAVE SEEN HIM BEFORE.
HOWEVER, HE WAS FROM OUT-SIDE THE CASTLE, SO I NEVER INTERACTED WITH HIM DIRECTLY.
I SEE.
CONSIDERING THE CONTENTS OF HIS RESEARCH, THIS TIME, YOU—

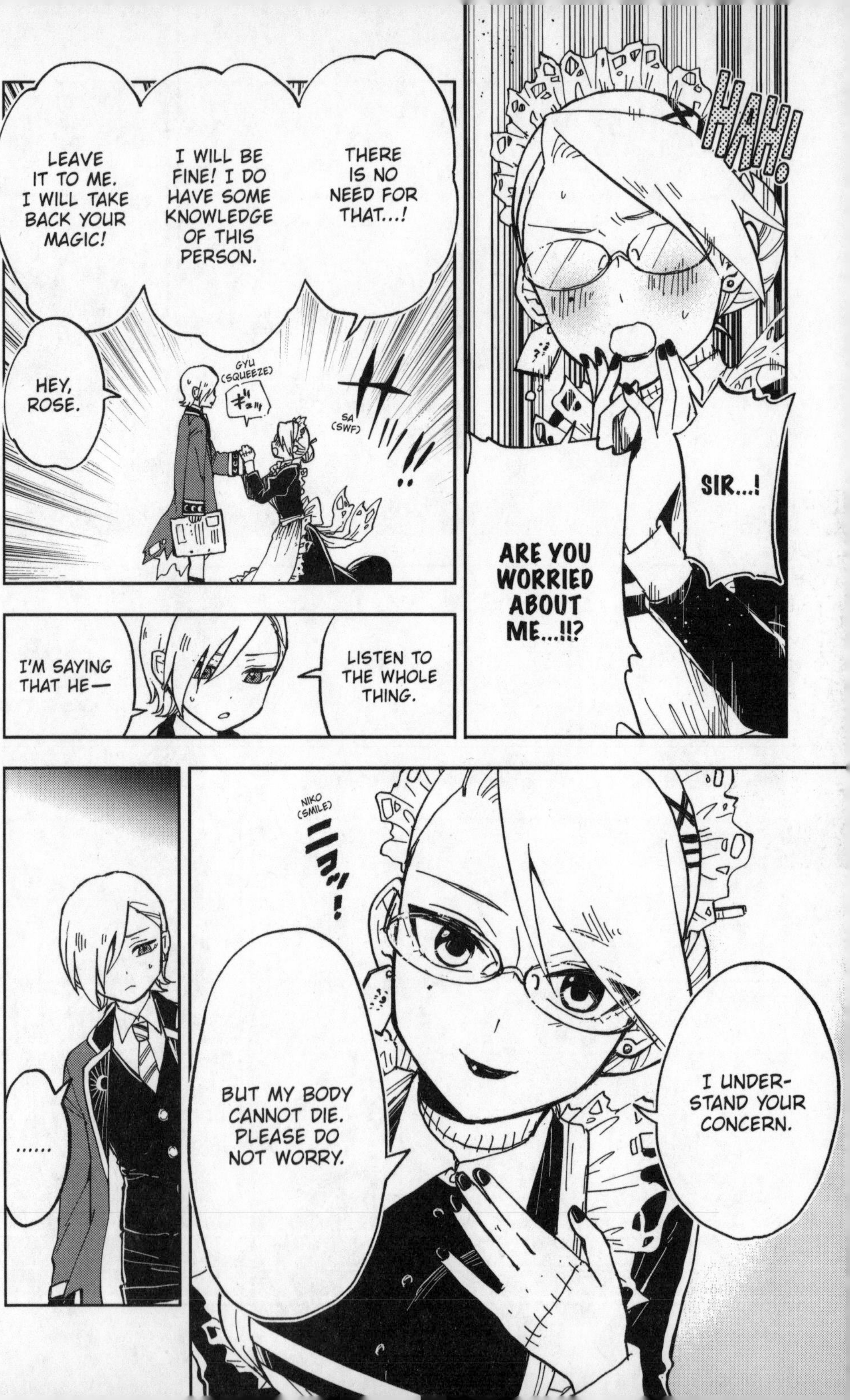
HAH!
SIR...!
ARE YOU WORRIED ABOUT ME...!!?
THERE IS NO NEED FOR THAT...!
I WILL BE FINE! I DO HAVE SOME KNOWLEDGE OF THIS PERSON.
LEAVE IT TO ME. I WILL TAKE BACK YOUR MAGIC!
SA (SWF)
!!
GYU (SQUEEZE)
HEY, ROSE.
LISTEN TO THE WHOLE THING.
I'M SAYING THAT HE—
I UNDER-STAND YOUR CONCERN.
NIKO (SMILE)
BUT MY BODY CANNOT DIE. PLEASE DO NOT WORRY.
......

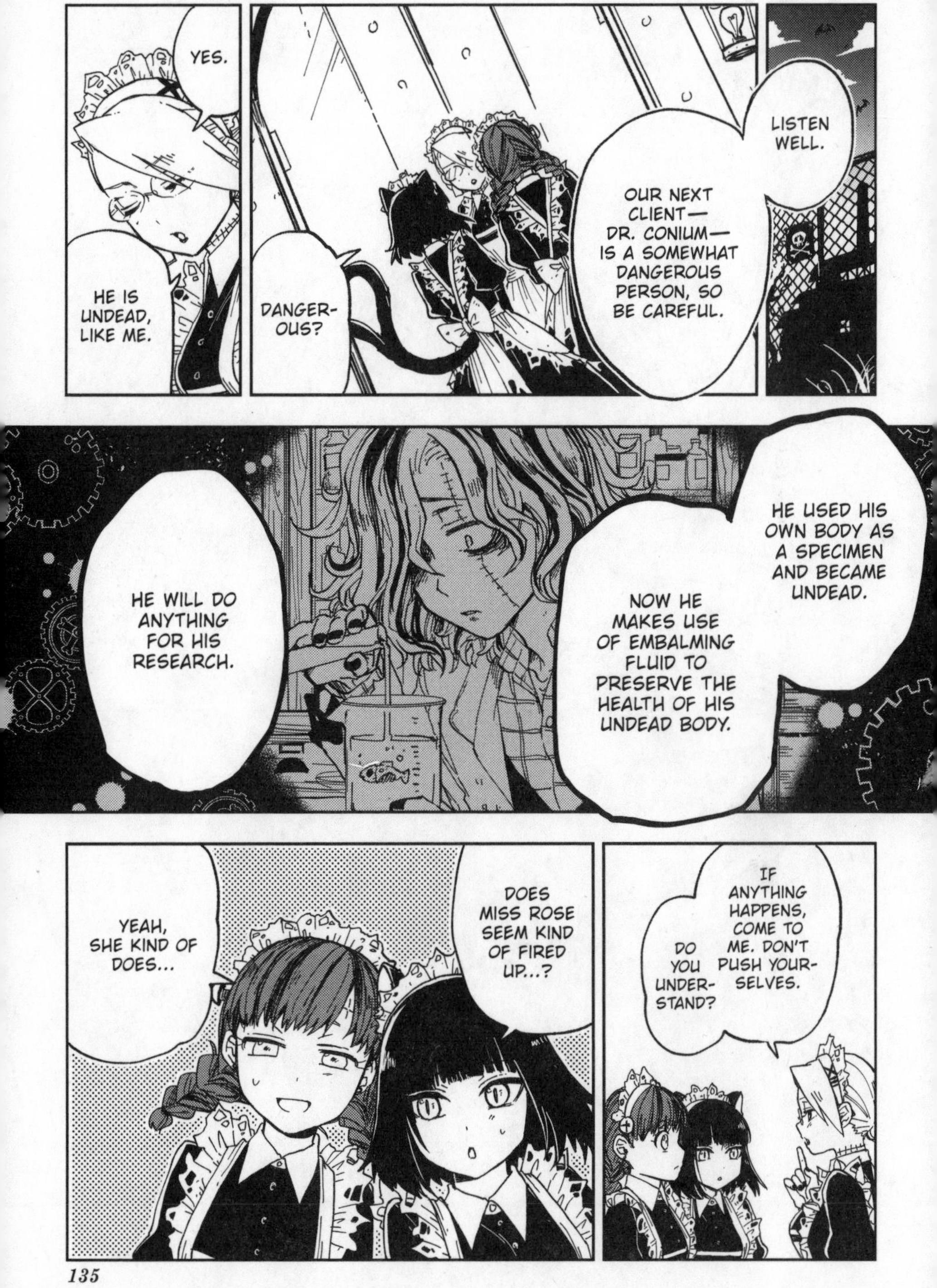
LISTEN WELL.
OUR NEXT CLIENT—DR. CONIUM—IS A SOMEWHAT DANGEROUS PERSON, SO BE CAREFUL.
DANGER-OUS?
YES.
HE IS UNDEAD, LIKE ME.
HE USED HIS OWN BODY AS A SPECIMEN AND BECAME UNDEAD.
NOW HE MAKES USE OF EMBALMING FLUID TO PRESERVE THE HEALTH OF HIS UNDEAD BODY.
HE WILL DO ANYTHING FOR HIS RESEARCH.
IF ANYTHING HAPPENS, COME TO ME. DON'T PUSH YOUR-SELVES.
DO YOU UNDER-STAND?
DOES MISS ROSE SEEM KIND OF FIRED UP...?
YEAH, SHE KIND OF DOES...

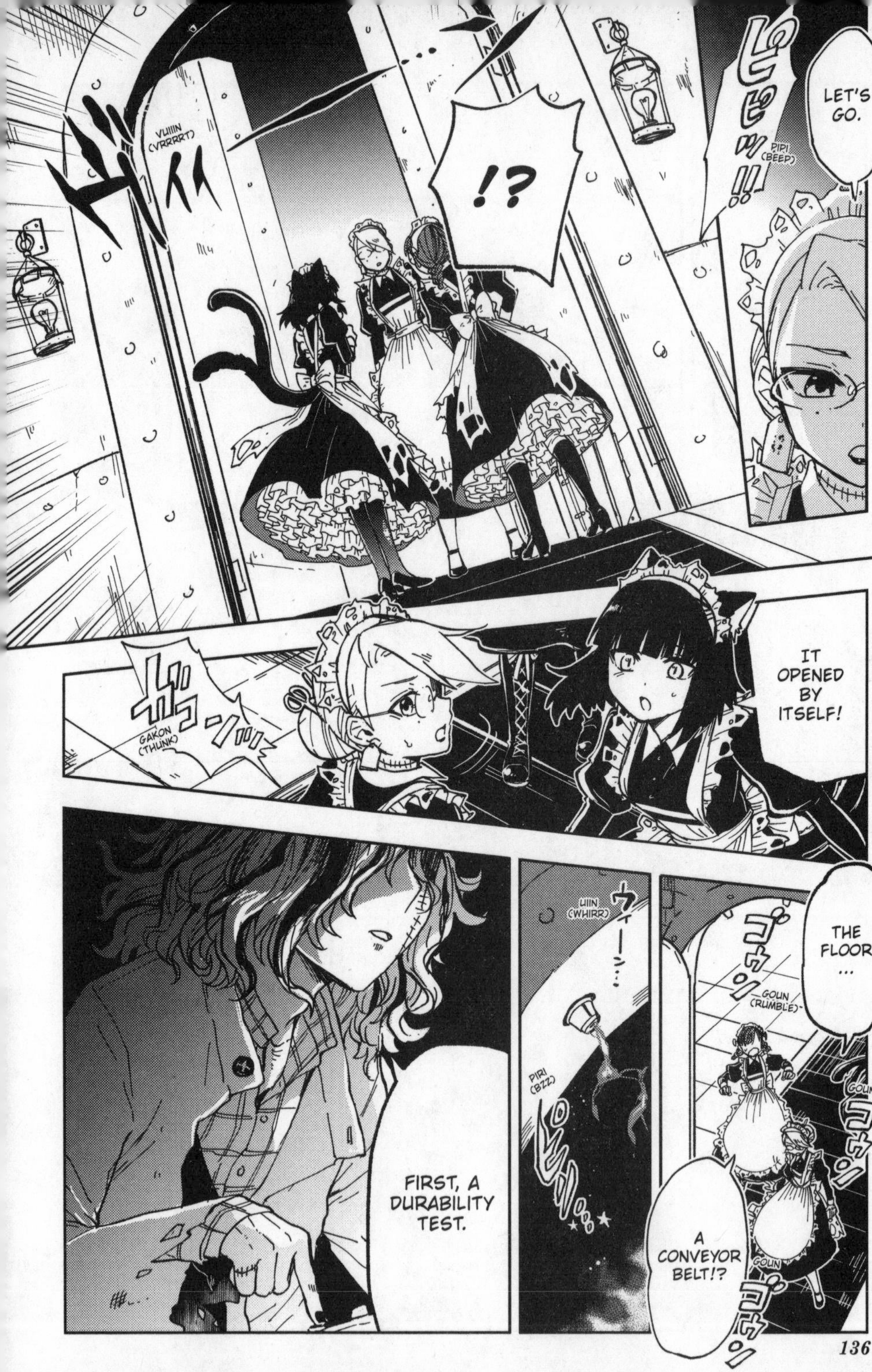
LET'S GO.
PIRI (BEEP)
VUIIIN (VRRRRT)
!?
IT OPENED BY ITSELF!
GAKON (THUNK)
THE FLOOR ...
GOUN (RUMBLE)
GOUN
A CONVEYOR BELT!?
GOUN
UIIN (WHIRR)
PIRI (BZZ)
FIRST, A DURABILITY TEST.

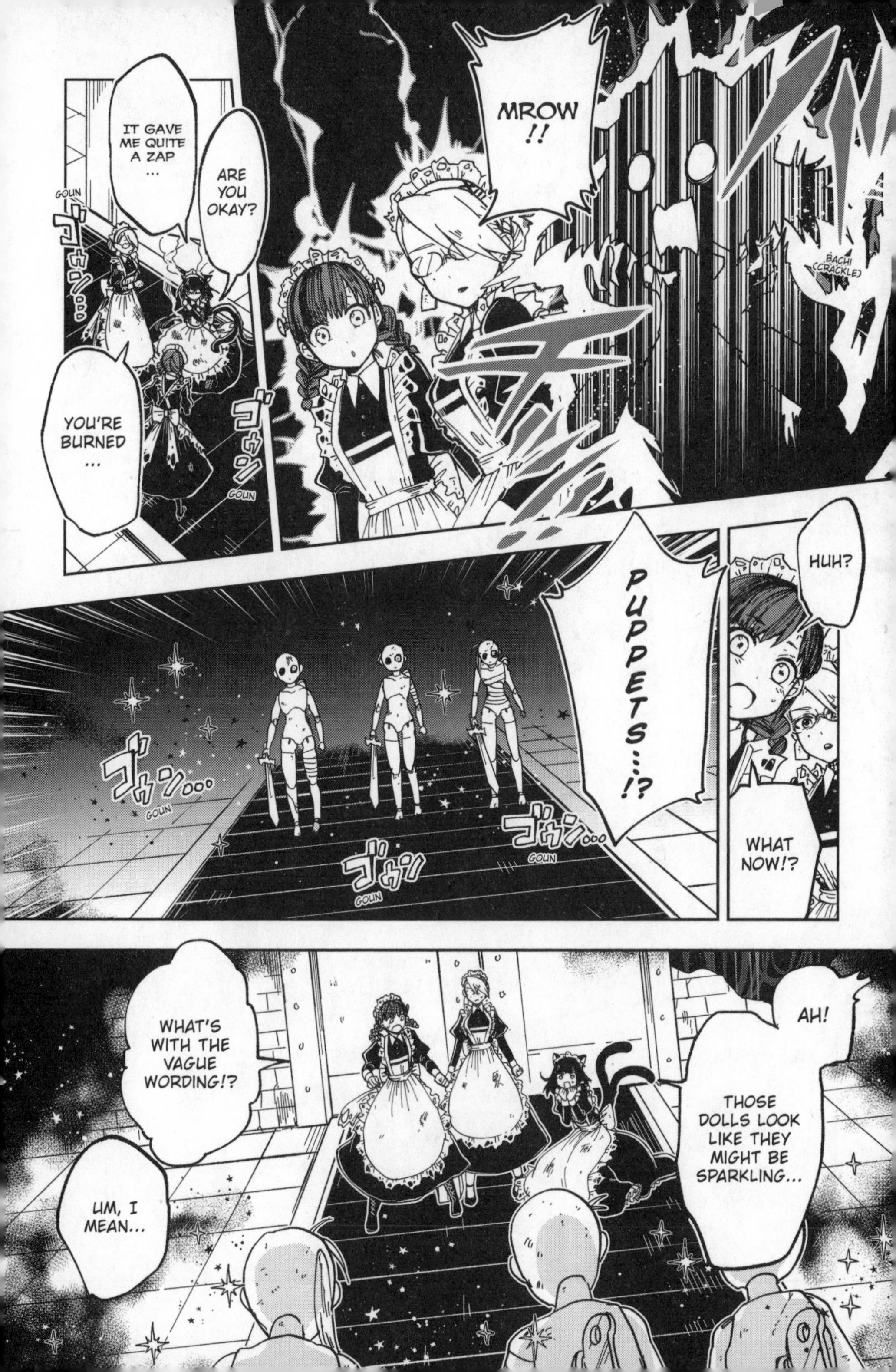
MROW !!
BACHI (CRACKLE)
ARE YOU OKAY?
IT GAVE ME QUITE A ZAP ...
GOUN
YOU'RE BURNED ...
GOUN
HUH?
WHAT NOW!?
PUPPETS...!?
GOUN
GOUN
GOUN
AH!
THOSE DOLLS LOOK LIKE THEY MIGHT BE SPARKLING...
WHAT'S WITH THE VAGUE WORDING!?
UM, I MEAN...

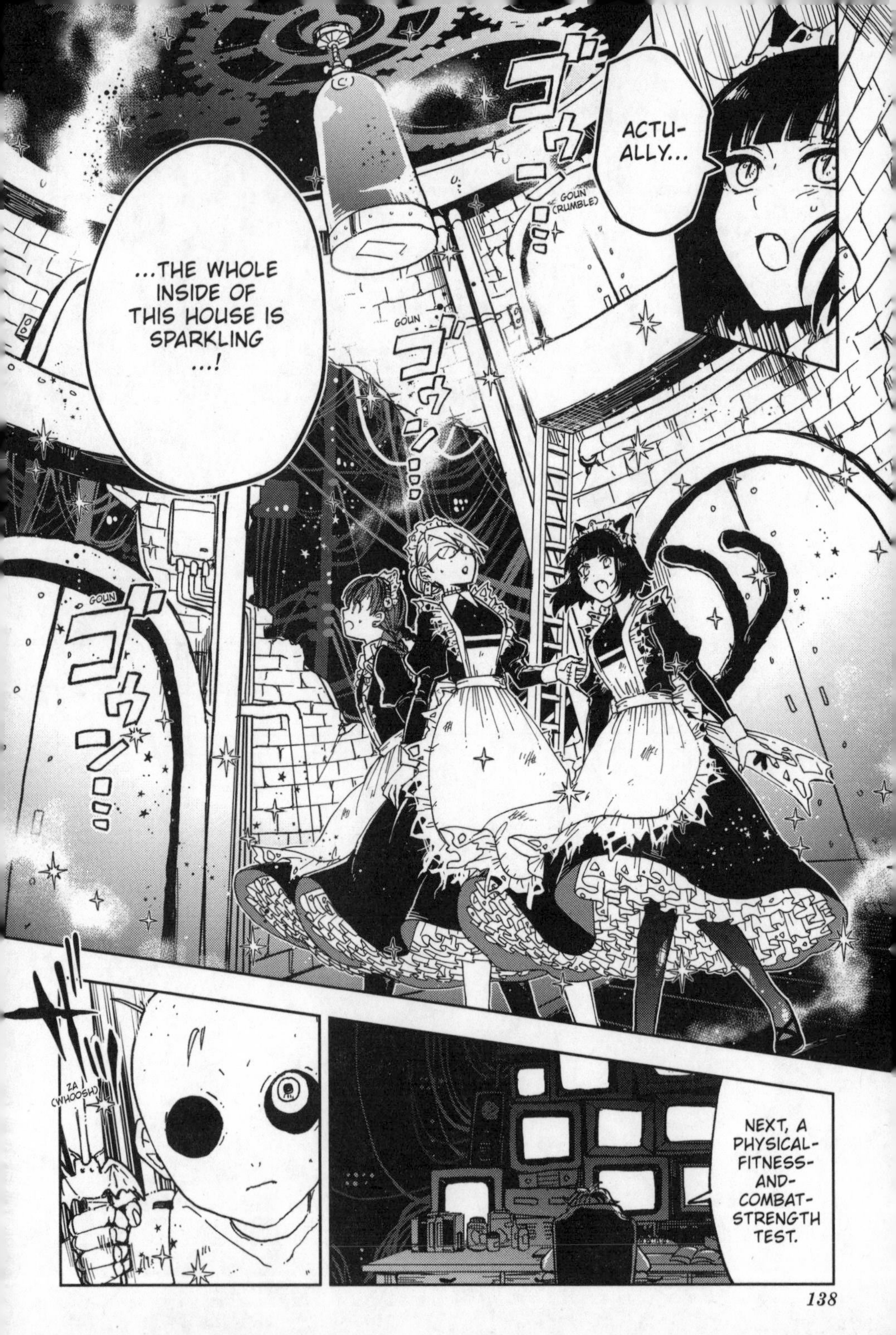
ACTU-ALLY...
GOUN (RUMBLE)
...THE WHOLE INSIDE OF THIS HOUSE IS SPARKLING ...!
GOUN
GOUN
NEXT, A PHYSICAL-FITNESS-AND-COMBAT-STRENGTH TEST.
ZA (WHOOSH)

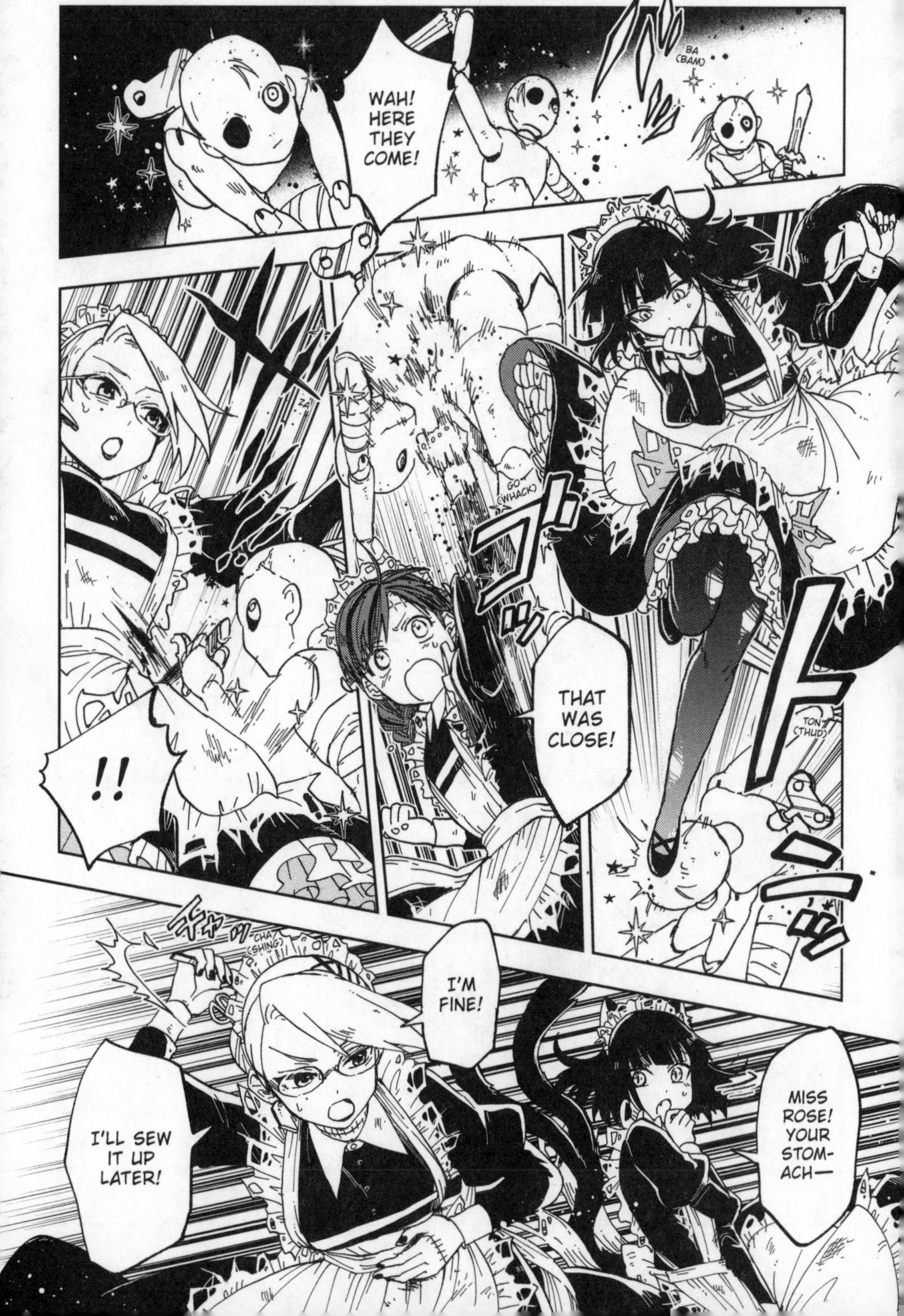
BA (BAM)
WAH! HERE THEY COME!
TON (THUD)
GO (WHACK)
THAT WAS CLOSE!
ZA
!!
MISS ROSE! YOUR STOMACH—
I'M FINE!
CHA (SHING)
I'LL SEW IT UP LATER!

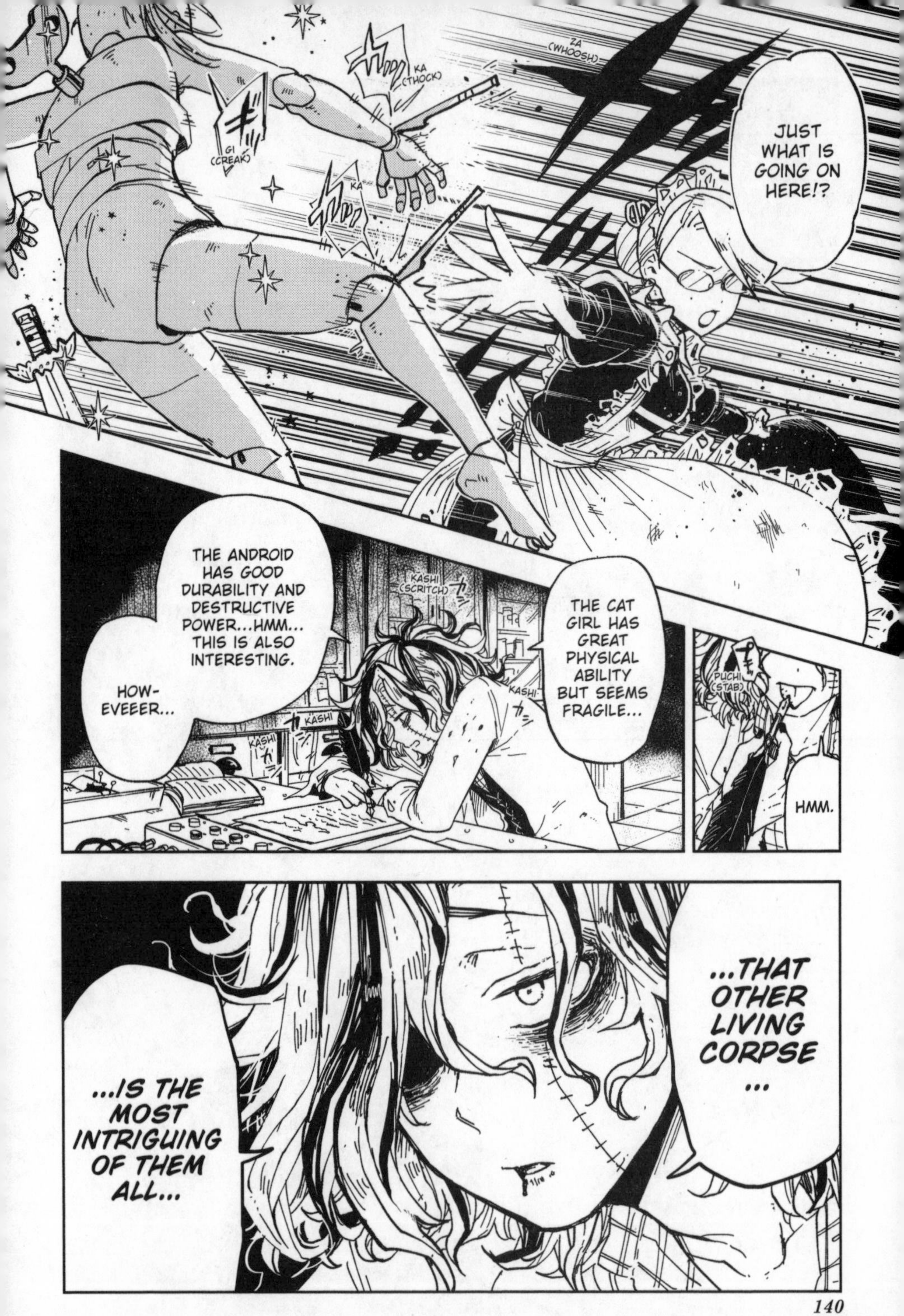
JUST WHAT IS GOING ON HERE!?
ZA (WHOOSH)
KA (THOCK)
GI (CREAK)
KA
PUCHI (STAB)
HMM.
THE CAT GIRL HAS GREAT PHYSICAL ABILITY BUT SEEMS FRAGILE...
KASHI (SCRITCH)
KASHI
THE ANDROID HAS GOOD DURABILITY AND DESTRUCTIVE POWER...HMM... THIS IS ALSO INTERESTING.
HOW-EVEEER...
KASHI
KASHI
...THAT OTHER LIVING CORPSE ...
...IS THE MOST INTRIGUING OF THEM ALL...

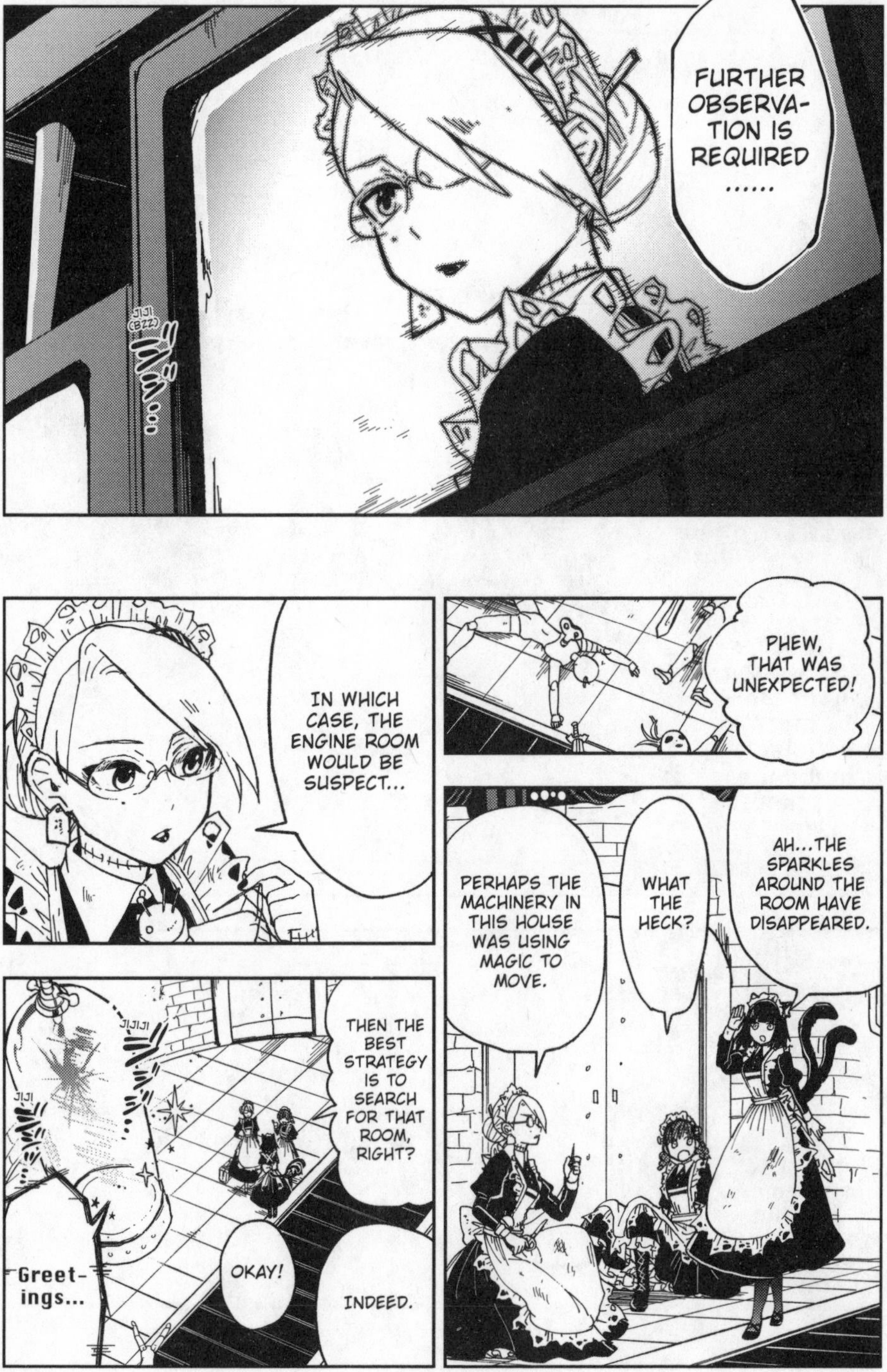
FURTHER OBSERVATION IS REQUIRED ......
JIJI (BZZ)
PHEW, THAT WAS UNEXPECTED!
AH...THE SPARKLES AROUND THE ROOM HAVE DISAPPEARED.
WHAT THE HECK?
PERHAPS THE MACHINERY IN THIS HOUSE WAS USING MAGIC TO MOVE.
IN WHICH CASE, THE ENGINE ROOM WOULD BE SUSPECT...
THEN THE BEST STRATEGY IS TO SEARCH FOR THAT ROOM, RIGHT?
OKAY!
INDEED.
JIJIJI
JIJI
Greet-ings...

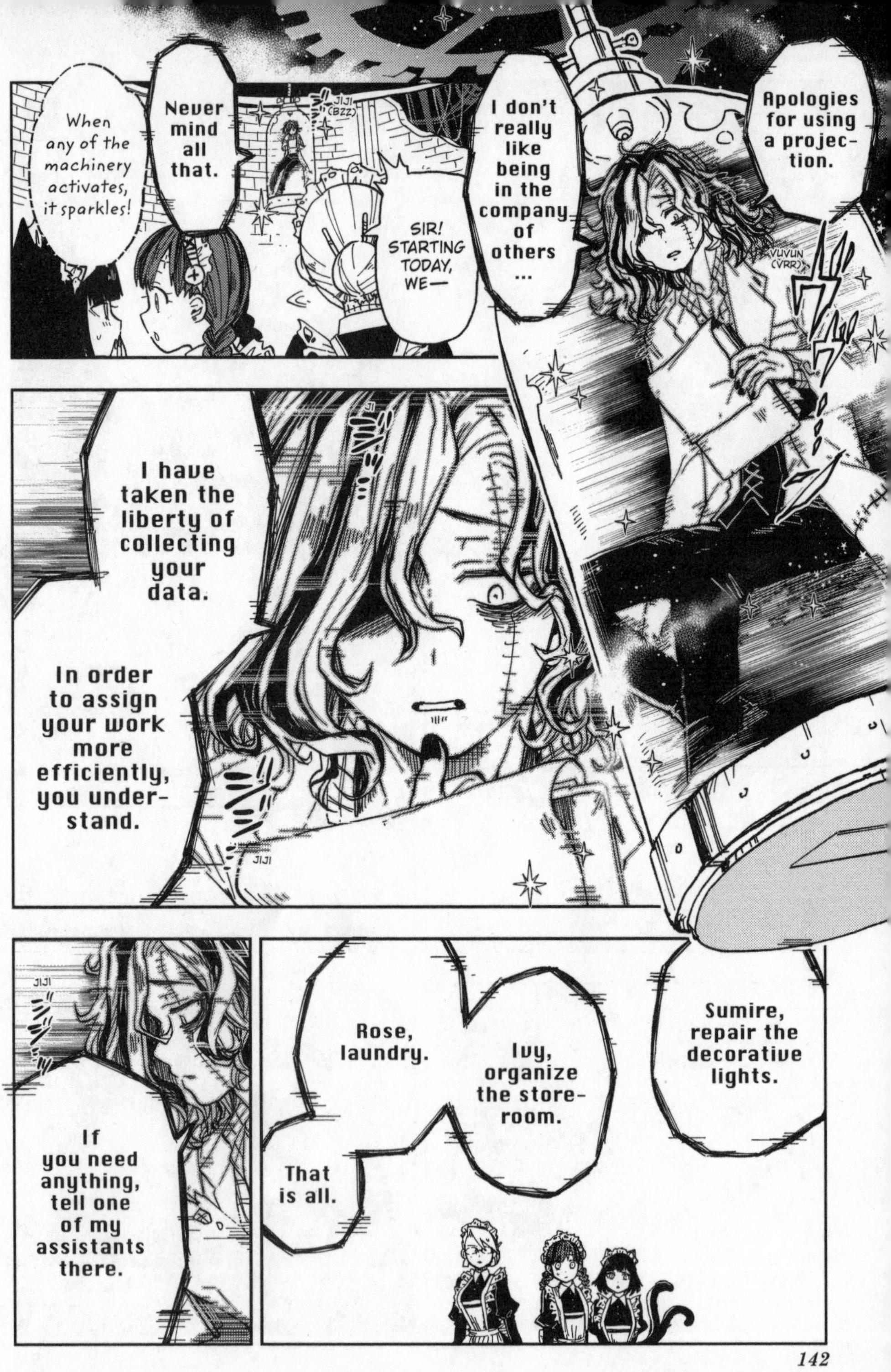
Apologies for using a projection.
I don't really like being in the company of others ...
VUVUN (VRR)
SIR! STARTING TODAY, WE—
JIJI (BZZ)
Never mind all that.
When any of the machinery activates, it sparkles!
I have taken the liberty of collecting your data.
In order to assign your work more efficiently, you understand.
JIJI
Sumire, repair the decorative lights.
Ivy, organize the storeroom.
Rose, laundry.
That is all.
JIJI
If you need anything, tell one of my assistants there.

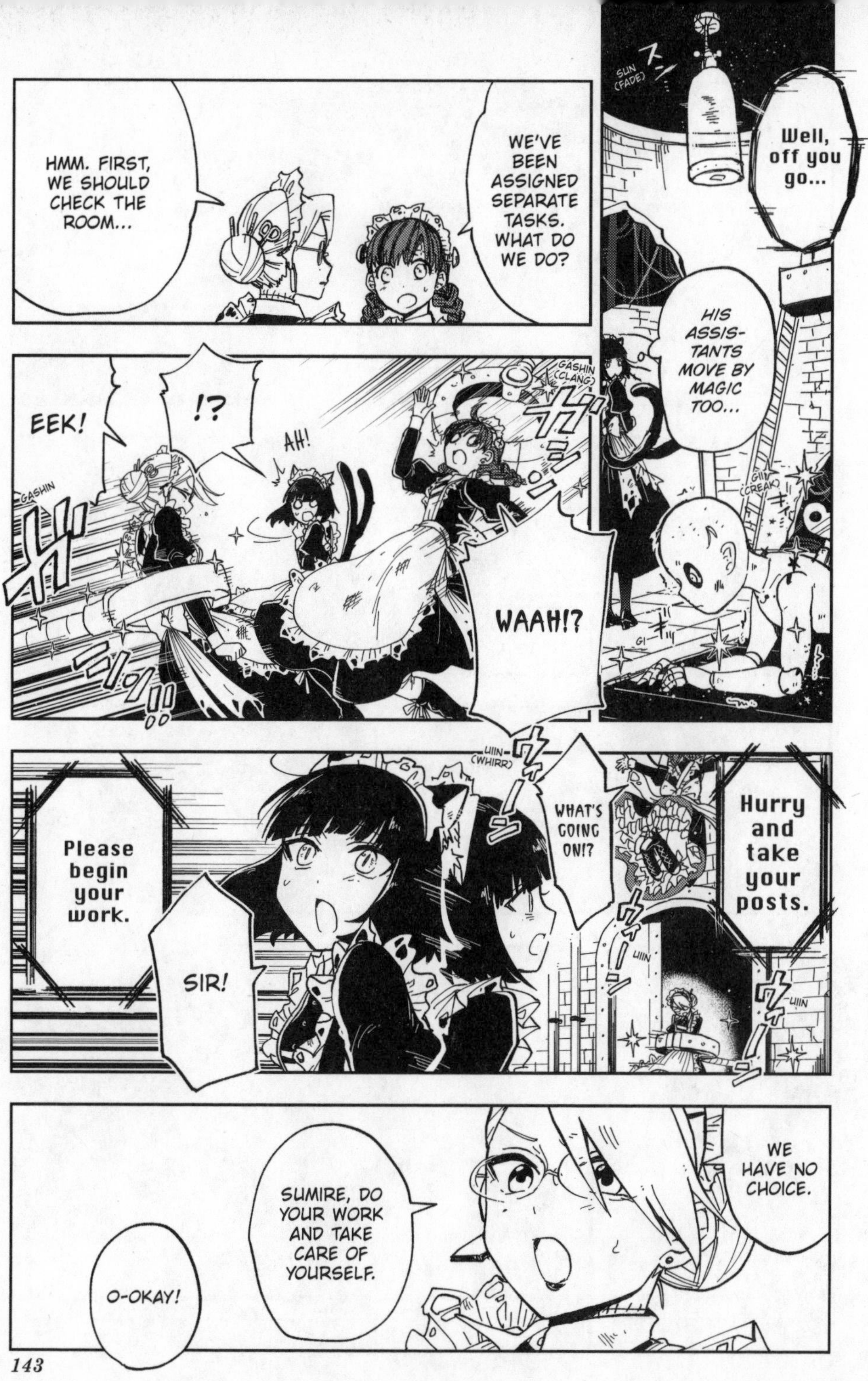
SUN (FADE)
Well, off you go...
HIS ASSIS-TANTS MOVE BY MAGIC TOO...
GIII (CREAK)
GI
WE'VE BEEN ASSIGNED SEPARATE TASKS. WHAT DO WE DO?
HMM. FIRST, WE SHOULD CHECK THE ROOM...
GASHIN (CLANG)
WAAH!?
AH!
!?
EEK!
GASHIN
Hurry and take your posts.
UIIN
WHAT'S GOING ON!?
UIIN (WHIRR)
SIR!
Please begin your work.
UIIN
WE HAVE NO CHOICE.
SUMIRE, DO YOUR WORK AND TAKE CARE OF YOURSELF.
O-OKAY!

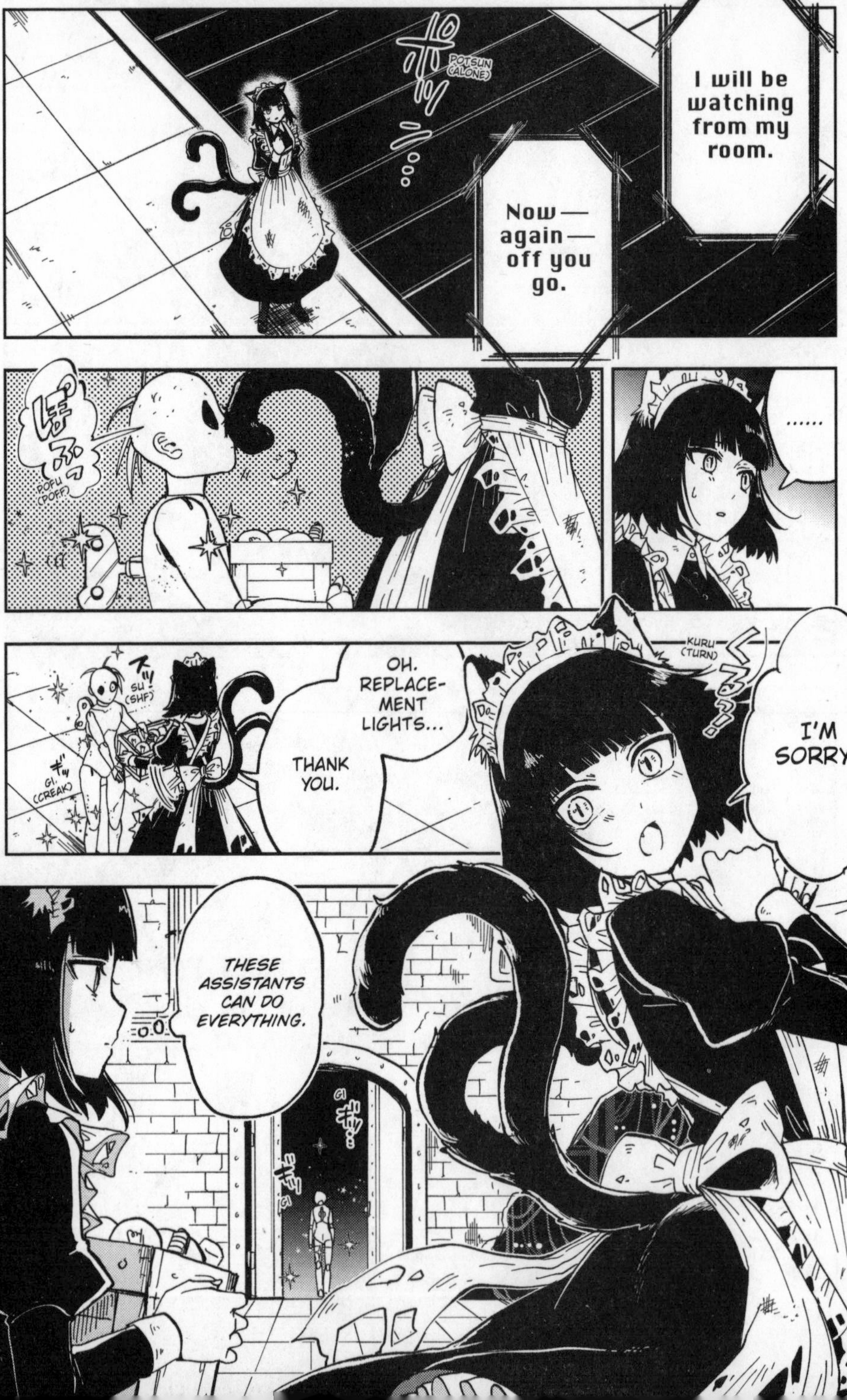
I will be watching from my room.
Now— again— off you go.
POTSUN (ALONE)
......
POFU (POFF)
KURU (TURN)
I'M SORRY!
OH. REPLACEMENT LIGHTS...
THANK YOU.
SU (SHF)
GI (CREAK)
THESE ASSISTANTS CAN DO EVERYTHING.

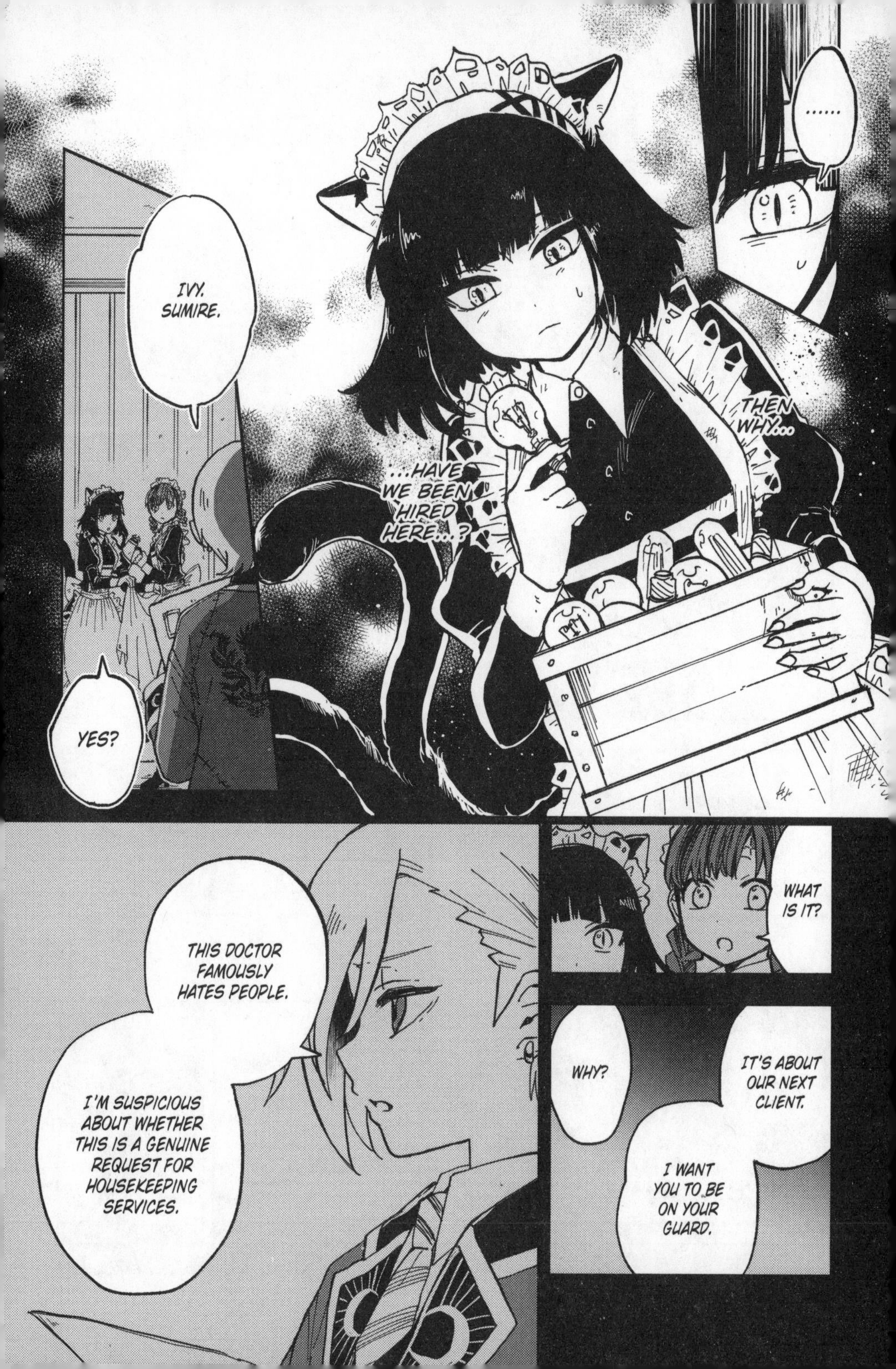
......
THEN WHY...
...HAVE WE BEEN HIRED HERE...?
IVY. SUMIRE.
YES?
WHAT IS IT?
IT'S ABOUT OUR NEXT CLIENT.
I WANT YOU TO BE ON YOUR GUARD.
WHY?
THIS DOCTOR FAMOUSLY HATES PEOPLE.
I'M SUSPICIOUS ABOUT WHETHER THIS IS A GENUINE REQUEST FOR HOUSEKEEPING SERVICES.

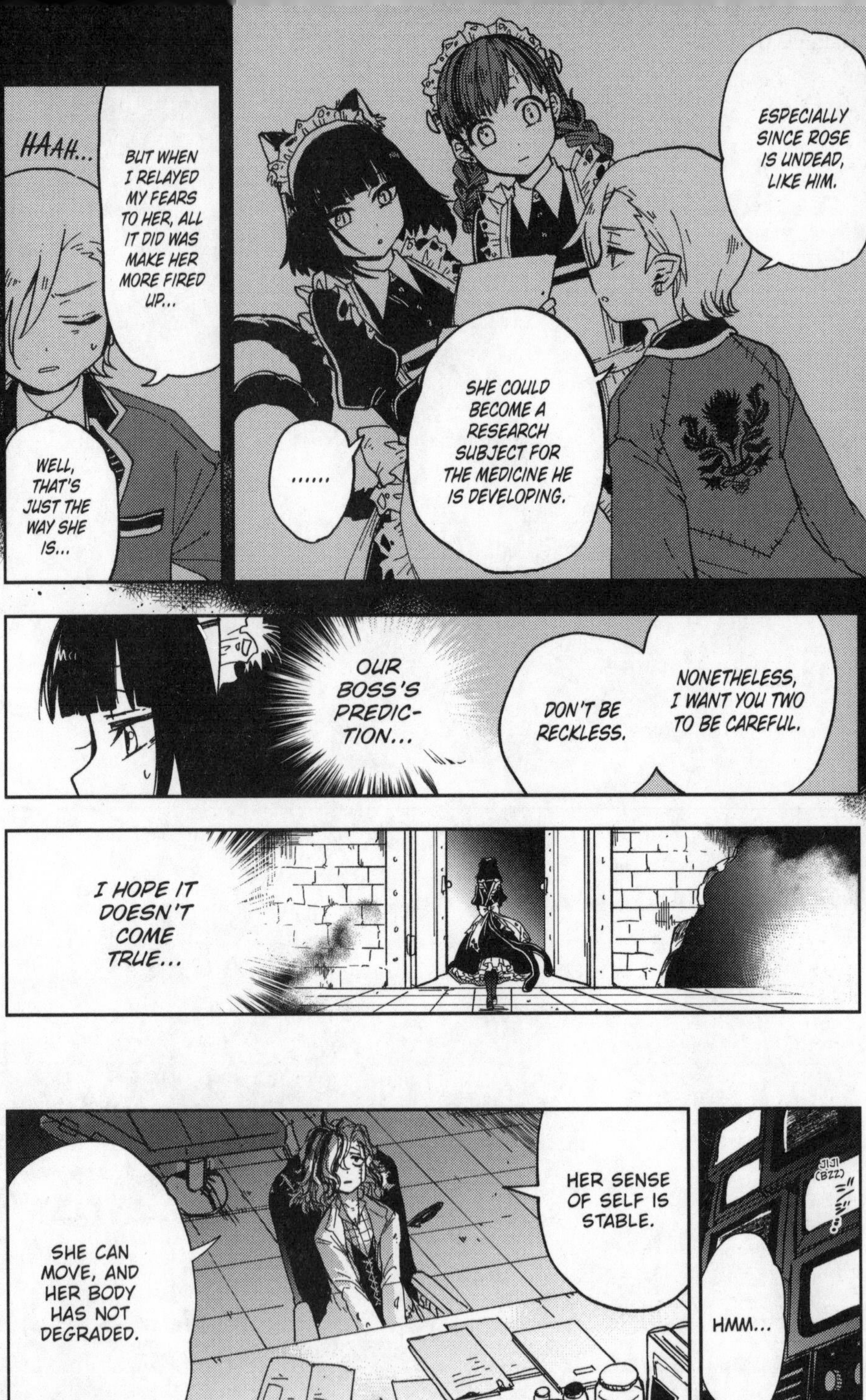
ESPECIALLY SINCE ROSE IS UNDEAD, LIKE HIM.
SHE COULD BECOME A RESEARCH SUBJECT FOR THE MEDICINE HE IS DEVELOPING.
......
HAAH...
BUT WHEN I RELAYED MY FEARS TO HER, ALL IT DID WAS MAKE HER MORE FIRED UP...
WELL, THAT'S JUST THE WAY SHE IS...
NONETHELESS, I WANT YOU TWO TO BE CAREFUL.
DON'T BE RECKLESS.
OUR BOSS'S PREDICTION...
I HOPE IT DOESN'T COME TRUE...
JIJI (BZZ)
HMM...
HER SENSE OF SELF IS STABLE.
SHE CAN MOVE, AND HER BODY HAS NOT DEGRADED.

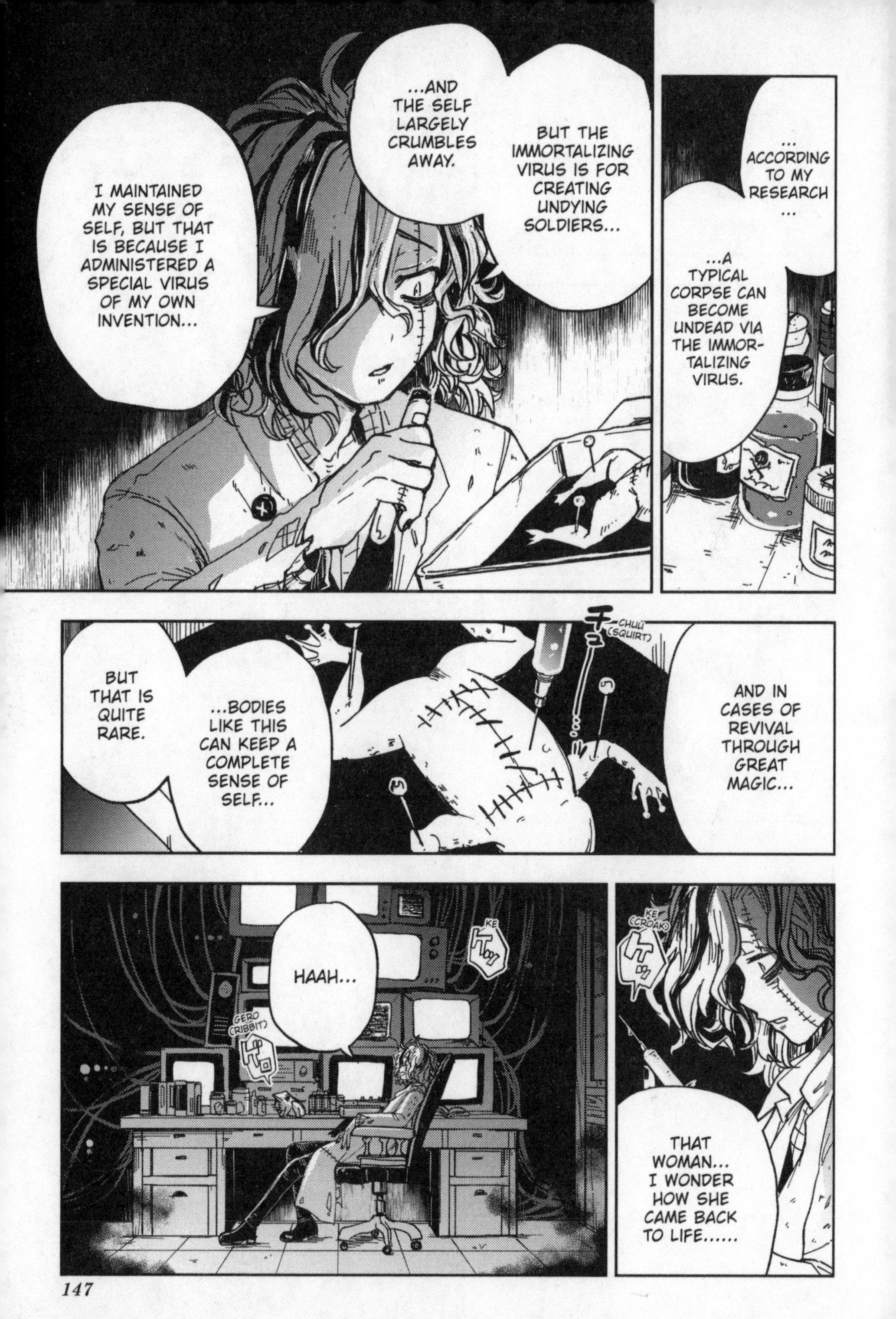
...ACCORDING TO MY RESEARCH...
...A TYPICAL CORPSE CAN BECOME UNDEAD VIA THE IMMORTALIZING VIRUS.
BUT THE IMMORTALIZING VIRUS IS FOR CREATING UNDYING SOLDIERS...
...AND THE SELF LARGELY CRUMBLES AWAY.
I MAINTAINED MY SENSE OF SELF, BUT THAT IS BECAUSE I ADMINISTERED A SPECIAL VIRUS OF MY OWN INVENTION...
AND IN CASES OF REVIVAL THROUGH GREAT MAGIC...
CHUU (SQUIRT)
...BODIES LIKE THIS CAN KEEP A COMPLETE SENSE OF SELF...
BUT THAT IS QUITE RARE.
KE (CROAK)
THAT WOMAN... I WONDER HOW SHE CAME BACK TO LIFE......
KE
HAAH...
GERO (RIBBIT)

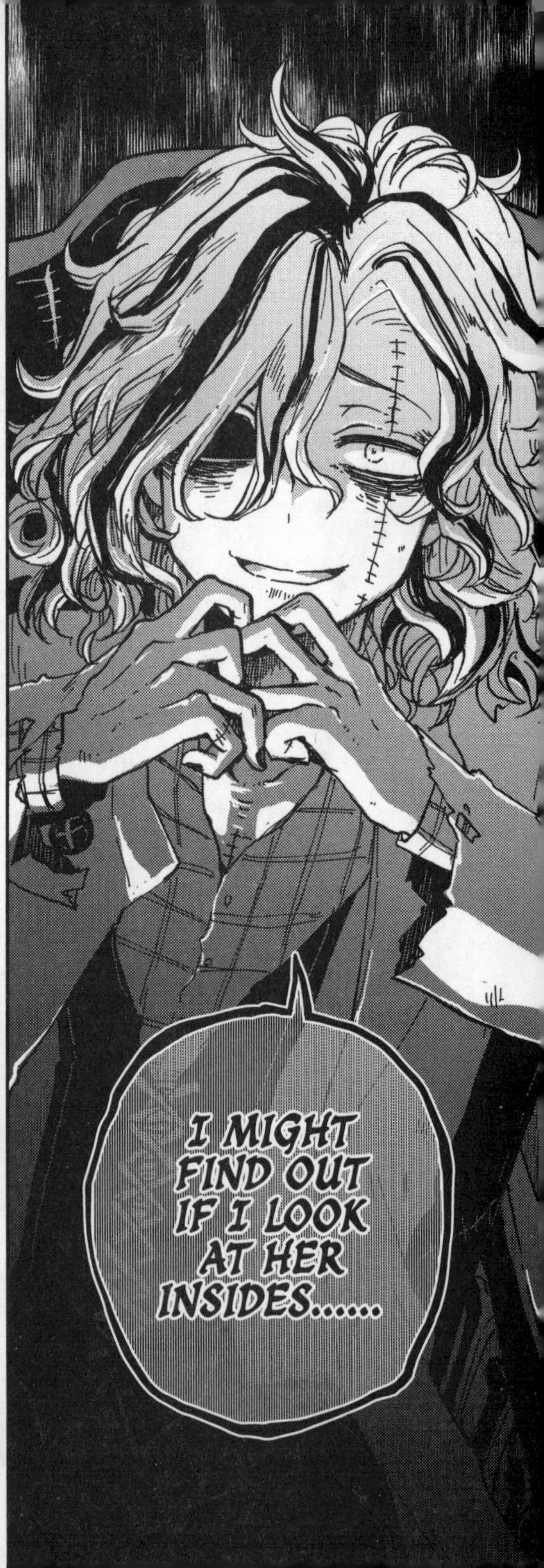
I MIGHT FIND OUT IF I LOOK AT HER INSIDES......

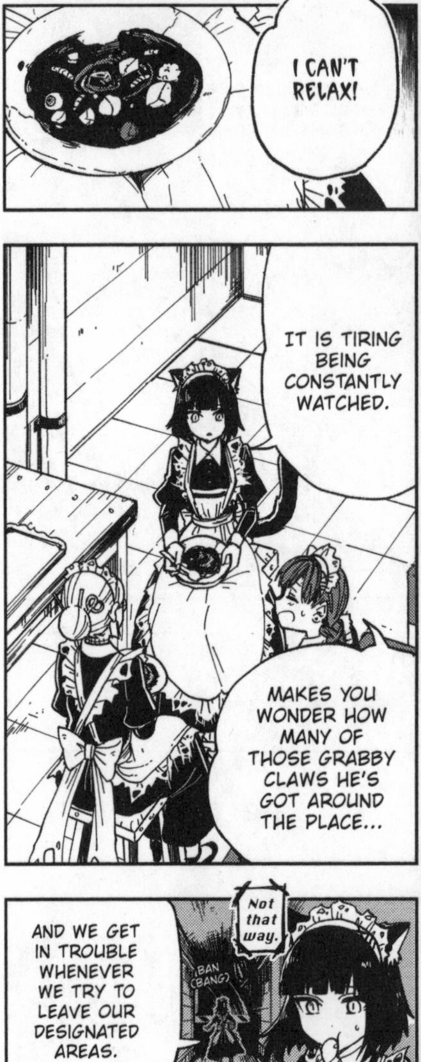
I CAN'T RELAX!
IT IS TIRING BEING CONSTANTLY WATCHED.
MAKES YOU WONDER HOW MANY OF THOSE GRABBY CLAWS HE'S GOT AROUND THE PLACE...
Not that way.
BAN (BANG)
AND WE GET IN TROUBLE WHENEVER WE TRY TO LEAVE OUR DESIGNATED AREAS.
HOW ARE WE SUPPOSED TO SEARCH FOR THE ENGINE ROOM!? ARGH!
YES, SINCE WE'RE BEING WATCHED ...

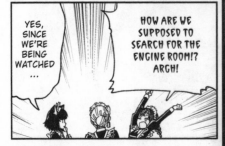

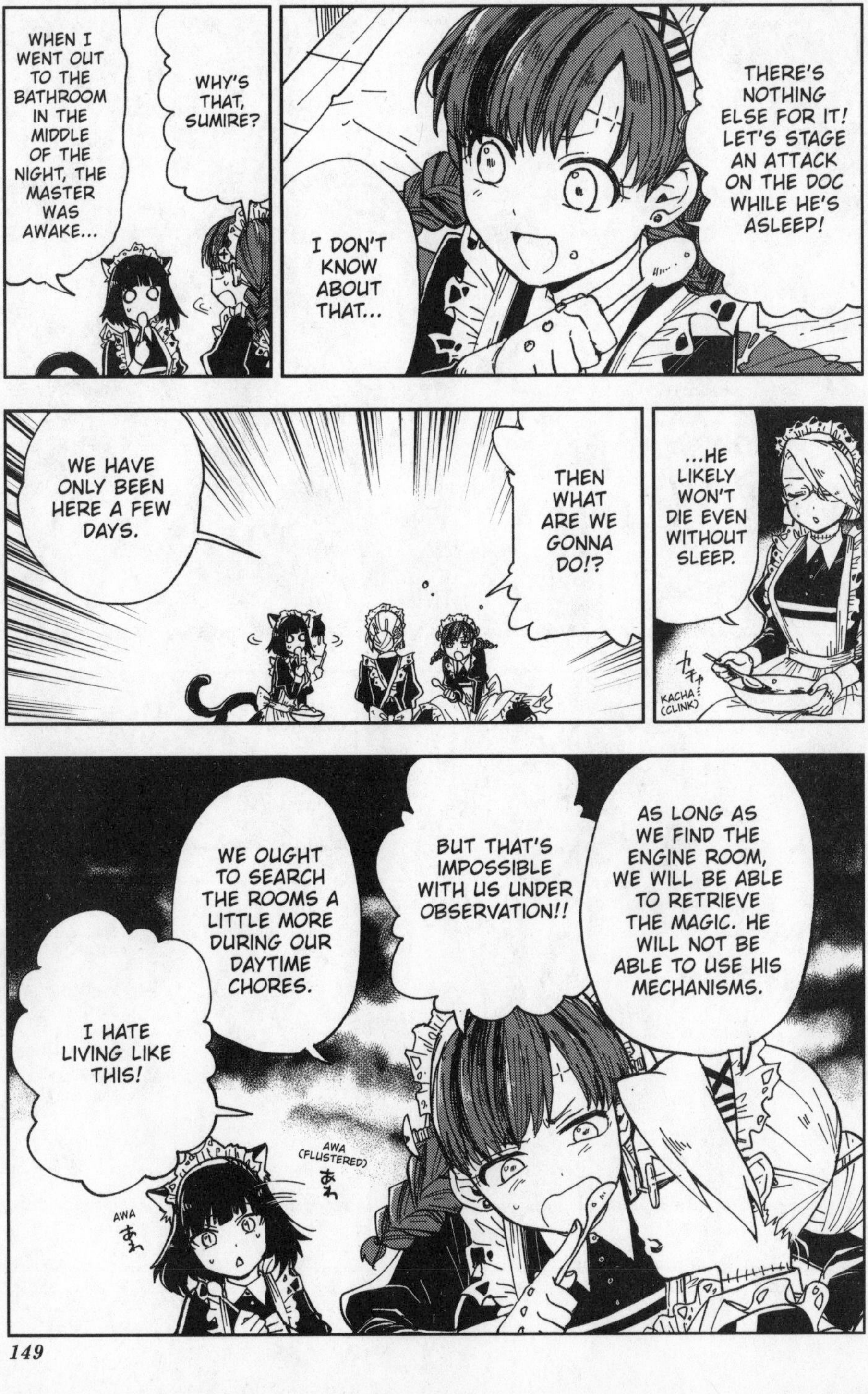
THERE'S NOTHING ELSE FOR IT! LET'S STAGE AN ATTACK ON THE DOC WHILE HE'S ASLEEP!
I DON'T KNOW ABOUT THAT...
WHY'S THAT, SUMIRE?
WHEN I WENT OUT TO THE BATHROOM IN THE MIDDLE OF THE NIGHT, THE MASTER WAS AWAKE...
...HE LIKELY WON'T DIE EVEN WITHOUT SLEEP.
カチャ
KACHA (CLINK)
THEN WHAT ARE WE GONNA DO!?
WE HAVE ONLY BEEN HERE A FEW DAYS.
AS LONG AS WE FIND THE ENGINE ROOM, WE WILL BE ABLE TO RETRIEVE THE MAGIC. HE WILL NOT BE ABLE TO USE HIS MECHANISMS.
BUT THAT'S IMPOSSIBLE WITH US UNDER OBSERVATION!!
WE OUGHT TO SEARCH THE ROOMS A LITTLE MORE DURING OUR DAYTIME CHORES.
I HATE LIVING LIKE THIS!
AWA (FLUSTERED)
あわ
AWA
あわ

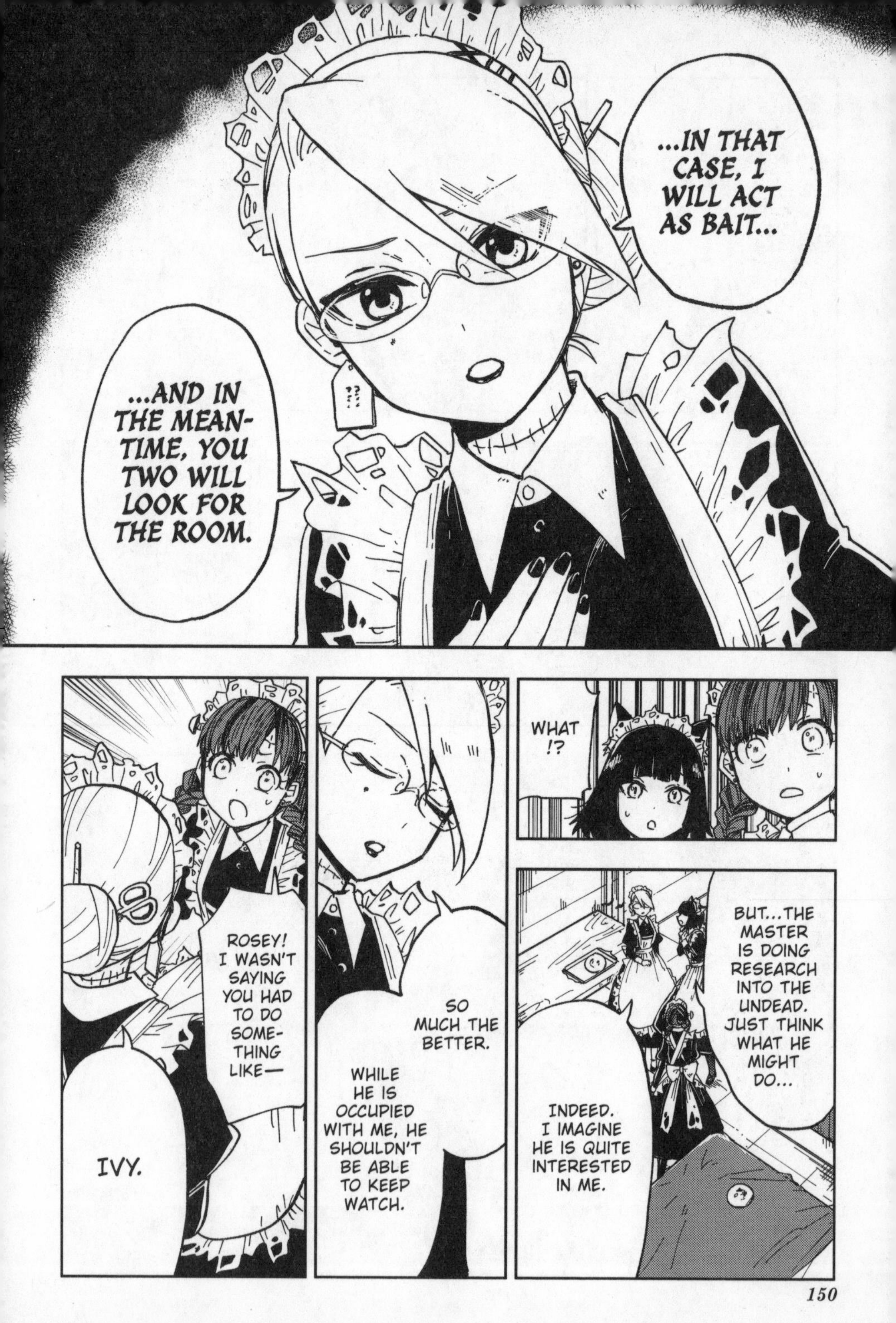
...IN THAT CASE, I WILL ACT AS BAIT...
...AND IN THE MEAN-TIME, YOU TWO WILL LOOK FOR THE ROOM.
WHAT!?
BUT...THE MASTER IS DOING RESEARCH INTO THE UNDEAD. JUST THINK WHAT HE MIGHT DO...
INDEED. I IMAGINE HE IS QUITE INTERESTED IN ME.
SO MUCH THE BETTER.
WHILE HE IS OCCUPIED WITH ME, HE SHOULDN'T BE ABLE TO KEEP WATCH.
ROSEY! I WASN'T SAYING YOU HAD TO DO SOME-THING LIKE—
IVY.

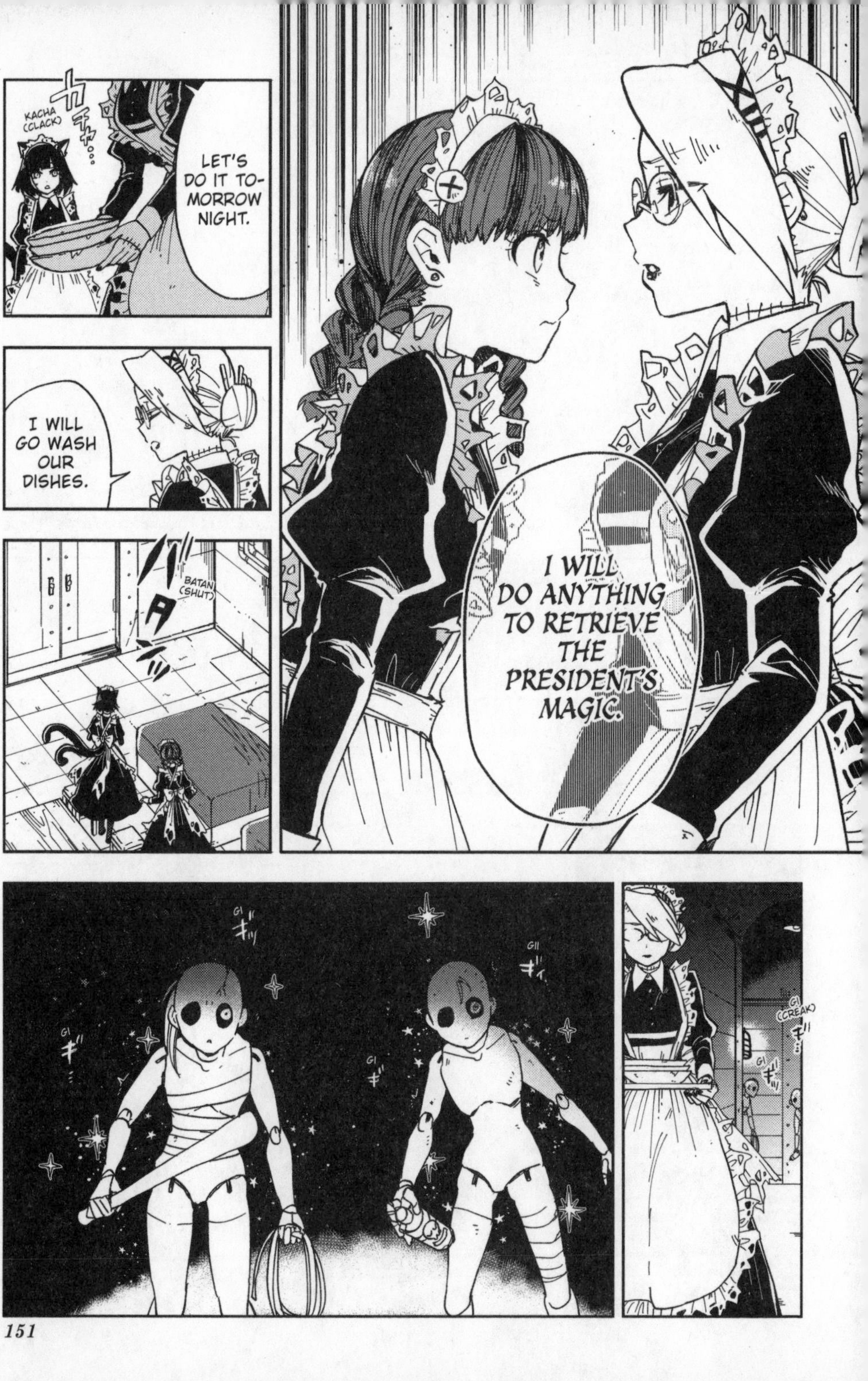
I WILL DO ANYTHING TO RETRIEVE THE PRESIDENT'S MAGIC.
KACHA (CLACK)
LET'S DO IT TO-MORROW NIGHT.
I WILL GO WASH OUR DISHES.
BATAN (SHUT)
GI (CREAK)
GI
GI
GII
GI
GI

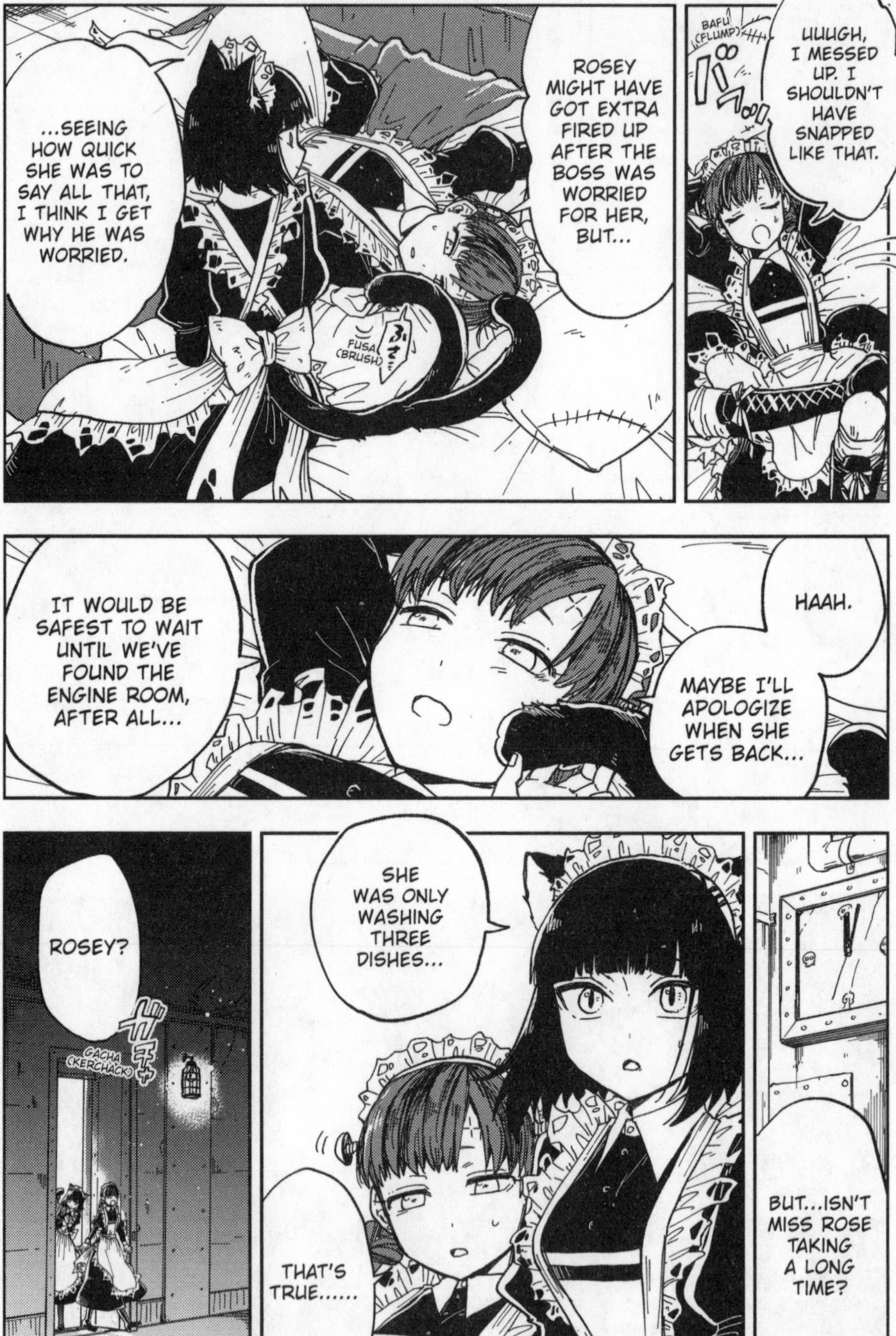
BAFU (FLUMP)
UUUGH, I MESSED UP. I SHOULDN'T HAVE SNAPPED LIKE THAT.
ROSEY MIGHT HAVE GOT EXTRA FIRED UP AFTER THE BOSS WAS WORRIED FOR HER, BUT...
...SEEING HOW QUICK SHE WAS TO SAY ALL THAT, I THINK I GET WHY HE WAS WORRIED.
FUSA (BRUSH)
HAAH.
MAYBE I'LL APOLOGIZE WHEN SHE GETS BACK...
IT WOULD BE SAFEST TO WAIT UNTIL WE'VE FOUND THE ENGINE ROOM, AFTER ALL...
BUT...ISN'T MISS ROSE TAKING A LONG TIME?
SHE WAS ONLY WASHING THREE DISHES...
THAT'S TRUE......
ROSEY?
GACHA (KERCHACK)

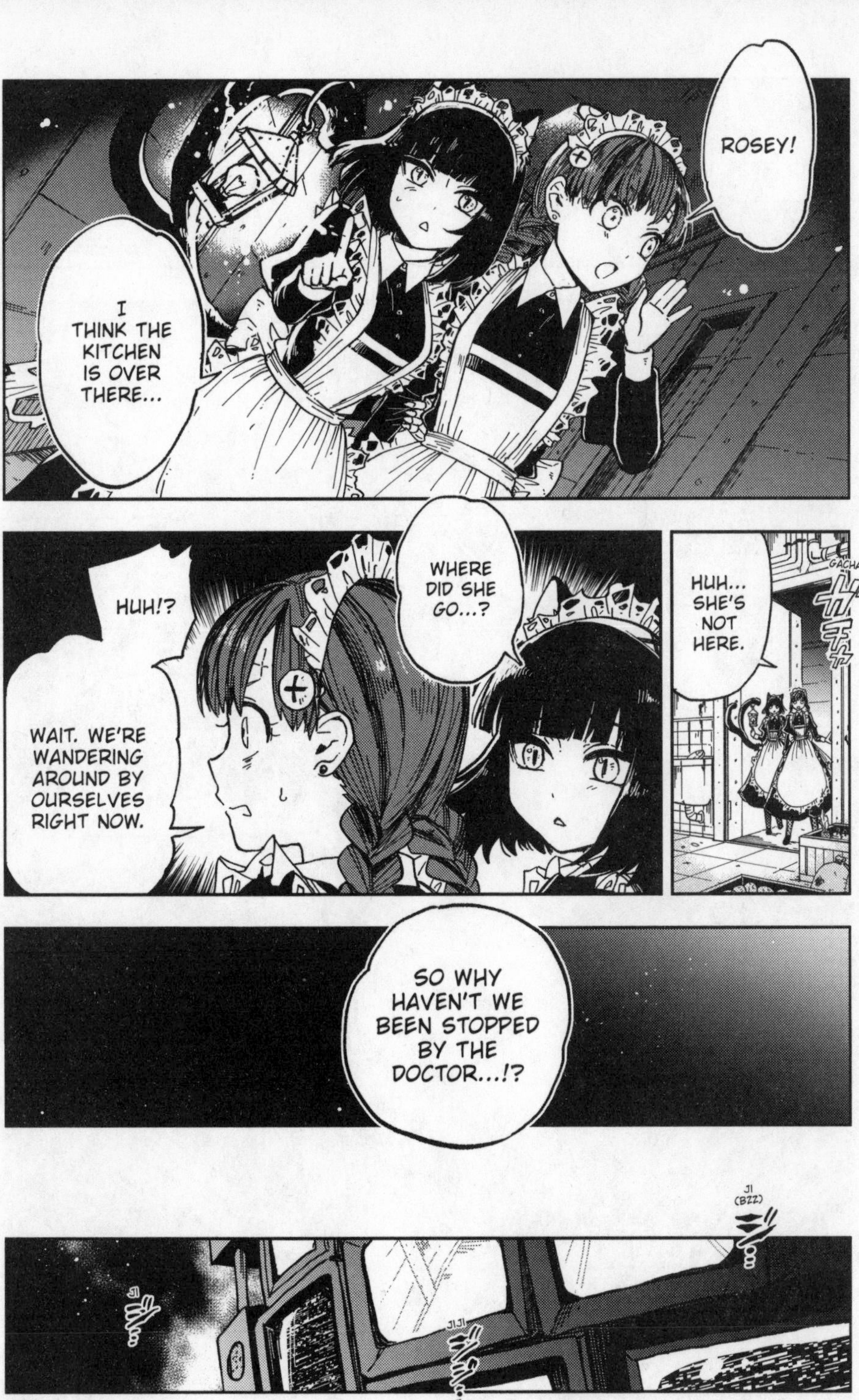

ROSEY!
I THINK THE KITCHEN IS OVER THERE...
GACHA
HUH... SHE'S NOT HERE.
WHERE DID SHE GO...?
HUH!?
WAIT. WE'RE WANDERING AROUND BY OURSELVES RIGHT NOW.
SO WHY HAVEN'T WE BEEN STOPPED BY THE DOCTOR...!?
JI (BZZ)
JI JI
JI

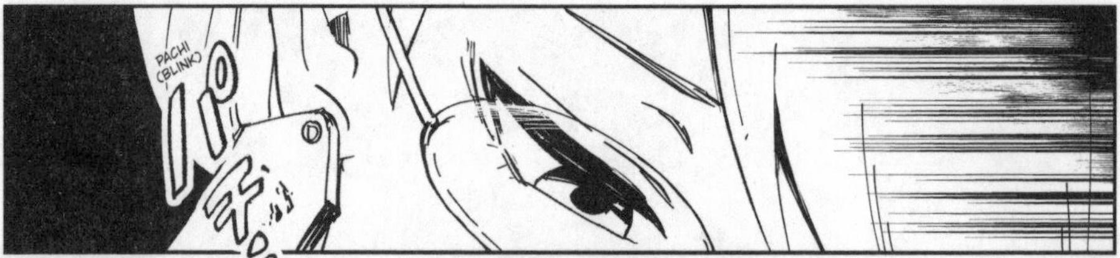
PACHI (BLINK)
パチ
DOOO
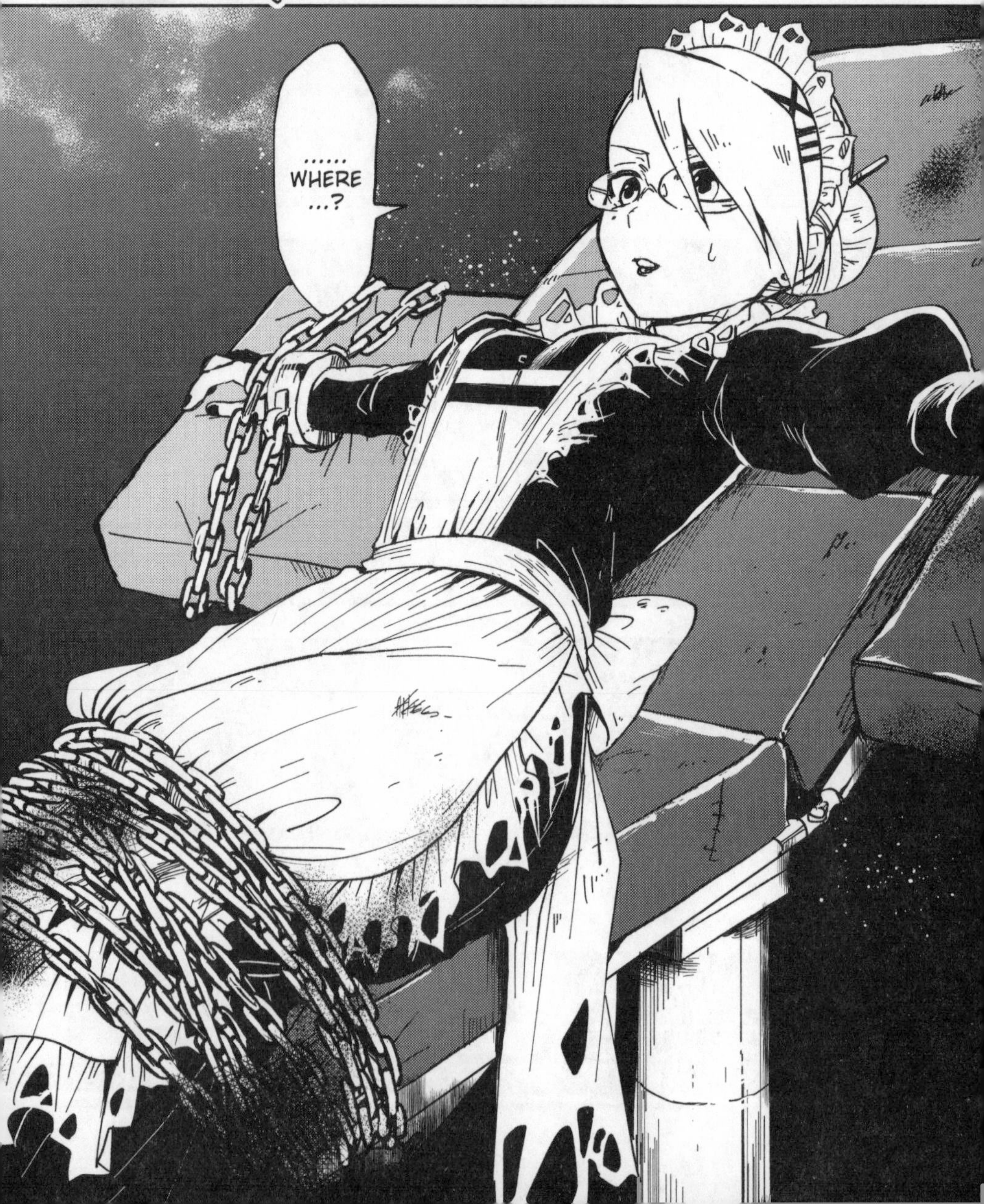
......
WHERE
...?

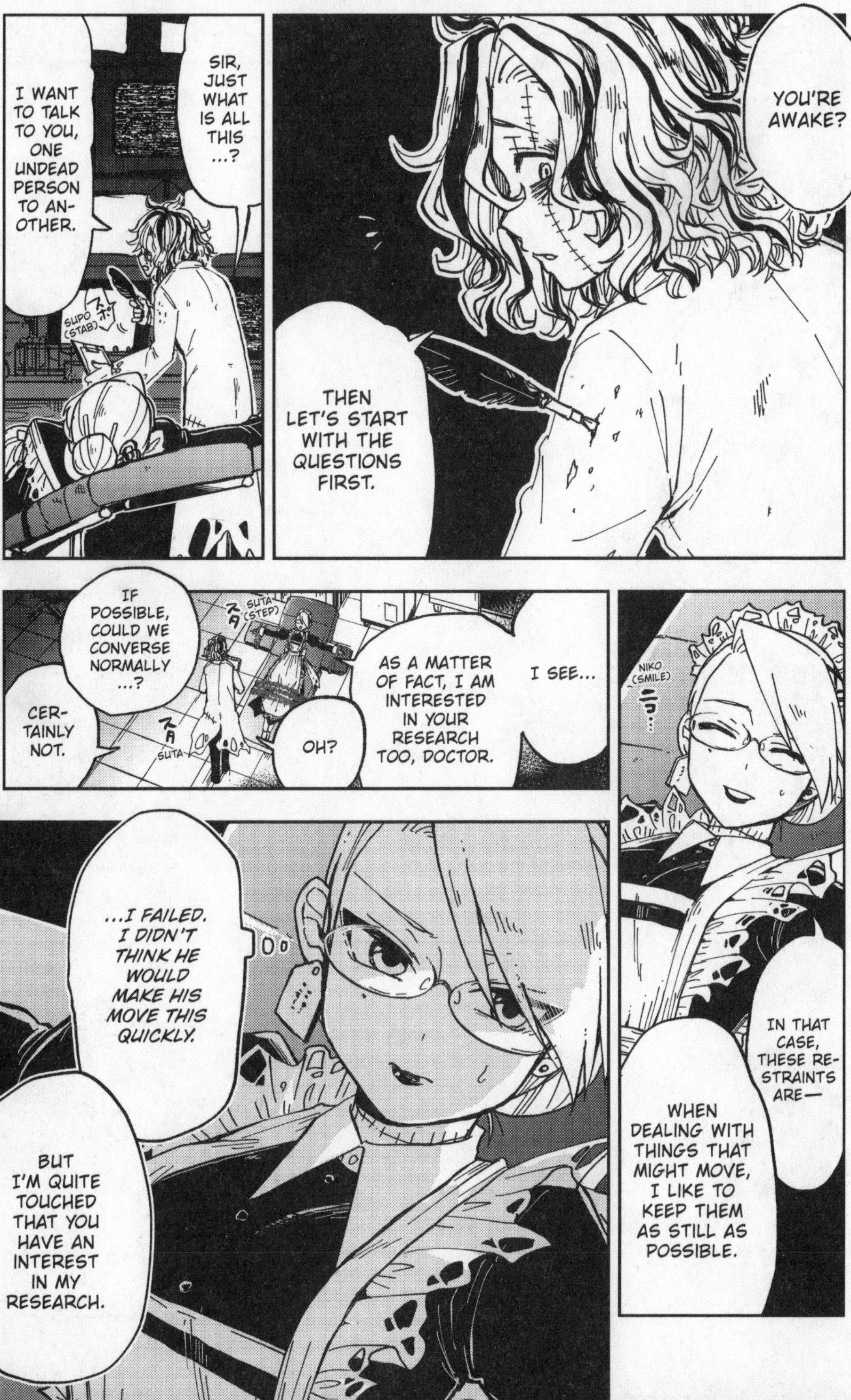
YOU'RE AWAKE?
THEN LET'S START WITH THE QUESTIONS FIRST.
SIR, JUST WHAT IS ALL THIS ...?
SUPO (STAB)
I WANT TO TALK TO YOU, ONE UNDEAD PERSON TO ANOTHER.
NIKO (SMILE)
IN THAT CASE, THESE RESTRAINTS ARE—
WHEN DEALING WITH THINGS THAT MIGHT MOVE, I LIKE TO KEEP THEM AS STILL AS POSSIBLE.
I SEE...
AS A MATTER OF FACT, I AM INTERESTED IN YOUR RESEARCH TOO, DOCTOR.
OH?
SUTA (STEP)
IF POSSIBLE, COULD WE CONVERSE NORMALLY ...?
SUTA
CERTAINLY NOT.
...I FAILED. I DIDN'T THINK HE WOULD MAKE HIS MOVE THIS QUICKLY.
BUT I'M QUITE TOUCHED THAT YOU HAVE AN INTEREST IN MY RESEARCH.

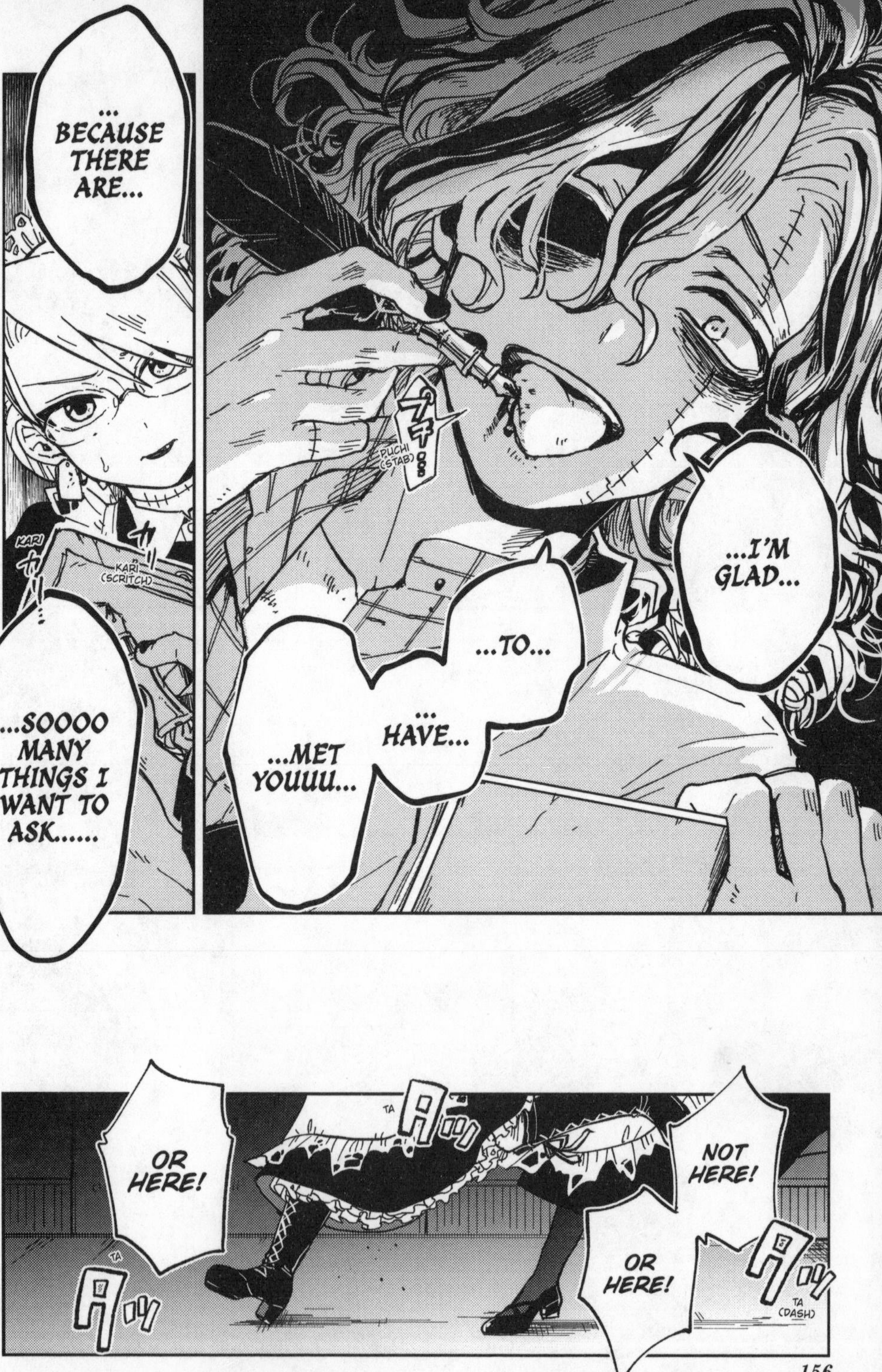
...I'M GLAD...
...TO...
...HAVE...
...MET YOUUU...
PUCHI (STAB)
...BECAUSE THERE ARE...
KARI
KARI (SCRITCH)
...SOOOO MANY THINGS I WANT TO ASK......
NOT HERE!
TA (DASH)
OR HERE!
TA
OR HERE!
TA

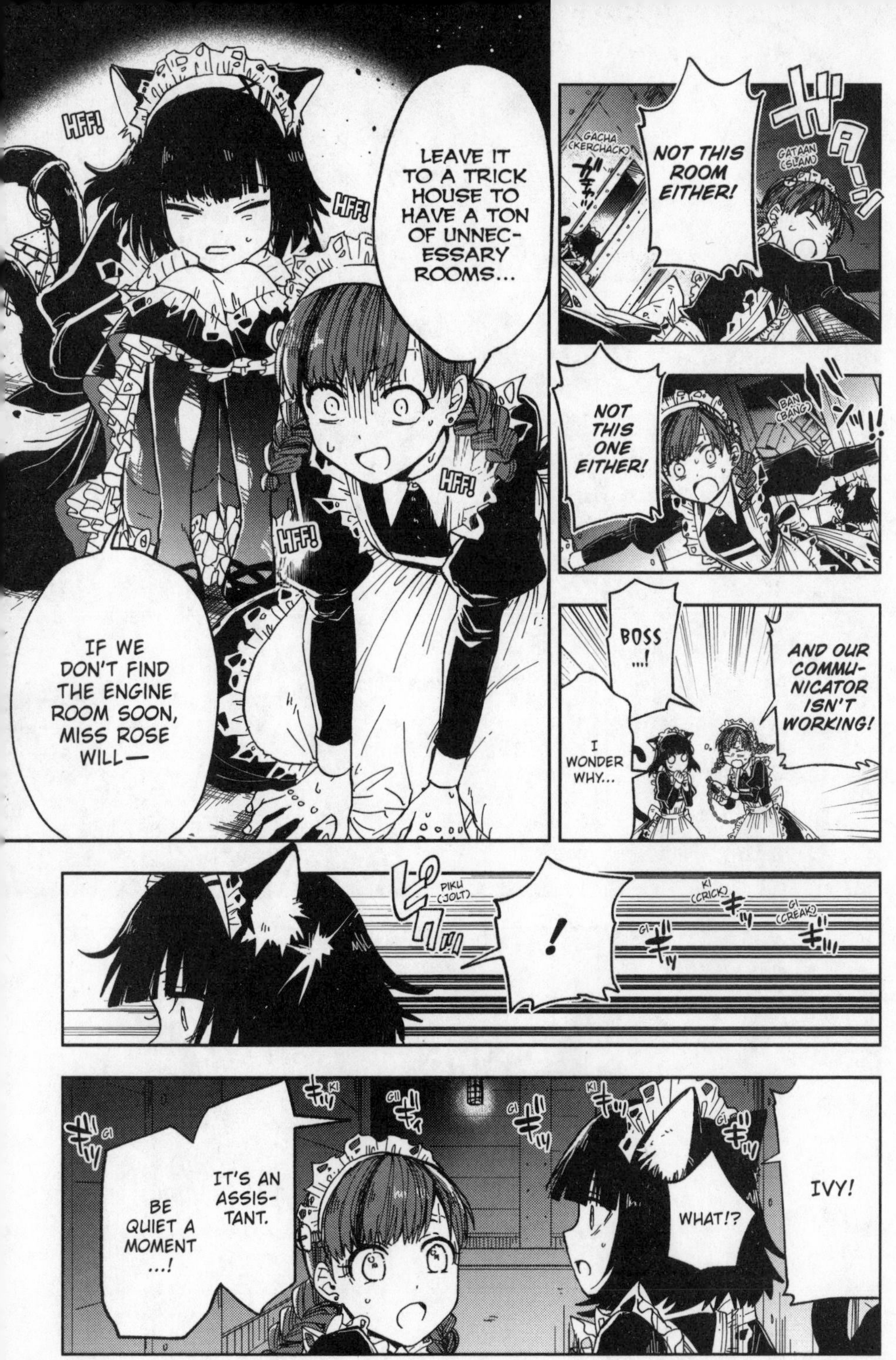
GATAAN (SLAM)
NOT THIS ROOM EITHER!
GACHA (KERCHACK)
BAN (BANG)
NOT THIS ONE EITHER!
AND OUR COMMUNICATOR ISN'T WORKING!
BOSS ...!
I WONDER WHY...
HFF!
LEAVE IT TO A TRICK HOUSE TO HAVE A TON OF UNNECESSARY ROOMS...
HFF!
HFF!
HFF!
IF WE DON'T FIND THE ENGINE ROOM SOON, MISS ROSE WILL—
GI (CREAK)
KI (CRICK)
GI
!
PIKU (JOLT)
IVY!
GI
KI
WHAT!?
GI
GI
KI
IT'S AN ASSISTANT.
BE QUIET A MOMENT ...!
GI

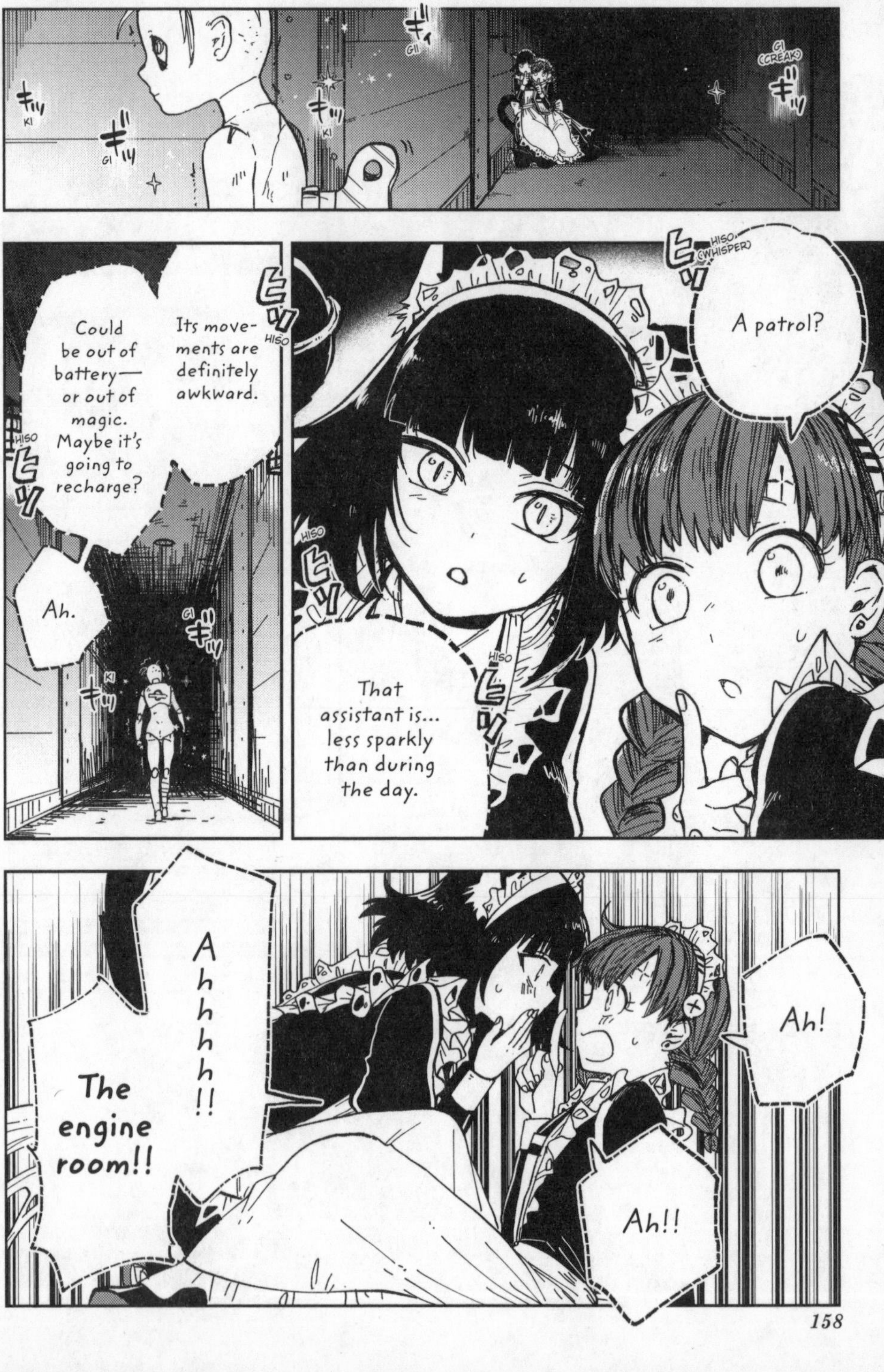
GI (CREAK)
ギッ
ギィ
GII
キッ
KI
キッ
KI
ギッ
GI
HISO (WHISPER)
ヒッ
A patrol?
HISO
ヒッ
HISO
ヒッ
That assistant is... less sparkly than during the day.
ヒッ
HISO
Its move-ments are definitely awkward.
Could be out of battery— or out of magic. Maybe it's going to recharge?
HISO
ヒッ
Ah.
GI
ギッ
KI
キッ
Ah!
Ah!!
Ahhhh!!
The engine room!!

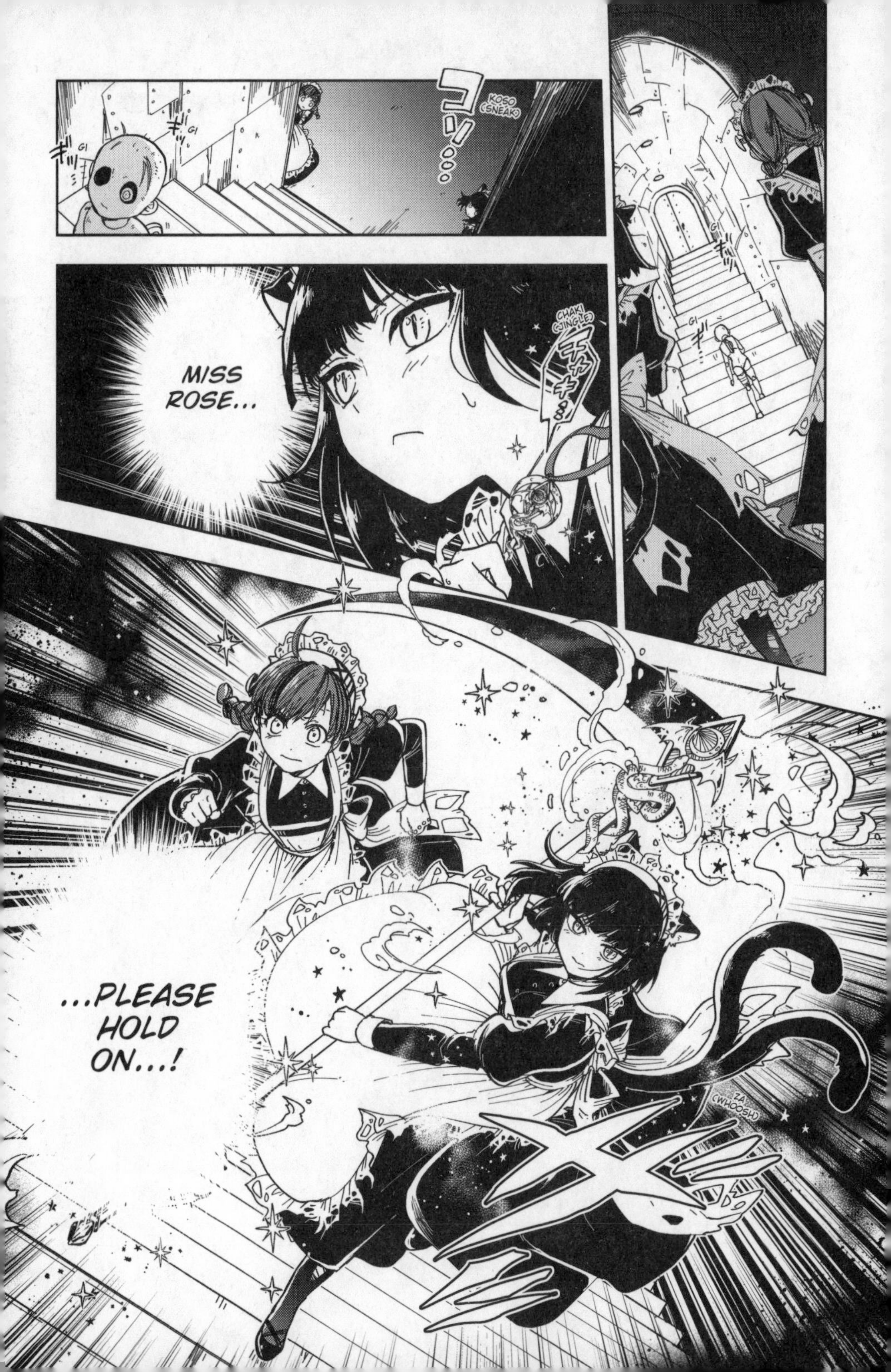
GI
GI
KOSO (SNEAK)
GI
GI
CHAKI (JINGLE)
MISS ROSE...
...PLEASE HOLD ON...!
ZA (WHOOSH)

The Splendid Work of a Monster Maid

GREETINGS

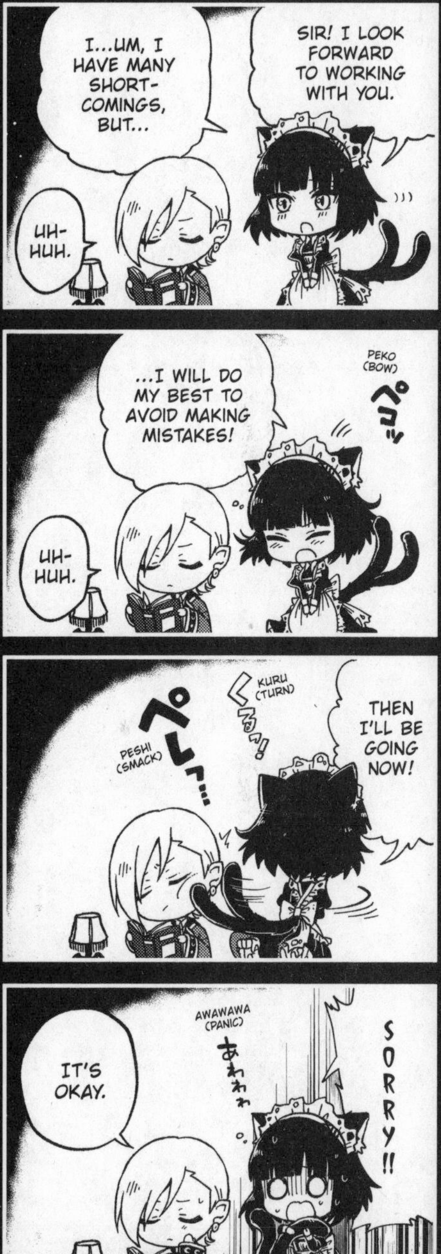
SIR! I LOOK FORWARD TO WORKING WITH YOU.
I...UM, I HAVE MANY SHORT-COMINGS, BUT...
UH-HUH.
PEKO (BOW)
...I WILL DO MY BEST TO AVOID MAKING MISTAKES!
UH-HUH.
THEN I'LL BE GOING NOW!
KURU (TURN)
PESHI (SMACK)
SORRY!!
AWAWAWA (PANIC)
IT'S OKAY.

TREE CLIMBING

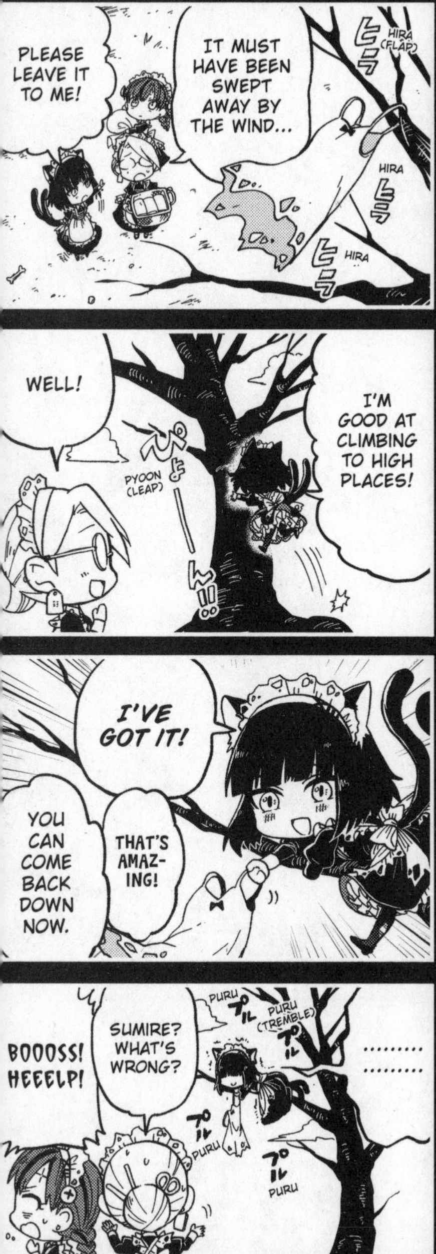
HIRA (FLAP)
HIRA
HIRA
IT MUST HAVE BEEN SWEPT AWAY BY THE WIND...
PLEASE LEAVE IT TO ME!
I'M GOOD AT CLIMBING TO HIGH PLACES!
PYOON (LEAP)
WELL!
I'VE GOT IT!
THAT'S AMAZ-ING!
YOU CAN COME BACK DOWN NOW.
....
....
PURU
PURU (TREMBLE)
PURU
PURU
SUMIRE? WHAT'S WRONG?
BOOOSS! HEEELP!

YARN

DO YOU THINK YOU COULD ROLL THIS YARN INTO BALLS FOR ME?
ABSO-LUTELY!
MAKI (ROLL)
まき
MAKI
まき
MAKI
まき
MAKI
まき
MAKI
まき
SHUBABABA (ZOOM)
POON (TOSS)
ぽーん!
FINISHED!
LET'S TAKE A BREAK!
UZU (FIDGET)
UZU
SOWA (TWITCH)
SOWA
NOW LOOK HERE!
GURUN (TUMBLE)
ぐるん
GURUN
ぐるん

SPECIAL THANKS

My editor

Everyone in the *Newtype* Editorial Department

Comic design / Kohei Nawata Design Office

Series logo design / Ayumi Sasaki

My friends

Everyone who supports me

You, for picking up this book

FAN LETTER

Attn: Yugata Tanabe
c/o Yen Press
150 West 30th Street, 19th Floor
New York, NY 10001

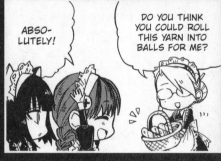

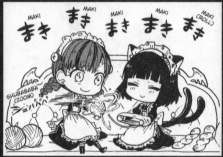

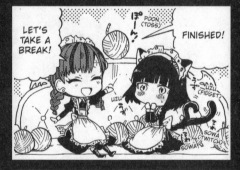

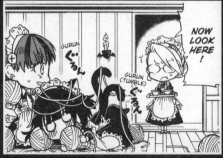

Translation Notes

General

Nekomata: A type of yokai, or Japanese ghoul. It is said that, when a cat reaches a certain age, it becomes a nekomata, gaining a forked tail and supernatural powers—including the ability to transform into a human.

Page 61

Custard Pudding: Known as "*purin*" in Japan, this is a popular cold custard dessert with runny caramel on top. Despite its name, its consistency is actually closer to flan, and it can hold its shape easily. It's usually sold upside down in cups and flipped right side up to eat, just as the president is doing. This ensures that the caramel remains on the very top.

The Splendid Work of a Monster Maid

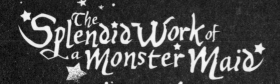

Yugata Tanabe

TRANSLATION: ELEANOR SUMMERS ★ LETTERING: LYS BLAKESLEE

KAIBUTSU MAID NO KAREI NARU OSHIGOTO Vol. 1
© Yugata Tanabe 2020
First published in Japan in 2020 by KADOKAWA CORPORATION, Tokyo.
English translation rights arranged with KADOKAWA CORPORATION, Tokyo
and Yen Press, LLC through Tuttle-Mori Agency, Inc.

English translation © 2021 by Yen Press, LLC

Yen Press
150 West 30th Street, 19th Floor
New York, NY 10001

Visit us at yenpress.com ✧ facebook.com/yenpress ✧ twitter.com/yenpress
yenpress.tumblr.com ✧ instagram.com/yenpress

First Yen Press Edition: November 2021

Yen Press is an imprint of Yen Press, LLC.
The Yen Press name and logo are trademarks of Yen Press, LLC.

Library of Congress Control Number: 2021945485

ISBNs: 978-1-9753-3497-0 (paperback)
978-1-9753-3498-7 (ebook)

10 9 8 7 6 5 4 3 2 1

WOR

Printed in the United States of America